La Corda d'Oro

4
Story & Art by Yuki Kure

La Corda d'Oro

CONTENTS
Volume 4

ff

Kahoko Hino
(General Education School, 2nd year)

The heroine. She knows nothing about music, but she still finds herself participating in the music competition equipped with a magic violin.

Ryotaro Tsuchiura
(General Education, 2nd year)

A member of the soccer team who seems to be looking after Kahoko as a fellow Gen Ed student.

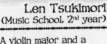

Len Tsukimori
(Music School, 2nd year)

A violin major and a cold perfectionist from a musical family of unquestionable talent.

Kazuki Hihara
(Music school, 3rd year)

An energetic and friendly trumpet major and a fan of anything fun.

Keiichi Shimizu
(Music school, 1st year)

A student of the cello who walks to the beat of his own drum and is often lost in the world of music. He is also often asleep.

Azuma Yunoki
(Music school, 3rd year)

A flute major and the son of a graceful and kind traditional flower arrangement master. He even has a dedicated fan club called "the Yunoki Guard."

Hiroto Kanazawa
(Music teacher)

The contest coordinator whose lazy demeanor suggests he is avoiding any hassle.

The music fairy Lili, who got Kahoko caught up in this affair. ↓

Story

Our story is set at Seisou Academy, which is split into the General Education School and Music School. One day Kahoko, a Gen Ed student, encounters a music fairy named Lili, who gives her a magic violin that anyone can play. All of a sudden, Kahoko finds herself in the school's music competition with good-looking, quirky Music School students as her fellow contestants! Kahoko eventually comes to accept this daunting task and actually finds herself enjoying music. But when the curtain rises on the first round, Kahoko's accompanist is nowhere to be found! Ryotaro surprisingly steps in to save the day, and is asked to join the competition. All the contestants attend a training camp to prepare for the second round. There, Len begins to take note of Kahoko. But the elegant and kind Azuma is...?

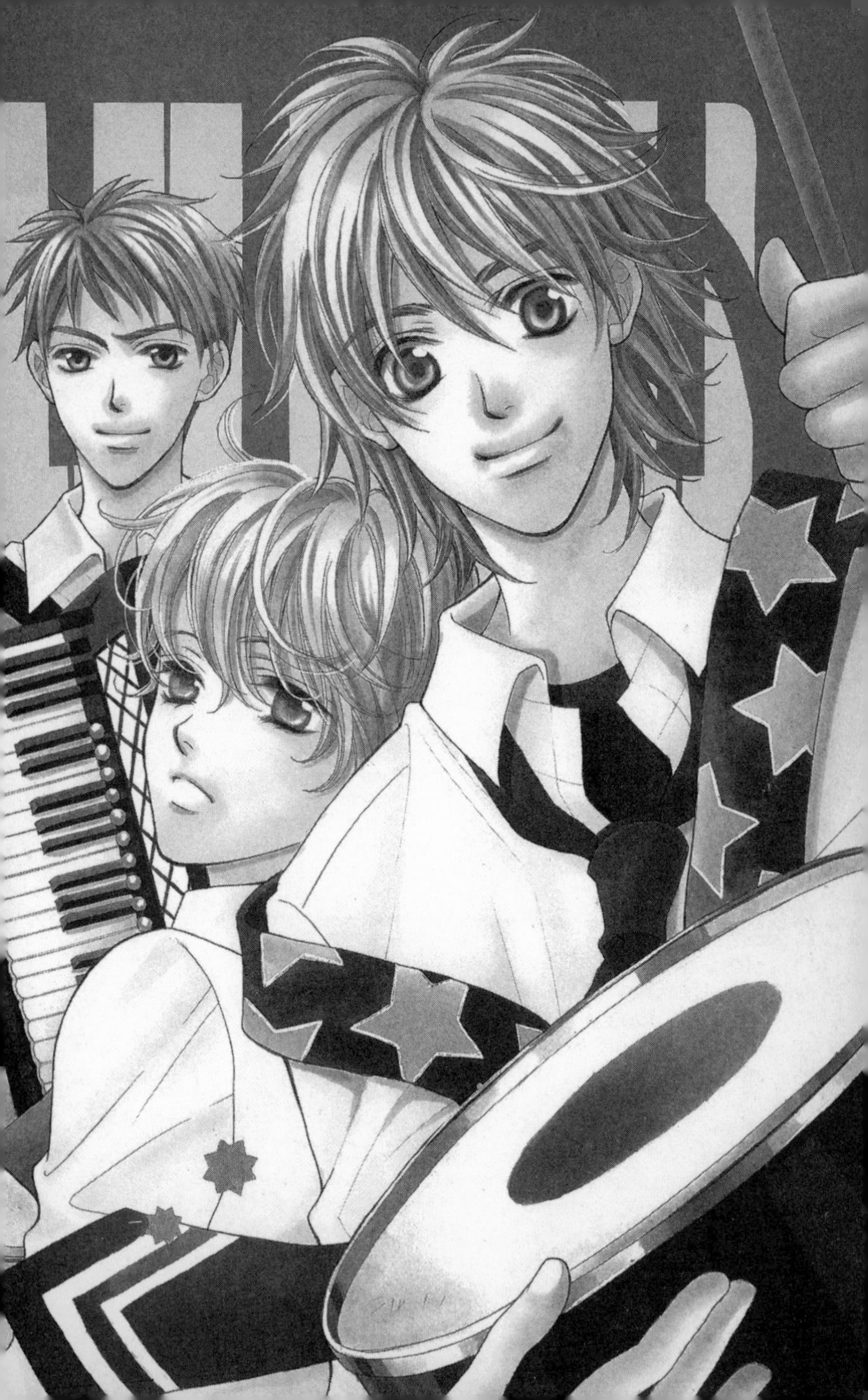

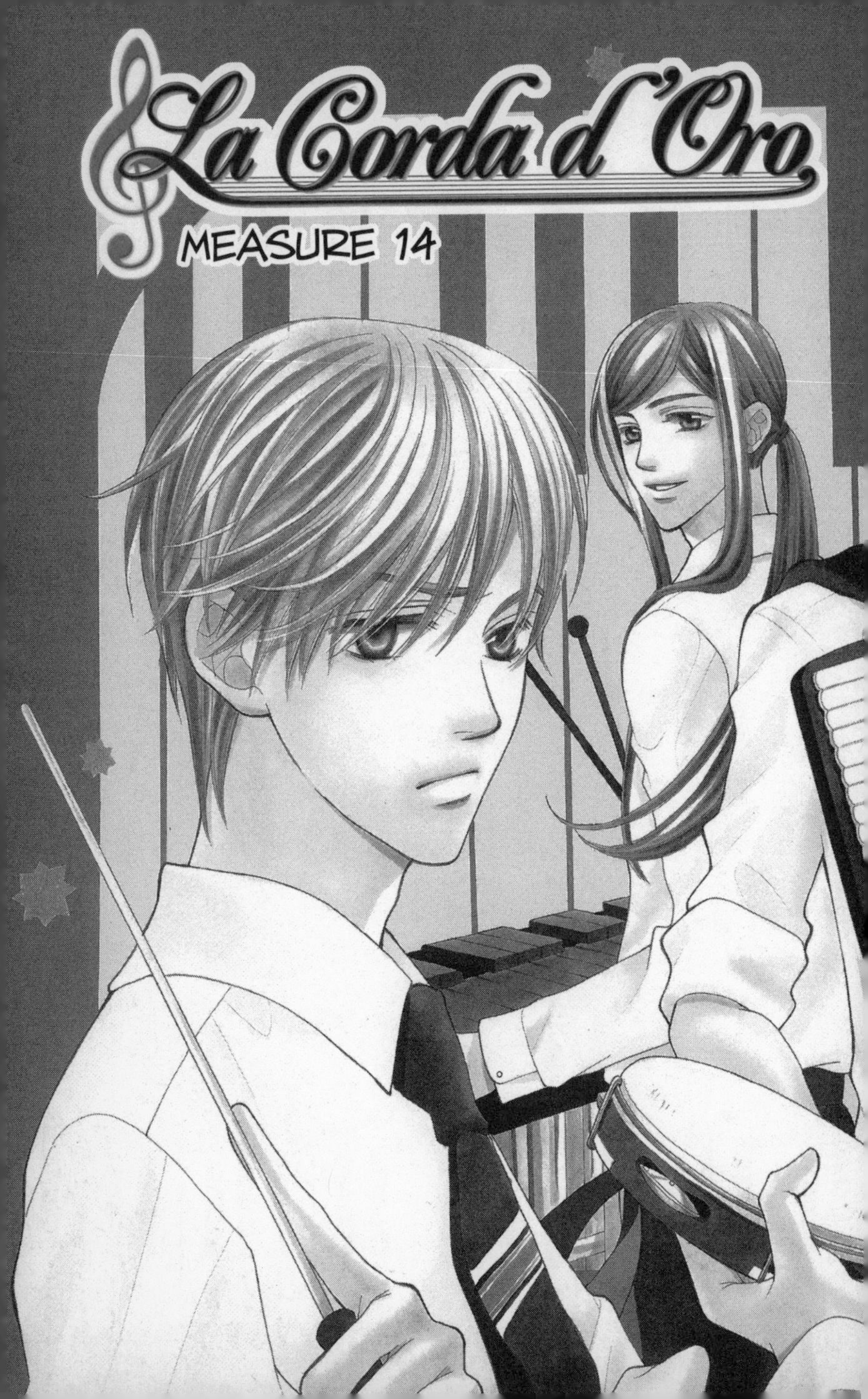
La Corda d'Oro
MEASURE 14

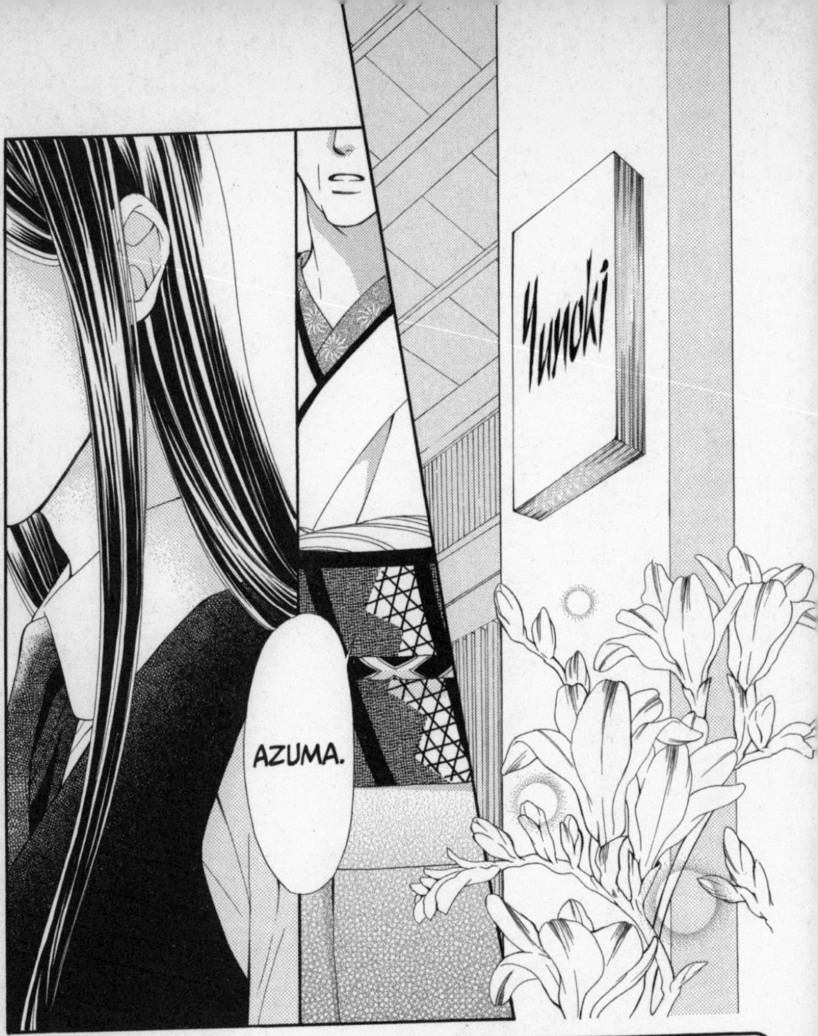
Yunoki
AZUMA.

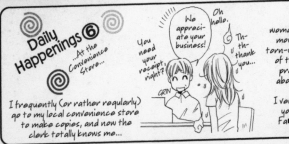

Daily Happenings 6

...At the Convenience Store...

I frequently (or rather regularly) go to my local convenience store to make copies, and now the clerk totally knows me...

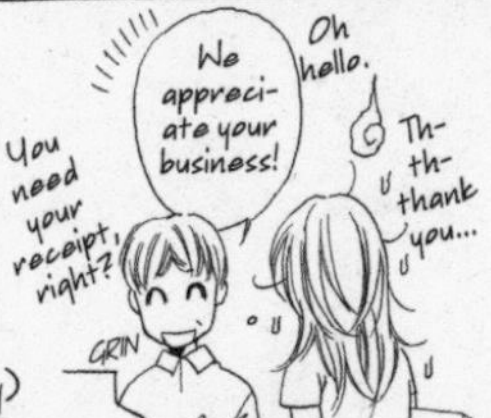
Oh hello.
We appreciate your business!
Th-th-thank you...
You need your receipt, right?
GRIN

I am the shady woman who goes to make mountains of copies in torn-up clothes at all hours of the day. I'm actually pretty embarrassed about it (a forced lol).

I very much appreciate your establishment, Fa[redacted]ly M[redacted]rt!! Thanks!

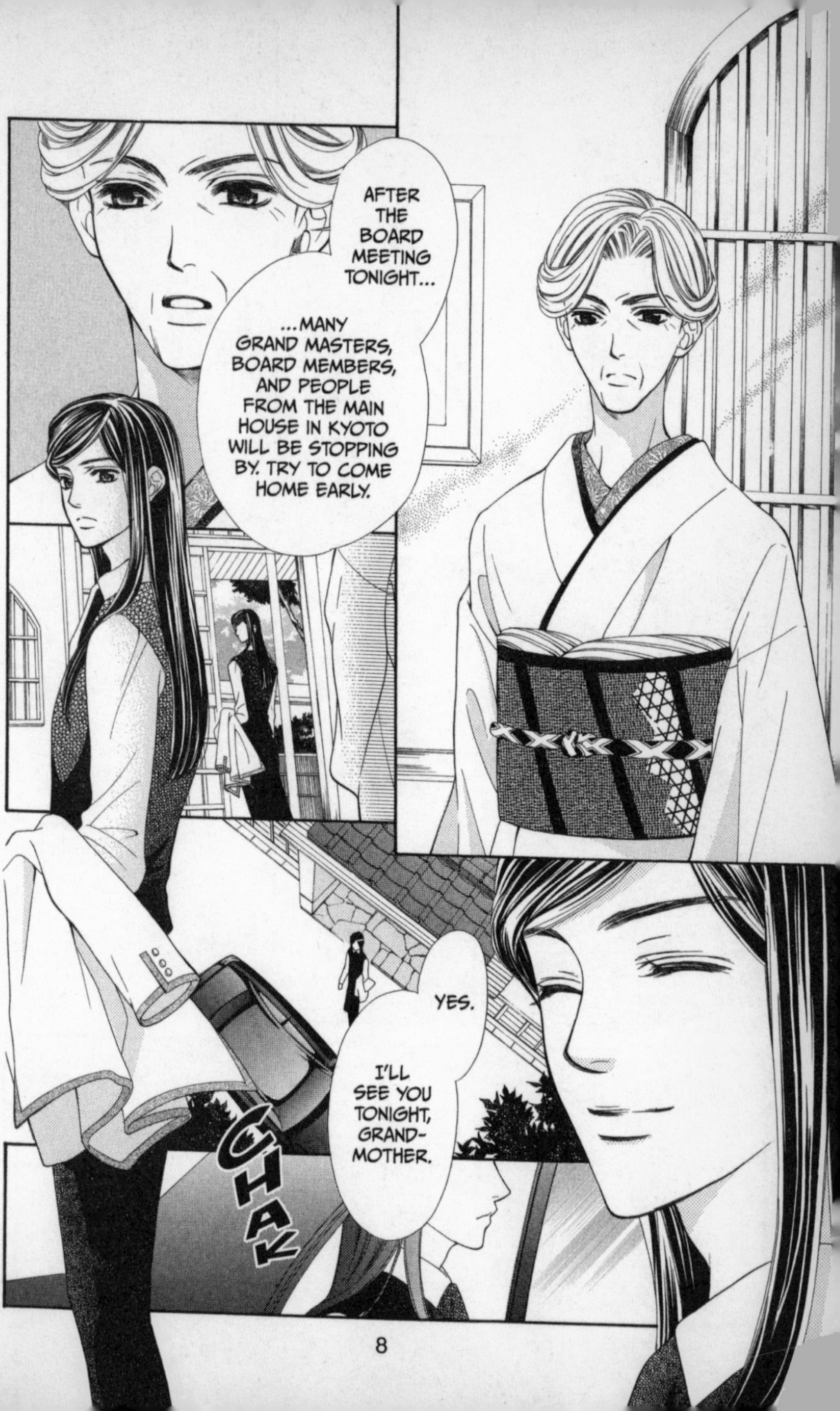
AFTER THE BOARD MEETING TONIGHT...
...MANY GRAND MASTERS, BOARD MEMBERS, AND PEOPLE FROM THE MAIN HOUSE IN KYOTO WILL BE STOPPING BY. TRY TO COME HOME EARLY.
YES.
I'LL SEE YOU TONIGHT, GRAND-MOTHER.
CHAK

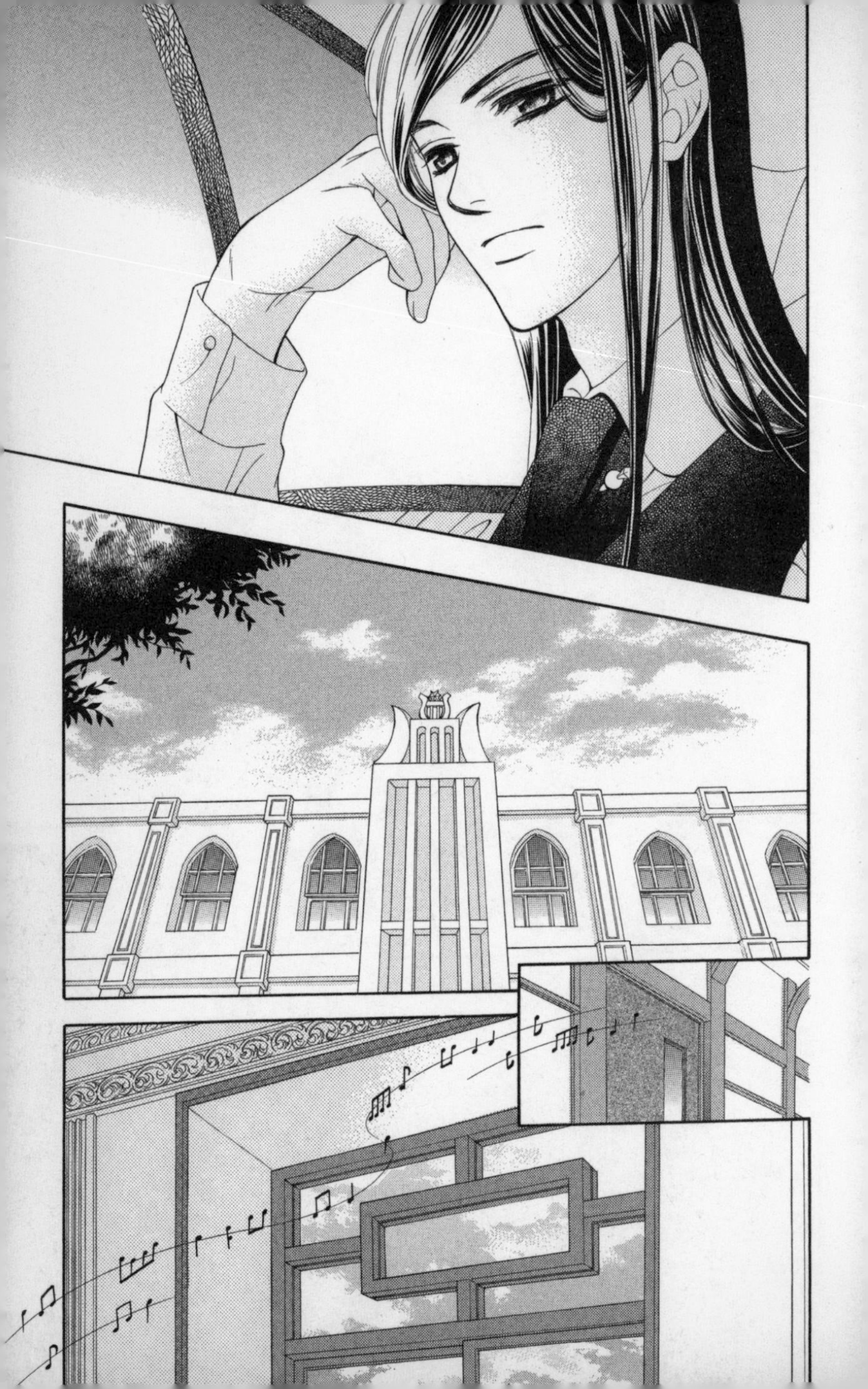

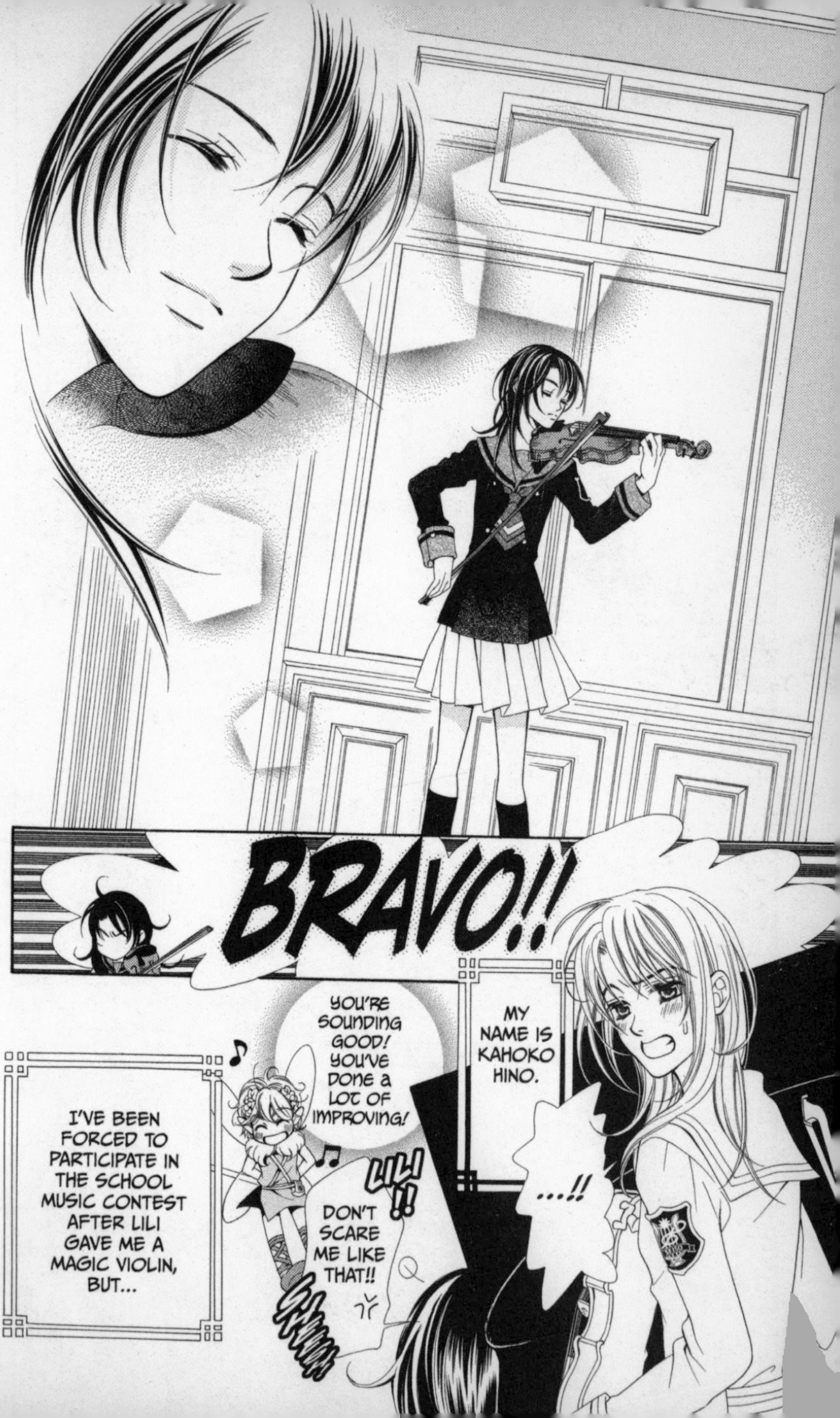
BRAVO!!
MY NAME IS KAHOKO HINO.
...!!
YOU'RE SOUNDING GOOD! YOU'VE DONE A LOT OF IMPROVING!
LILI!!
DON'T SCARE ME LIKE THAT!!
I'VE BEEN FORCED TO PARTICIPATE IN THE SCHOOL MUSIC CONTEST AFTER LILI GAVE ME A MAGIC VIOLIN, BUT...

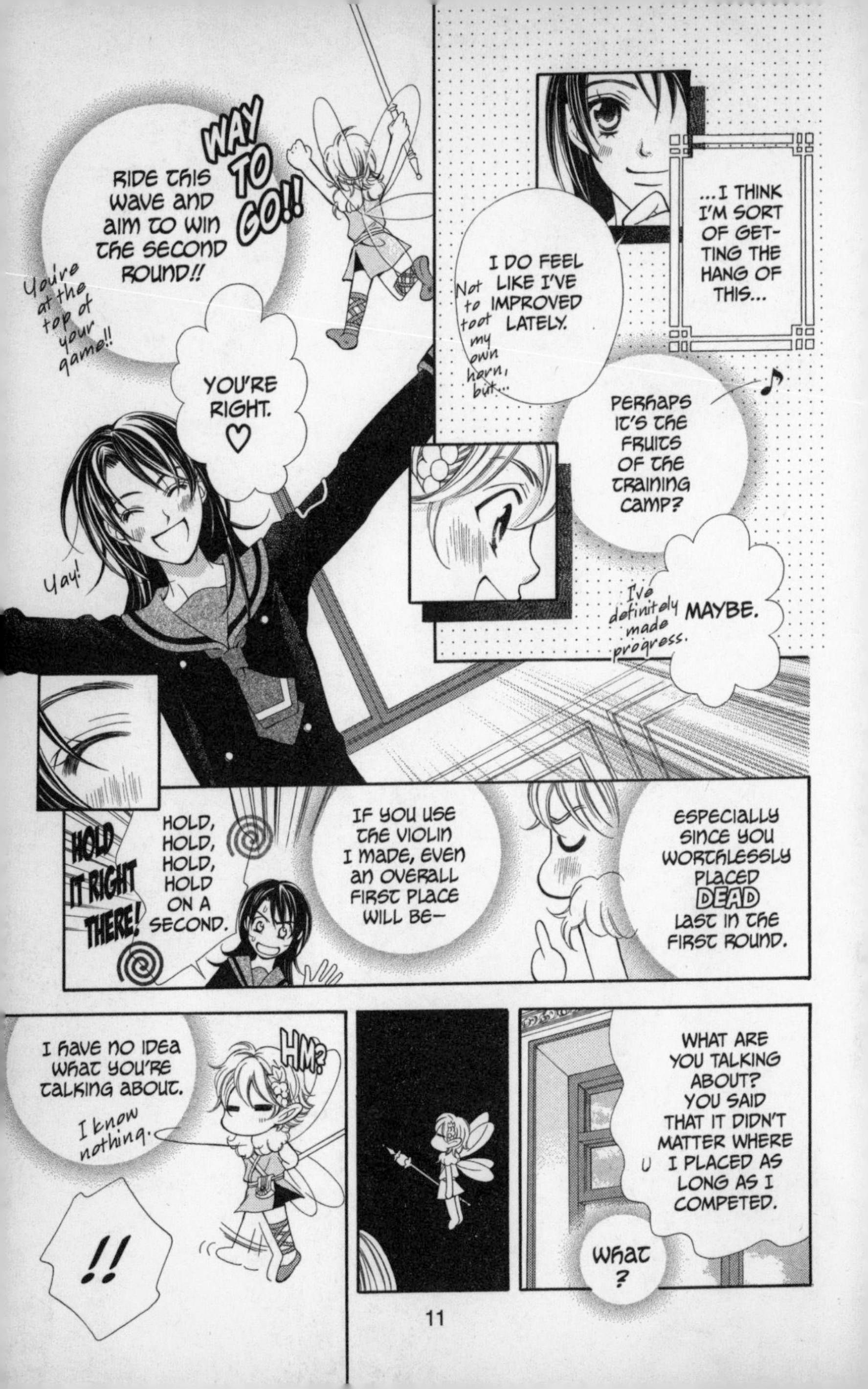
...I THINK I'M SORT OF GETTING THE HANG OF THIS...
I DO FEEL LIKE I'VE IMPROVED LATELY.
Not to toot my own horn, but...
PERHAPS IT'S THE FRUITS OF THE TRAINING CAMP? ♪
MAYBE.
I've definitely made progress.
YOU'RE RIGHT. ♡
WAY TO GO!!
RIDE THIS WAVE AND AIM TO WIN THE SECOND ROUND!!
You're at the top of your game!!
Yay!
ESPECIALLY SINCE YOU WORTHLESSLY PLACED DEAD LAST IN THE FIRST ROUND.
IF YOU USE THE VIOLIN I MADE, EVEN AN OVERALL FIRST PLACE WILL BE—
HOLD, HOLD, HOLD, HOLD ON A SECOND.
HOLD IT RIGHT THERE!
WHAT ARE YOU TALKING ABOUT? YOU SAID THAT IT DIDN'T MATTER WHERE I PLACED AS LONG AS I COMPETED.
WHAT?
HM?
I HAVE NO IDEA WHAT YOU'RE TALKING ABOUT.
I know nothing.
!!

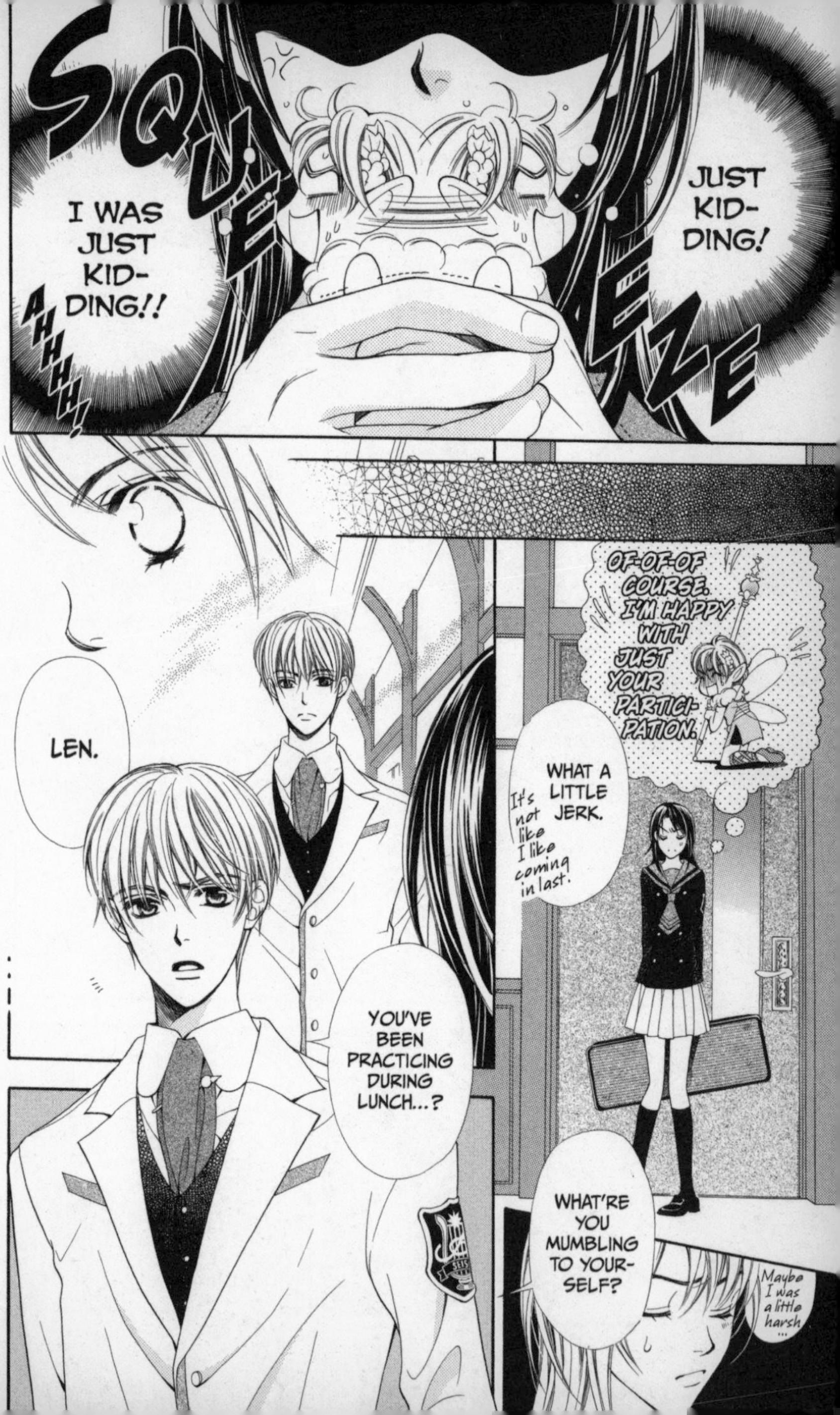
JUST KID-DING!
I WAS JUST KID-DING!!
SQUEEZE
AHHHH!
OF-OF-OF COURSE. I'M HAPPY WITH JUST YOUR PARTICI-PATION.
WHAT A LITTLE JERK.
It's not like I like coming in last.
WHAT'RE YOU MUMBLING TO YOUR-SELF?
Maybe I was a little harsh...
LEN.
...!
YOU'VE BEEN PRACTICING DURING LUNCH...?

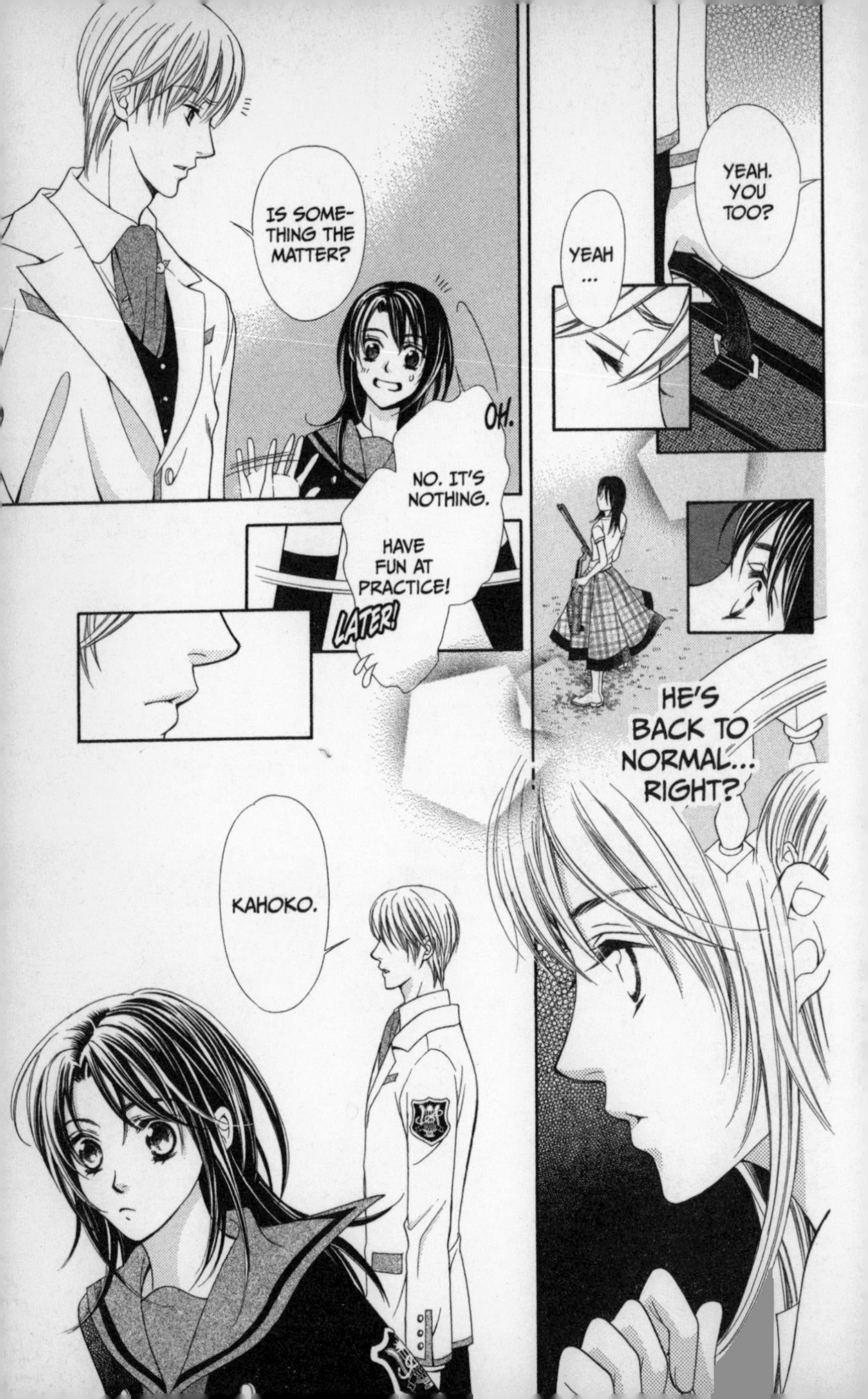
YEAH. YOU TOO?
YEAH ...
HE'S BACK TO NORMAL... RIGHT?
IS SOME-THING THE MATTER?
OH.
NO. IT'S NOTHING.
HAVE FUN AT PRACTICE!
LATER!
KAHOKO.

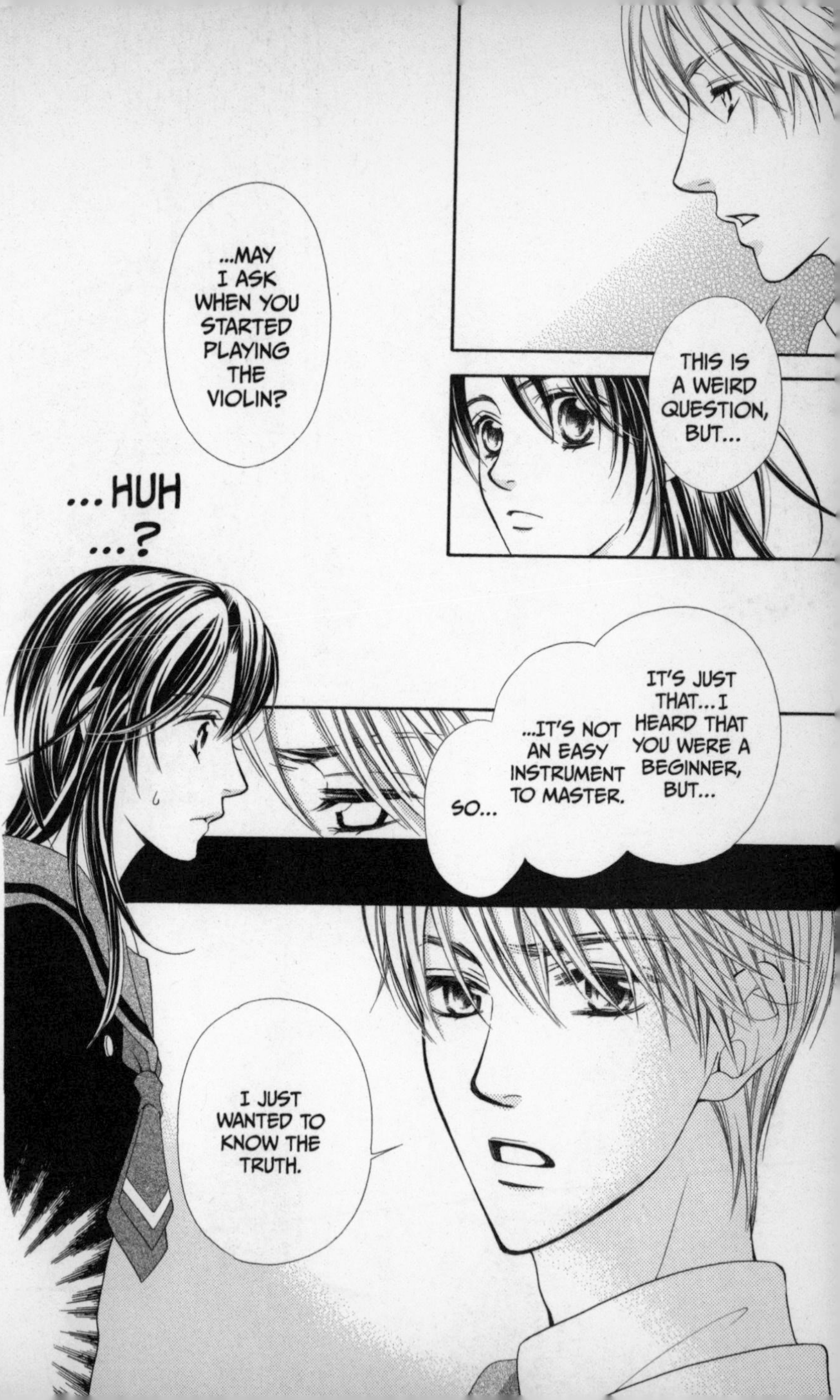
THIS IS A WEIRD QUESTION, BUT...
...MAY I ASK WHEN YOU STARTED PLAYING THE VIOLIN?
...HUH ...?
IT'S JUST THAT...I HEARD THAT YOU WERE A BEGINNER, BUT...
...IT'S NOT AN EASY INSTRUMENT TO MASTER.
SO...
I JUST WANTED TO KNOW THE TRUTH.

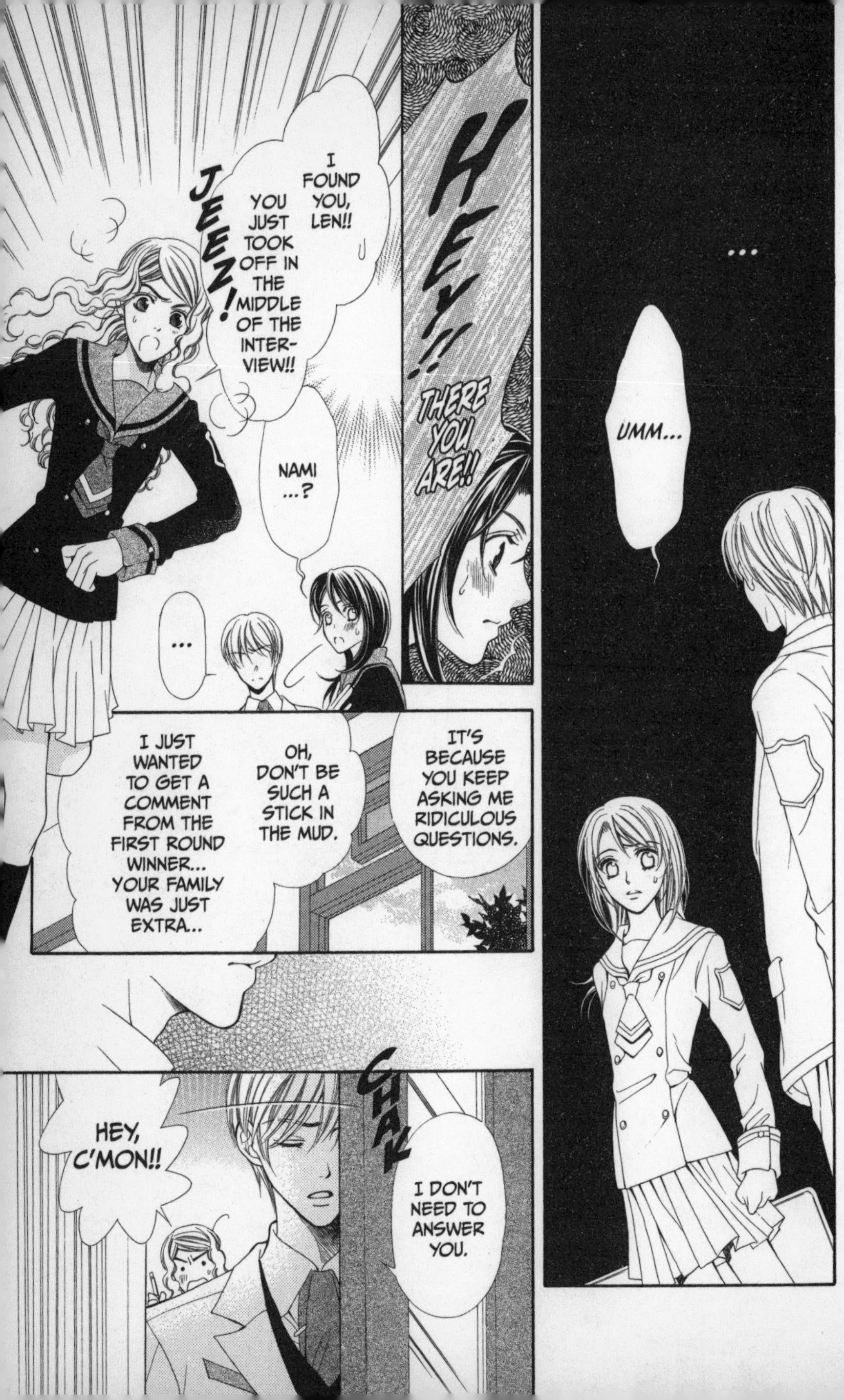
...
UMM...
HEY!!
THERE YOU ARE!!
I FOUND YOU, LEN!!
JEEZ!
YOU JUST TOOK OFF IN THE MIDDLE OF THE INTER-VIEW!!
NAMI ...?
...
IT'S BECAUSE YOU KEEP ASKING ME RIDICULOUS QUESTIONS.
OH, DON'T BE SUCH A STICK IN THE MUD.
I JUST WANTED TO GET A COMMENT FROM THE FIRST ROUND WINNER... YOUR FAMILY WAS JUST EXTRA...
CHAK
I DON'T NEED TO ANSWER YOU.
HEY, C'MON!!

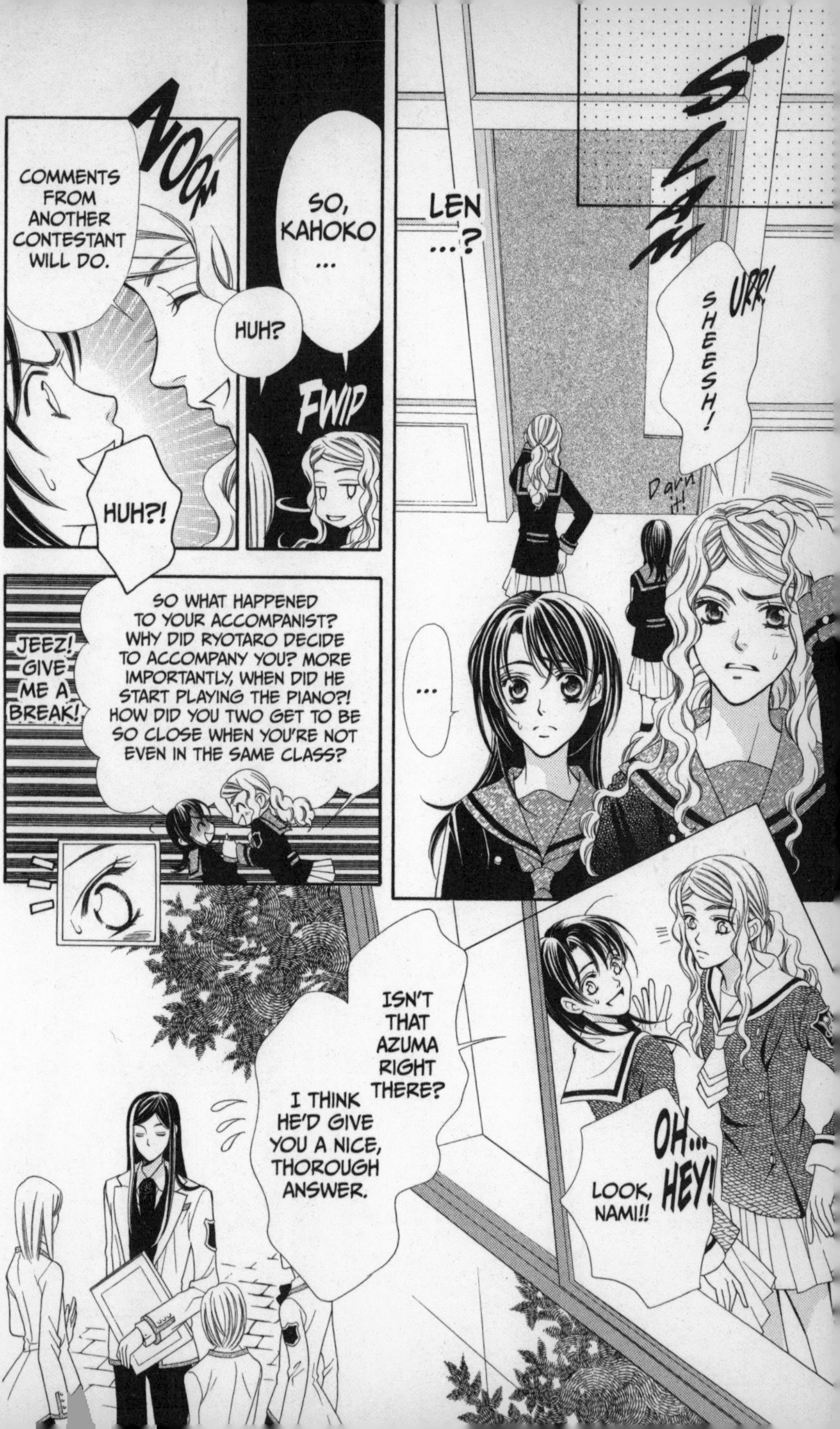
SLAM
SHEESH!
URR!
Darn it!
LEN ...?
...
SO, KAHOKO ...
HUH?
FWIP
NOOM
COMMENTS FROM ANOTHER CONTESTANT WILL DO.
HUH?!
SO WHAT HAPPENED TO YOUR ACCOMPANIST? WHY DID RYOTARO DECIDE TO ACCOMPANY YOU? MORE IMPORTANTLY, WHEN DID HE START PLAYING THE PIANO?! HOW DID YOU TWO GET TO BE SO CLOSE WHEN YOU'RE NOT EVEN IN THE SAME CLASS?
JEEZ! GIVE ME A BREAK!
LOOK, NAMI!!
OH... HEY!
ISN'T THAT AZUMA RIGHT THERE?
I THINK HE'D GIVE YOU A NICE, THOROUGH ANSWER.

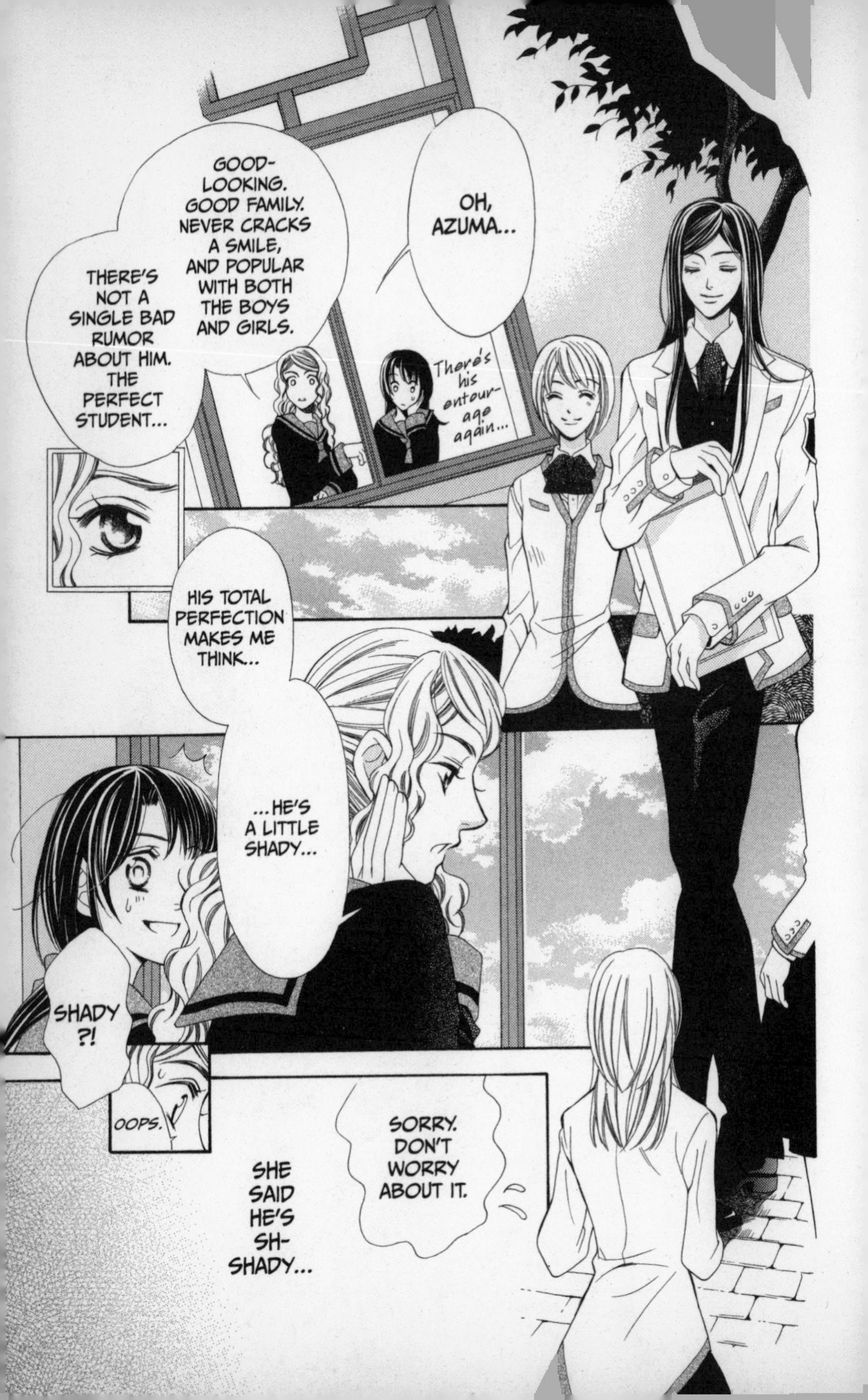
OH, AZUMA...
There's his entourage again...
GOOD-LOOKING. GOOD FAMILY. NEVER CRACKS A SMILE, AND POPULAR WITH BOTH THE BOYS AND GIRLS.
THERE'S NOT A SINGLE BAD RUMOR ABOUT HIM. THE PERFECT STUDENT...
HIS TOTAL PERFECTION MAKES ME THINK...
...HE'S A LITTLE SHADY...
SHADY?!
OOPS.
SORRY. DON'T WORRY ABOUT IT.
SHE SAID HE'S SH-SHADY...

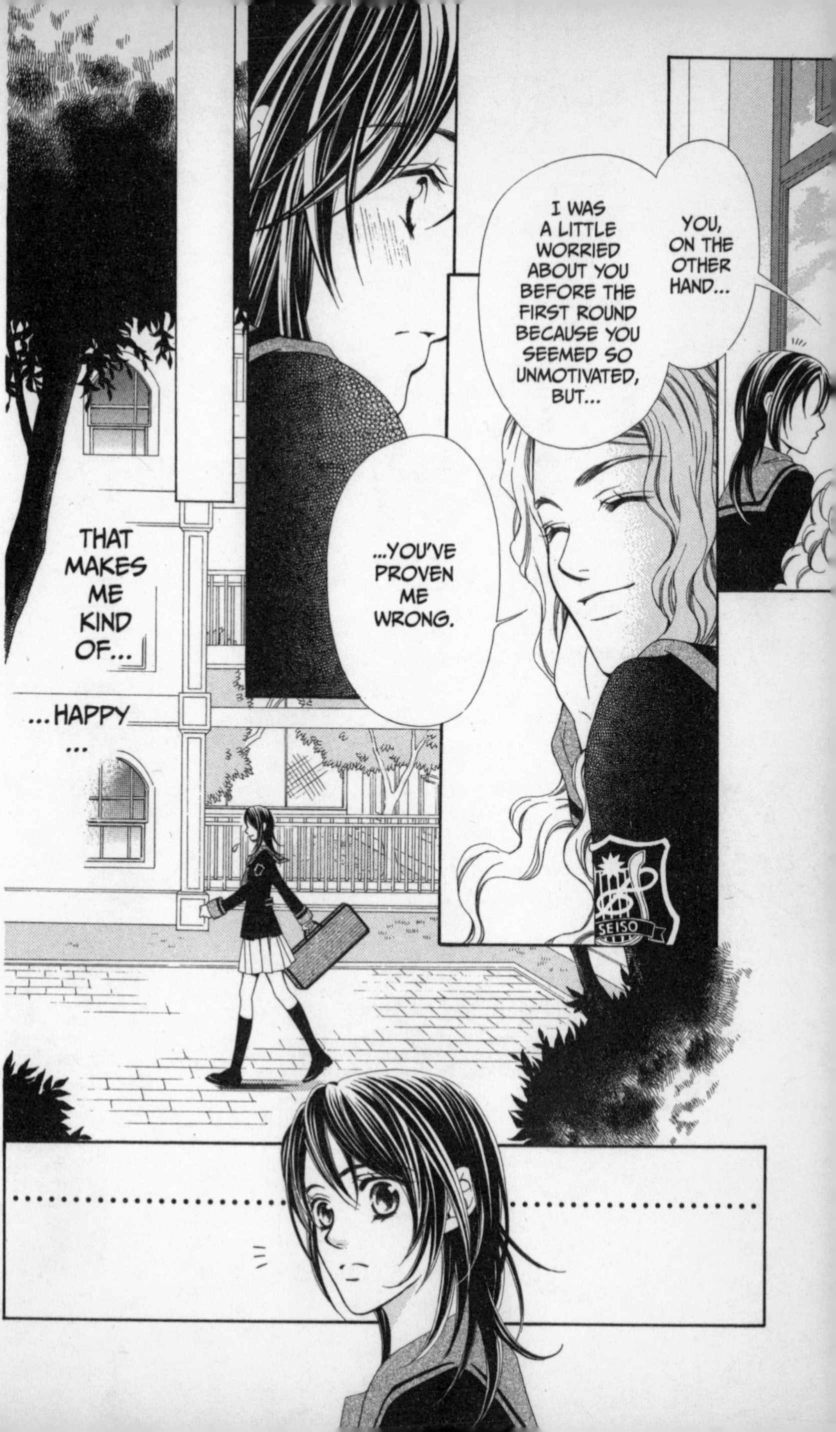
YOU, ON THE OTHER HAND...
I WAS A LITTLE WORRIED ABOUT YOU BEFORE THE FIRST ROUND BECAUSE YOU SEEMED SO UNMOTIVATED, BUT...
...YOU'VE PROVEN ME WRONG.
SEISO
THAT MAKES ME KIND OF...
...HAPPY...
....

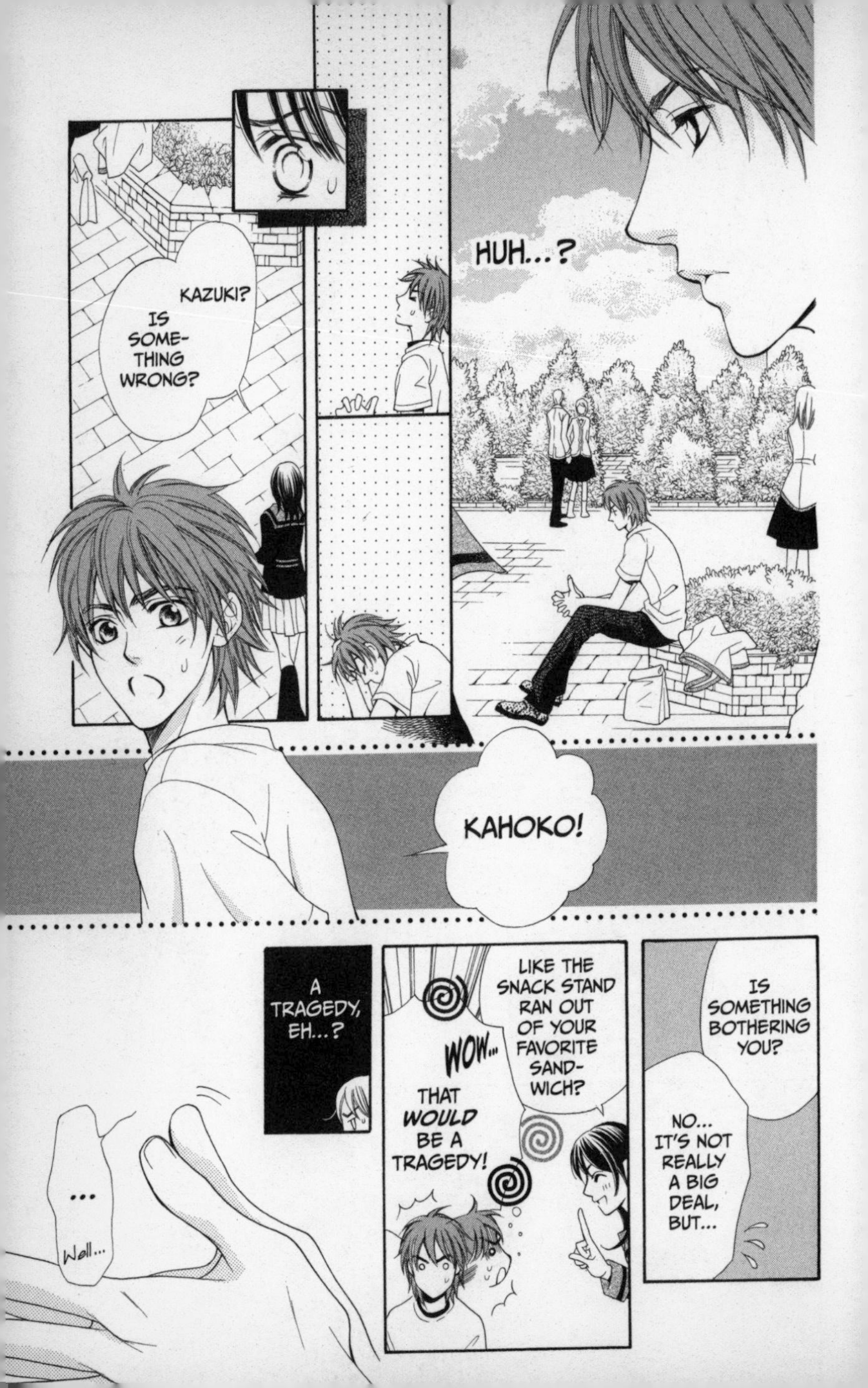
HUH...?
KAZUKI? IS SOMETHING WRONG?
KAHOKO!
IS SOMETHING BOTHERING YOU?
NO... IT'S NOT REALLY A BIG DEAL, BUT...
LIKE THE SNACK STAND RAN OUT OF YOUR FAVORITE SANDWICH?
WOW...
THAT WOULD BE A TRAGEDY!
A TRAGEDY, EH...?
...
Well...

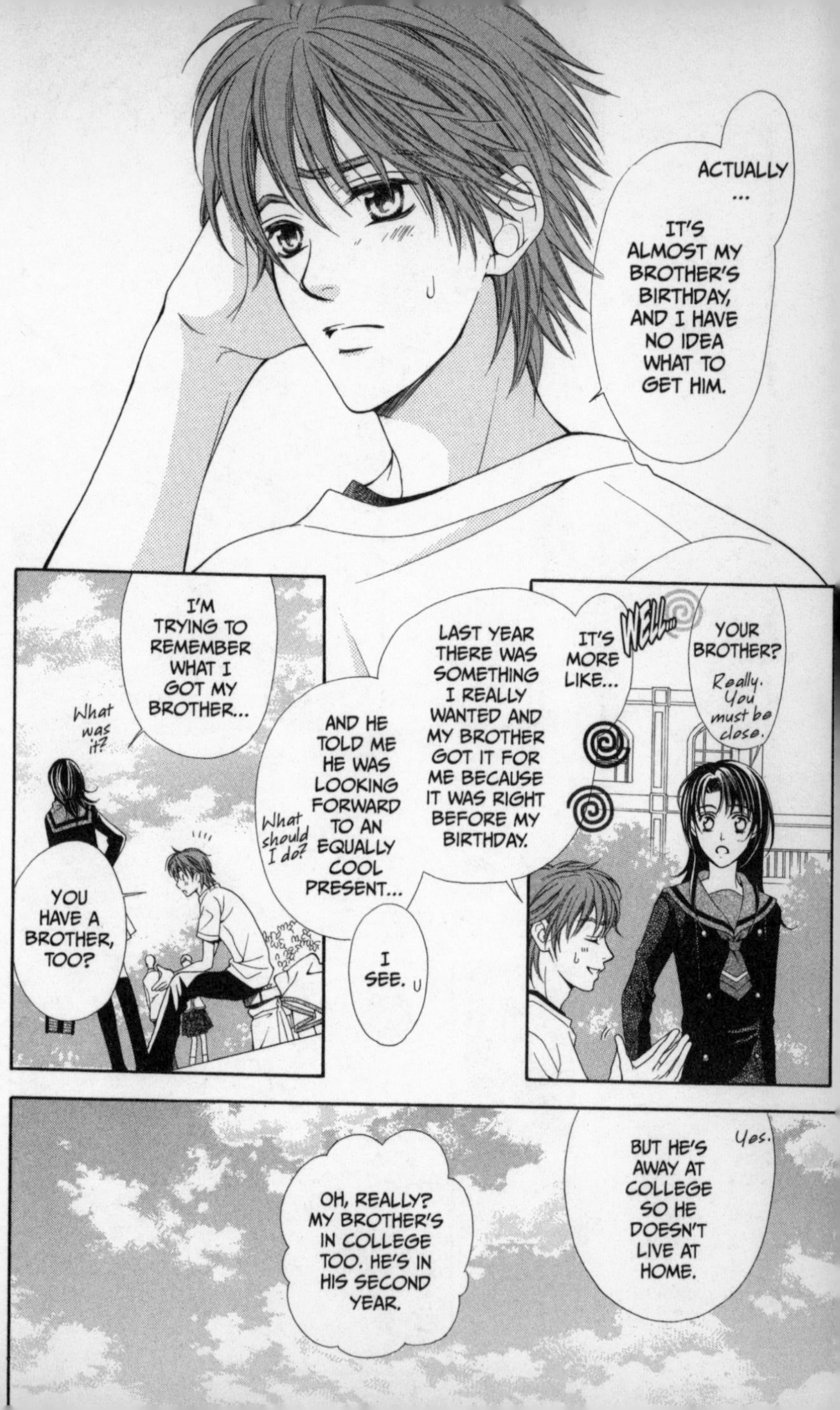
ACTUALLY ...
IT'S ALMOST MY BROTHER'S BIRTHDAY, AND I HAVE NO IDEA WHAT TO GET HIM.
YOUR BROTHER?
Really. You must be close.
WELL...
IT'S MORE LIKE...
LAST YEAR THERE WAS SOMETHING I REALLY WANTED AND MY BROTHER GOT IT FOR ME BECAUSE IT WAS RIGHT BEFORE MY BIRTHDAY.
AND HE TOLD ME HE WAS LOOKING FORWARD TO AN EQUALLY COOL PRESENT...
What should I do?
I SEE.
I'M TRYING TO REMEMBER WHAT I GOT MY BROTHER...
What was it?
YOU HAVE A BROTHER, TOO?
Yes.
BUT HE'S AWAY AT COLLEGE SO HE DOESN'T LIVE AT HOME.
OH, REALLY? MY BROTHER'S IN COLLEGE TOO. HE'S IN HIS SECOND YEAR.

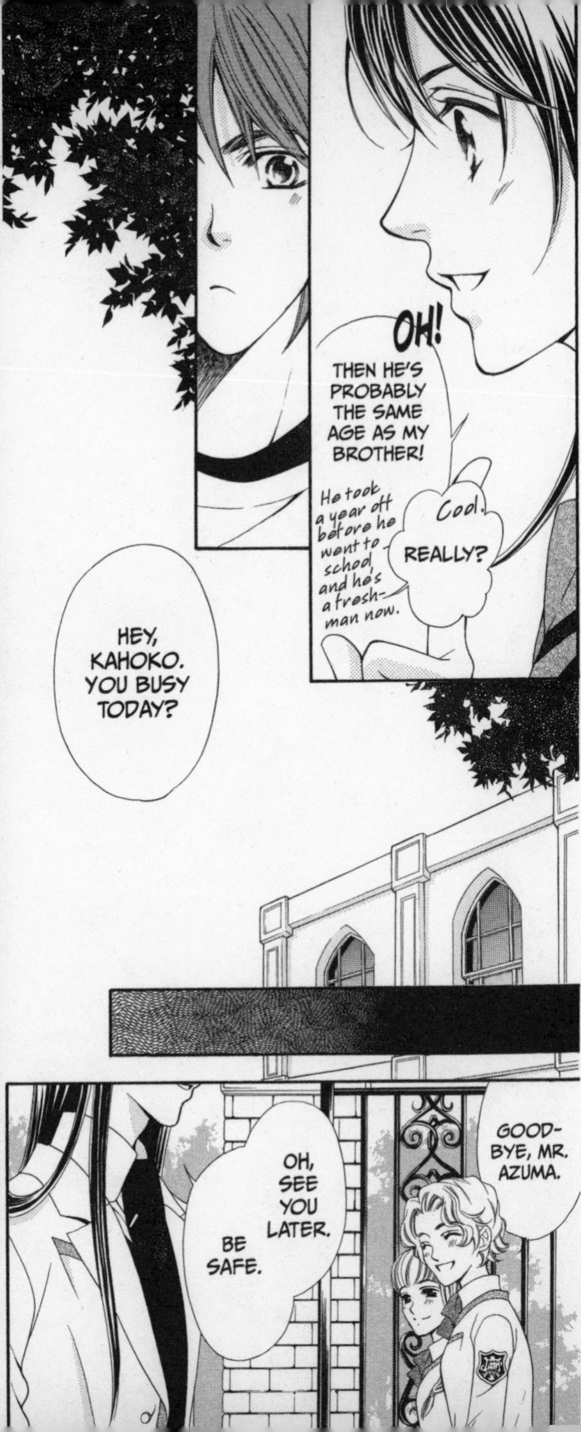
OH!
THEN HE'S PROBABLY THE SAME AGE AS MY BROTHER!
He took a year off before he went to school and he's a fresh-man now.
Cool.
REALLY?
HEY, KAHOKO. YOU BUSY TODAY?
GOOD-BYE, MR. AZUMA.
OH, SEE YOU LATER.
BE SAFE.

ONE

Long time no see. This is Yuki Kure. Thank you for buying volume 4 of *La Corda*.

I wrote in the author's column in volume 3 that Azuma would play a bigger role in this volume, and so he's appearing much more than he has in the past.

Well, I hope you enjoy this volume.

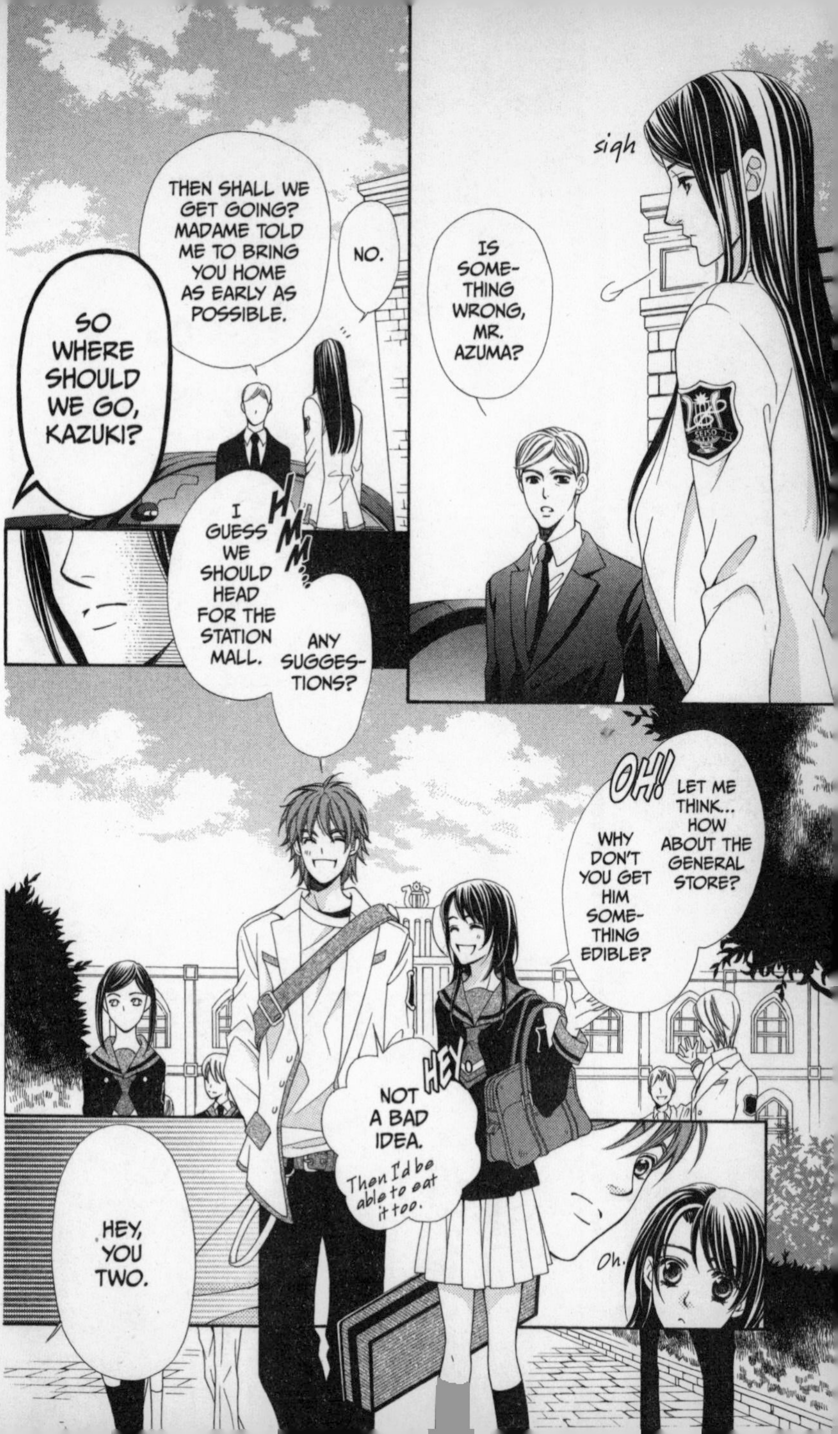
sigh
IS SOMETHING WRONG, MR. AZUMA?
NO.
THEN SHALL WE GET GOING? MADAME TOLD ME TO BRING YOU HOME AS EARLY AS POSSIBLE.
SO WHERE SHOULD WE GO, KAZUKI?
HMM...
I GUESS WE SHOULD HEAD FOR THE STATION MALL.
ANY SUGGESTIONS?
OH!
LET ME THINK... HOW ABOUT THE GENERAL STORE?
WHY DON'T YOU GET HIM SOMETHING EDIBLE?
HEY
NOT A BAD IDEA.
Then I'd be able to eat it too.
Oh.
HEY, YOU TWO.

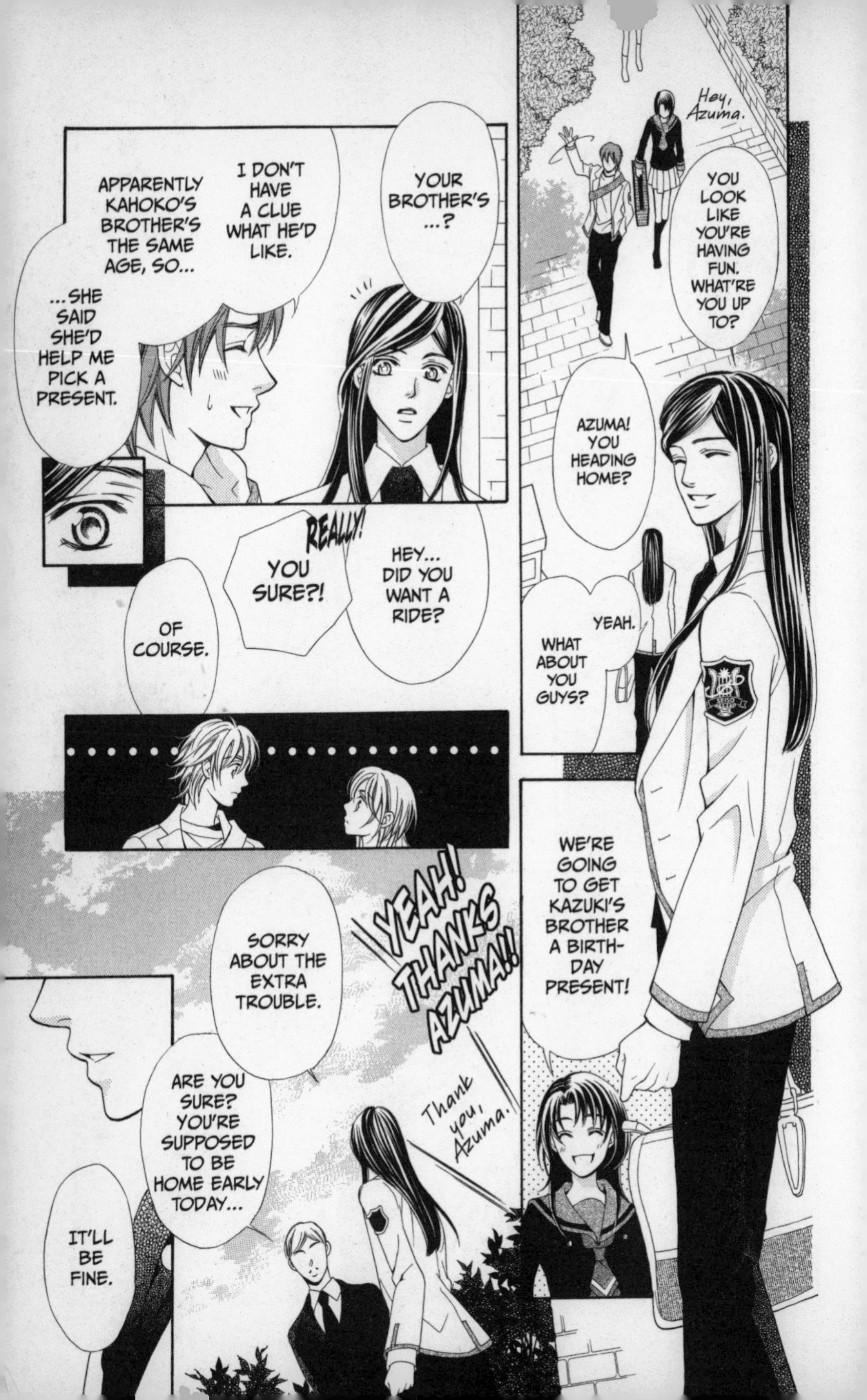
Hey, Azuma.
YOU LOOK LIKE YOU'RE HAVING FUN. WHAT'RE YOU UP TO?
AZUMA! YOU HEADING HOME?
YEAH.
WHAT ABOUT YOU GUYS?
WE'RE GOING TO GET KAZUKI'S BROTHER A BIRTH-DAY PRESENT!
Thank you, Azuma.
YOUR BROTHER'S ...?
I DON'T HAVE A CLUE WHAT HE'D LIKE.
APPARENTLY KAHOKO'S BROTHER'S THE SAME AGE, SO...
...SHE SAID SHE'D HELP ME PICK A PRESENT.
HEY... DID YOU WANT A RIDE?
REALLY!
YOU SURE?!
OF COURSE.
YEAH! THANKS AZUMA!!
SORRY ABOUT THE EXTRA TROUBLE.
ARE YOU SURE? YOU'RE SUPPOSED TO BE HOME EARLY TODAY...
IT'LL BE FINE.

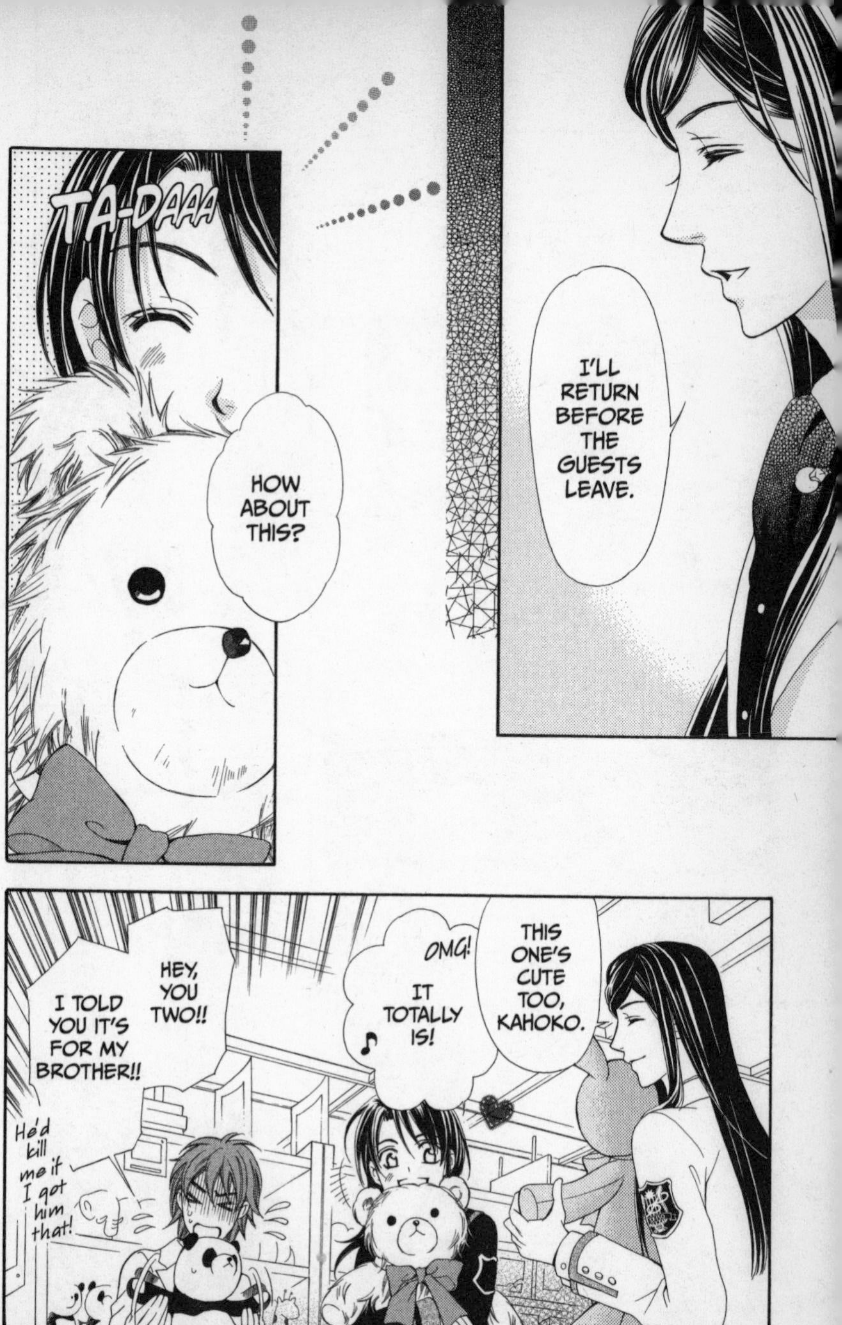
I'LL RETURN BEFORE THE GUESTS LEAVE.
TA-DAAA
HOW ABOUT THIS?
THIS ONE'S CUTE TOO, KAHOKO.
OMG!
IT TOTALLY IS!
HEY, YOU TWO!!
I TOLD YOU IT'S FOR MY BROTHER!!
He'd kill me if I got him that!

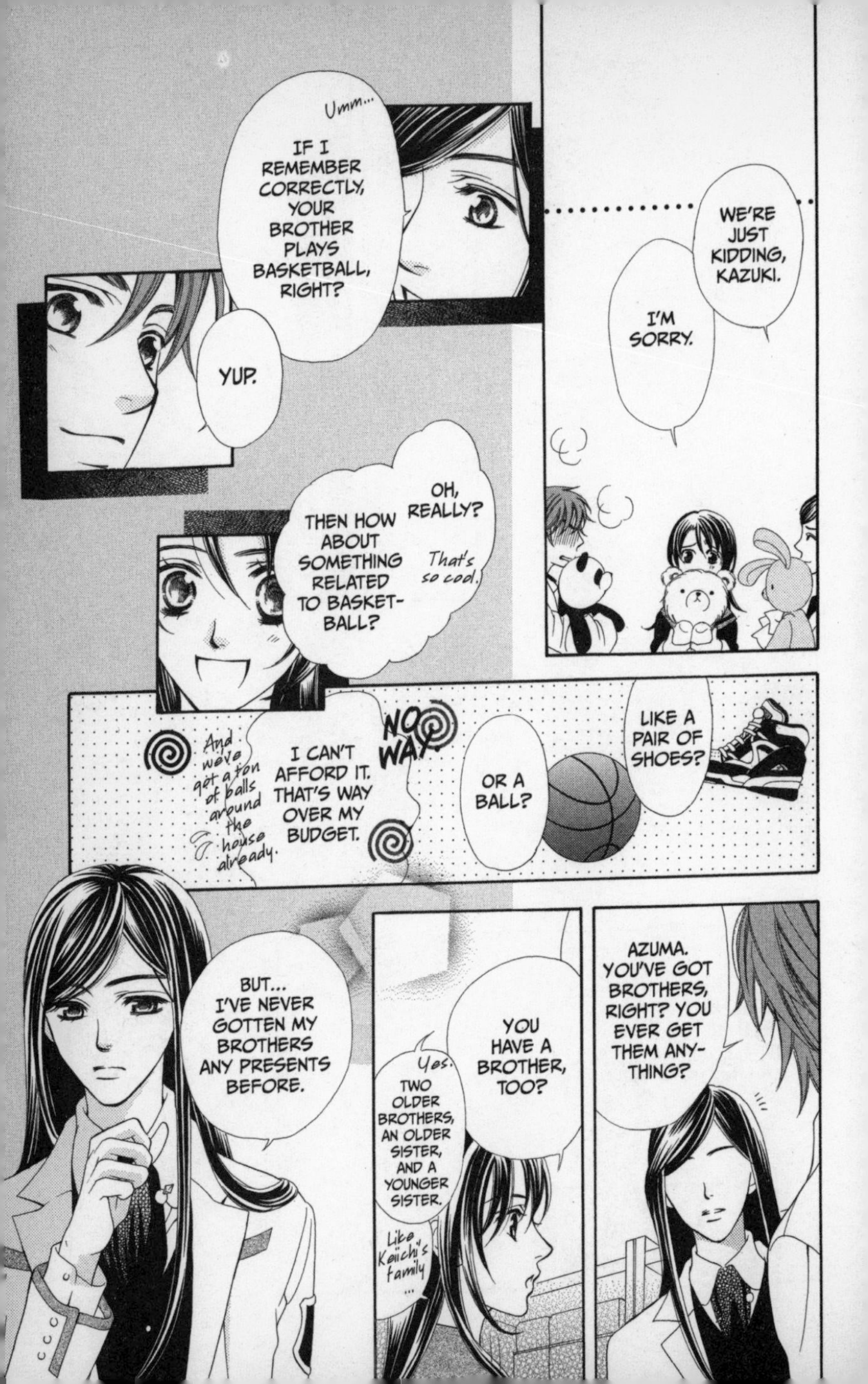
WE'RE JUST KIDDING, KAZUKI.
I'M SORRY.
Umm...
IF I REMEMBER CORRECTLY, YOUR BROTHER PLAYS BASKETBALL, RIGHT?
YUP.
OH, REALLY?
That's so cool.
THEN HOW ABOUT SOMETHING RELATED TO BASKET-BALL?
LIKE A PAIR OF SHOES?
OR A BALL?
NO WAY.
I CAN'T AFFORD IT. THAT'S WAY OVER MY BUDGET.
And we've got a ton of balls around the house already.
AZUMA. YOU'VE GOT BROTHERS, RIGHT? YOU EVER GET THEM ANY-THING?
YOU HAVE A BROTHER, TOO?
Yes.
TWO OLDER BROTHERS, AN OLDER SISTER, AND A YOUNGER SISTER.
Like Keiichi's family...
BUT... I'VE NEVER GOTTEN MY BROTHERS ANY PRESENTS BEFORE.

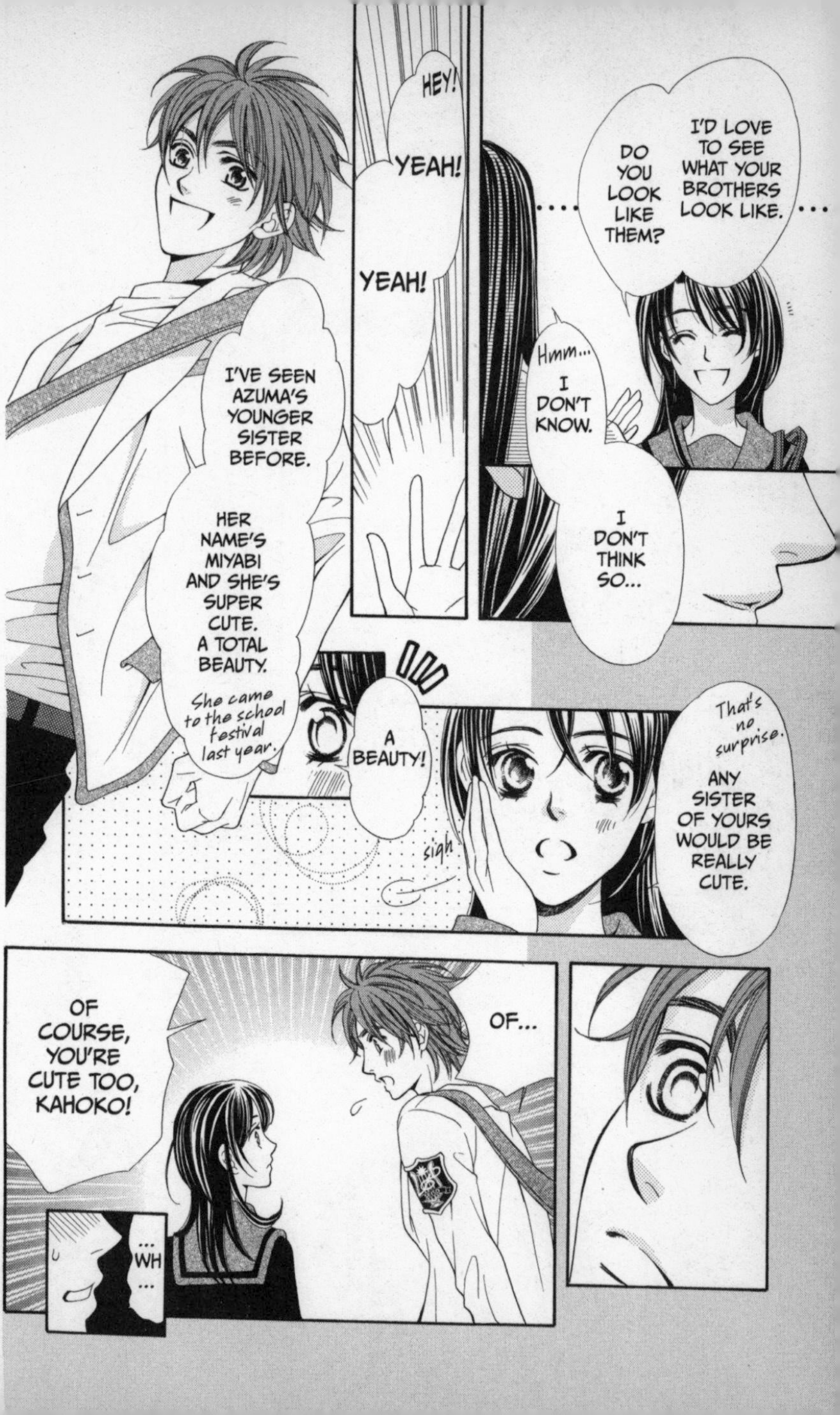
I'D LOVE TO SEE WHAT YOUR BROTHERS LOOK LIKE.
DO YOU LOOK LIKE THEM?
Hmm... I DON'T KNOW.
I DON'T THINK SO...
HEY!
YEAH!
YEAH!
I'VE SEEN AZUMA'S YOUNGER SISTER BEFORE.
HER NAME'S MIYABI AND SHE'S SUPER CUTE. A TOTAL BEAUTY.
She came to the school festival last year.
That's no surprise.
ANY SISTER OF YOURS WOULD BE REALLY CUTE.
sigh
A BEAUTY!
OF...
OF COURSE, YOU'RE CUTE TOO, KAHOKO!
...WH...

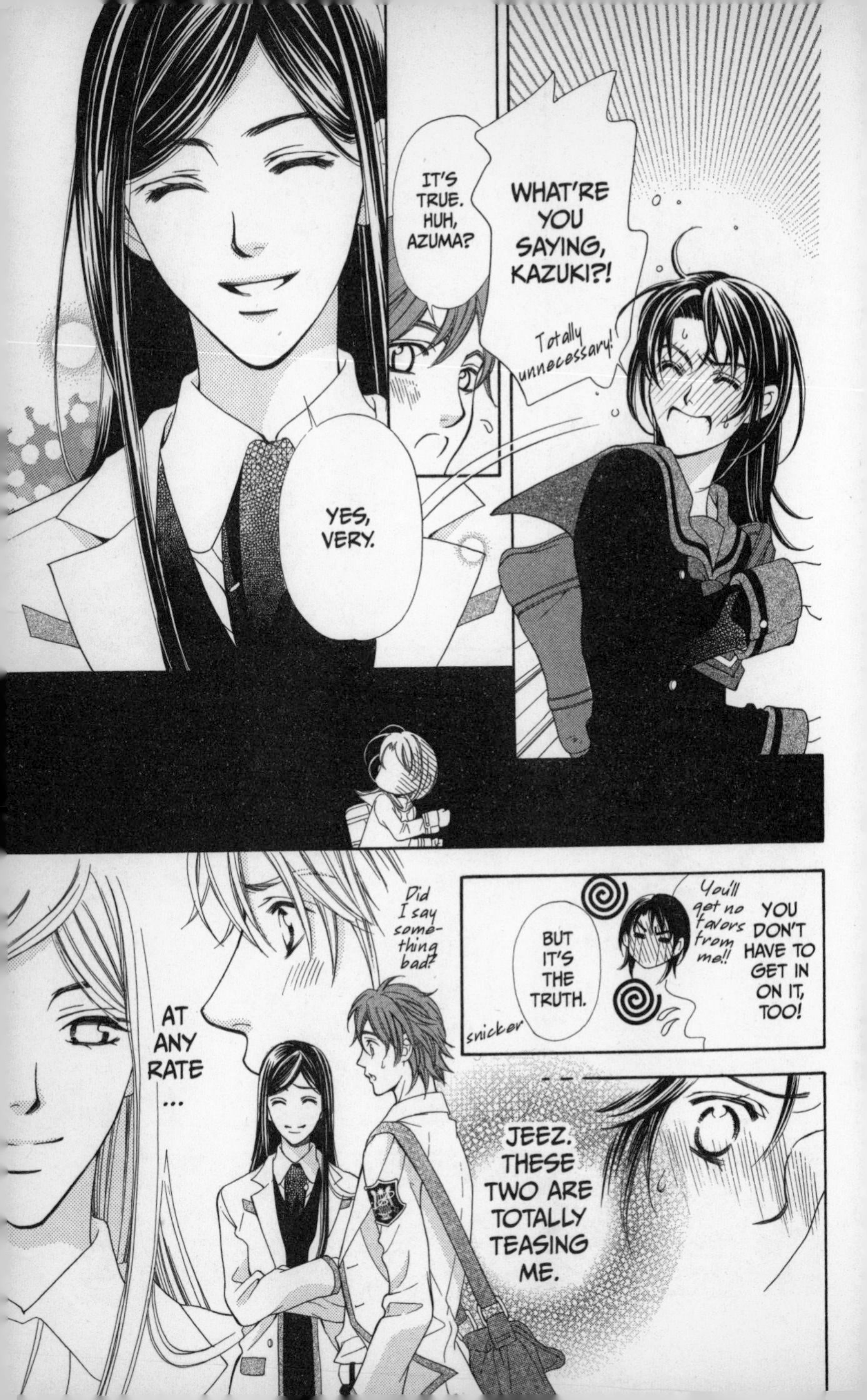
WHAT'RE YOU SAYING, KAZUKI?!
Totally unnecessary!
IT'S TRUE. HUH, AZUMA?
YES, VERY.
YOU DON'T HAVE TO GET IN ON IT, TOO!
You'll get no favors from me!!
BUT IT'S THE TRUTH.
snicker
JEEZ. THESE TWO ARE TOTALLY TEASING ME.
Did I say some-thing bad?
AT ANY RATE ...

HERE YOU GO. Is this the one you want?

...I CAN'T BELIEVE HOW CLOSE KAZUKI AND AZUMA ARE EVEN THOUGH THEY'RE SO DIFFERENT.

SLIP

Jeez...

And... I CAN'T HELP BUT NOTICE THE GIRLS CHECKING THEM OUT...

ESPECIALLY AZUMA...

They do stand out.

NOT THAT I BLAME THEM.

Even a child is no match for him...

WOW...

28

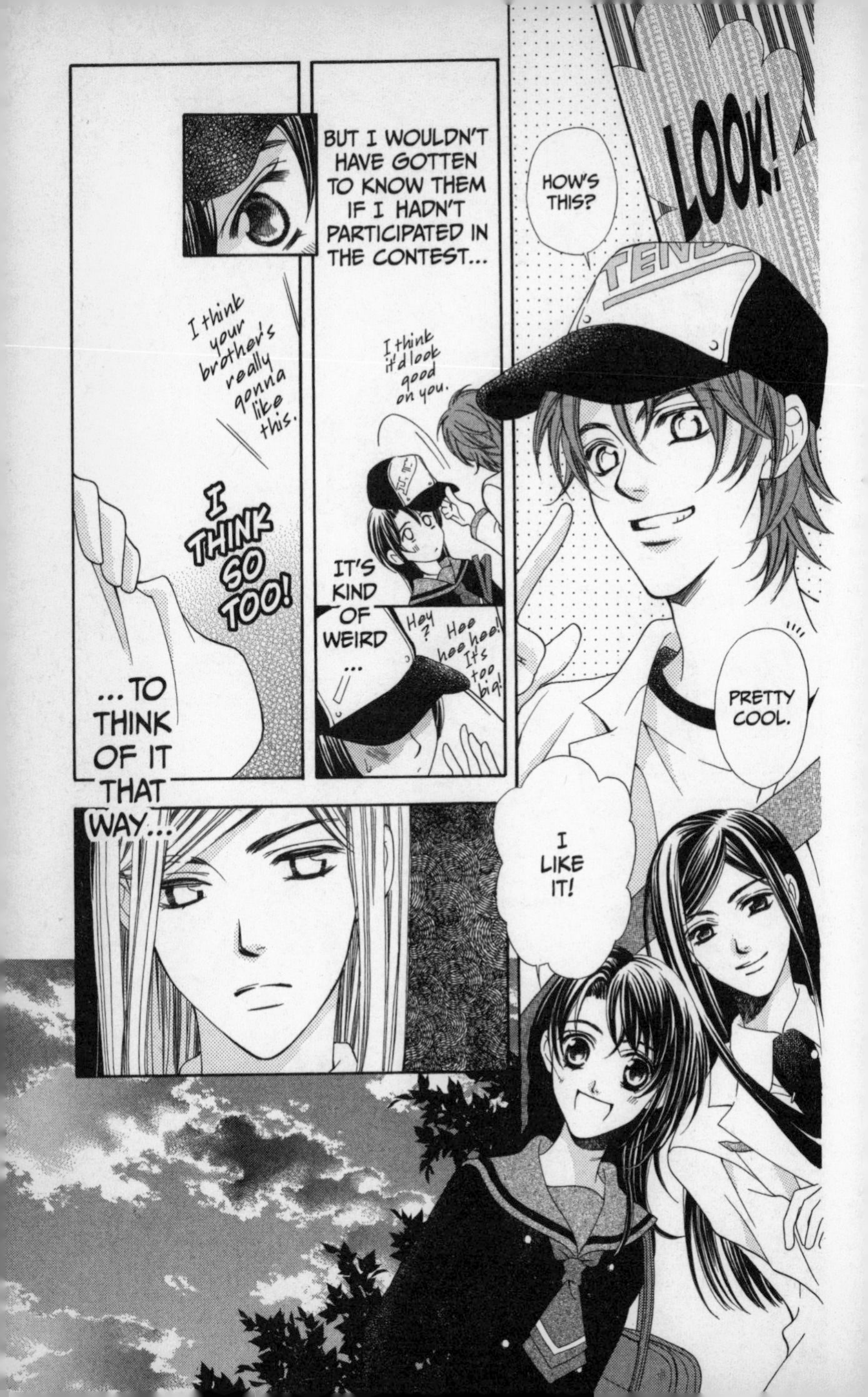
LOOK!
HOW'S THIS?
PRETTY COOL.
I LIKE IT!
BUT I WOULDN'T HAVE GOTTEN TO KNOW THEM IF I HADN'T PARTICIPATED IN THE CONTEST...
I think it'd look good on you.
IT'S KIND OF WEIRD...
Hey?
Hee hee hee! It's too big!
I think your brother's really gonna like this.
I THINK SO TOO!
...TO THINK OF IT THAT WAY...

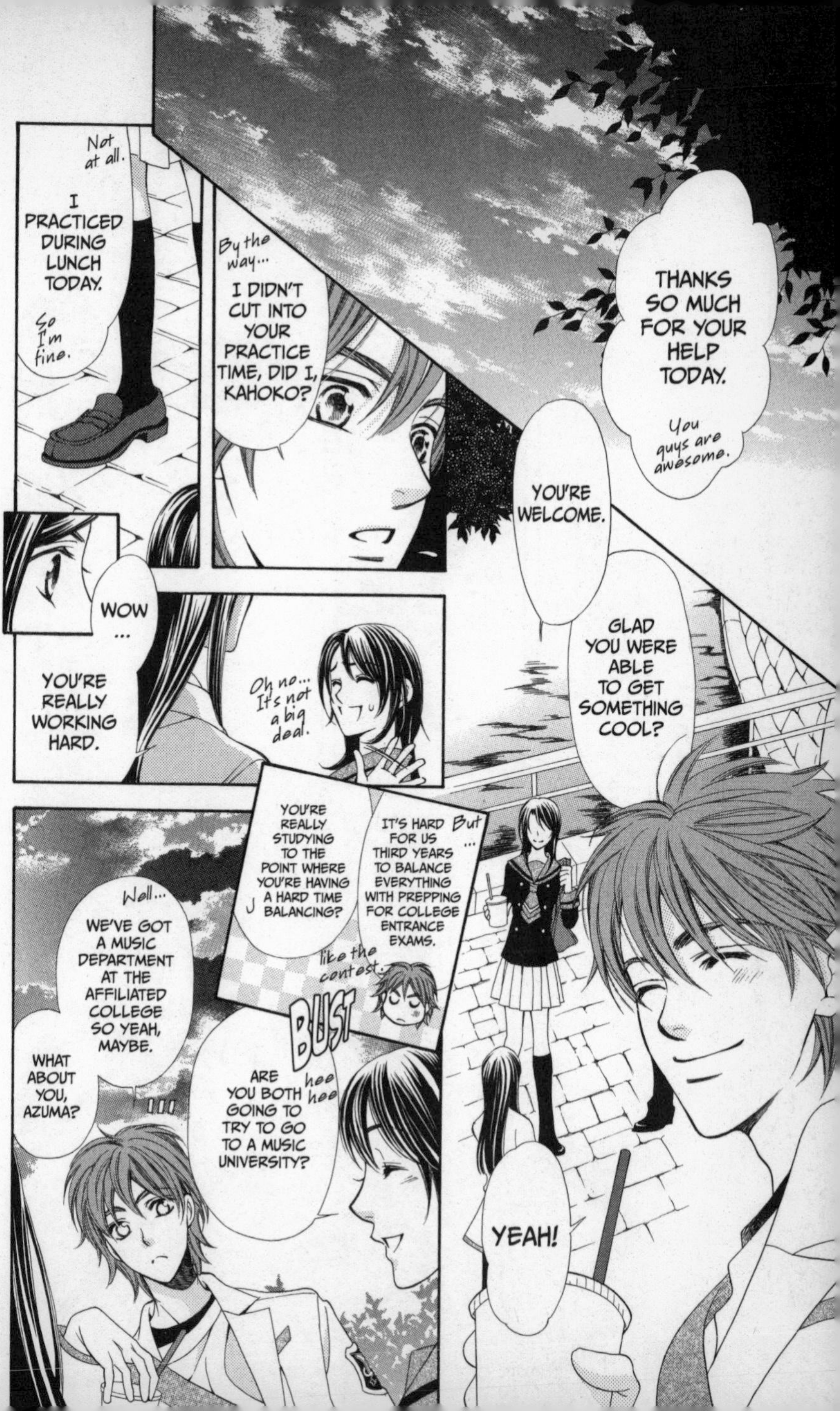
THANKS SO MUCH FOR YOUR HELP TODAY.
You guys are awesome.
YOU'RE WELCOME.
GLAD YOU WERE ABLE TO GET SOMETHING COOL?
YEAH!
By the way...
I DIDN'T CUT INTO YOUR PRACTICE TIME, DID I, KAHOKO?
Not at all.
I PRACTICED DURING LUNCH TODAY.
So I'm fine.
WOW...
YOU'RE REALLY WORKING HARD.
Oh no... It's not a big deal.
But...
IT'S HARD FOR US THIRD YEARS TO BALANCE EVERYTHING WITH PREPPING FOR COLLEGE ENTRANCE EXAMS.
YOU'RE REALLY STUDYING TO THE POINT WHERE YOU'RE HAVING A HARD TIME BALANCING?
like the contest.
BUST
ARE YOU BOTH GOING TO TRY TO GO TO A MUSIC UNIVERSITY?
hee hee
Well...
WE'VE GOT A MUSIC DEPARTMENT AT THE AFFILIATED COLLEGE SO YEAH, MAYBE.
WHAT ABOUT YOU, AZUMA?

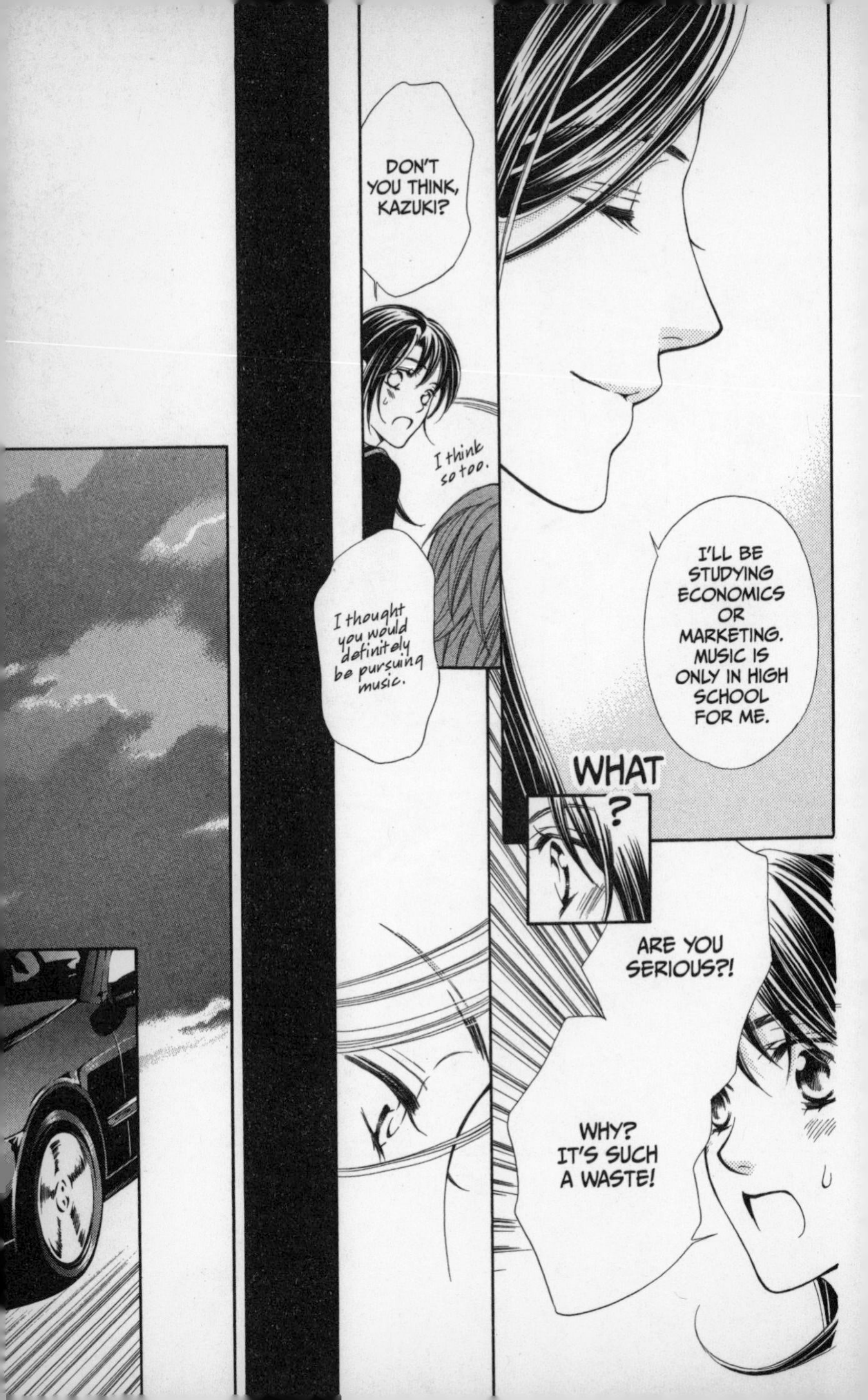
DON'T YOU THINK, KAZUKI?
I think so too.
I thought you would definitely be pursuing music.
I'LL BE STUDYING ECONOMICS OR MARKETING. MUSIC IS ONLY IN HIGH SCHOOL FOR ME.
WHAT?
ARE YOU SERIOUS?!
WHY? IT'S SUCH A WASTE!

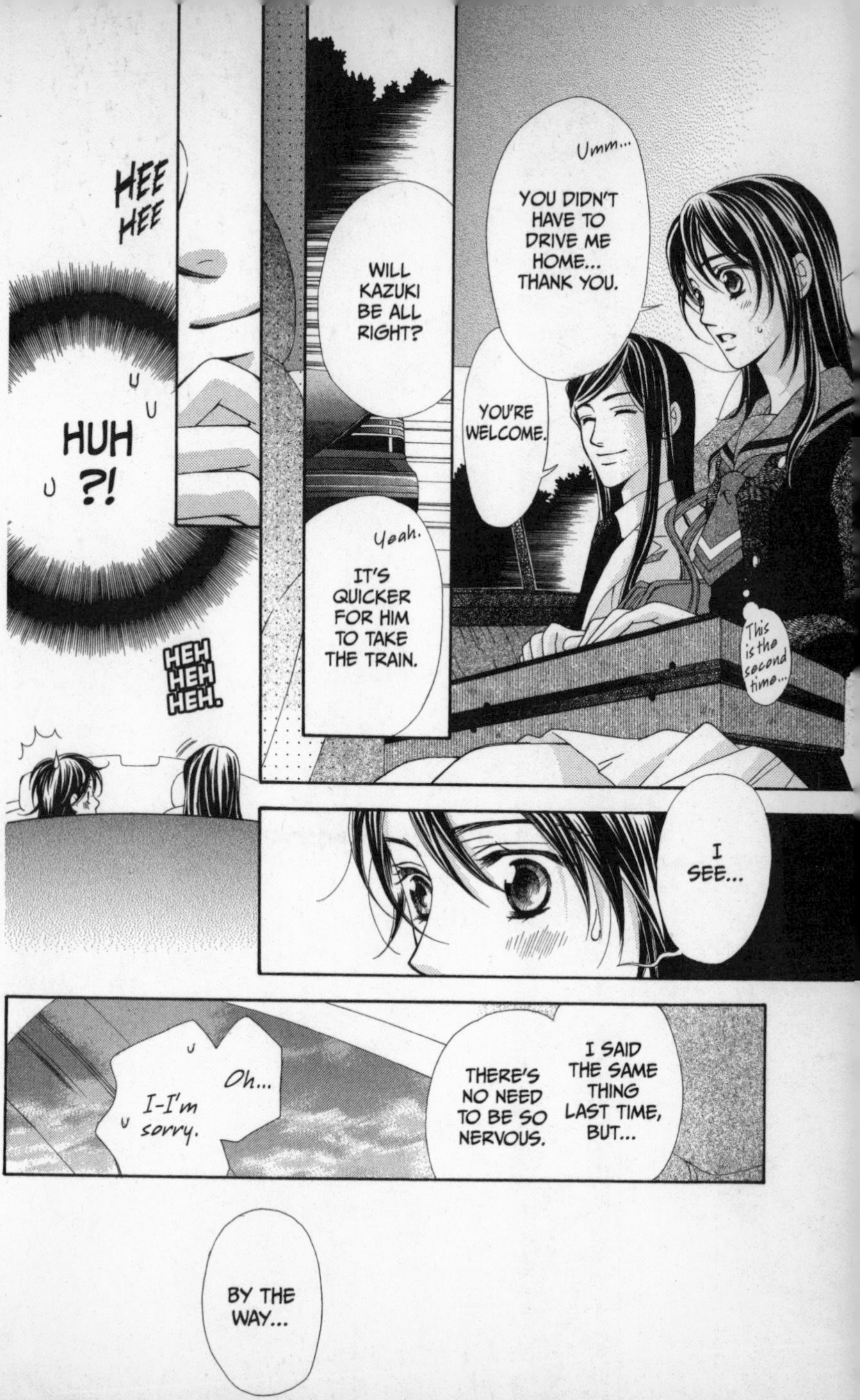
Umm...
YOU DIDN'T HAVE TO DRIVE ME HOME... THANK YOU.
YOU'RE WELCOME.
This is the second time...
WILL KAZUKI BE ALL RIGHT?
Yeah.
IT'S QUICKER FOR HIM TO TAKE THE TRAIN.
I SEE...
HEE HEE
HUH ?!
HEH HEH HEH.
I SAID THE SAME THING LAST TIME, BUT...
THERE'S NO NEED TO BE SO NERVOUS.
Oh...
I-I'm sorry.
BY THE WAY...

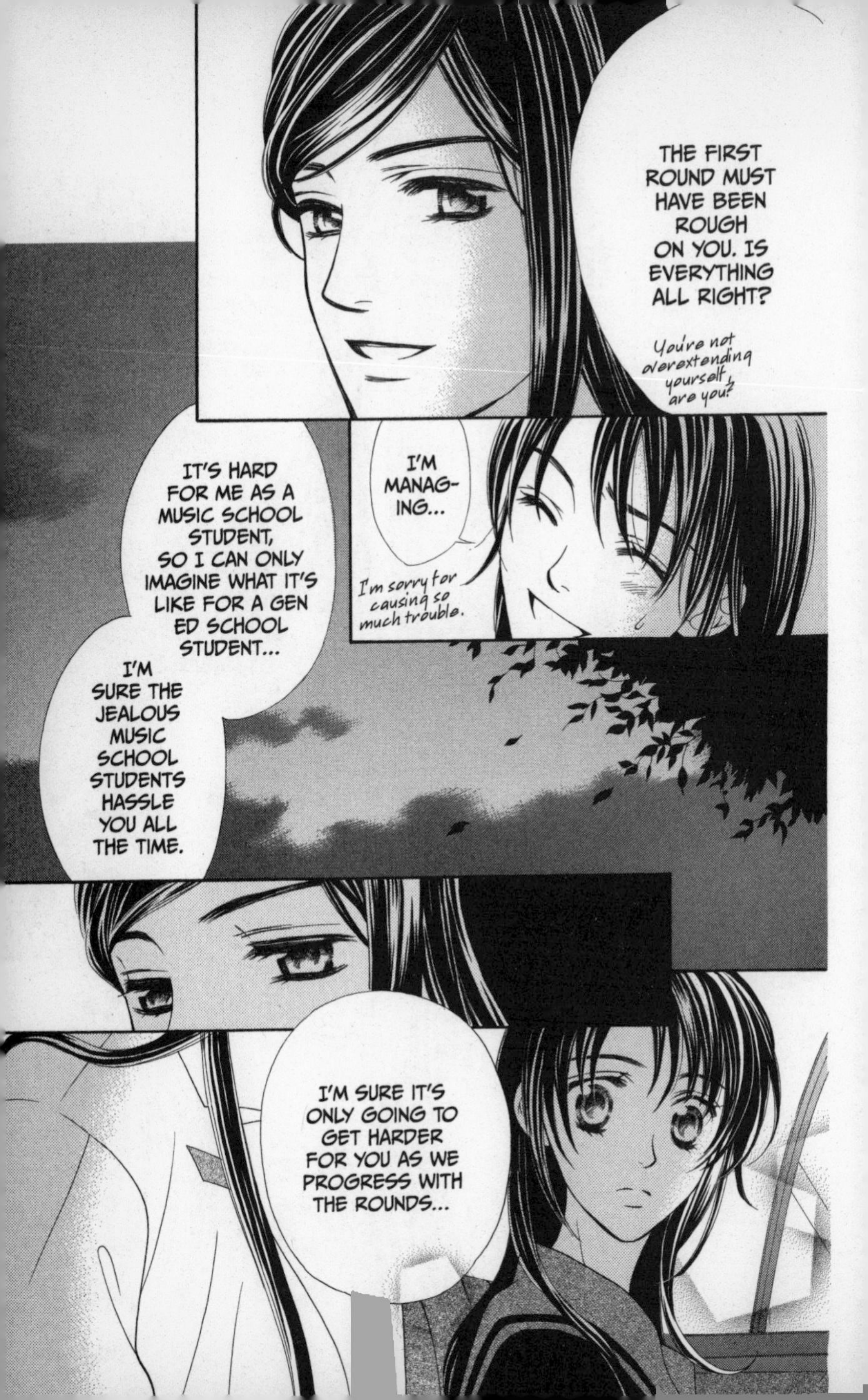
THE FIRST ROUND MUST HAVE BEEN ROUGH ON YOU. IS EVERYTHING ALL RIGHT?
You're not overextending yourself, are you?
I'M MANAG-ING...
I'm sorry for causing so much trouble.
IT'S HARD FOR ME AS A MUSIC SCHOOL STUDENT, SO I CAN ONLY IMAGINE WHAT IT'S LIKE FOR A GEN ED SCHOOL STUDENT...
I'M SURE THE JEALOUS MUSIC SCHOOL STUDENTS HASSLE YOU ALL THE TIME.
I'M SURE IT'S ONLY GOING TO GET HARDER FOR YOU AS WE PROGRESS WITH THE ROUNDS...

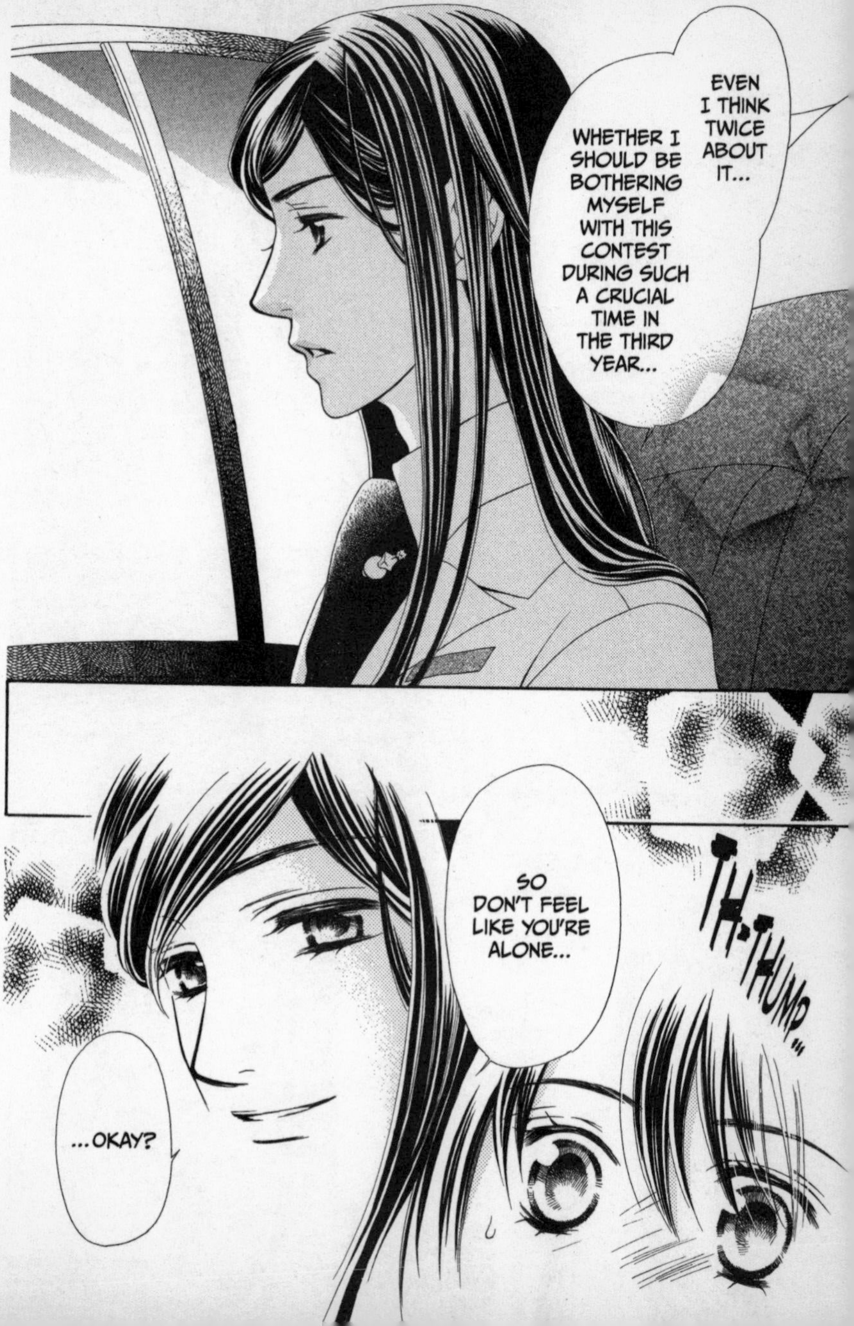
EVEN I THINK TWICE ABOUT IT...
WHETHER I SHOULD BE BOTHERING MYSELF WITH THIS CONTEST DURING SUCH A CRUCIAL TIME IN THE THIRD YEAR...
TH-THUMP...
SO DON'T FEEL LIKE YOU'RE ALONE...
...OKAY?

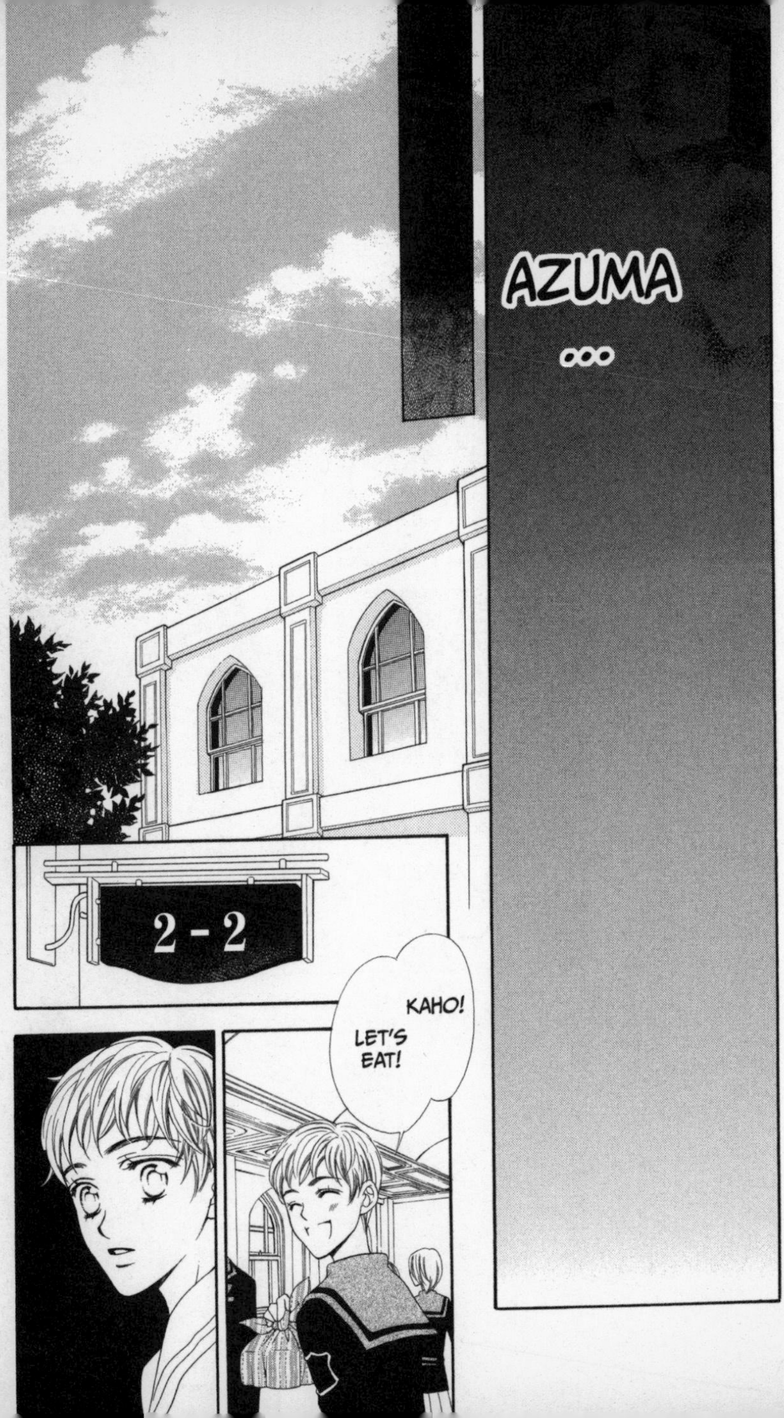
AZUMA
...
2-2
KAHO!
LET'S EAT!

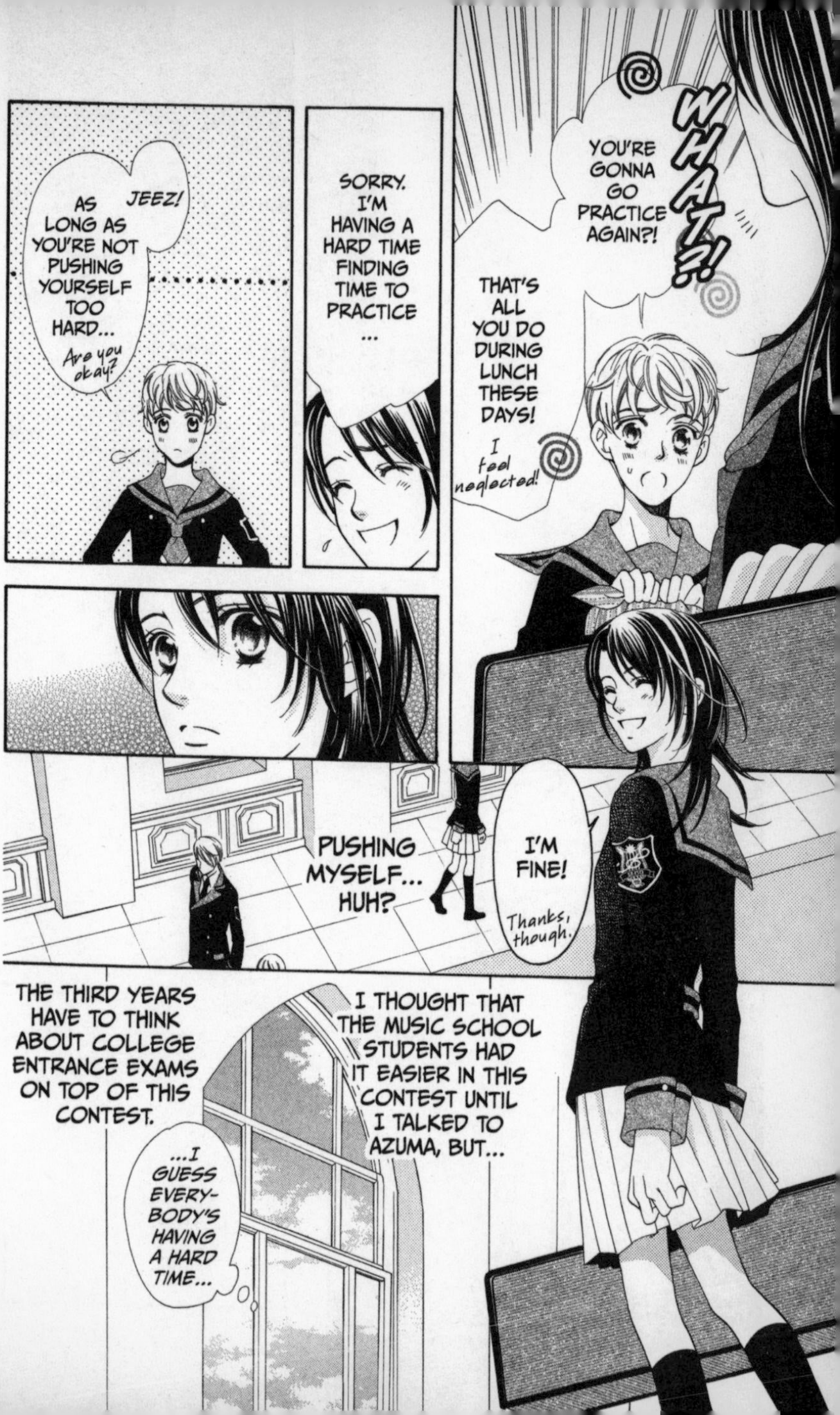
YOU'RE GONNA GO PRACTICE AGAIN?!
WHAT?!
THAT'S ALL YOU DO DURING LUNCH THESE DAYS!
I feel neglected!
SORRY. I'M HAVING A HARD TIME FINDING TIME TO PRACTICE...
JEEZ!
AS LONG AS YOU'RE NOT PUSHING YOURSELF TOO HARD...
Are you okay?
I'M FINE!
Thanks, though.
PUSHING MYSELF... HUH?
I THOUGHT THAT THE MUSIC SCHOOL STUDENTS HAD IT EASIER IN THIS CONTEST UNTIL I TALKED TO AZUMA, BUT...
THE THIRD YEARS HAVE TO THINK ABOUT COLLEGE ENTRANCE EXAMS ON TOP OF THIS CONTEST.
...I GUESS EVERYBODY'S HAVING A HARD TIME...

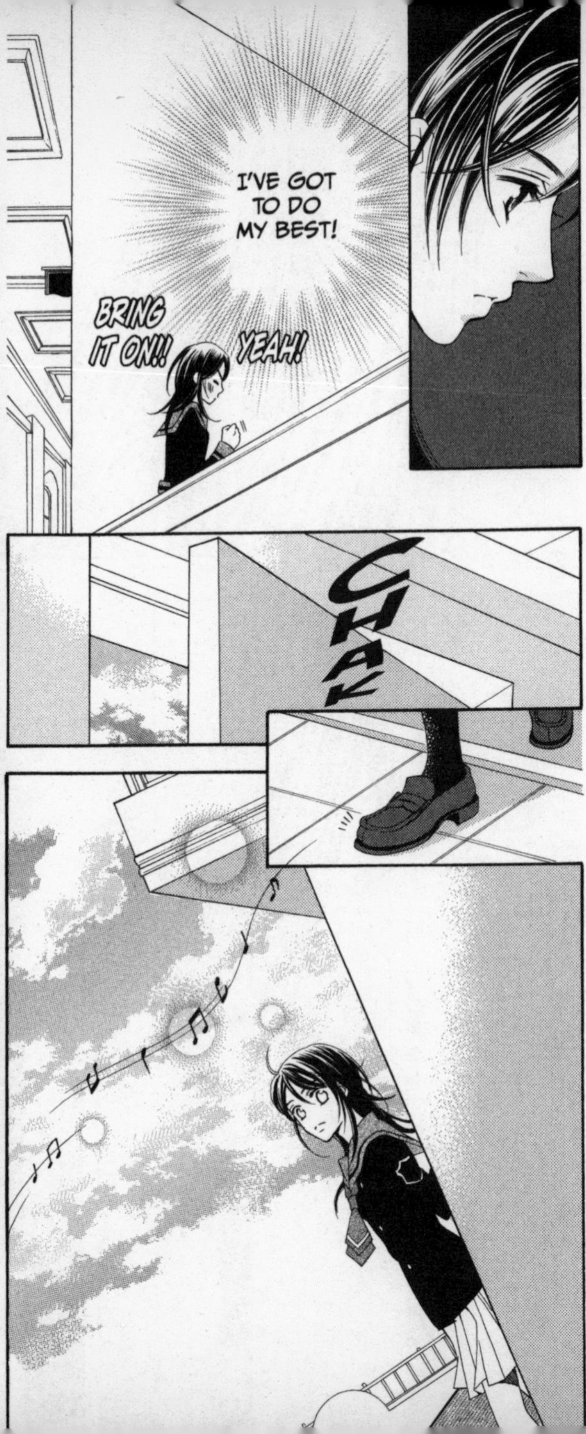
I'VE GOT TO DO MY BEST!
YEAH!
BRING IT ON!!
CHAK

TWO

♛

The inspiration for the Meaure 14 cover page is... "La Corda Marching Band Unites!! Miss? Would you like to put in a request?" I started off with a rough draft where they had castanets and triangles... All instruments that kindergarten kids would have... but I decided to switch over to bigger instruments. Len with a pair of castanets just looked ridiculous... Especially with his expression. I was going to have Azuma play the glockenspiel or the marimba, but when I started coloring, he ended up with a xylophone.

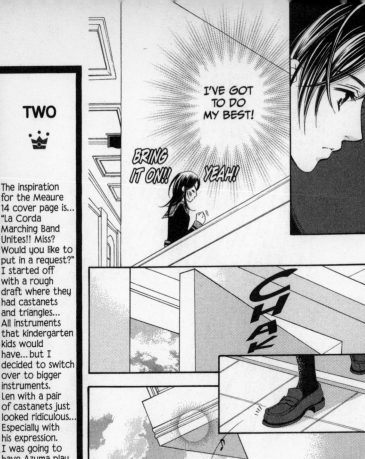

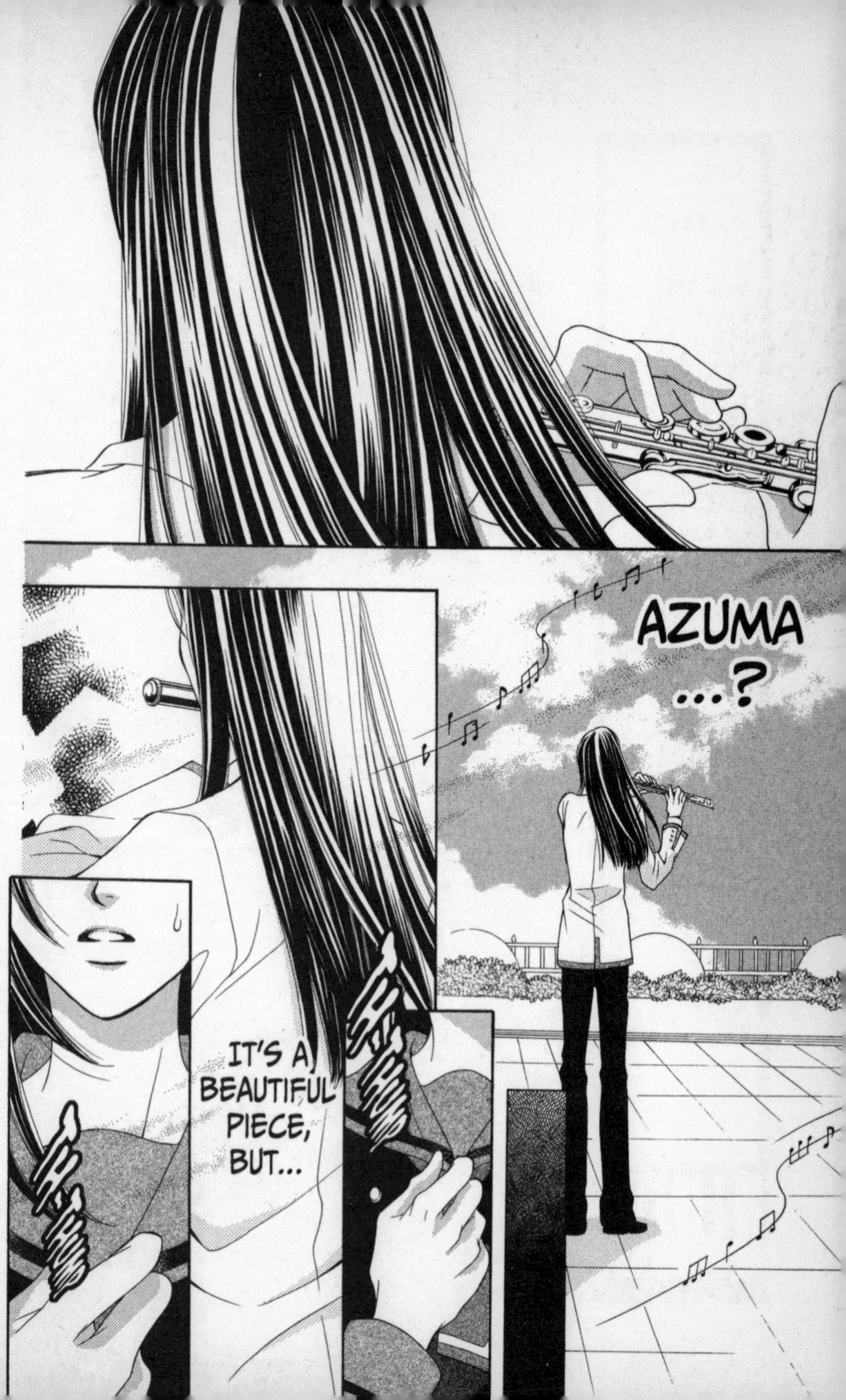
AZUMA ...?
IT'S A BEAUTIFUL PIECE, BUT...

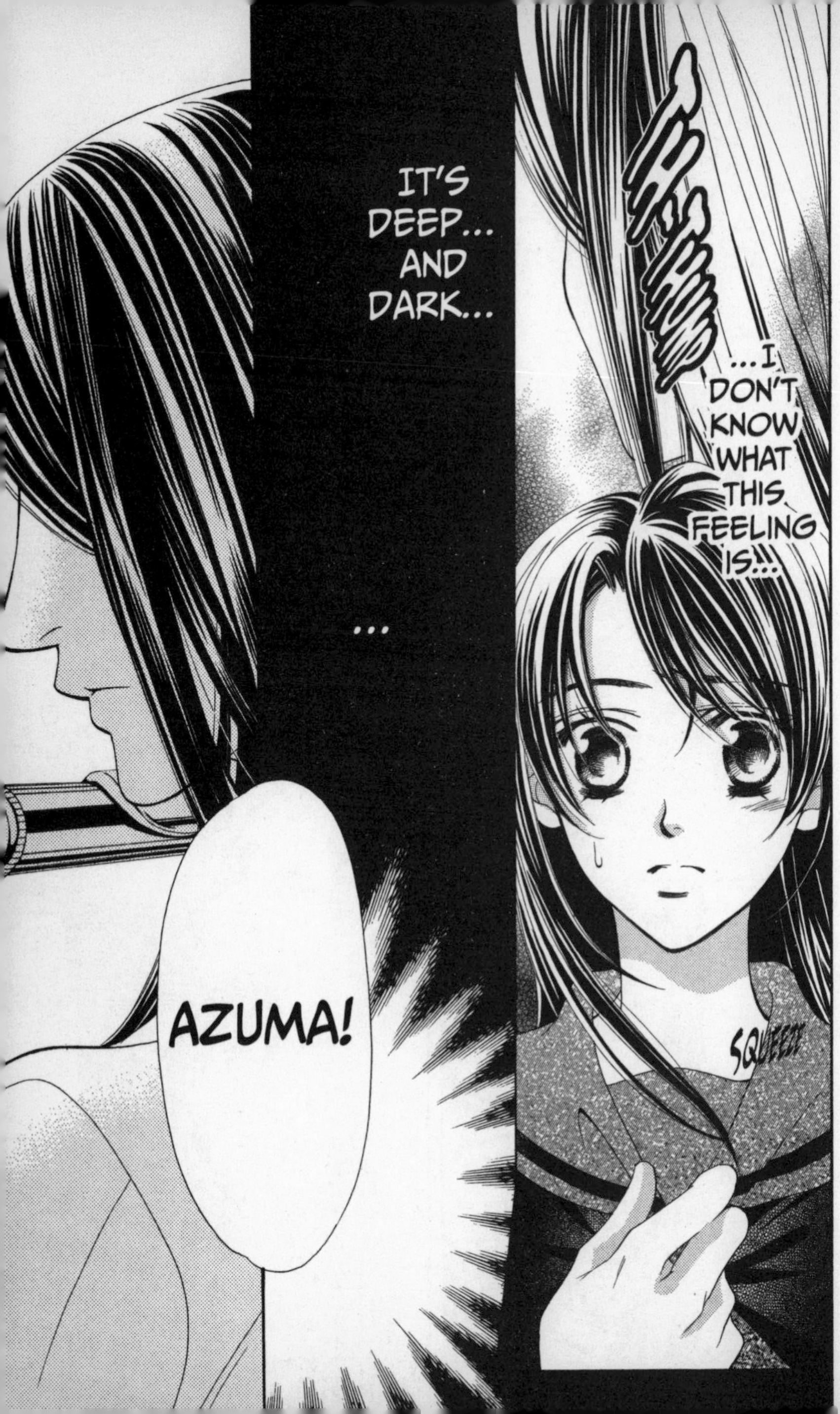

...I DON'T KNOW WHAT THIS FEELING IS...
SQUEEZE
IT'S DEEP... AND DARK...
...
AZUMA!

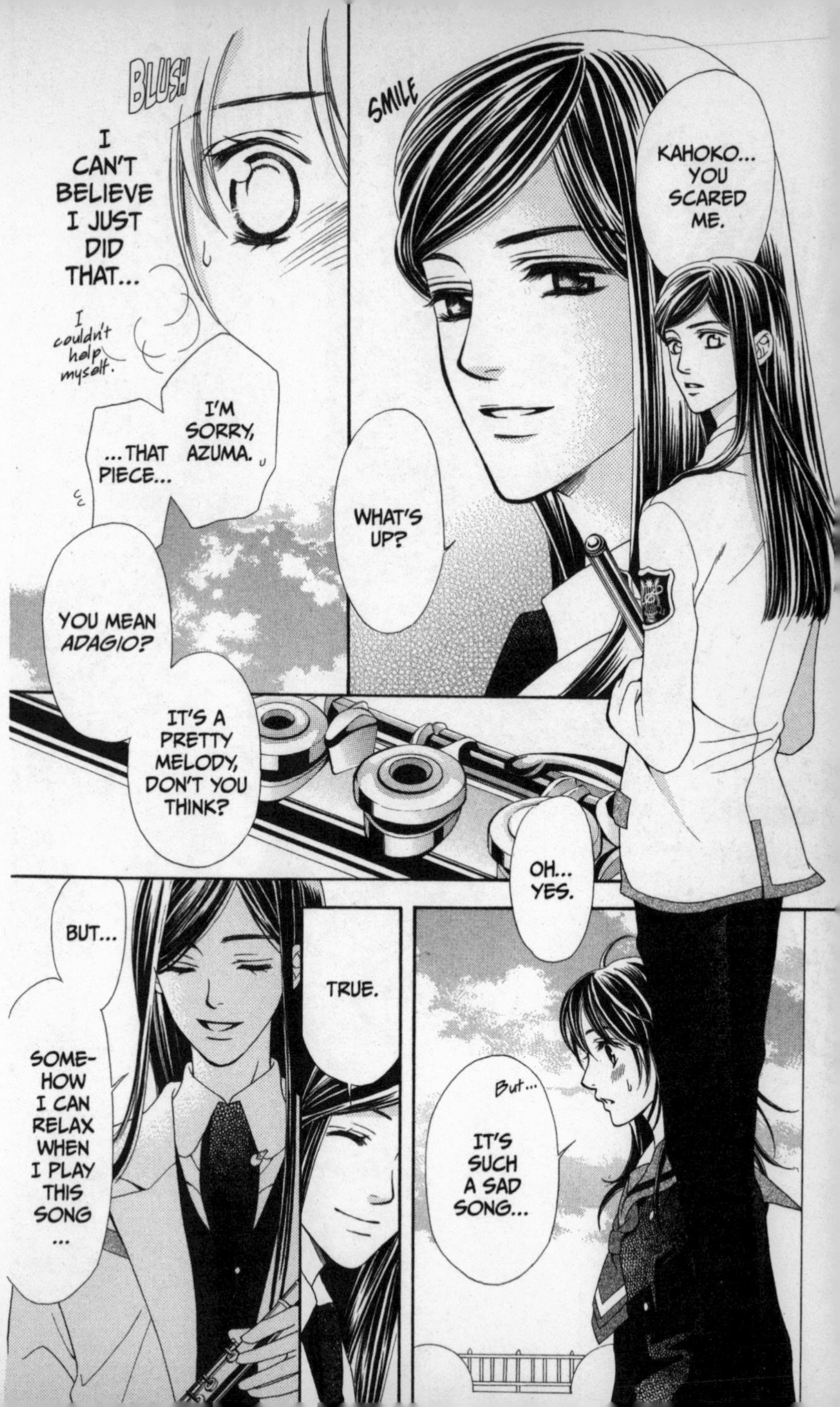
SMILE
KAHOKO... YOU SCARED ME.
WHAT'S UP?
BLUSH
I CAN'T BELIEVE I JUST DID THAT...
I couldn't help myself.
I'M SORRY, AZUMA.
...THAT PIECE...
YOU MEAN ADAGIO?
IT'S A PRETTY MELODY, DON'T YOU THINK?
OH... YES.
But...
IT'S SUCH A SAD SONG...
TRUE.
BUT...
SOME-HOW I CAN RELAX WHEN I PLAY THIS SONG ...

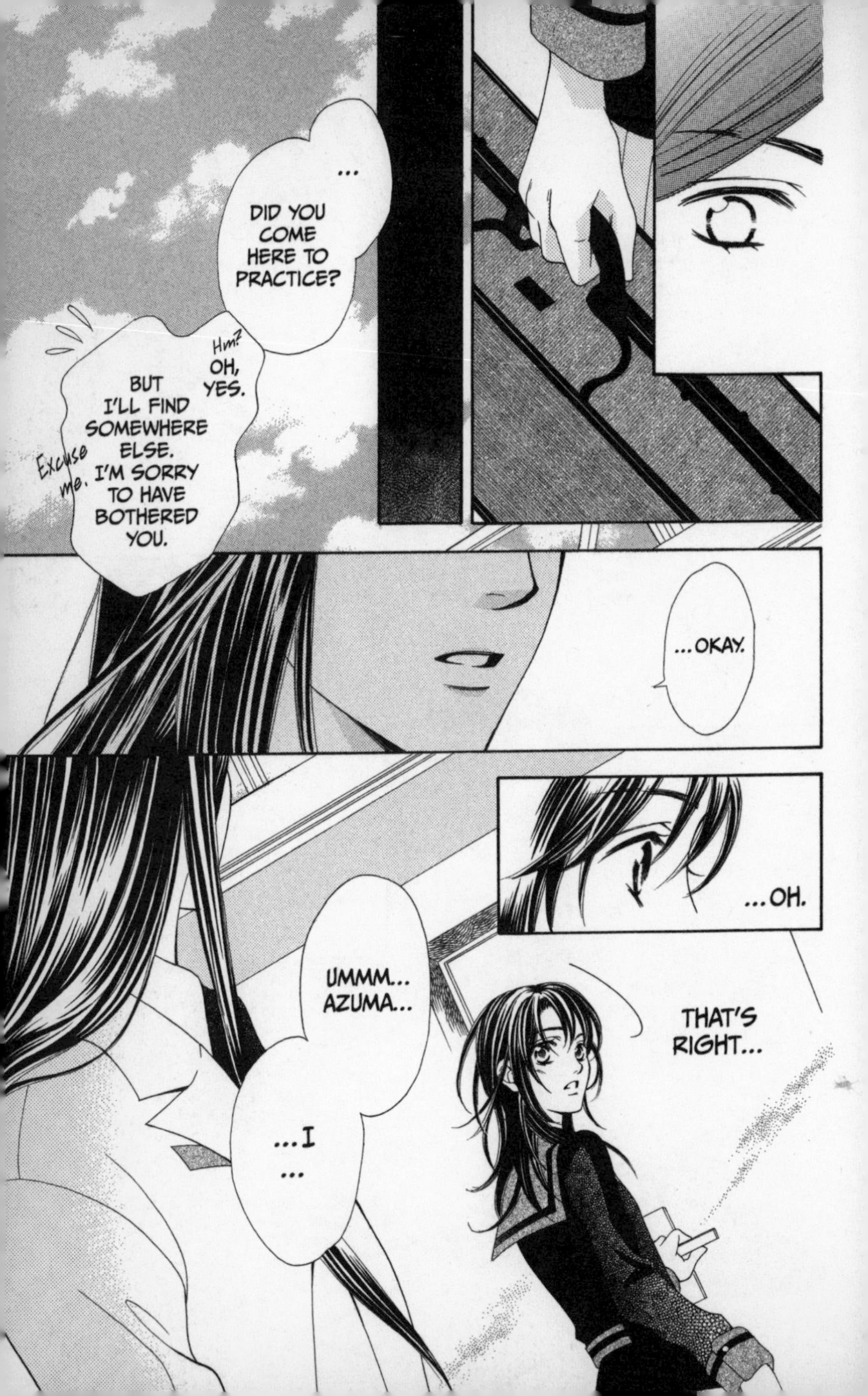
...
DID YOU COME HERE TO PRACTICE?
Hm?
OH, YES.
BUT I'LL FIND SOMEWHERE ELSE.
I'M SORRY TO HAVE BOTHERED YOU.
Excuse me.
...OKAY.
...OH.
THAT'S RIGHT...
UMMM... AZUMA...
...I
...

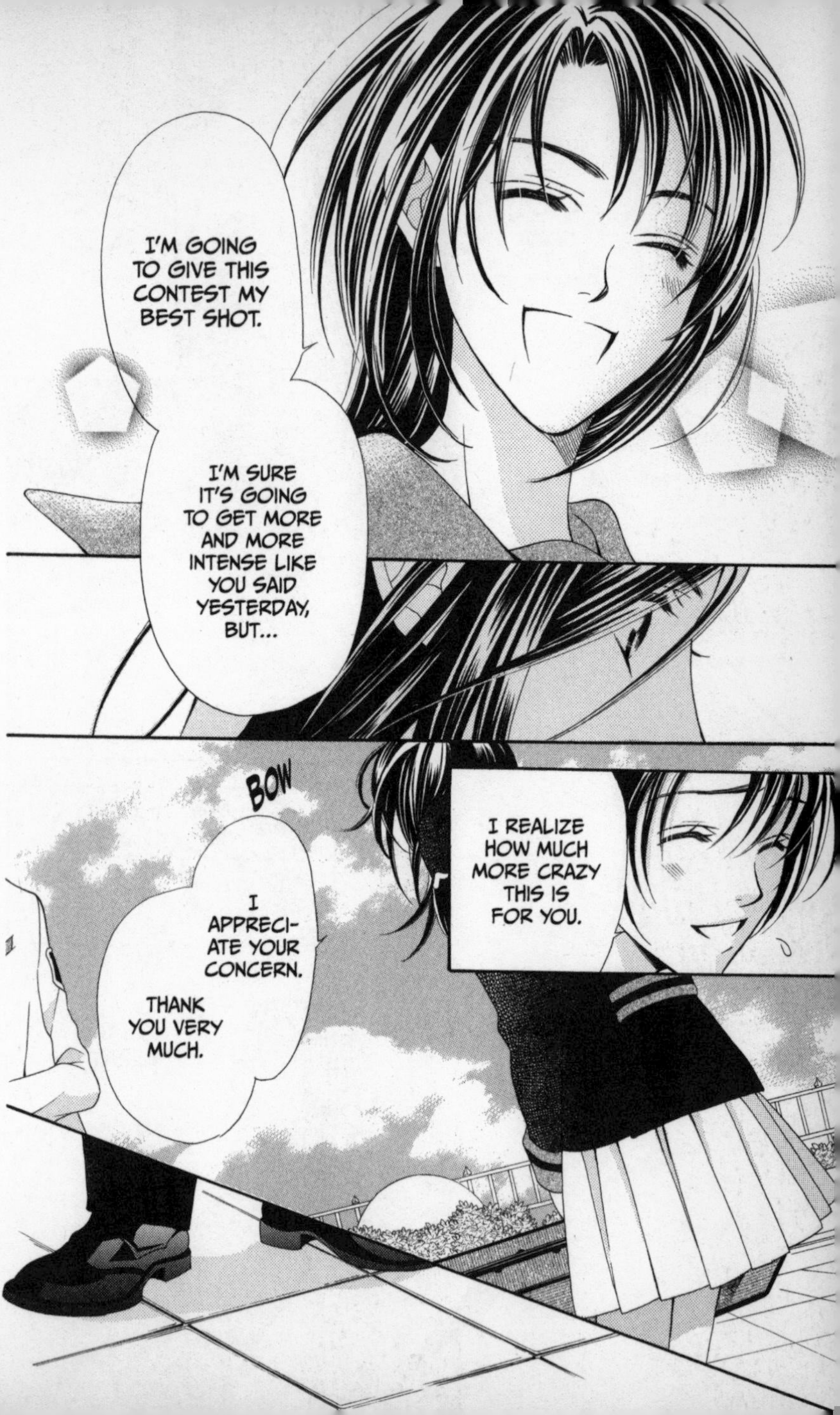
I'M GOING TO GIVE THIS CONTEST MY BEST SHOT.
I'M SURE IT'S GOING TO GET MORE AND MORE INTENSE LIKE YOU SAID YESTERDAY, BUT...
I REALIZE HOW MUCH MORE CRAZY THIS IS FOR YOU.
BOW
I APPRECIATE YOUR CONCERN.
THANK YOU VERY MUCH.

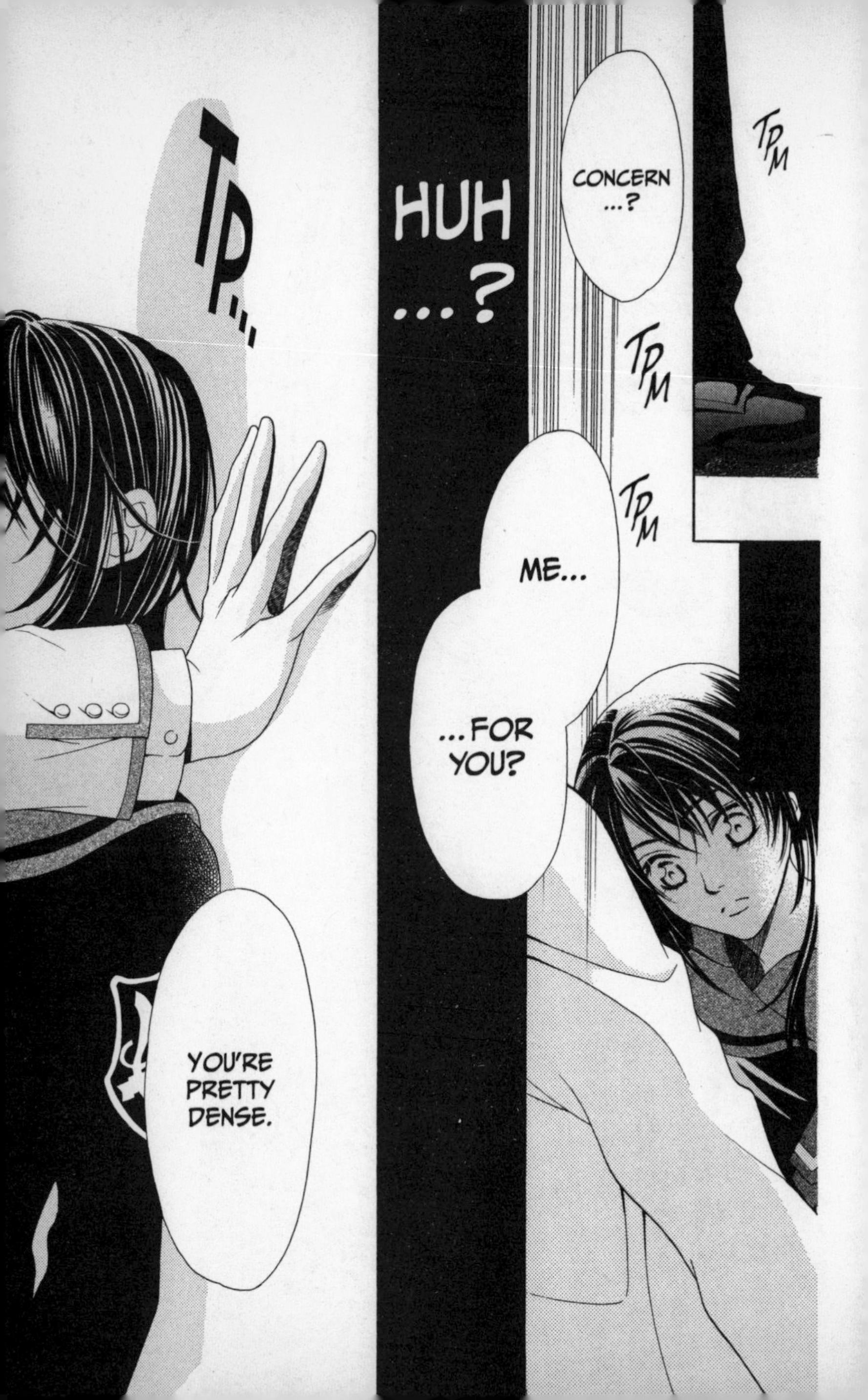
TPM
CONCERN ...?
TPM
TPM
ME...
...FOR YOU?
HUH ...?
TP...
YOU'RE PRETTY DENSE.

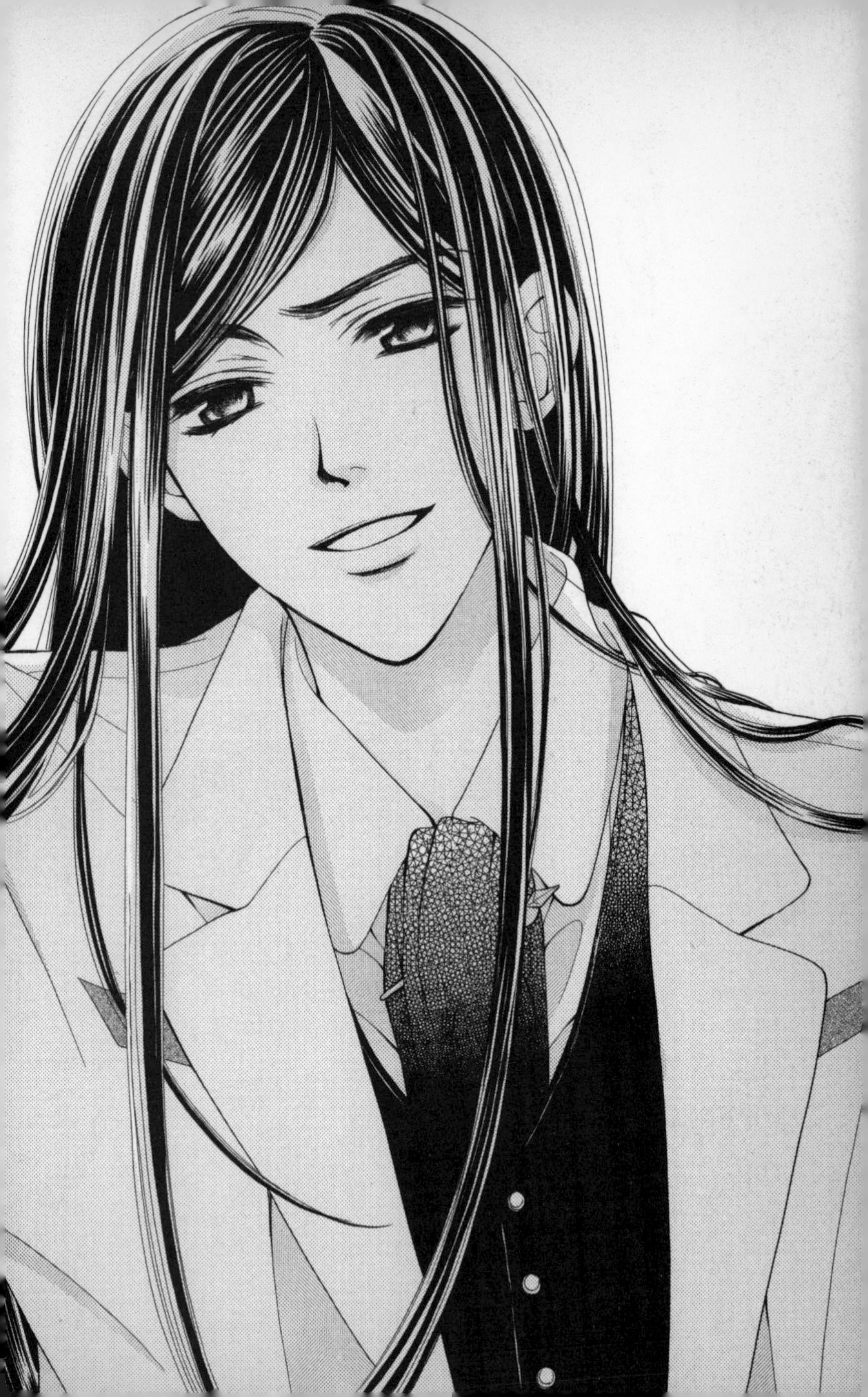

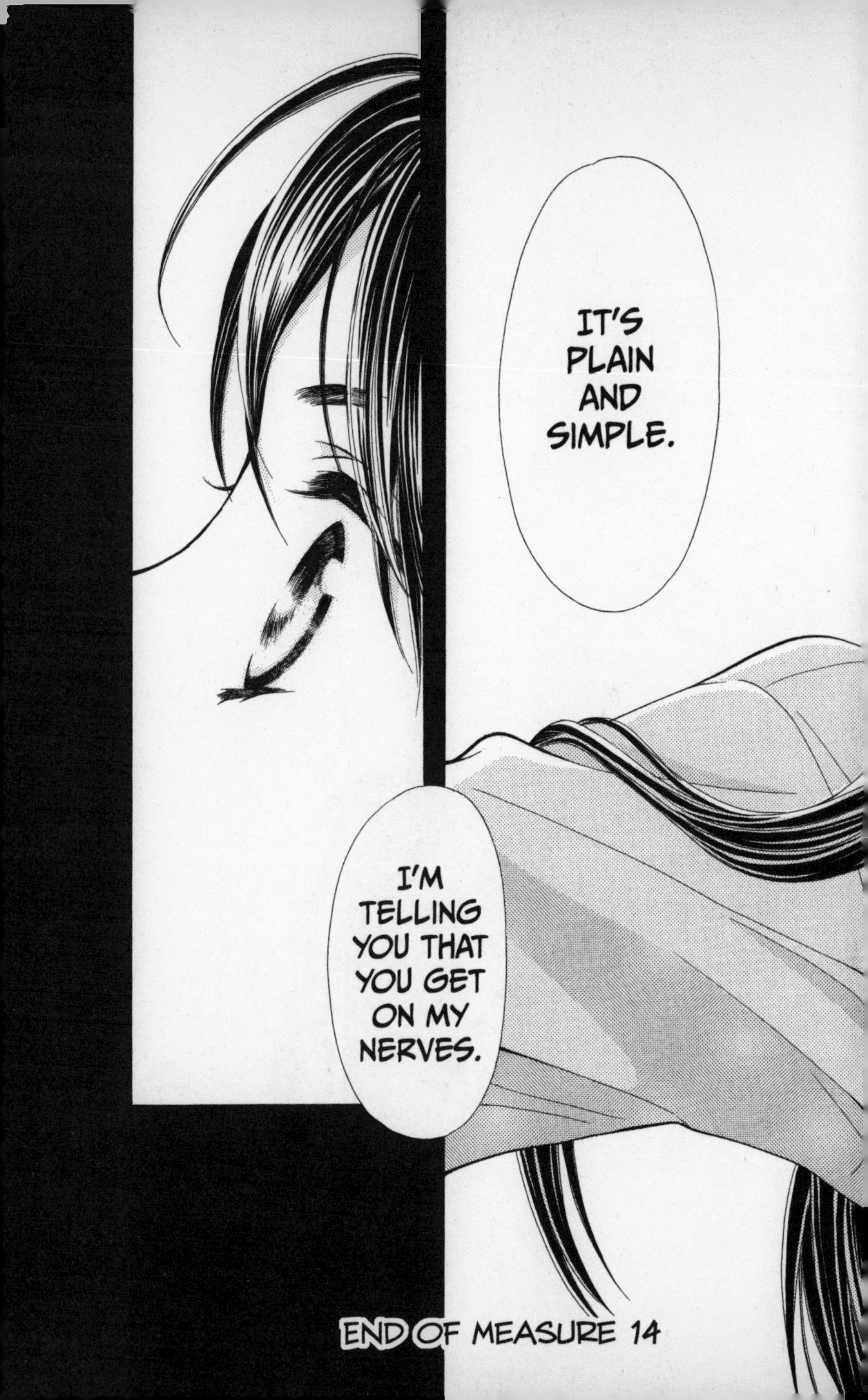
IT'S PLAIN AND SIMPLE.
I'M TELLING YOU THAT YOU GET ON MY NERVES.
END OF MEASURE 14

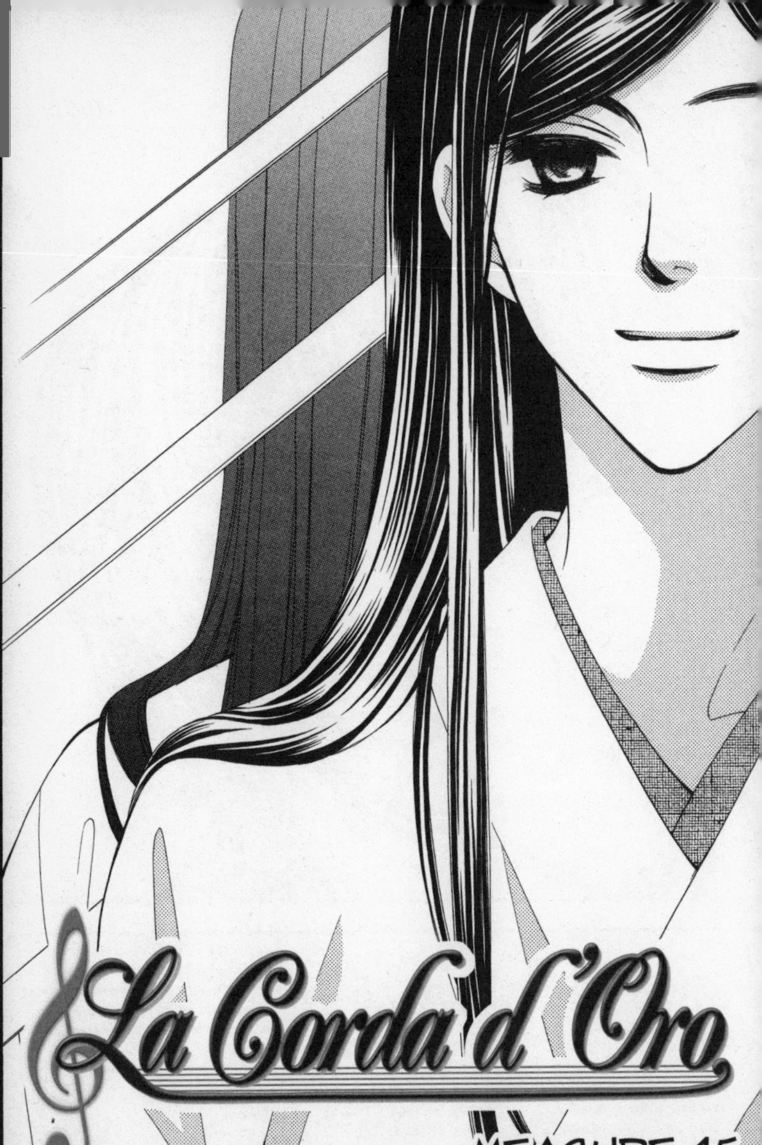
La Corda d'Oro
MEASURE 15

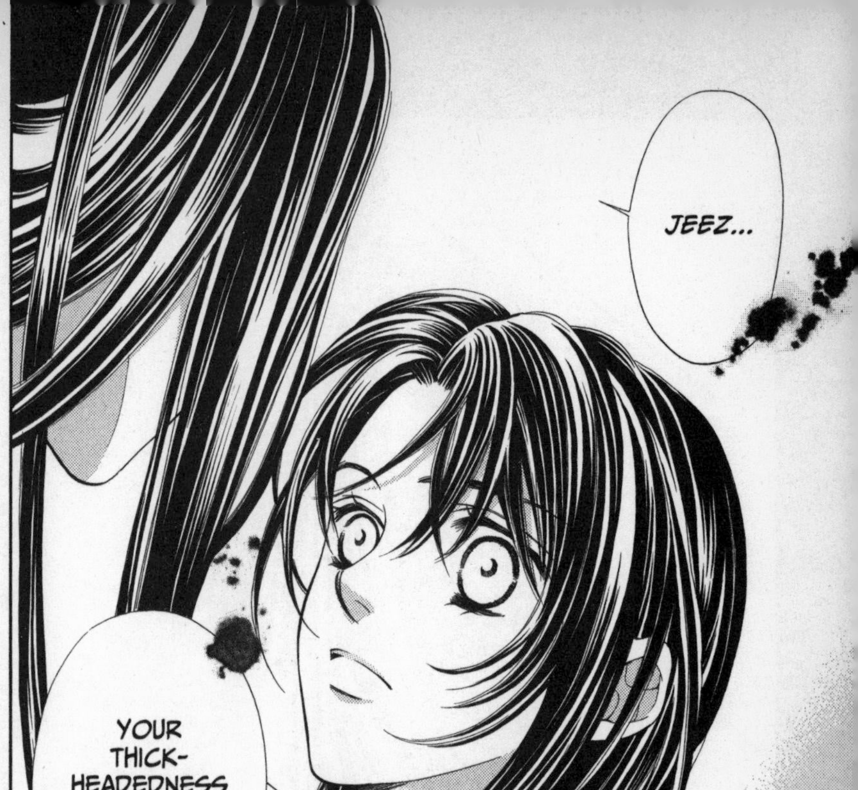
JEEZ...
YOUR THICK-HEADEDNESS IS GETTING REALLY ANNOYING...

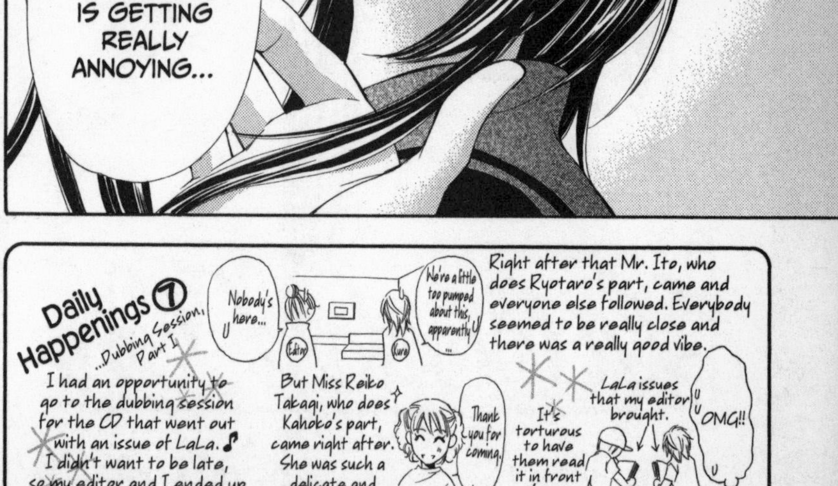
Daily Happenings 7
...Dubbing Session, Part I
I had an opportunity to go to the dubbing session for the CD that went out with an issue of LaLa. ♪ I didn't want to be late, so my editor and I ended up being the first ones there.
Nobody's here...
We're a little too pumped about this, apparently...
Editor
Kure
But Miss Reiko Takagi, who does Kahoko's part, came right after. She was such a delicate and adorable nice lady.
Thank you for coming.
Right after that Mr. Ito, who does Ryotaro's part, came and everyone else followed. Everybody seemed to be really close and there was a really good vibe.
It's torturous to have them read it in front of me...
LaLa issues that my editor brought.
OMG!!

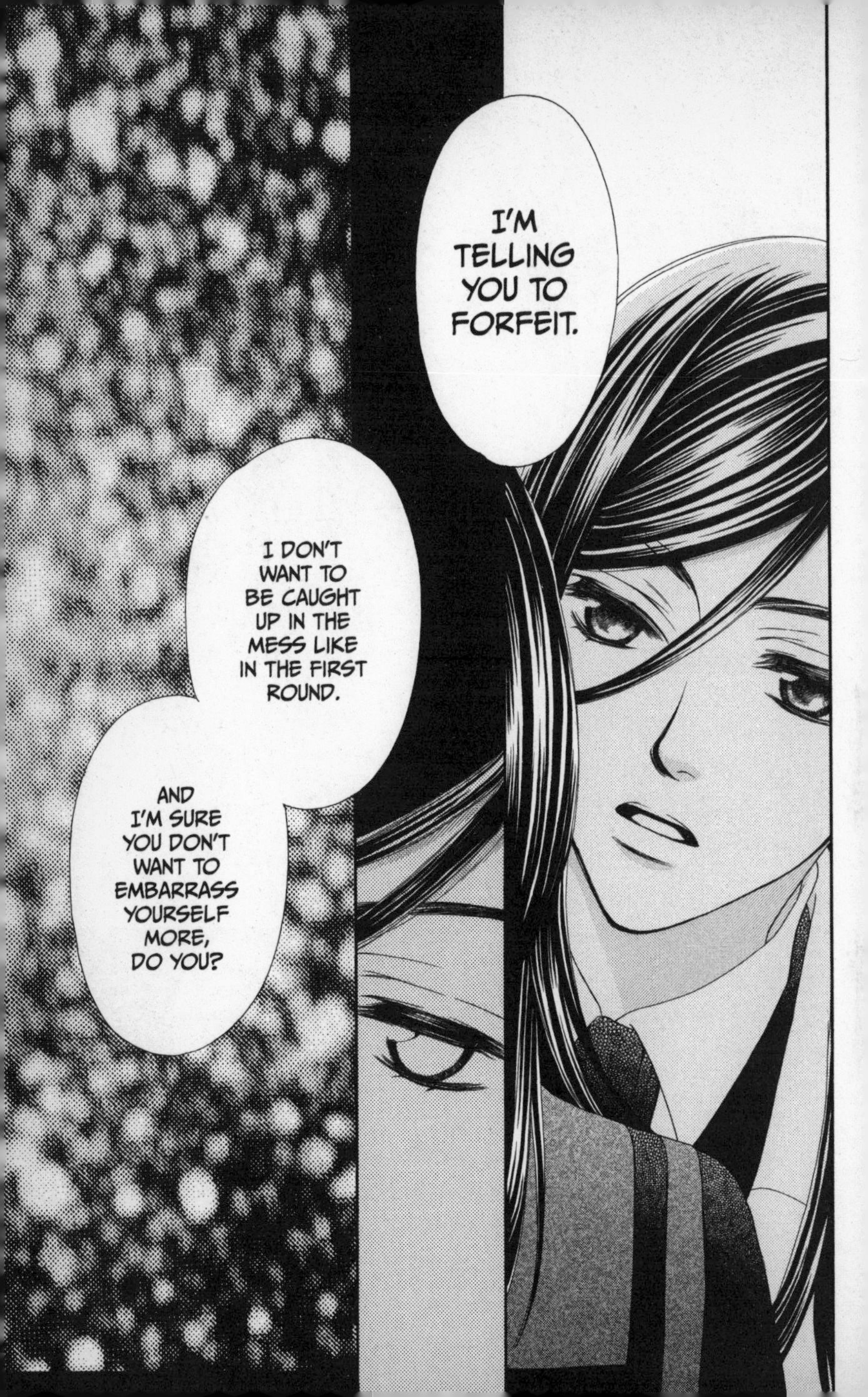
I'M TELLING YOU TO FORFEIT.
I DON'T WANT TO BE CAUGHT UP IN THE MESS LIKE IN THE FIRST ROUND.
AND I'M SURE YOU DON'T WANT TO EMBARRASS YOURSELF MORE, DO YOU?

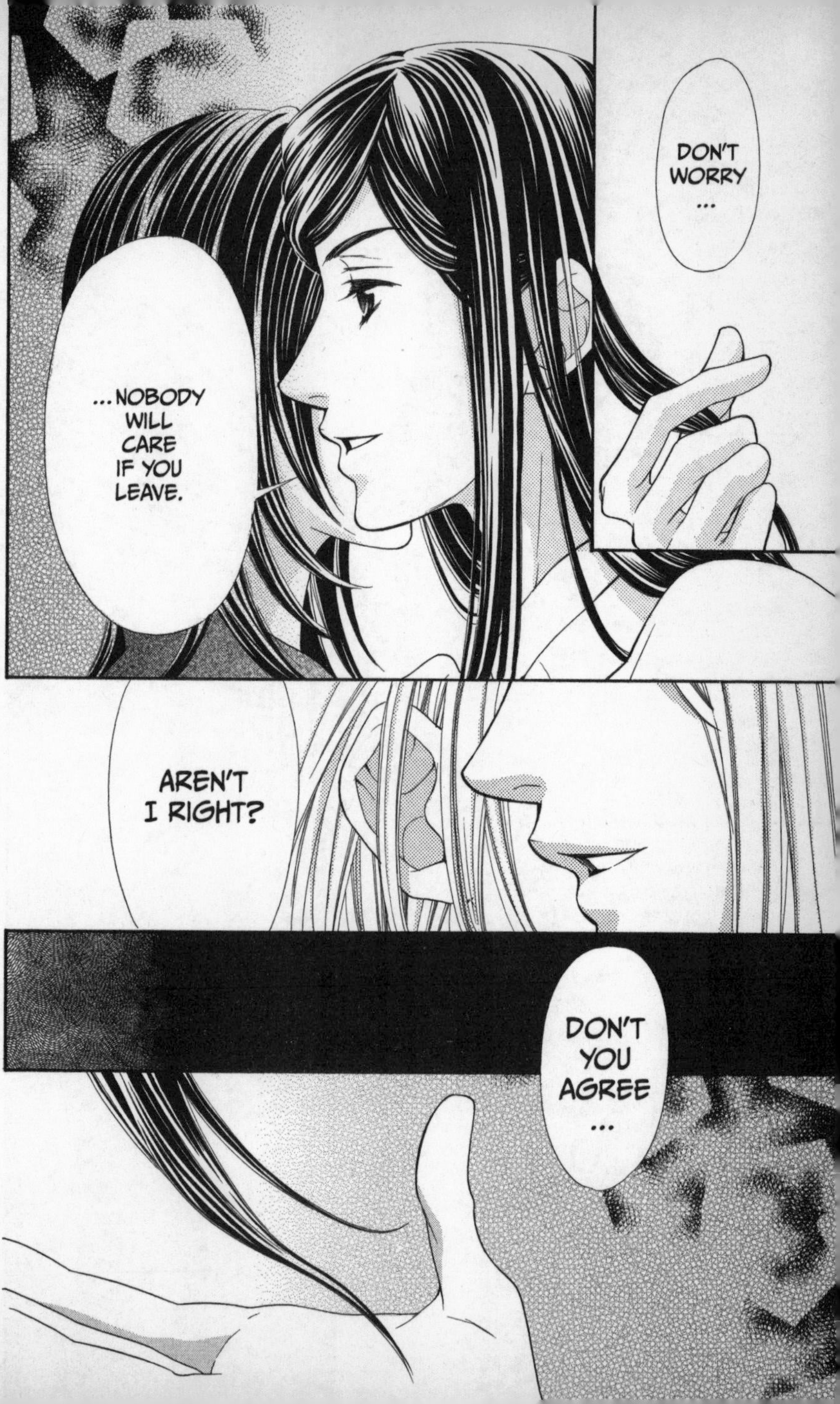
DON'T WORRY ...
...NOBODY WILL CARE IF YOU LEAVE.
AREN'T I RIGHT?
DON'T YOU AGREE ...

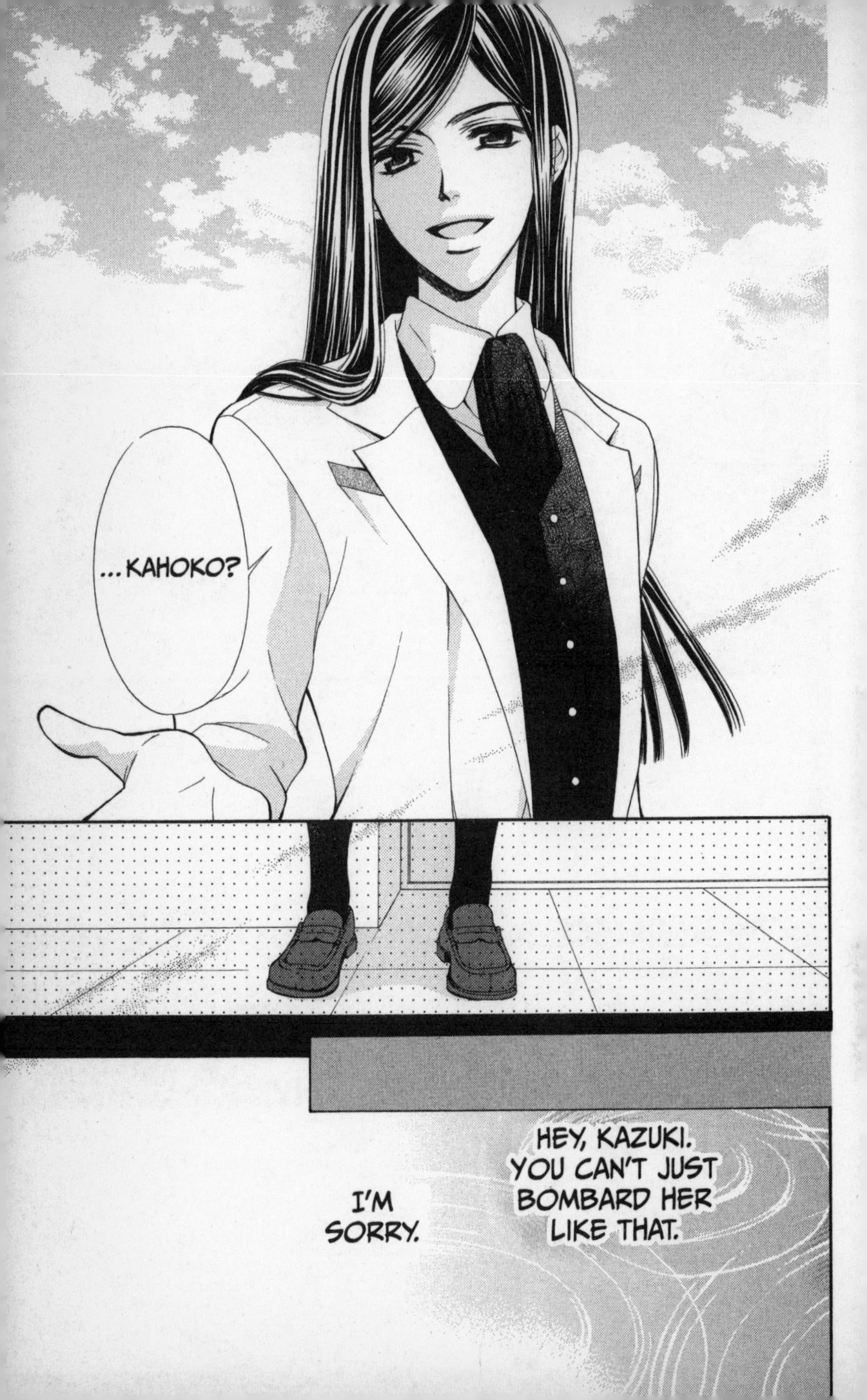
...KAHOKO?
HEY, KAZUKI. YOU CAN'T JUST BOMBARD HER LIKE THAT.
I'M SORRY.

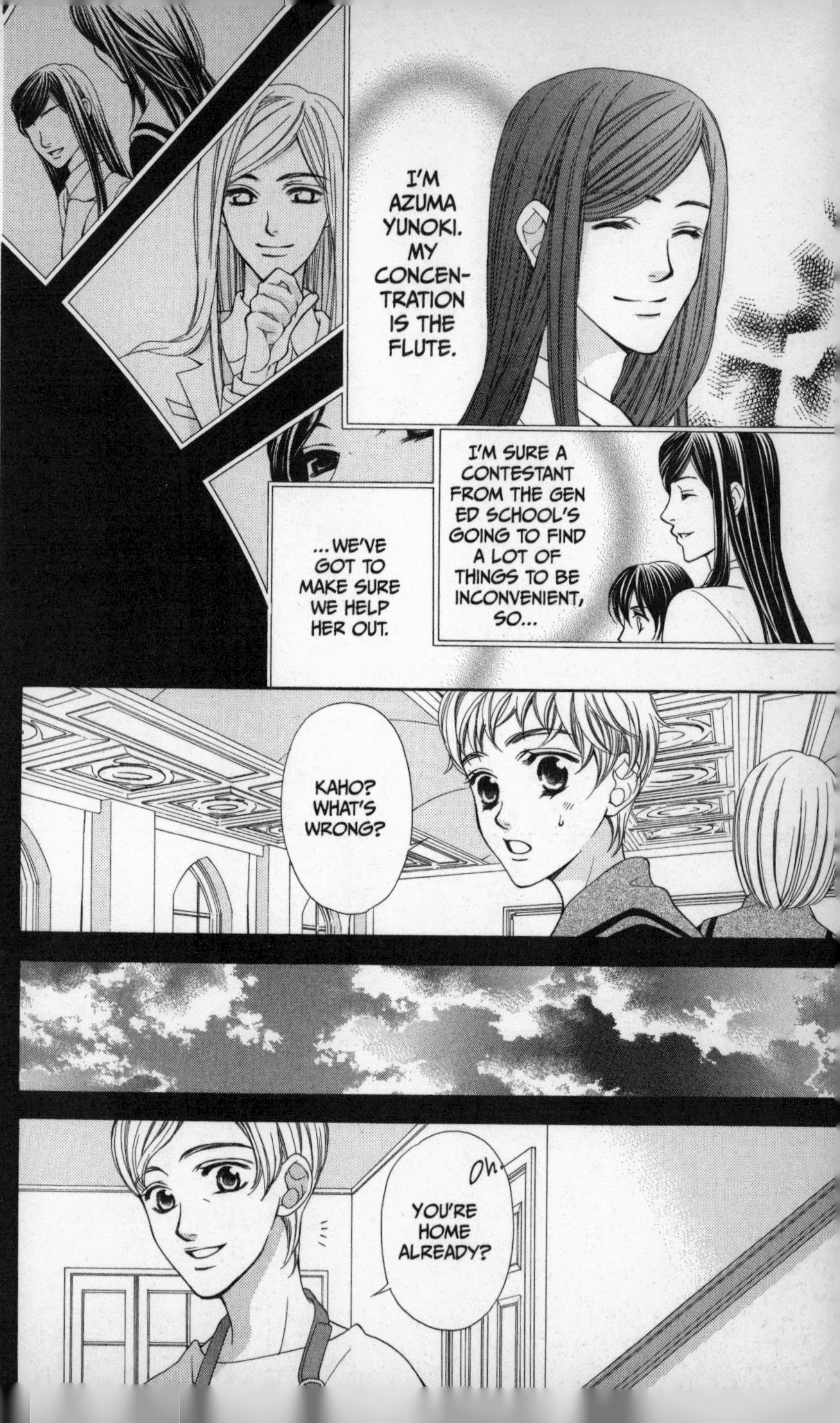
I'M AZUMA YUNOKI. MY CONCEN-TRATION IS THE FLUTE.
I'M SURE A CONTESTANT FROM THE GEN ED SCHOOL'S GOING TO FIND A LOT OF THINGS TO BE INCONVENIENT, SO...
...WE'VE GOT TO MAKE SURE WE HELP HER OUT.
KAHO? WHAT'S WRONG?
Oh.
YOU'RE HOME ALREADY?

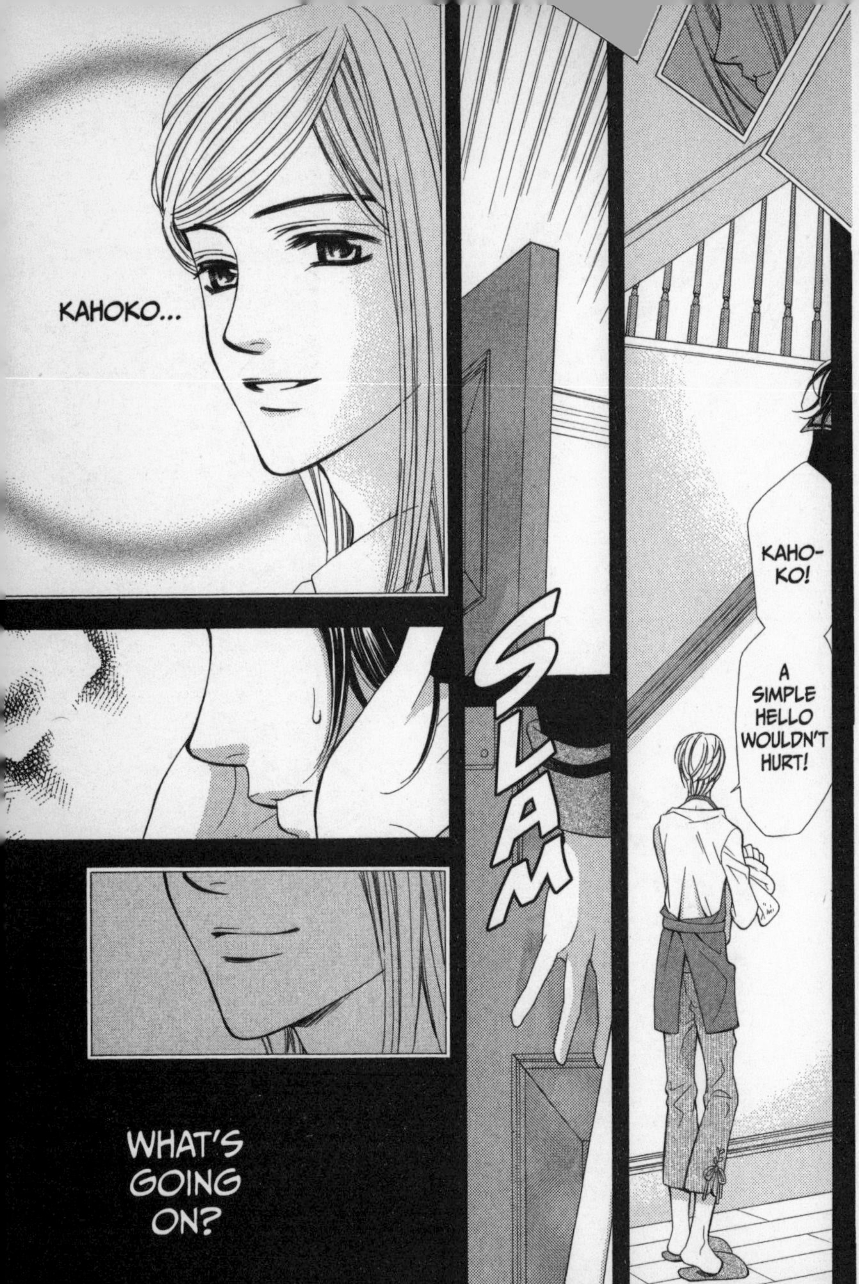
KAHO-KO!
A SIMPLE HELLO WOULDN'T HURT!
SLAM
KAHOKO...
WHAT'S GOING ON?

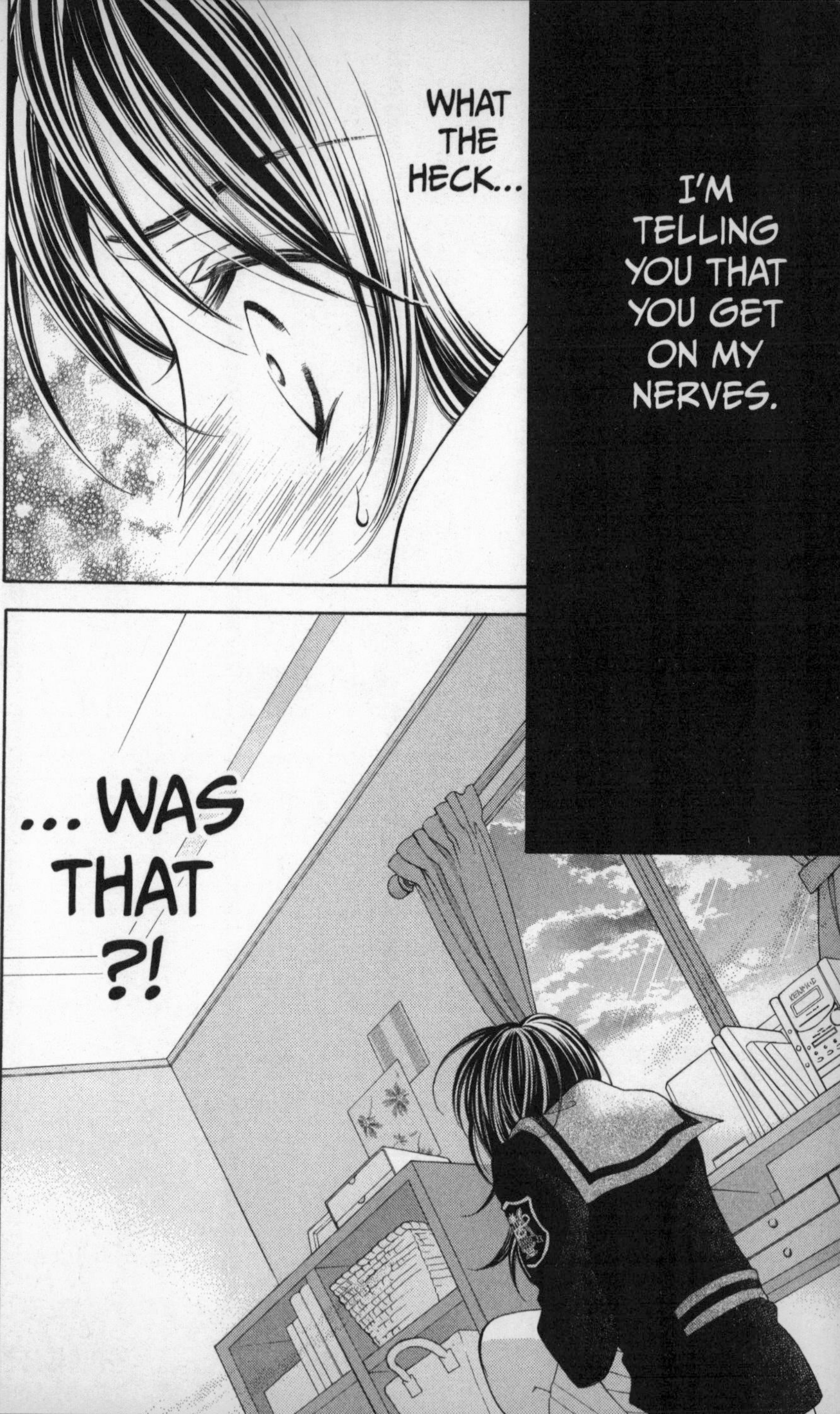
I'M TELLING YOU THAT YOU GET ON MY NERVES.
WHAT THE HECK...
...WAS THAT?!

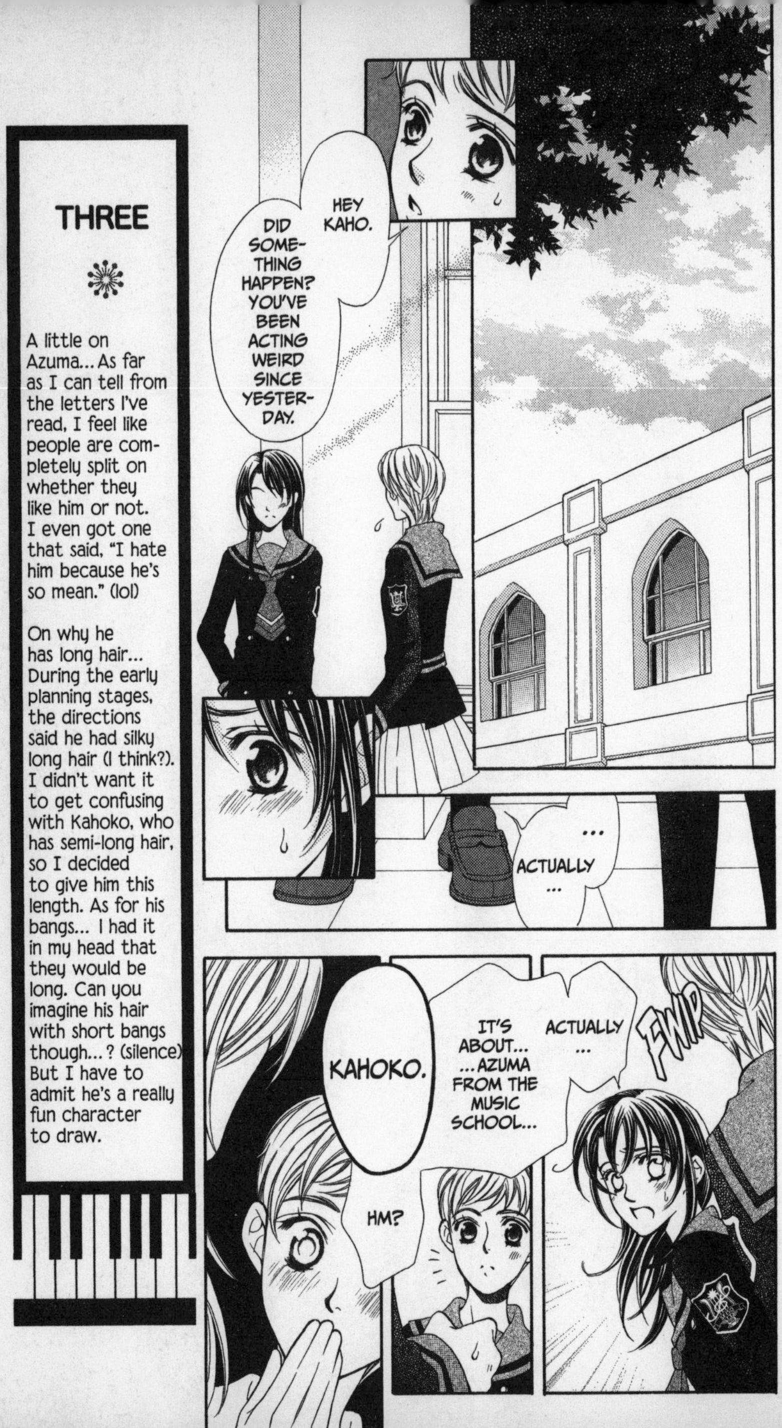
HEY KAHO.
DID SOMETHING HAPPEN? YOU'VE BEEN ACTING WEIRD SINCE YESTERDAY.
... ACTUALLY ...
ACTUALLY ...
IT'S ABOUT... ...AZUMA FROM THE MUSIC SCHOOL...
FWIP
HM?
KAHOKO.

THREE

A little on Azuma... As far as I can tell from the letters I've read, I feel like people are completely split on whether they like him or not. I even got one that said, "I hate him because he's so mean." (lol)

On why he has long hair... During the early planning stages, the directions said he had silky long hair (I think?). I didn't want it to get confusing with Kahoko, who has semi-long hair, so I decided to give him this length. As for his bangs... I had it in my head that they would be long. Can you imagine his hair with short bangs though...? (silence) But I have to admit he's a really fun character to draw.

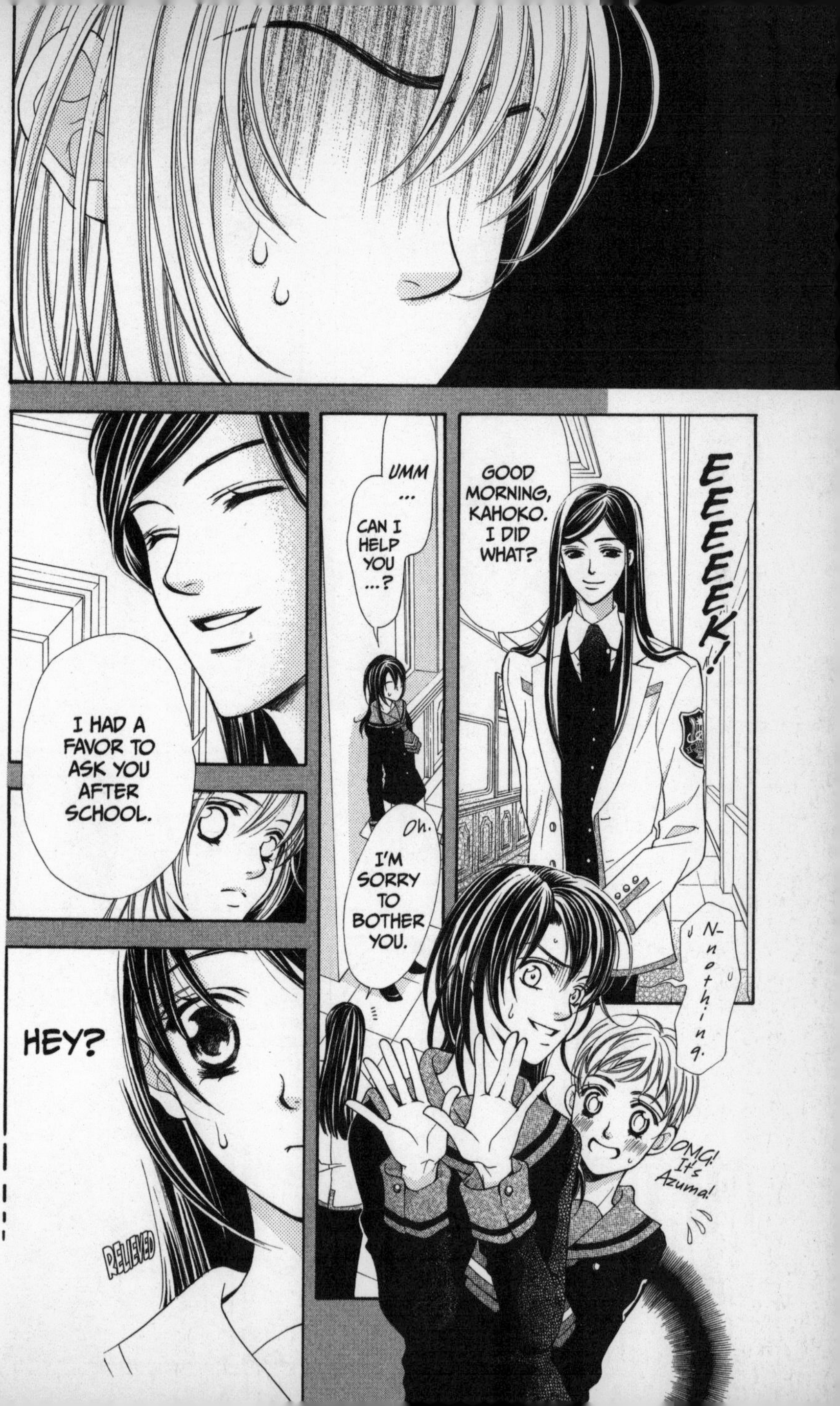
EEEEEEK!
GOOD MORNING, KAHOKO. I DID WHAT?
N-nothing.
OMG! It's Azuma!
UMM... CAN I HELP YOU...?
Oh. I'M SORRY TO BOTHER YOU.
I HAD A FAVOR TO ASK YOU AFTER SCHOOL.
HEY?
RELIEVED

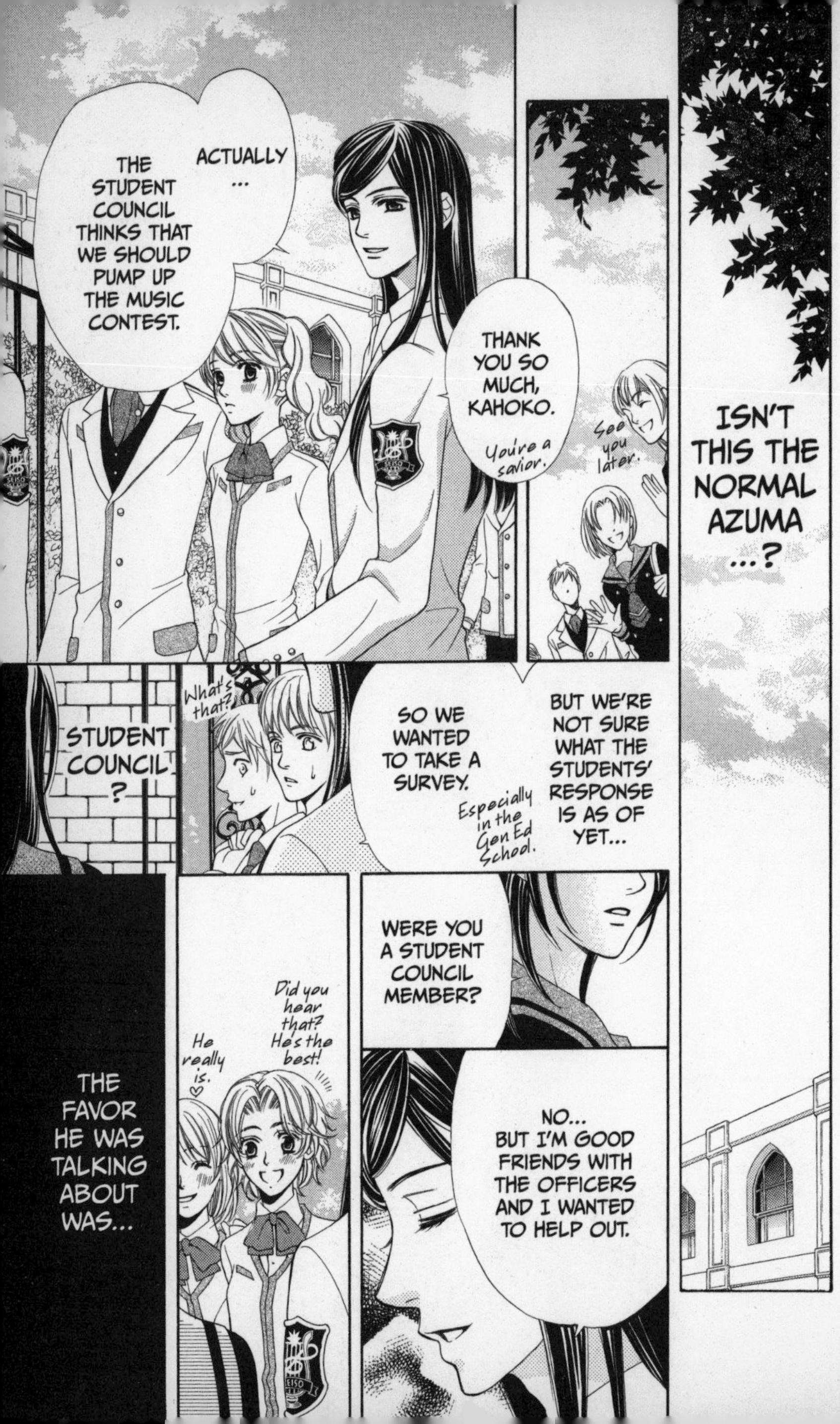
ISN'T THIS THE NORMAL AZUMA ...?
See you later.
THANK YOU SO MUCH, KAHOKO.
You're a savior.
ACTUALLY ...
THE STUDENT COUNCIL THINKS THAT WE SHOULD PUMP UP THE MUSIC CONTEST.
BUT WE'RE NOT SURE WHAT THE STUDENTS' RESPONSE IS AS OF YET...
SO WE WANTED TO TAKE A SURVEY.
Especially in the Gen Ed School.
What's that?
STUDENT COUNCIL ?
WERE YOU A STUDENT COUNCIL MEMBER?
NO... BUT I'M GOOD FRIENDS WITH THE OFFICERS AND I WANTED TO HELP OUT.
Did you hear that? He's the best!
He really is. ♡
THE FAVOR HE WAS TALKING ABOUT WAS...

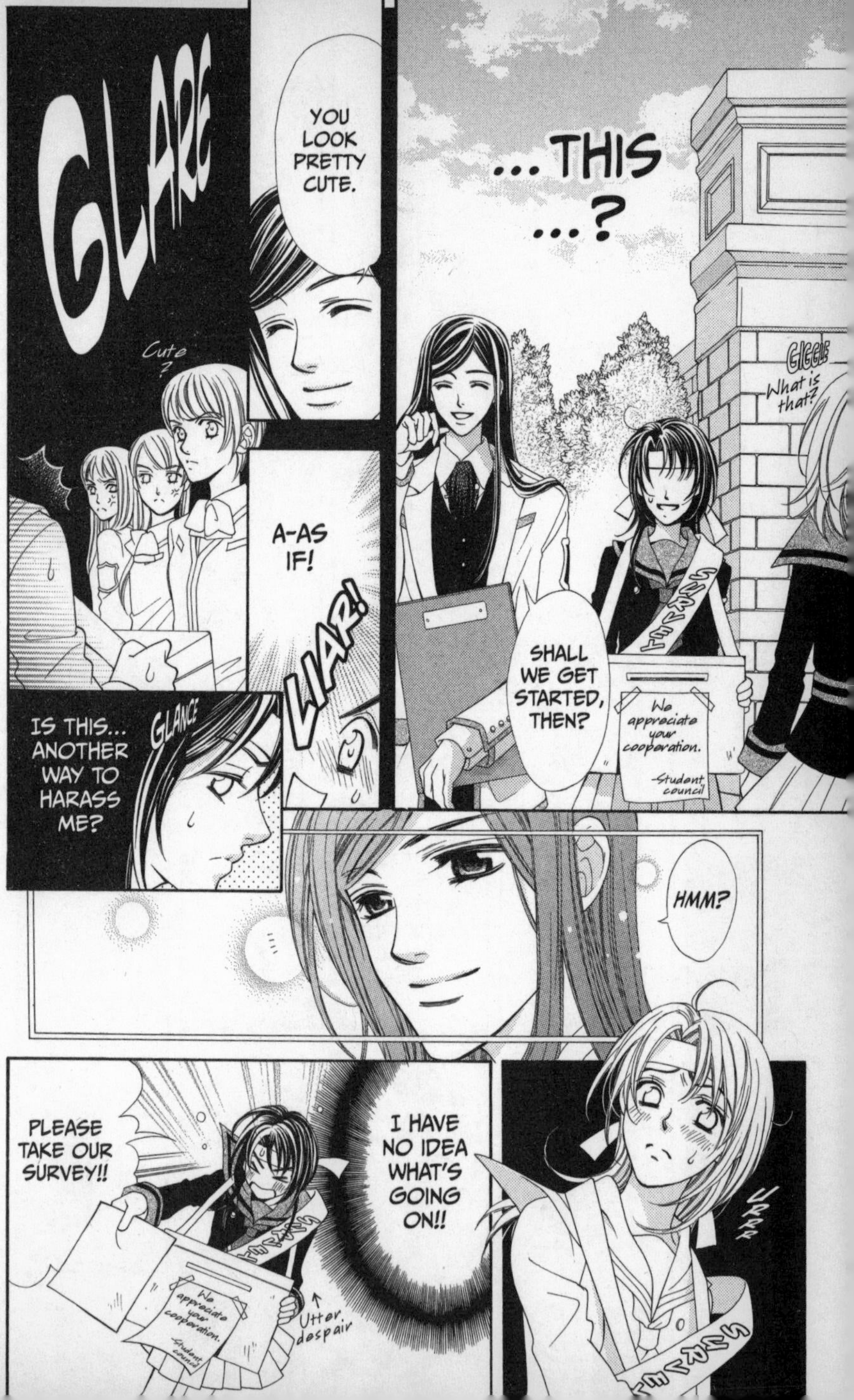
...THIS ...?
GIGGLE
What is that?
SURVEY
SHALL WE GET STARTED, THEN?
We appreciate your cooperation. -Student council
YOU LOOK PRETTY CUTE.
A-AS IF!
LIAR!
GLARE
Cute?
GLANCE
IS THIS... ANOTHER WAY TO HARASS ME?
HMM?
URRR
I HAVE NO IDEA WHAT'S GOING ON!!
PLEASE TAKE OUR SURVEY!!
We appreciate your cooperation. -Student council
Utter despair

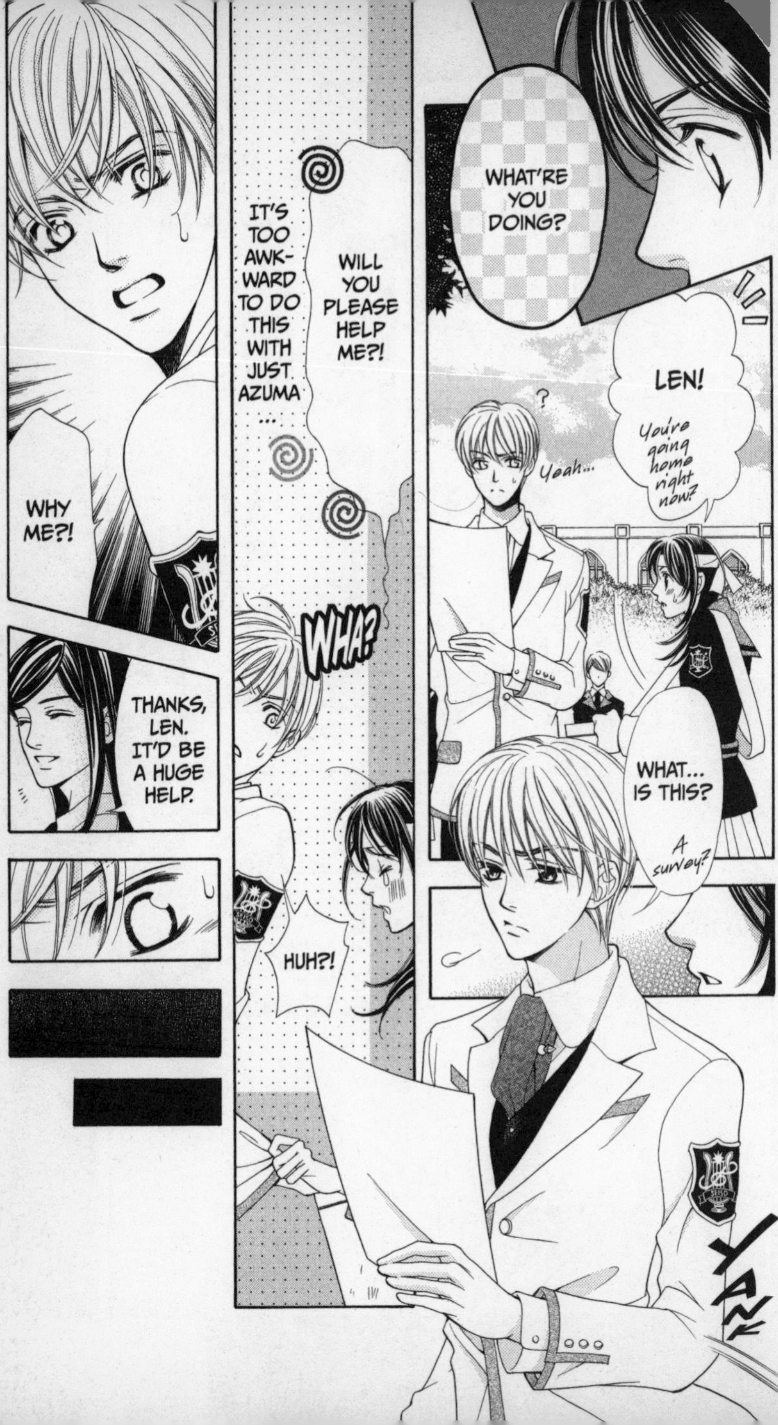

WHAT'RE YOU DOING?
LEN!
You're going home right now?
?
Yeah...
WHAT... IS THIS?
A survey?
YANK
WILL YOU PLEASE HELP ME?!
IT'S TOO AWK-WARD TO DO THIS WITH JUST AZUMA...
WHA?
HUH?!
WHY ME?!
THANKS, LEN. IT'D BE A HUGE HELP.

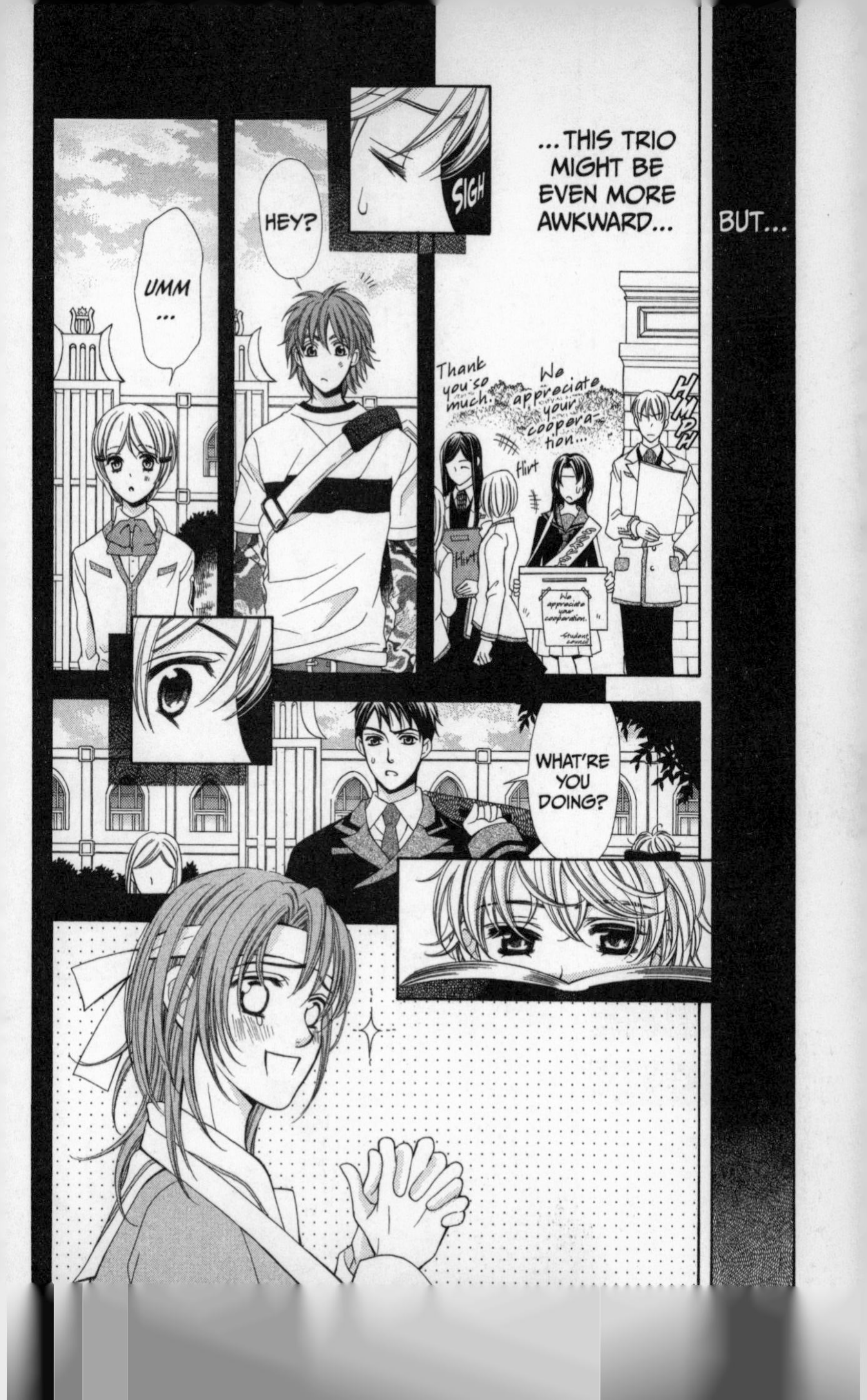
BUT...
...THIS TRIO MIGHT BE EVEN MORE AWKWARD...
HMPH
Thank you so much.
We appreciate your cooperation...
We appreciate your cooperation.
-Student council
SIGH
HEY?
UMM ...
WHAT'RE YOU DOING?

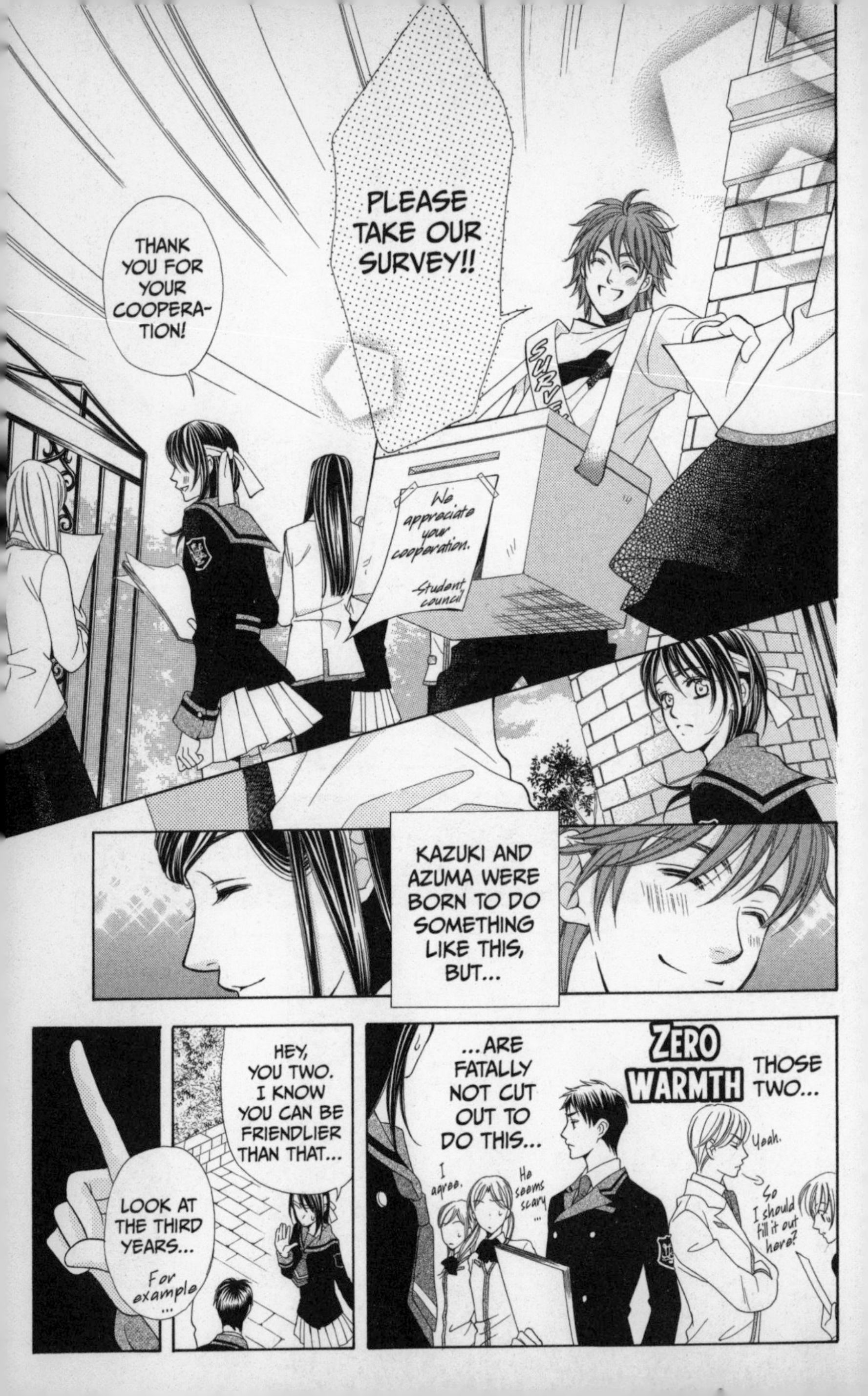
PLEASE TAKE OUR SURVEY!!
THANK YOU FOR YOUR COOPERATION!
We appreciate your cooperation. Student council
KAZUKI AND AZUMA WERE BORN TO DO SOMETHING LIKE THIS, BUT...
THOSE TWO...
ZERO WARMTH
...ARE FATALLY NOT CUT OUT TO DO THIS...
Yeah.
So I should fill it out here?
He seems scary ...
I agree.
HEY, YOU TWO. I KNOW YOU CAN BE FRIENDLIER THAN THAT...
LOOK AT THE THIRD YEARS...
For example ...

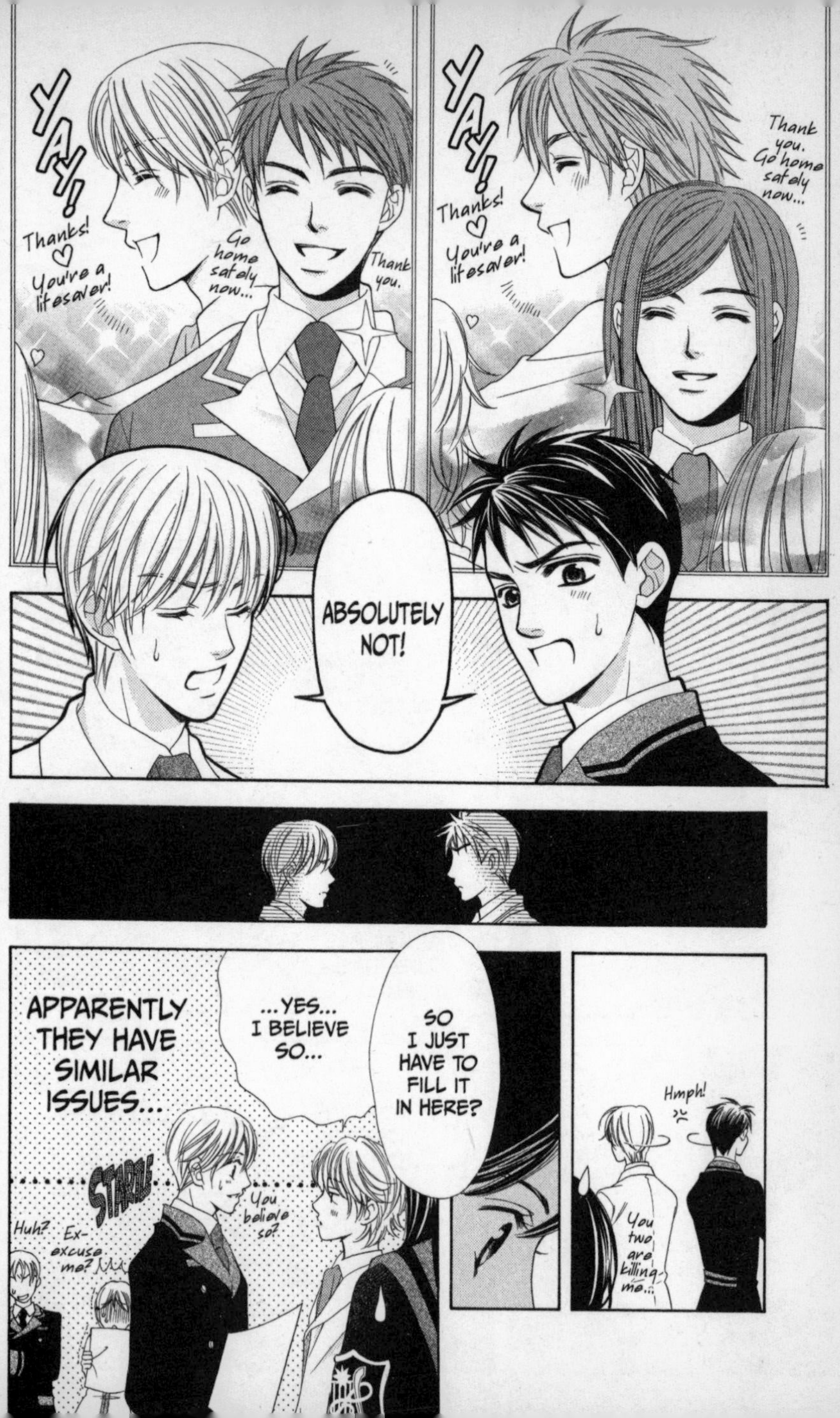
YAY!
Thanks! ♡ You're a lifesaver!
Thank you. Go home safely now...
YAY!
Thanks! ♡ You're a lifesaver!
Go home safely now...
Thank you.
ABSOLUTELY NOT!
Hmph!
You two are killing me...
SO I JUST HAVE TO FILL IT IN HERE?
...YES... I BELIEVE SO...
APPARENTLY THEY HAVE SIMILAR ISSUES...
STARTLE
You believe so?
Huh?
Ex-excuse me?

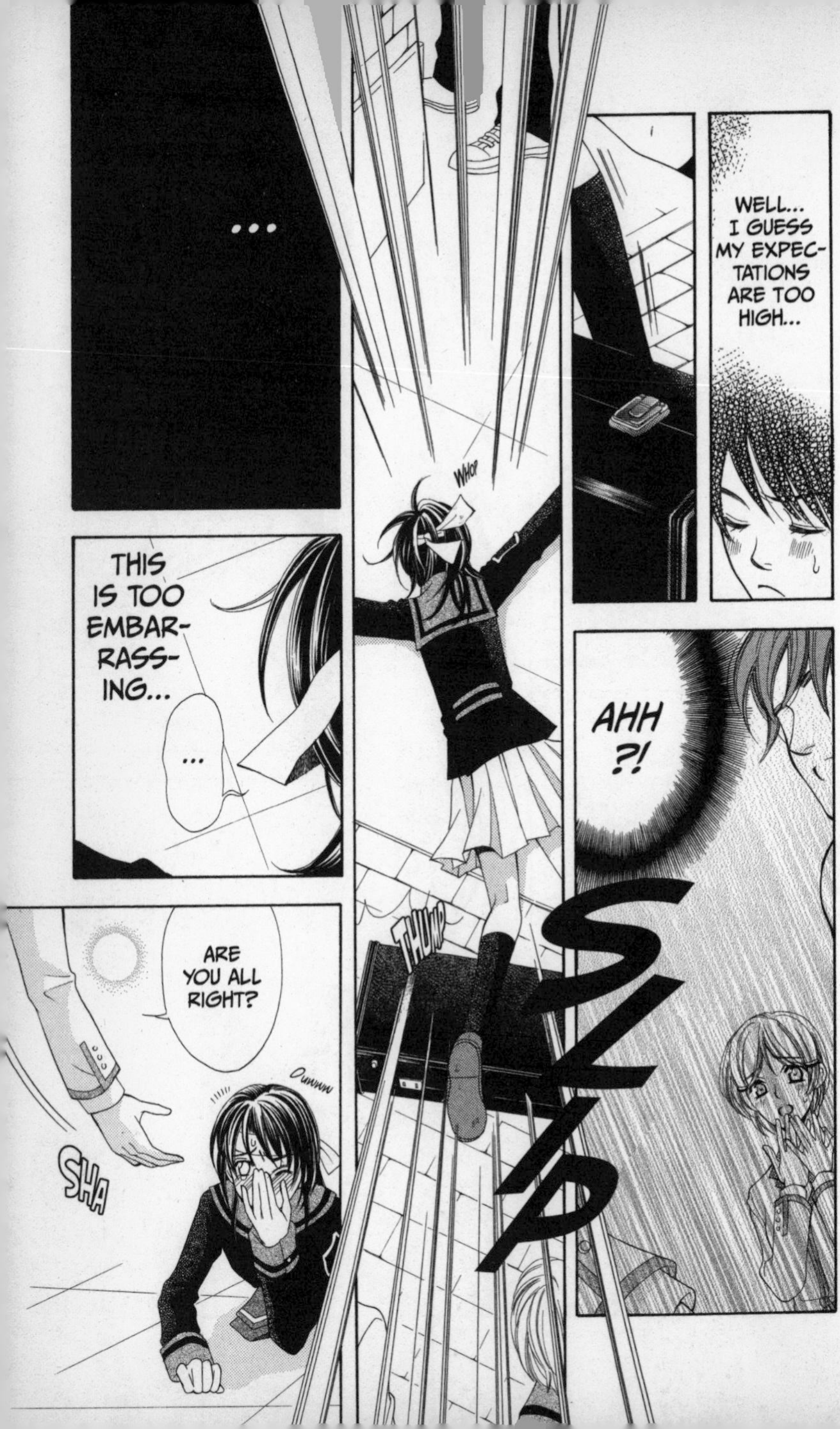

WELL... I GUESS MY EXPECTATIONS ARE TOO HIGH...
AHH ?!
SLIP
WHOP
THUMP
...
THIS IS TOO EMBARRASSING...
...
ARE YOU ALL RIGHT?
Owwww
SHA

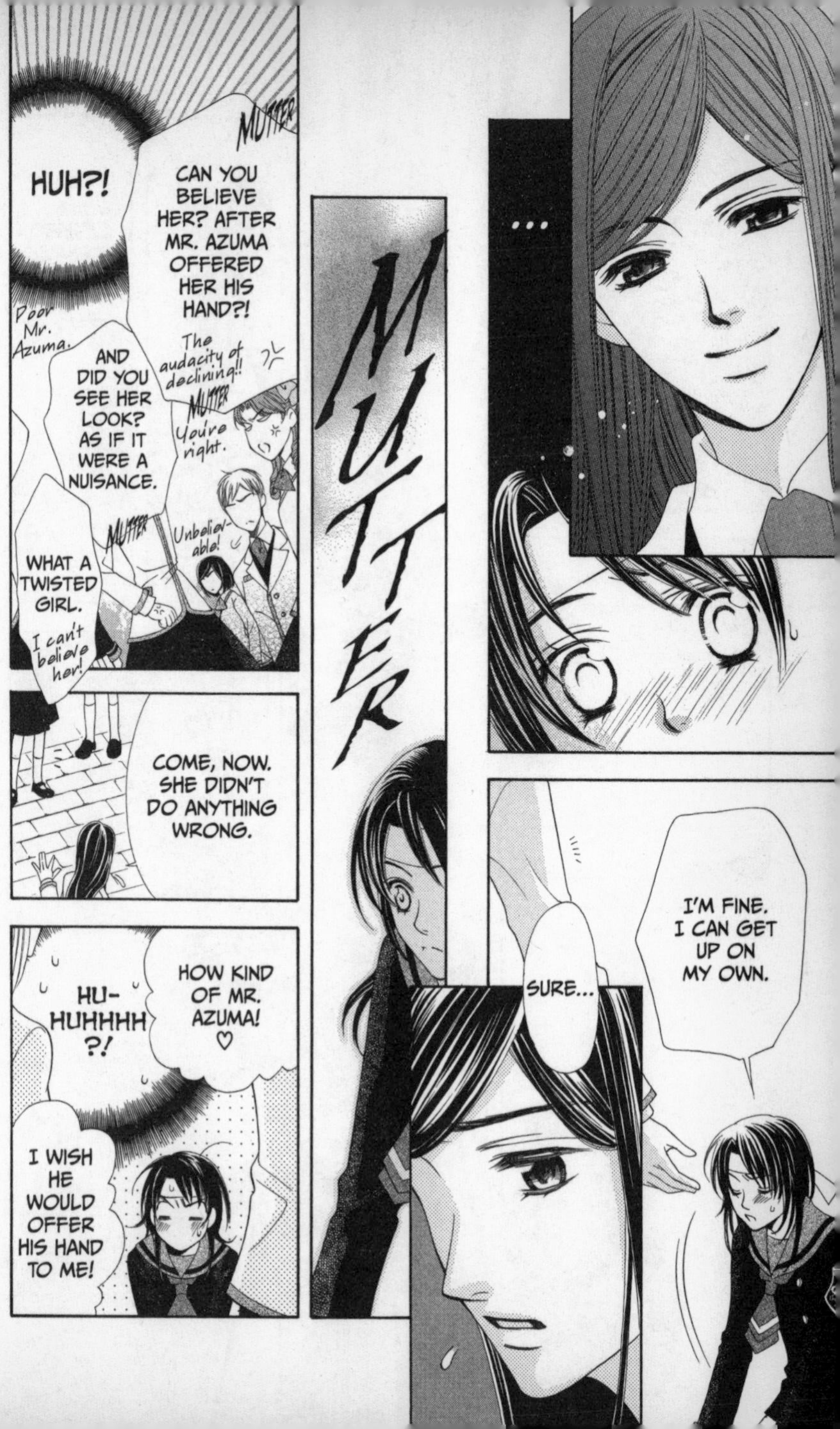
...
I'M FINE. I CAN GET UP ON MY OWN.
SURE...
MUTTER
MUTTER
CAN YOU BELIEVE HER? AFTER MR. AZUMA OFFERED HER HIS HAND?!
HUH?!
Poor Mr. Azuma.
The audacity of declining!!
MUTTER
You're right.
AND DID YOU SEE HER LOOK? AS IF IT WERE A NUISANCE.
Unbelievable!
MUTTER
WHAT A TWISTED GIRL.
I can't believe her!
COME, NOW. SHE DIDN'T DO ANYTHING WRONG.
HOW KIND OF MR. AZUMA! ♡
HU-HUHHHH?!
I WISH HE WOULD OFFER HIS HAND TO ME!

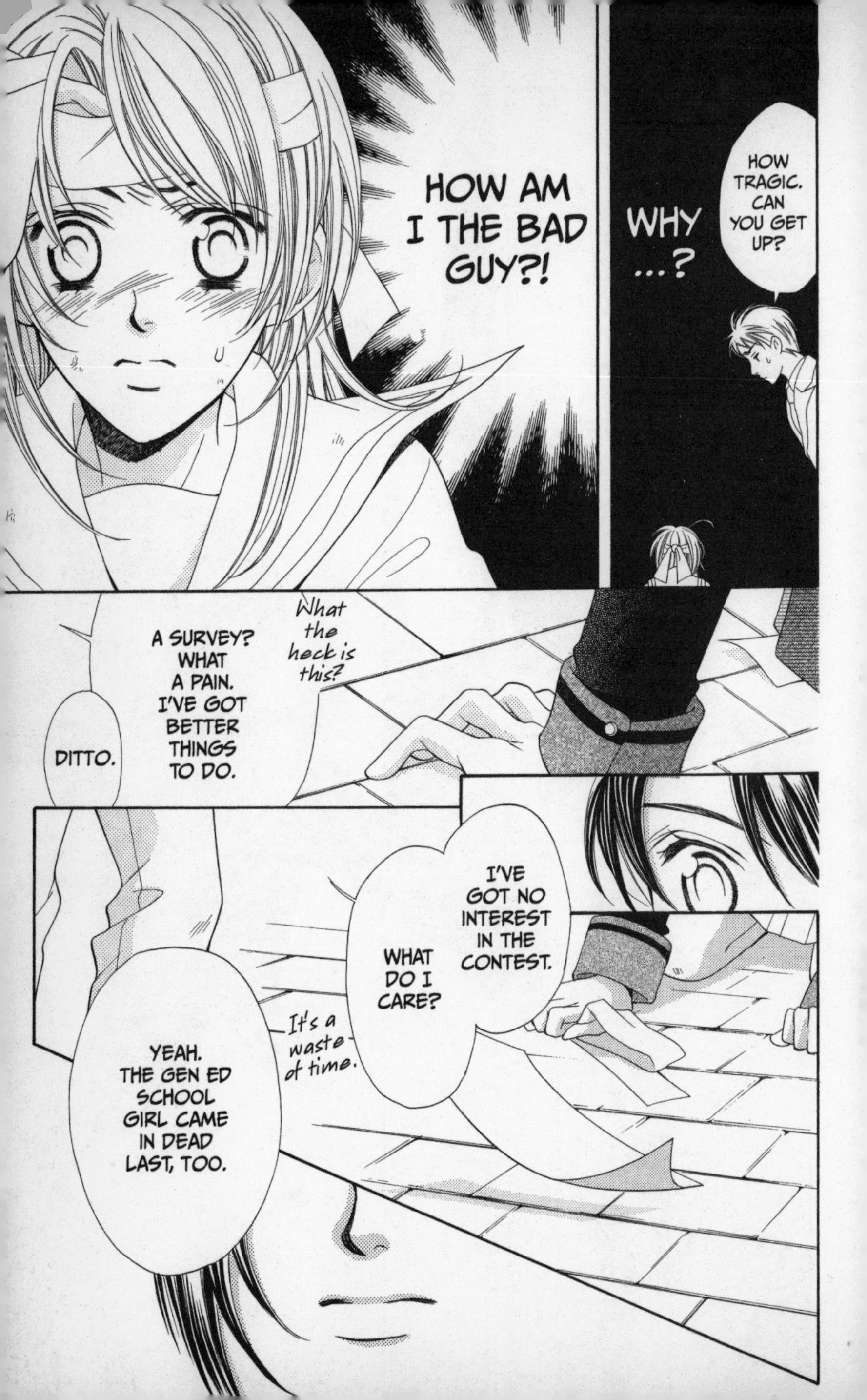
HOW TRAGIC. CAN YOU GET UP?
WHY ...?
HOW AM I THE BAD GUY?!
What the heck is this?
A SURVEY? WHAT A PAIN. I'VE GOT BETTER THINGS TO DO.
DITTO.
I'VE GOT NO INTEREST IN THE CONTEST.
WHAT DO I CARE?
It's a waste of time.
YEAH. THE GEN ED SCHOOL GIRL CAME IN DEAD LAST, TOO.

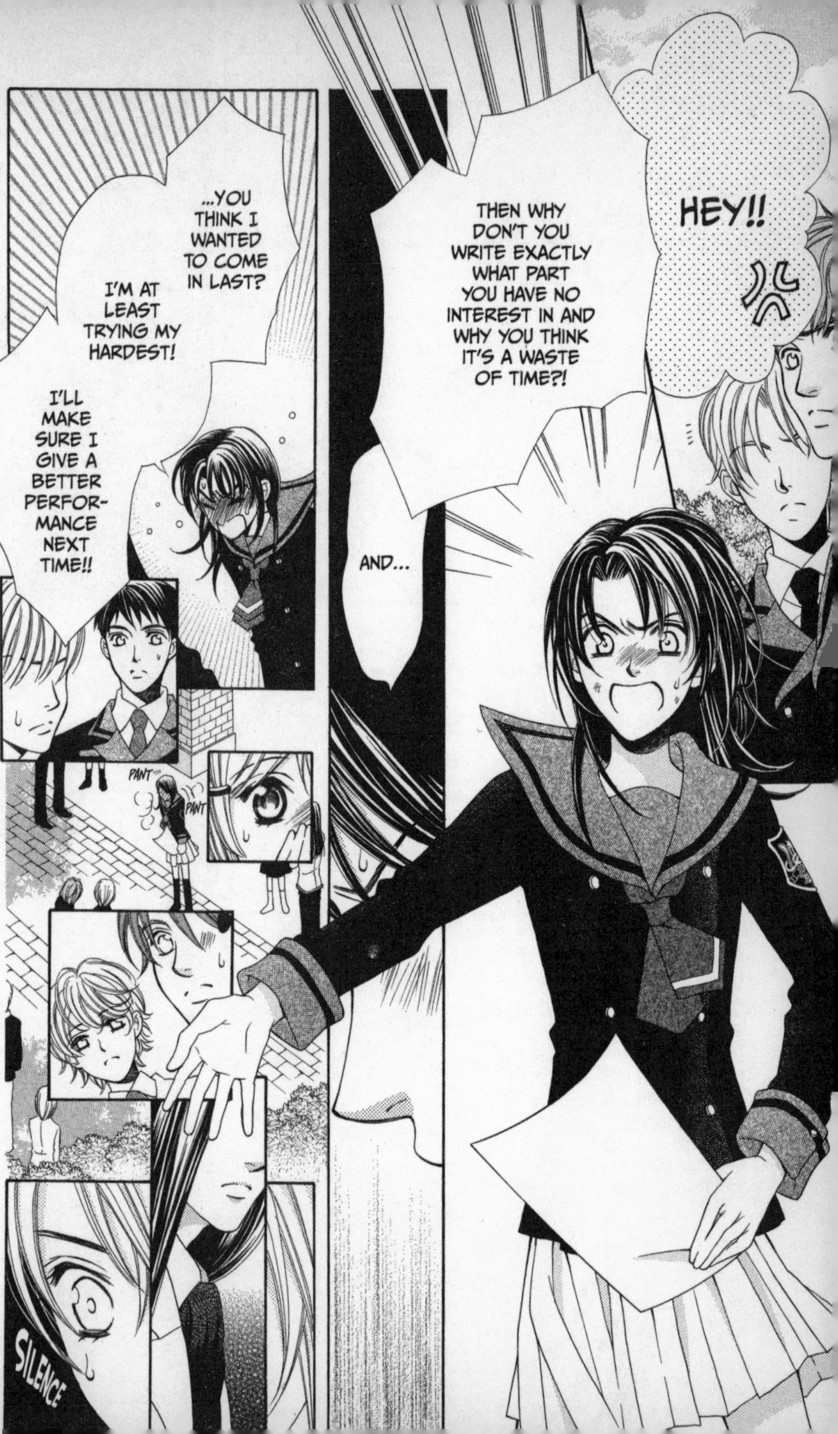
HEY!!
THEN WHY DON'T YOU WRITE EXACTLY WHAT PART YOU HAVE NO INTEREST IN AND WHY YOU THINK IT'S A WASTE OF TIME?!
AND...
...YOU THINK I WANTED TO COME IN LAST?
I'M AT LEAST TRYING MY HARDEST!
I'LL MAKE SURE I GIVE A BETTER PERFORMANCE NEXT TIME!!
PANT
PANT
SILENCE

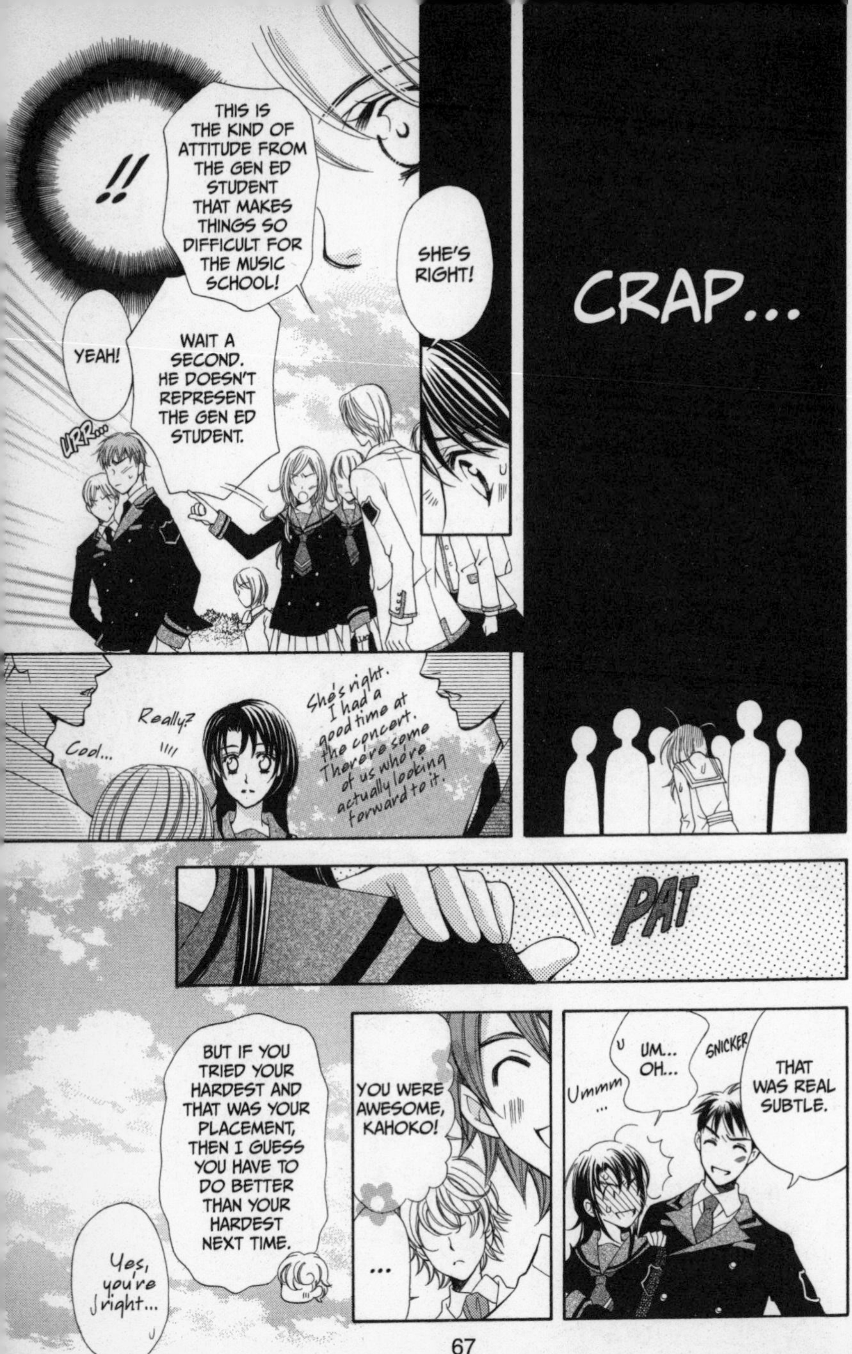
CRAP...
SHE'S RIGHT!
THIS IS THE KIND OF ATTITUDE FROM THE GEN ED STUDENT THAT MAKES THINGS SO DIFFICULT FOR THE MUSIC SCHOOL!
!!
WAIT A SECOND. HE DOESN'T REPRESENT THE GEN ED STUDENT.
YEAH!
URRR...
She's right. I had a good time at the concert. There're some of us who're actually looking forward to it.
Really?
Cool...
PAT
THAT WAS REAL SUBTLE.
SNICKER
UM... OH...
Ummm...
YOU WERE AWESOME, KAHOKO!
...
BUT IF YOU TRIED YOUR HARDEST AND THAT WAS YOUR PLACEMENT, THEN I GUESS YOU HAVE TO DO BETTER THAN YOUR HARDEST NEXT TIME.
Yes, you're right...

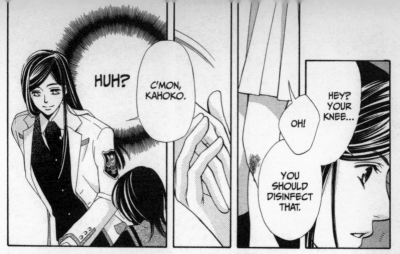

HUH?

C'MON, KAHOKO.

OH!

HEY? YOUR KNEE...

YOU SHOULD DISINFECT THAT.

WHAT?!

W-WAIT A SECOND.

AZUMA!

Hold on a second.

INFIRMARY

...

THANK YOU.

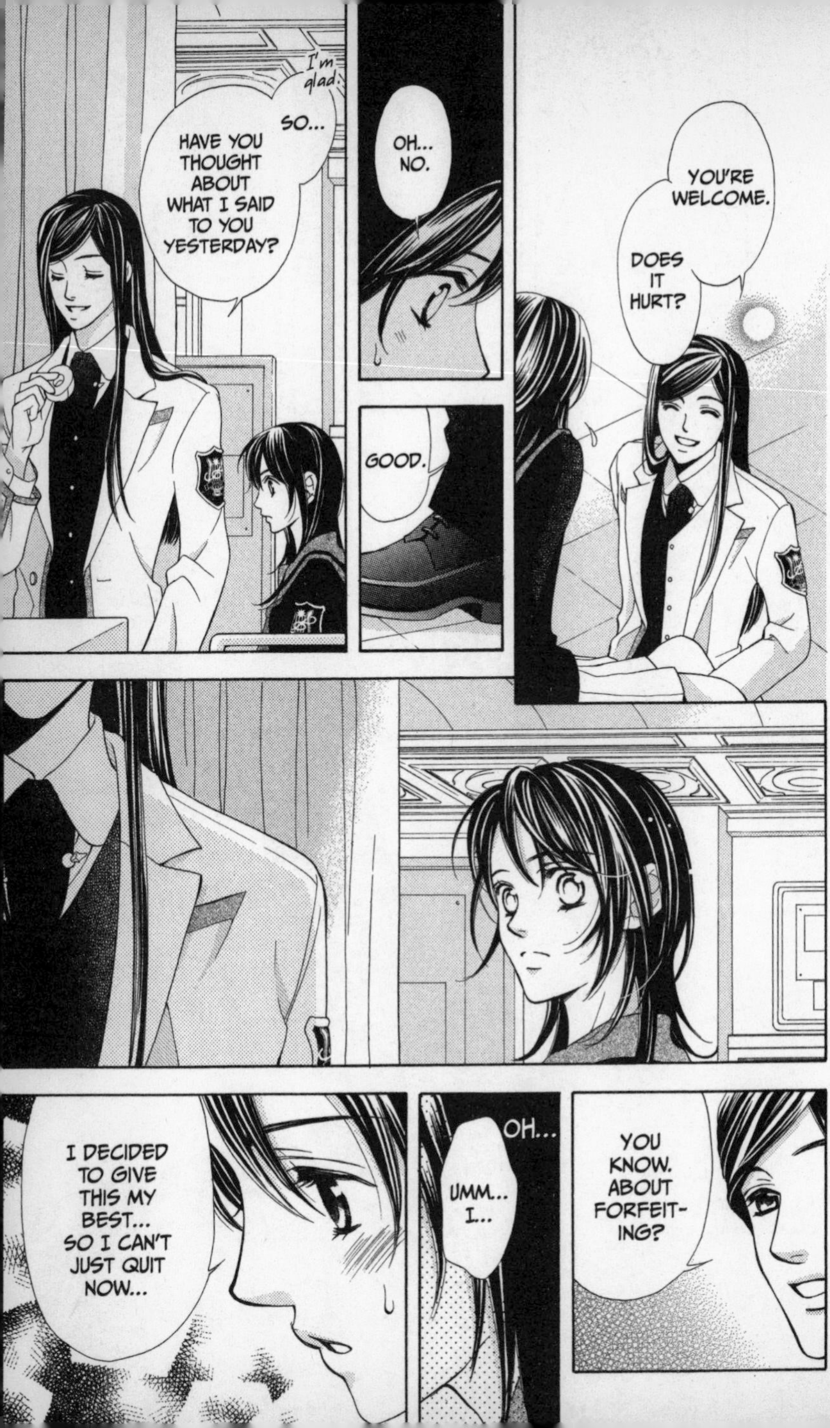
YOU'RE WELCOME.
DOES IT HURT?
OH... NO.
GOOD.
I'm glad.
SO...
HAVE YOU THOUGHT ABOUT WHAT I SAID TO YOU YESTERDAY?
YOU KNOW. ABOUT FORFEIT-ING?
OH...
UMM... I...
I DECIDED TO GIVE THIS MY BEST... SO I CAN'T JUST QUIT NOW...

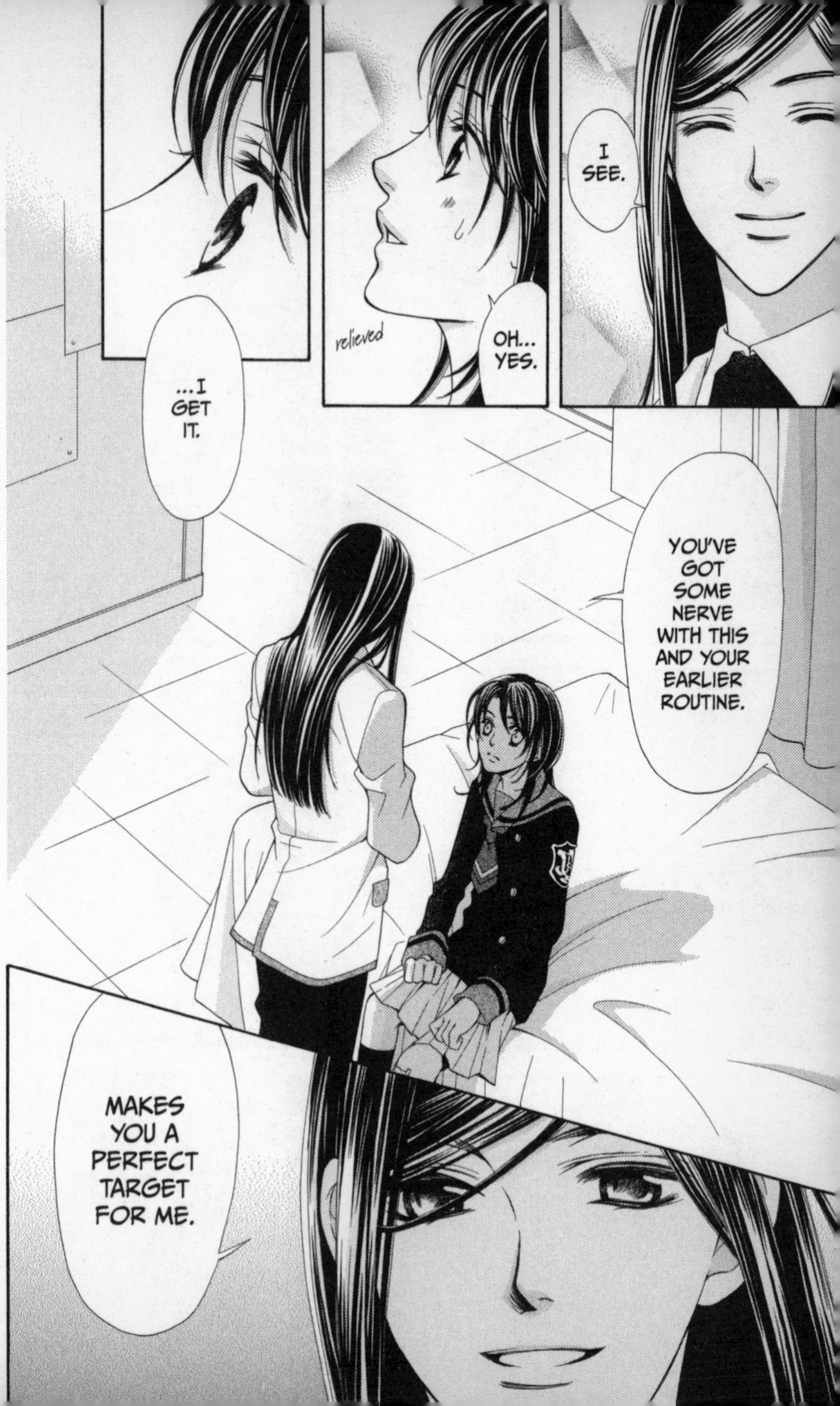
I SEE.
relieved
OH... YES.
...I GET IT.
YOU'VE GOT SOME NERVE WITH THIS AND YOUR EARLIER ROUTINE.
MAKES YOU A PERFECT TARGET FOR ME.

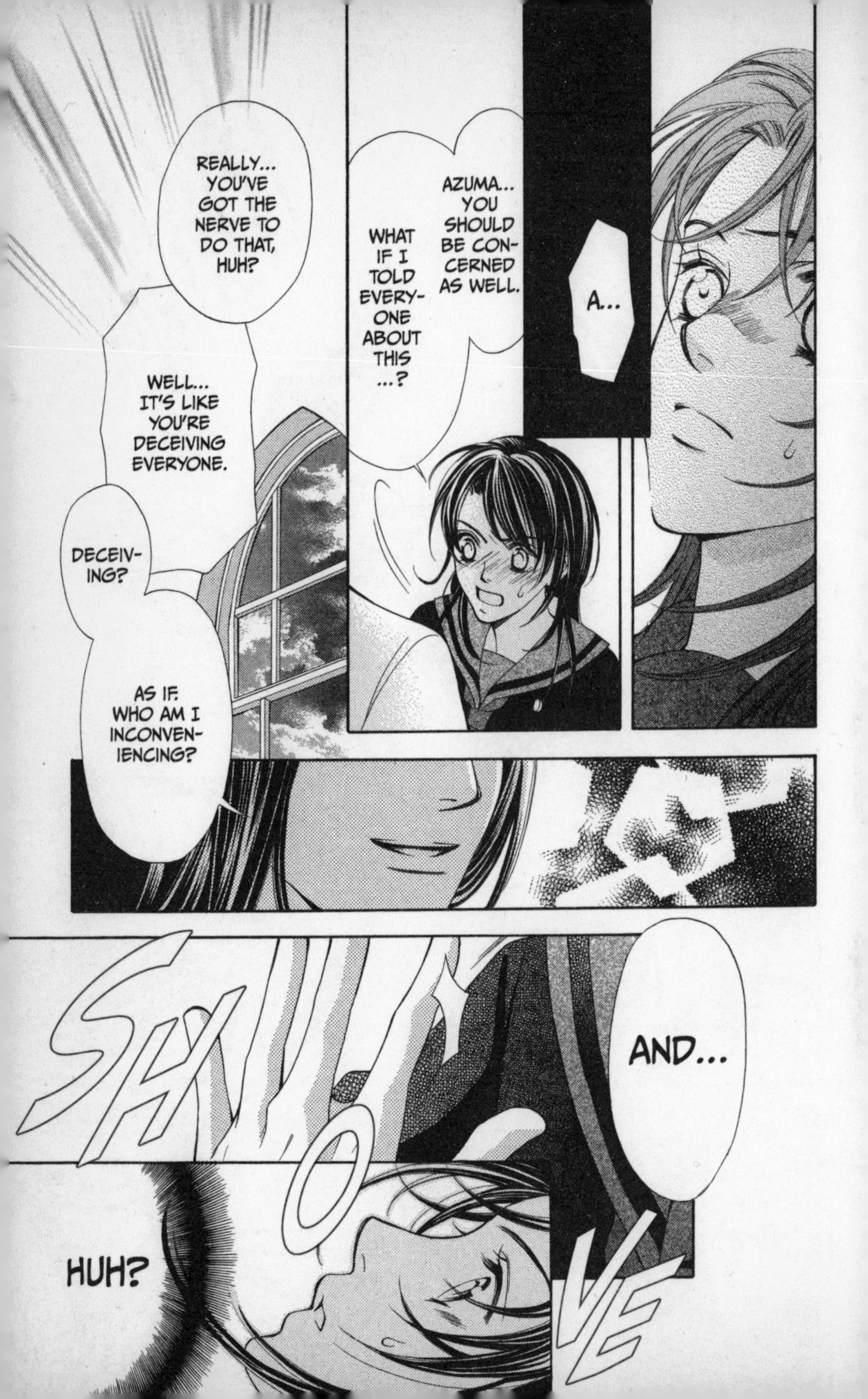
A...
AZUMA... YOU SHOULD BE CON-CERNED AS WELL.
WHAT IF I TOLD EVERY-ONE ABOUT THIS ...?
REALLY... YOU'VE GOT THE NERVE TO DO THAT, HUH?
WELL... IT'S LIKE YOU'RE DECEIVING EVERYONE.
DECEIV-ING?
AS IF. WHO AM I INCONVEN-IENCING?
AND...
SHOVE
HUH?

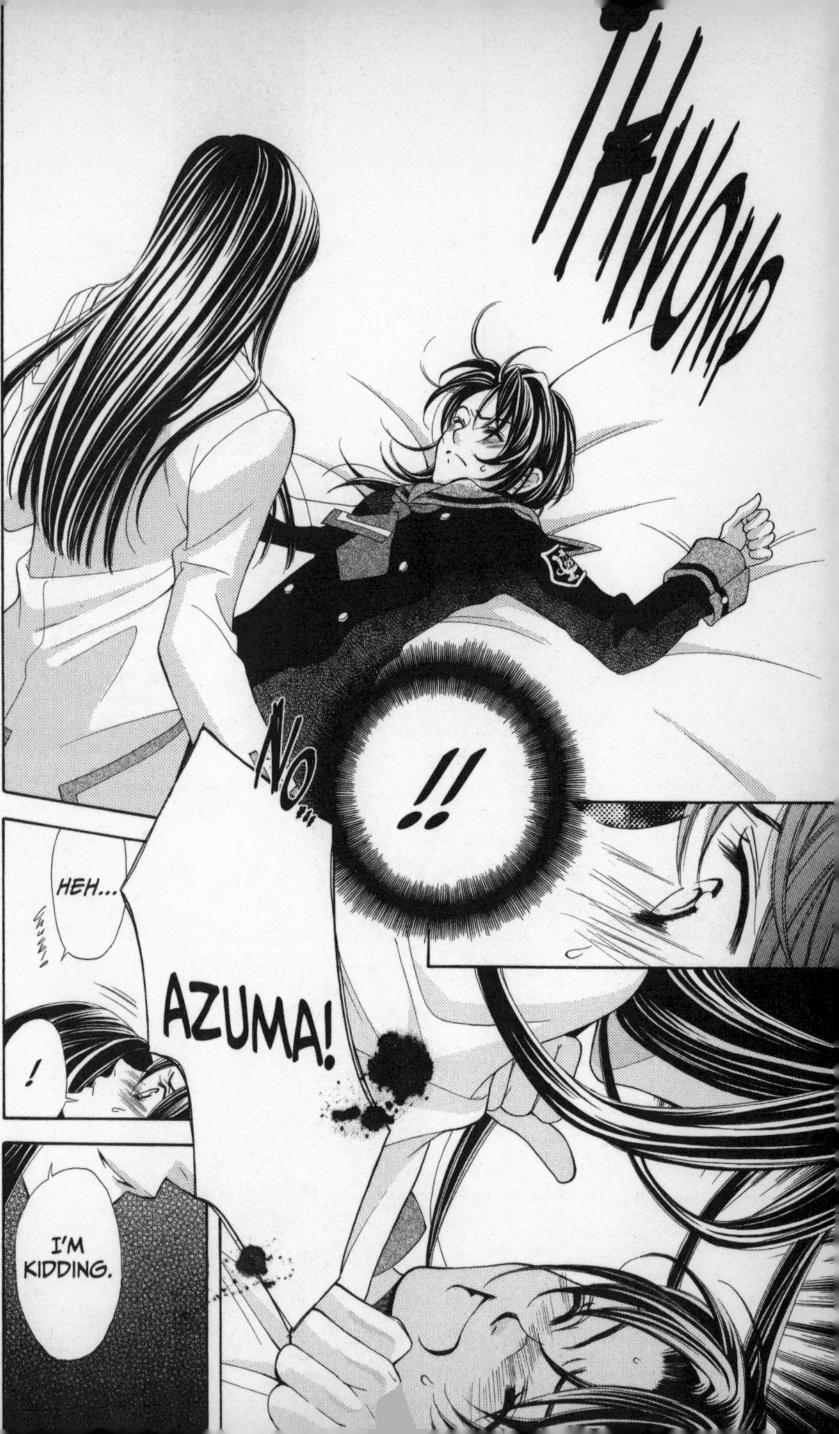
THWOMP
NO...
!!
HEH...
AZUMA!
!
I'M KIDDING.

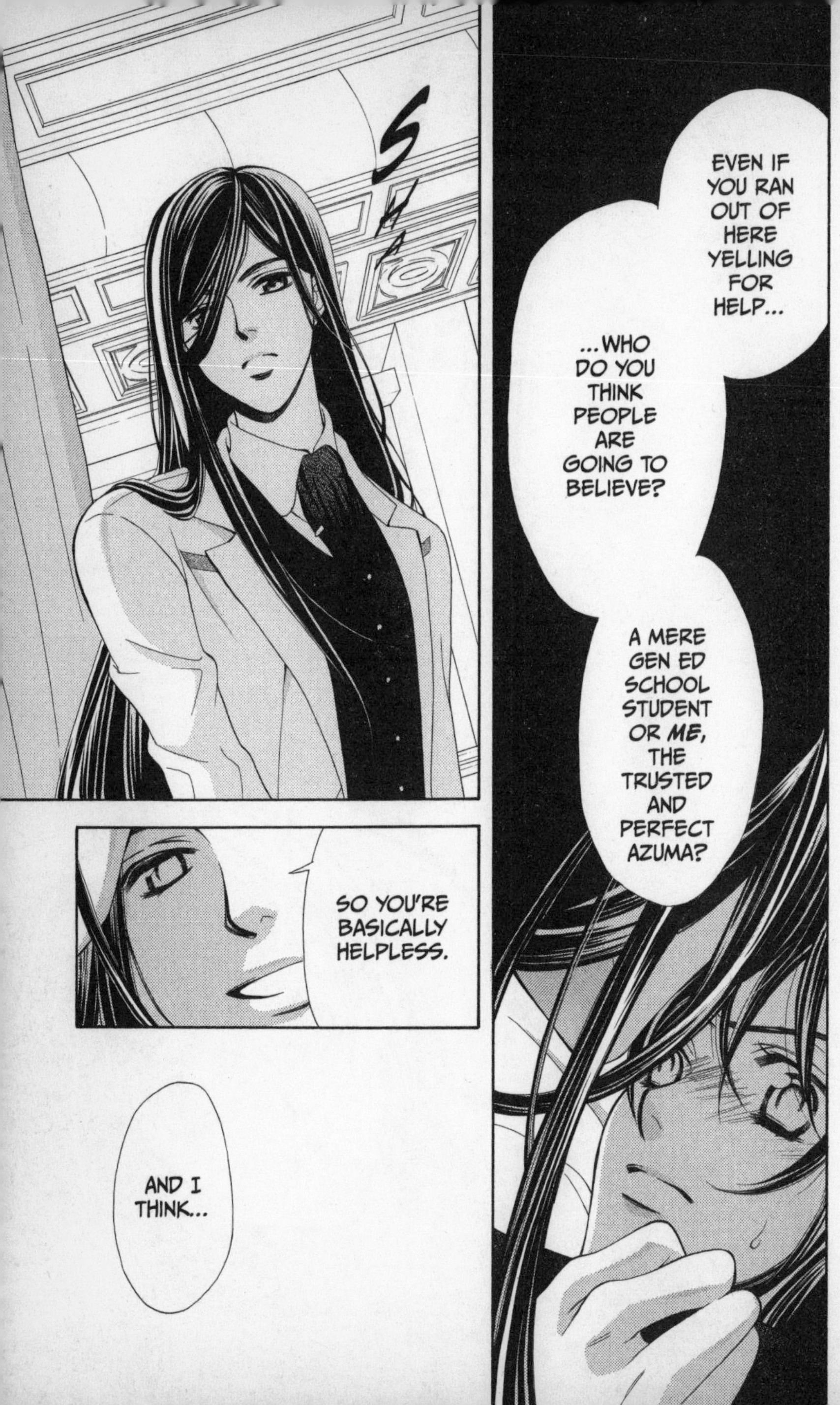

EVEN IF YOU RAN OUT OF HERE YELLING FOR HELP...
...WHO DO YOU THINK PEOPLE ARE GOING TO BELIEVE?
A MERE GEN ED SCHOOL STUDENT OR *ME*, THE TRUSTED AND PERFECT AZUMA?
SHA
SO YOU'RE BASICALLY HELPLESS.
AND I THINK...

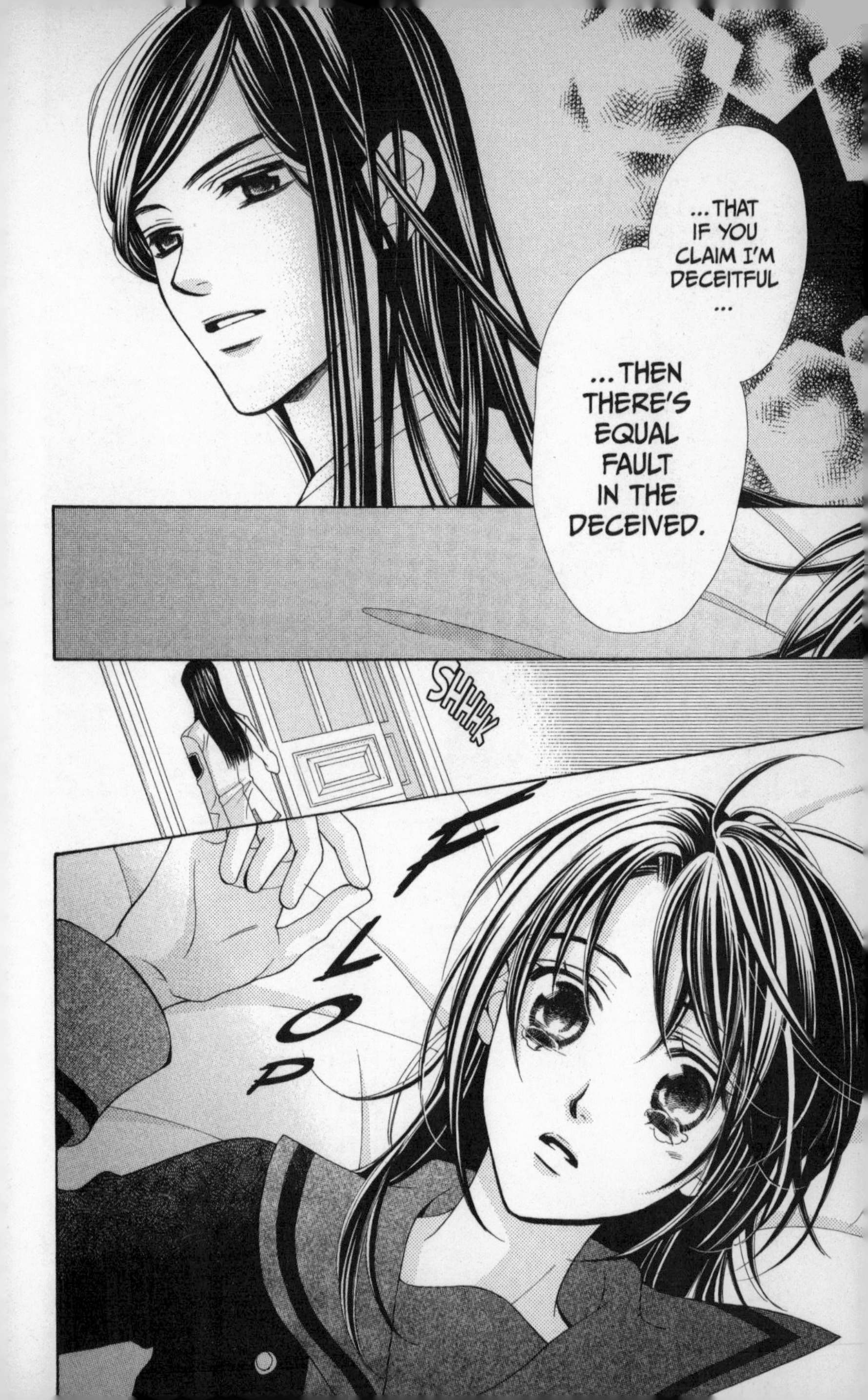
...THAT IF YOU CLAIM I'M DECEITFUL ...
...THEN THERE'S EQUAL FAULT IN THE DECEIVED.
SHHHK
FLOOP

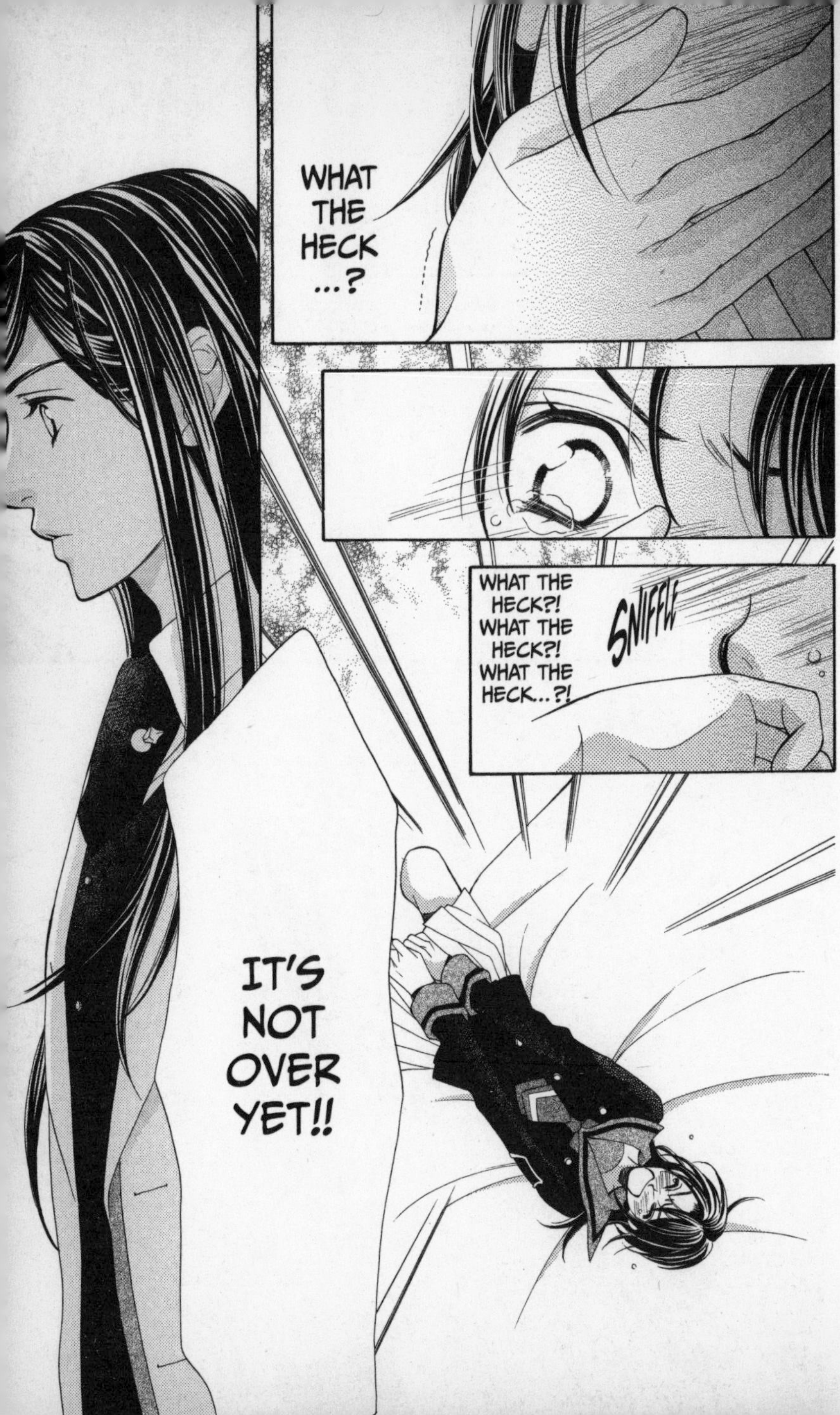
WHAT THE HECK ...?
WHAT THE HECK?! WHAT THE HECK?! WHAT THE HECK...?!
SNIFFLE
IT'S NOT OVER YET!!

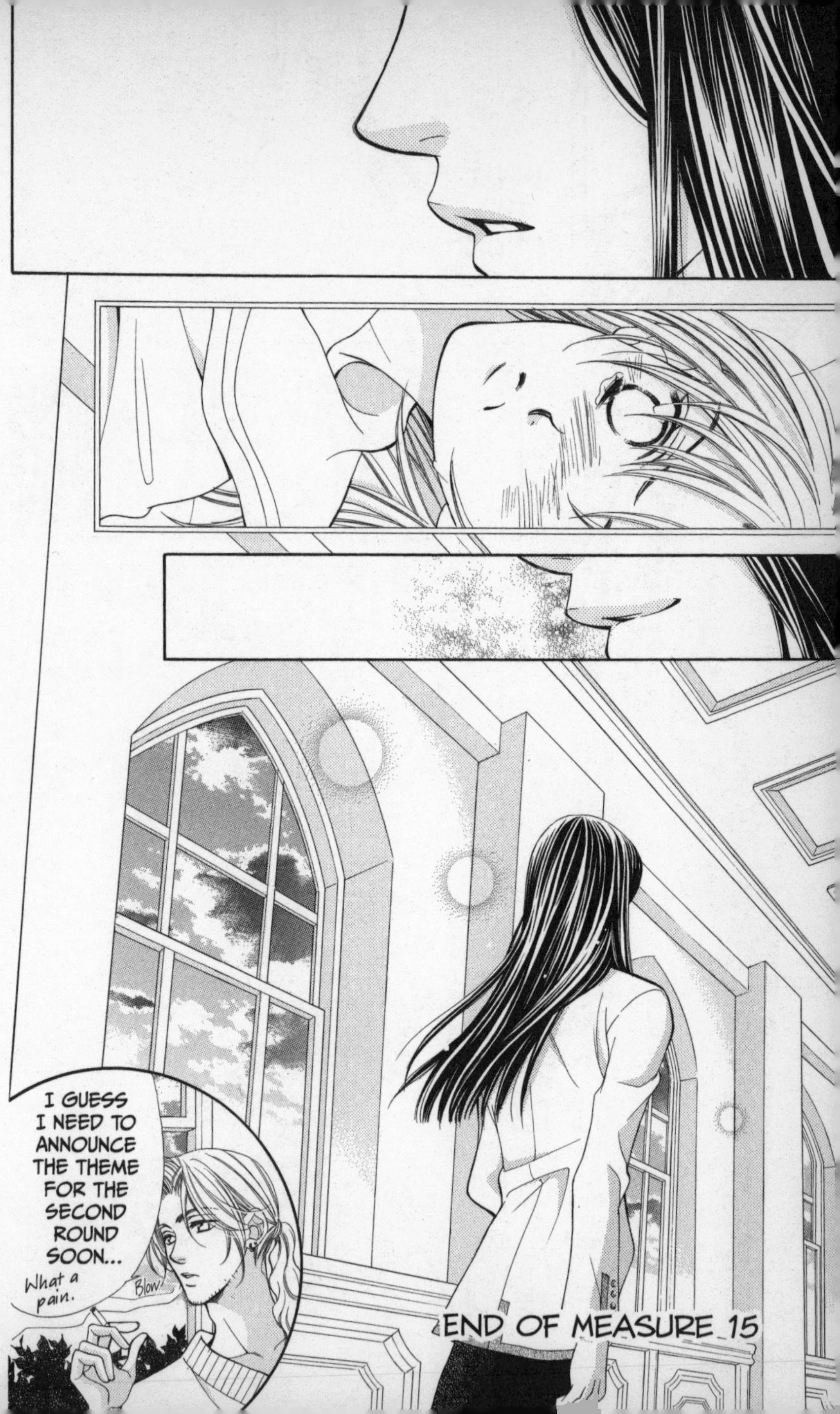
I GUESS I NEED TO ANNOUNCE THE THEME FOR THE SECOND ROUND SOON...
Blow
What a pain.
END OF MEASURE 15

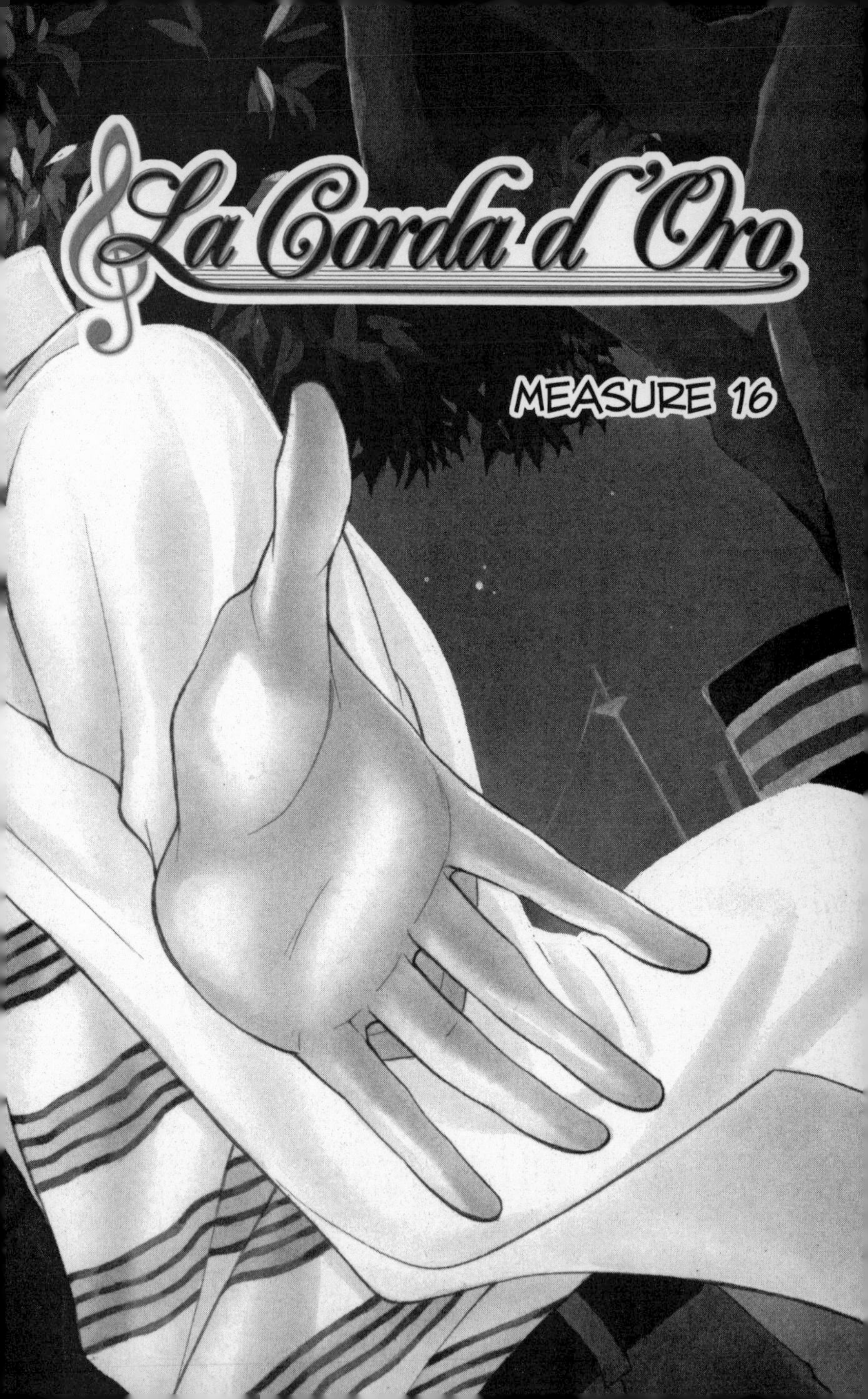
La Corda d'Oro
MEASURE 16

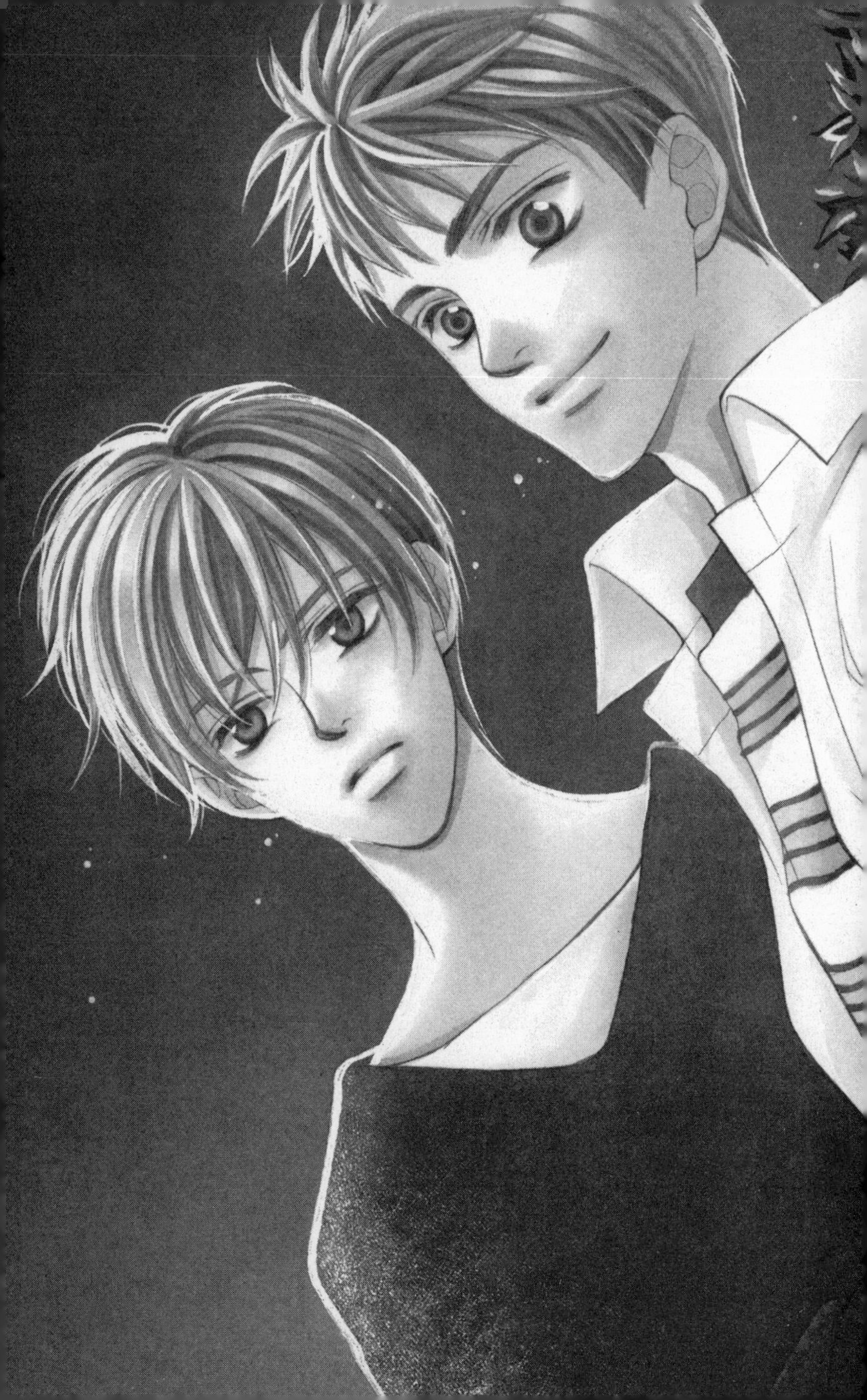

CHAK
SIGH

Daily Happenings ⑧
...Dubbing Session, Part II

The dubbing session progressed smoothly. It was professional work at its best, and I was impressed at the ease with which everyone was able to answer the producer's little requests.

Azuma! You're a little too dark there! Think grey tones!
...
I was in awe...

The CD content was drama and free talk and the allocated time for the free talk portion was about seven minutes (for everybody). But the lead off hitter, Mr. Morita, who plays Kazuki, went over seven minutes alone, which I thought was hilarious. (lol)

I had such a good time. Thank you so much for all your hard work, everyone!

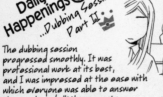

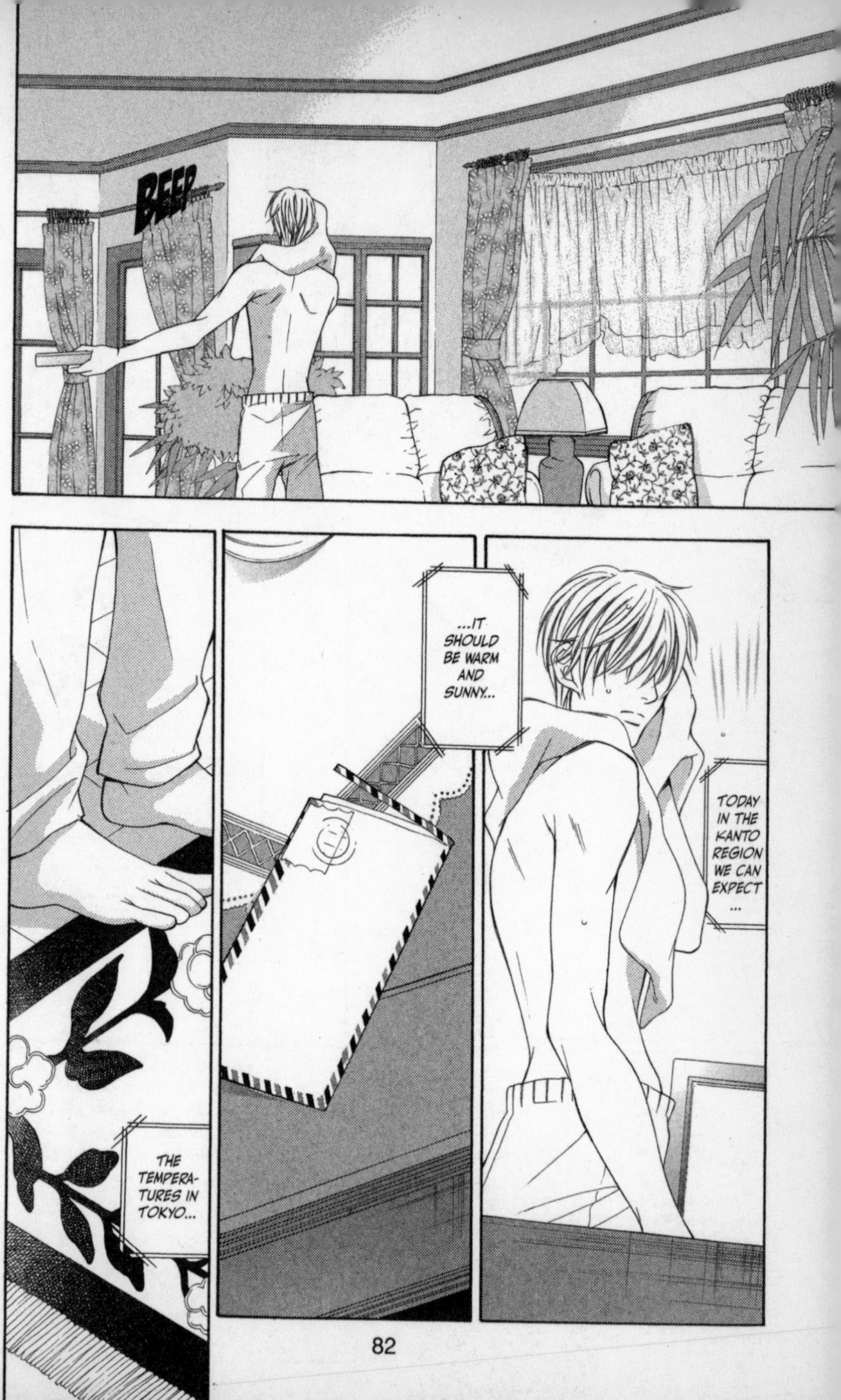
BEEP
TODAY IN THE KANTO REGION WE CAN EXPECT ...
...IT SHOULD BE WARM AND SUNNY...
THE TEMPERA-TURES IN TOKYO...

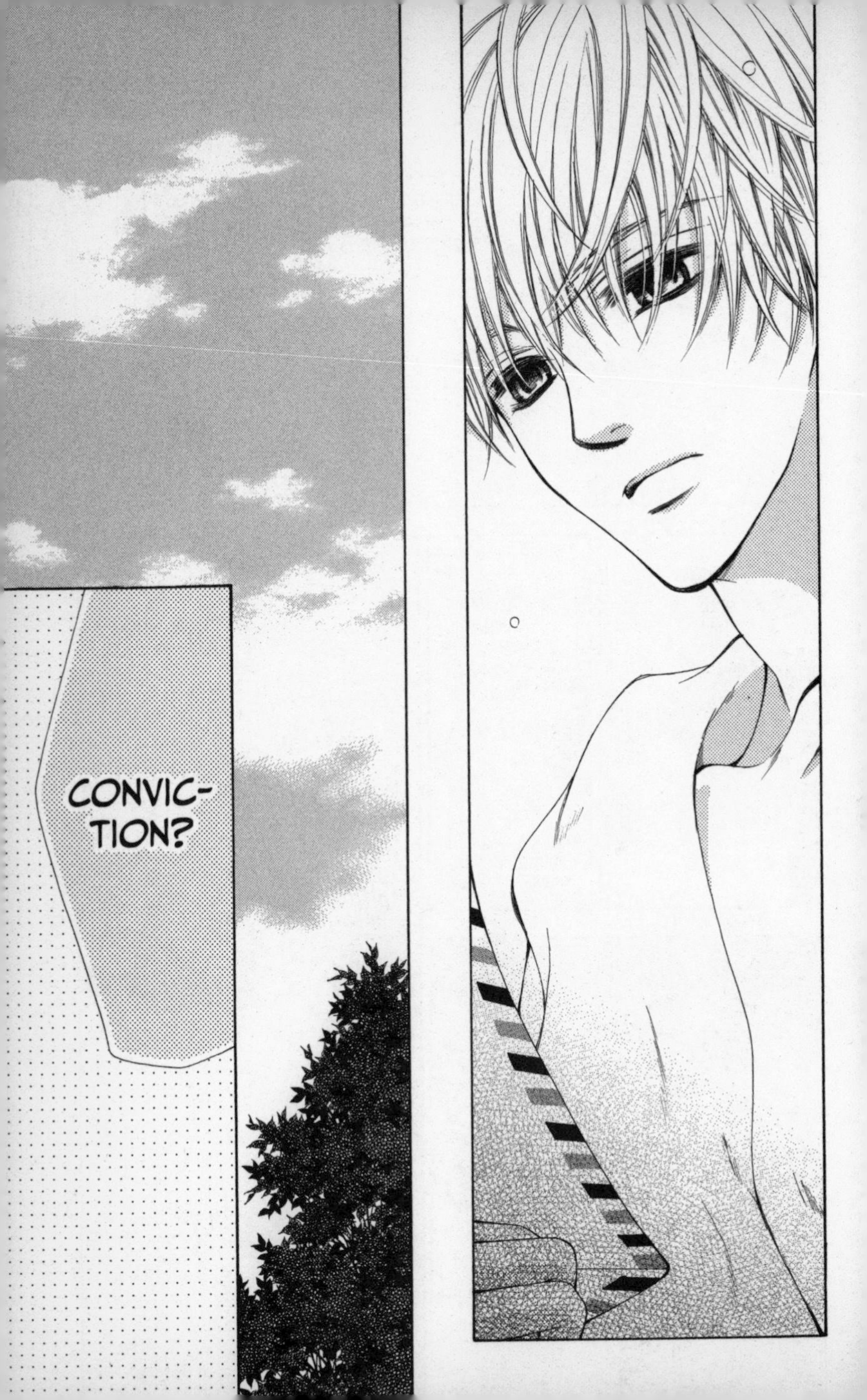
CONVIC-
TION?

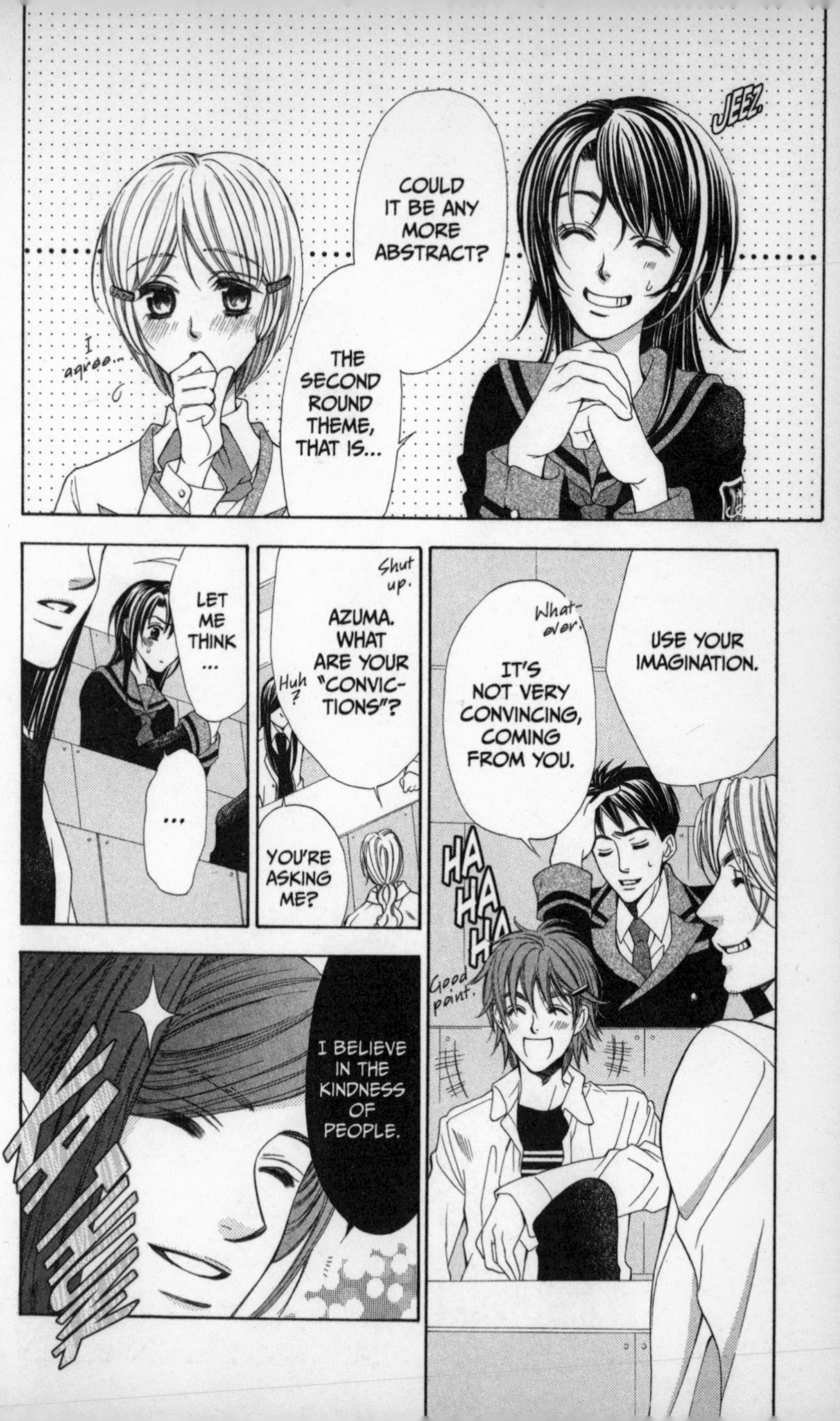
JEEZ
COULD IT BE ANY MORE ABSTRACT?
THE SECOND ROUND THEME, THAT IS...
I agree...
USE YOUR IMAGINATION.
What-ever.
IT'S NOT VERY CONVINCING, COMING FROM YOU.
HAHAHA
Good point.
Shut up.
AZUMA. WHAT ARE YOUR "CONVICTIONS"?
Huh?
YOU'RE ASKING ME?
LET ME THINK...
...
I BELIEVE IN THE KINDNESS OF PEOPLE.

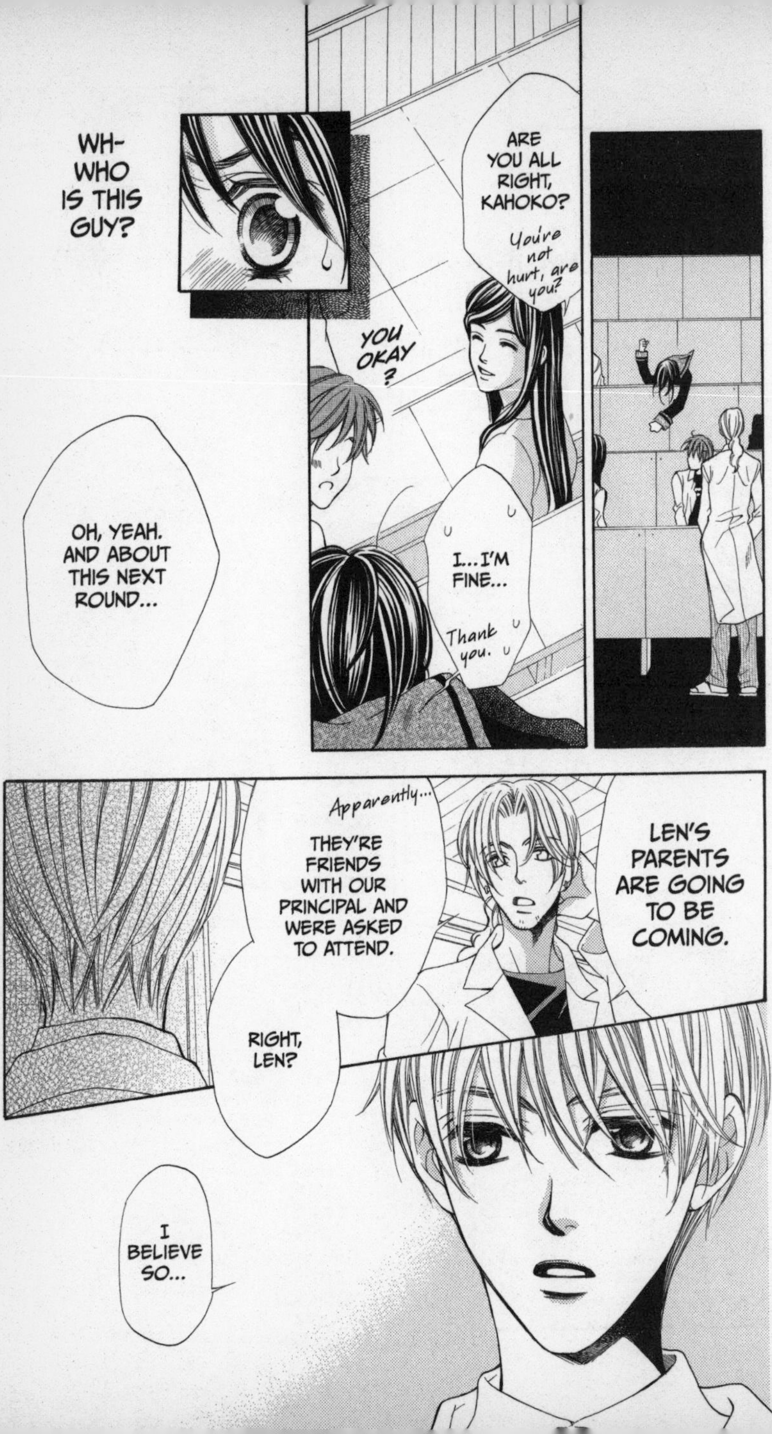
ARE YOU ALL RIGHT, KAHOKO?
You're not hurt, are you?
YOU OKAY?
I...I'M FINE...
Thank you.
WH-WHO IS THIS GUY?
OH, YEAH. AND ABOUT THIS NEXT ROUND...
LEN'S PARENTS ARE GOING TO BE COMING.
Apparently...
THEY'RE FRIENDS WITH OUR PRINCIPAL AND WERE ASKED TO ATTEND.
RIGHT, LEN?
I BELIEVE SO...

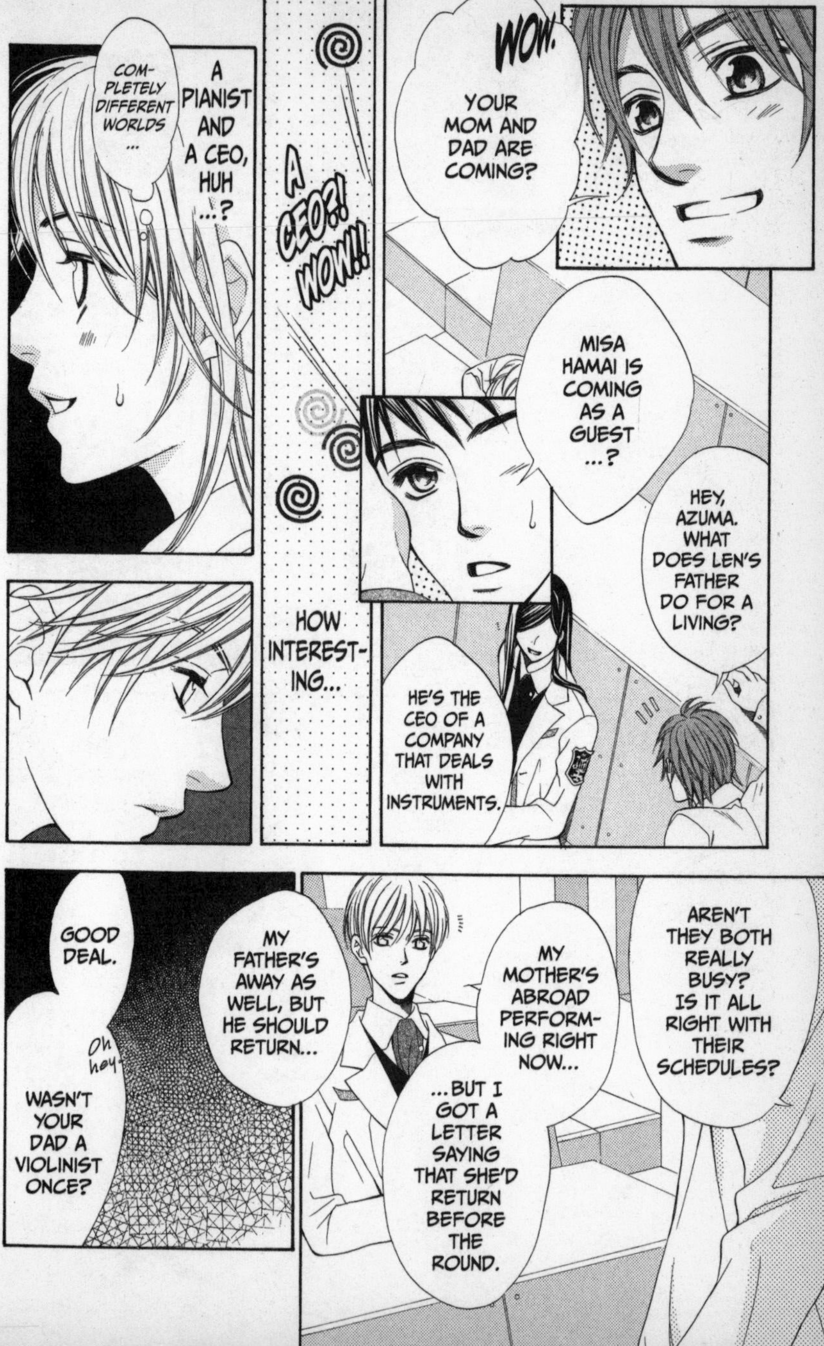
WOW.
YOUR MOM AND DAD ARE COMING?
MISA HAMAI IS COMING AS A GUEST ...?
HEY, AZUMA. WHAT DOES LEN'S FATHER DO FOR A LIVING?
HE'S THE CEO OF A COMPANY THAT DEALS WITH INSTRUMENTS.
A CEO?! WOW!!
HOW INTEREST-ING...
A PIANIST AND A CEO, HUH ...?
COM-PLETELY DIFFERENT WORLDS ...
AREN'T THEY BOTH REALLY BUSY? IS IT ALL RIGHT WITH THEIR SCHEDULES?
MY MOTHER'S ABROAD PERFORM-ING RIGHT NOW...
...BUT I GOT A LETTER SAYING THAT SHE'D RETURN BEFORE THE ROUND.
MY FATHER'S AWAY AS WELL, BUT HE SHOULD RETURN...
GOOD DEAL.
Oh hey-
WASN'T YOUR DAD A VIOLINIST ONCE?

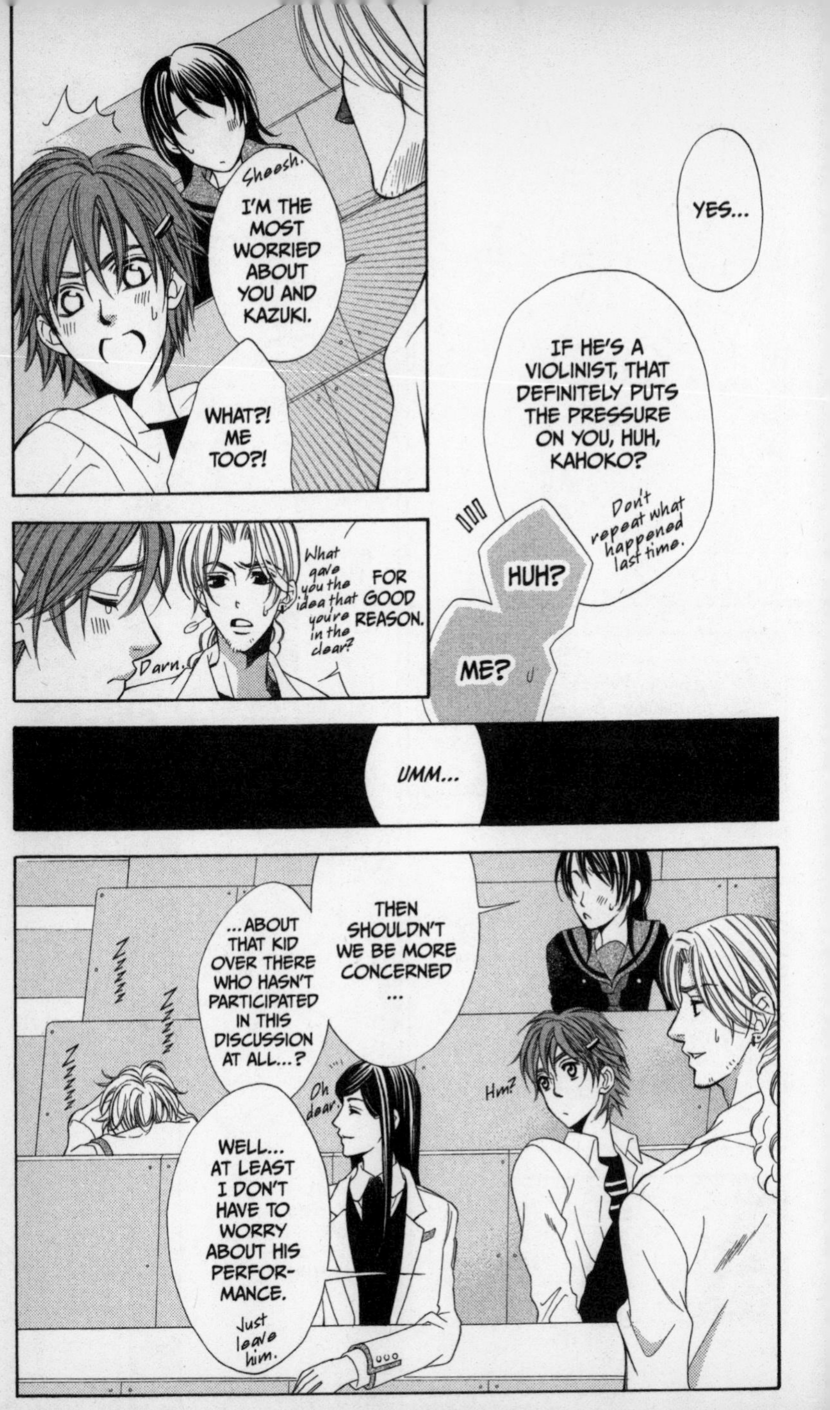
YES...
IF HE'S A VIOLINIST, THAT DEFINITELY PUTS THE PRESSURE ON YOU, HUH, KAHOKO?
Don't repeat what happened last time.
HUH?
ME?
Sheesh.
I'M THE MOST WORRIED ABOUT YOU AND KAZUKI.
WHAT?! ME TOO?!
FOR GOOD REASON.
What gave you the idea that you're in the clear?
Darn.
UMM...
THEN SHOULDN'T WE BE MORE CONCERNED ...
...ABOUT THAT KID OVER THERE WHO HASN'T PARTICIPATED IN THIS DISCUSSION AT ALL...?
Hm?
Oh dear.
WELL... AT LEAST I DON'T HAVE TO WORRY ABOUT HIS PERFORMANCE.
Just leave him.

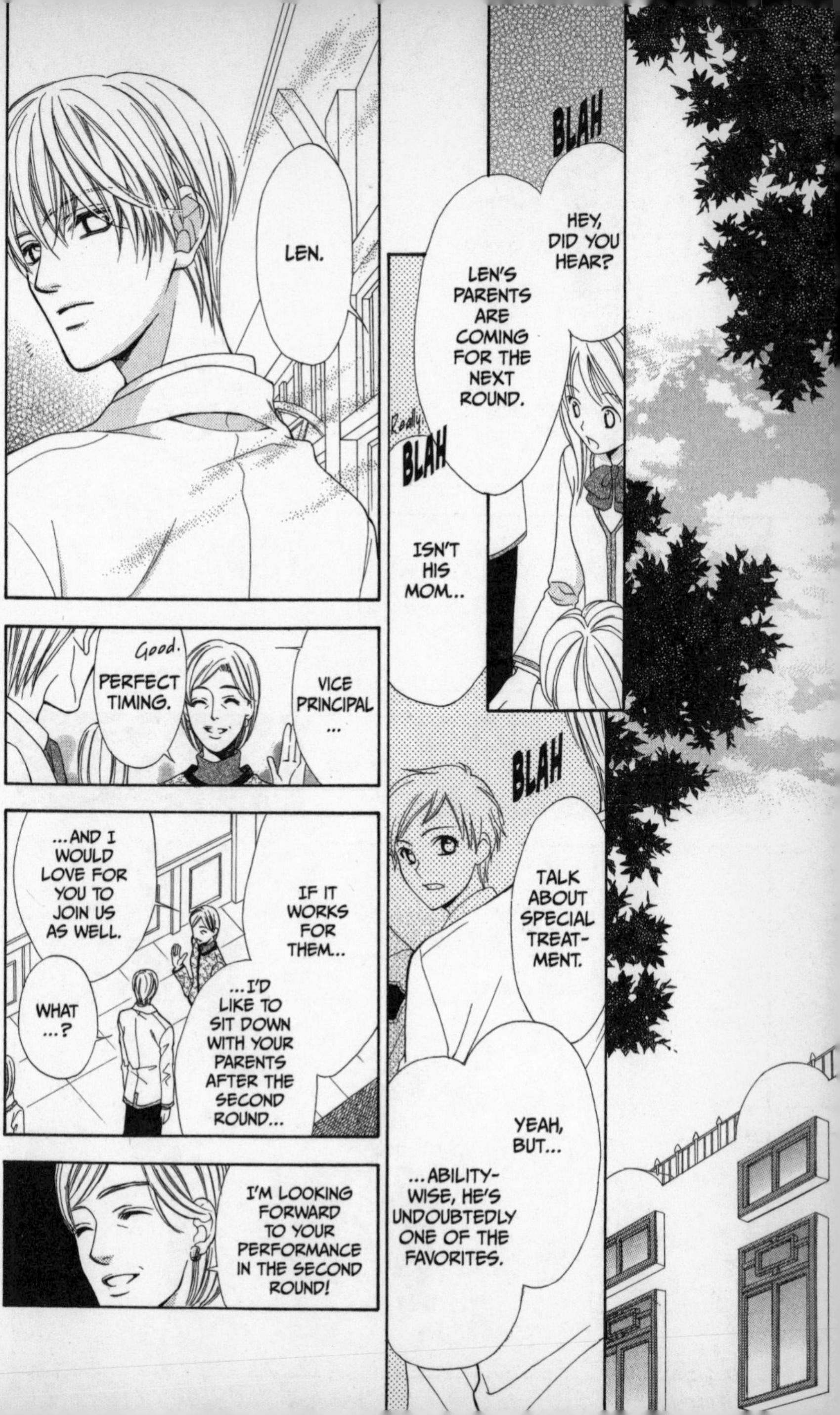
BLAH
HEY, DID YOU HEAR?
LEN'S PARENTS ARE COMING FOR THE NEXT ROUND.
Really.
BLAH
ISN'T HIS MOM...
BLAH
TALK ABOUT SPECIAL TREATMENT.
YEAH, BUT...
...ABILITY-WISE, HE'S UNDOUBTEDLY ONE OF THE FAVORITES.
LEN.
VICE PRINCIPAL ...
Good.
PERFECT TIMING.
IF IT WORKS FOR THEM...
...I'D LIKE TO SIT DOWN WITH YOUR PARENTS AFTER THE SECOND ROUND...
...AND I WOULD LOVE FOR YOU TO JOIN US AS WELL.
WHAT ...?
I'M LOOKING FORWARD TO YOUR PERFORMANCE IN THE SECOND ROUND!

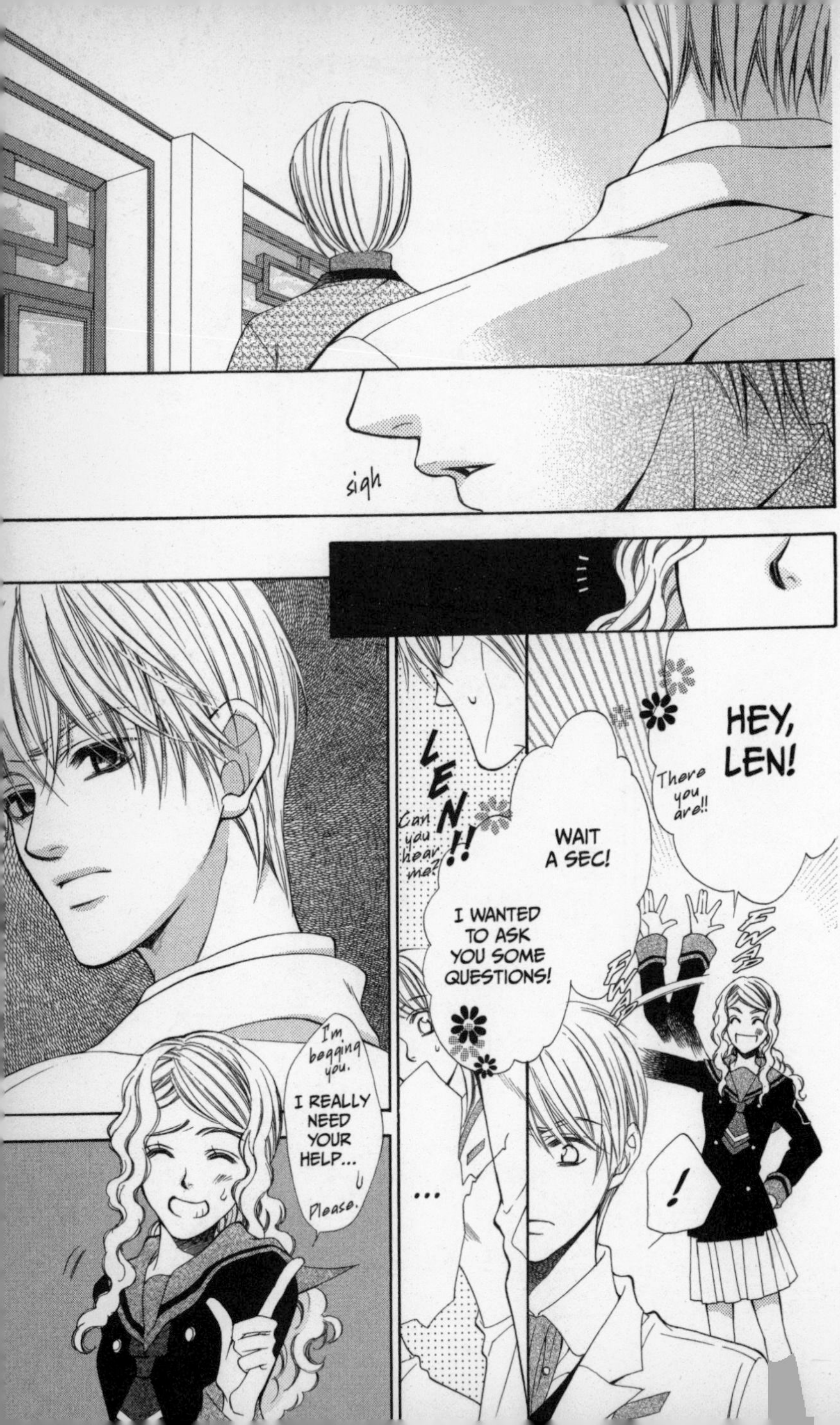
sigh
HEY, LEN!
There you are!!
WAIT A SEC!
I WANTED TO ASK YOU SOME QUESTIONS!
!
LEN!!
Can you hear me?
...
I'm begging you.
I REALLY NEED YOUR HELP...
Please.

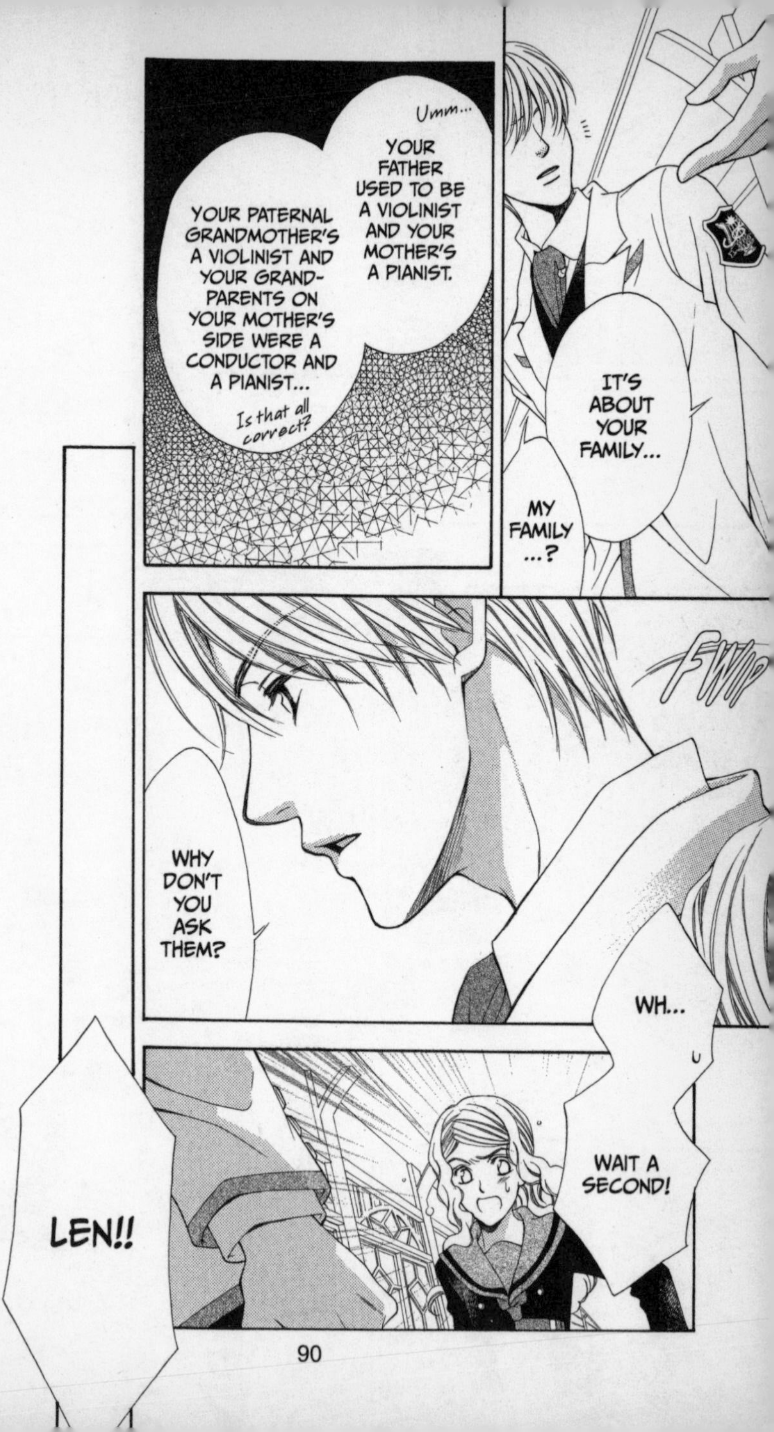
IT'S ABOUT YOUR FAMILY...
MY FAMILY ...?
Umm...
YOUR FATHER USED TO BE A VIOLINIST AND YOUR MOTHER'S A PIANIST.
YOUR PATERNAL GRANDMOTHER'S A VIOLINIST AND YOUR GRAND-PARENTS ON YOUR MOTHER'S SIDE WERE A CONDUCTOR AND A PIANIST...
Is that all correct?
FWIP
WHY DON'T YOU ASK THEM?
WH...
WAIT A SECOND!
LEN!!

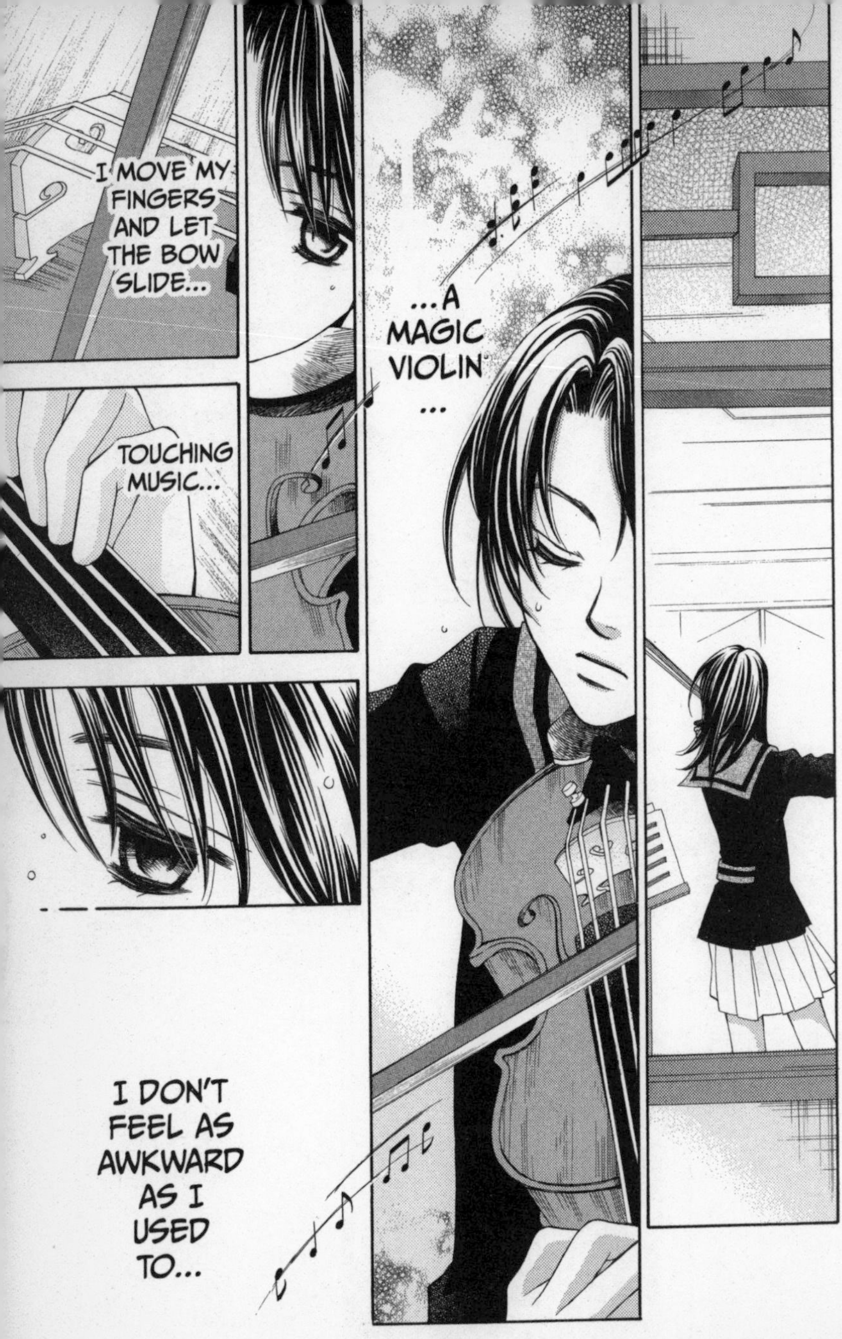
...A MAGIC VIOLIN ...
I MOVE MY FINGERS AND LET THE BOW SLIDE...
TOUCHING MUSIC...
I DON'T FEEL AS AWKWARD AS I USED TO...

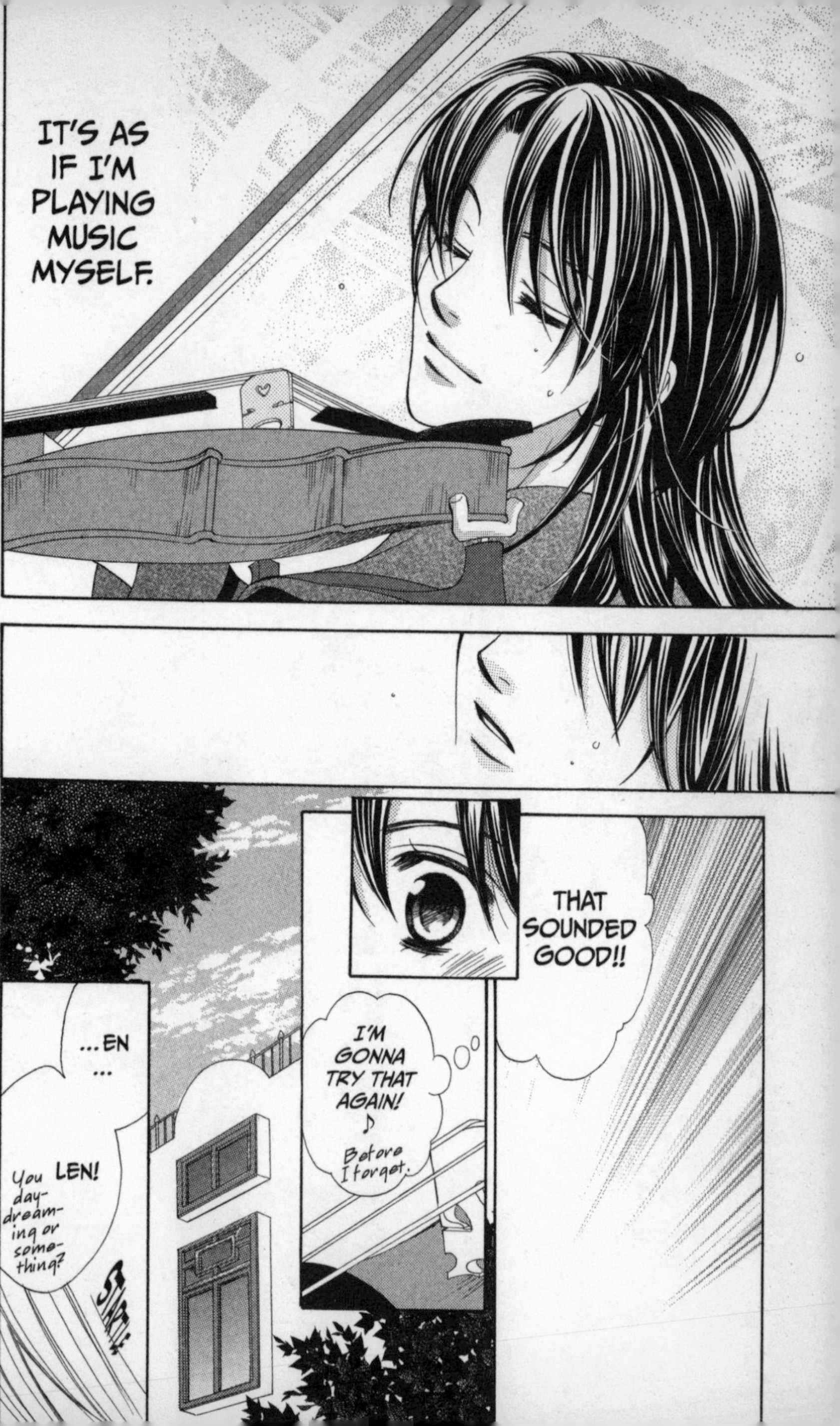
IT'S AS IF I'M PLAYING MUSIC MYSELF.
THAT SOUNDED GOOD!!
I'M GONNA TRY THAT AGAIN! ♪
Before I forget.
...EN ...
LEN!
You day-dreaming or some-thing?

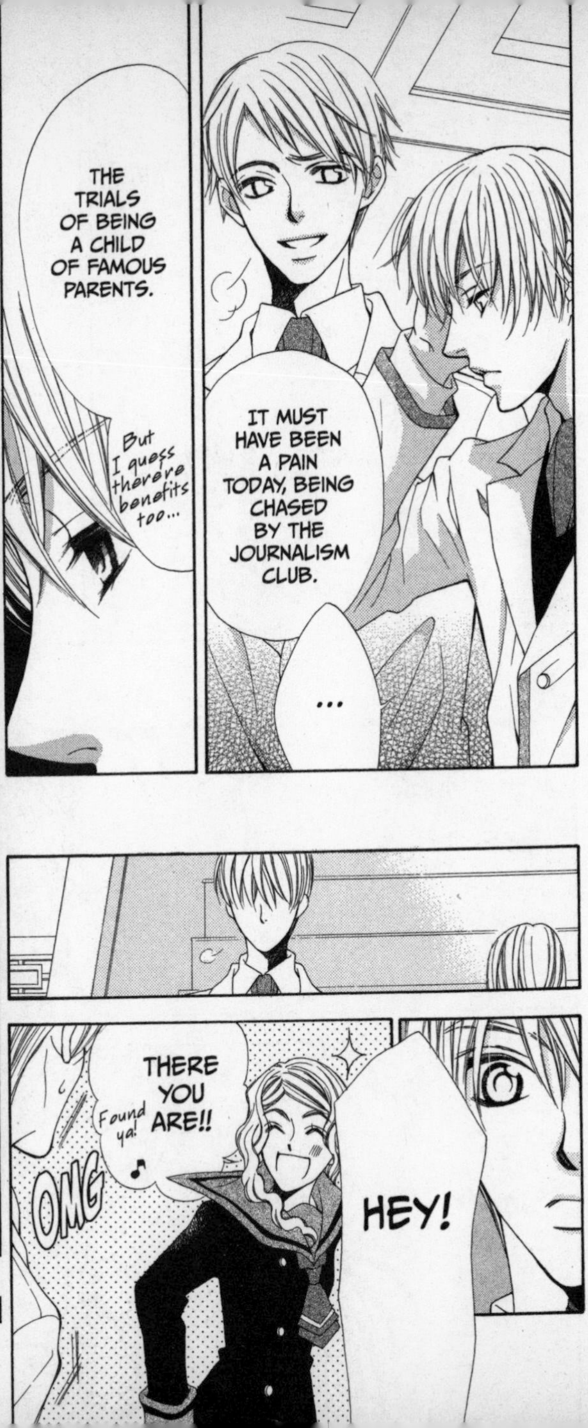
IT MUST HAVE BEEN A PAIN TODAY, BEING CHASED BY THE JOURNALISM CLUB.
...
THE TRIALS OF BEING A CHILD OF FAMOUS PARENTS.
But I guess there're benefits too...
HEY!
THERE YOU ARE!!
Found ya! ♪
OMG

FOUR

A little more on Azuma... I wrote in my previous column (THREE) that he was a really fun character to draw, but he's also a source of agony for me before deadlines. Coloring in his hair to be specific... (the horrors...)

I mean, for the most part I don't mind, but when Azuma and Kahoko are on a page together... You wouldn't believe how much time it takes. I'm just at it for hours with my brush pen.

But the character that takes the most time is Miyabi, who made a brief appearance in volume 3.

Apparently my assistants struggle with Kazuki's hair.

They ominously refer to it as "the Kazuki head..." Sorry, guys! But I really do appreciate your help!

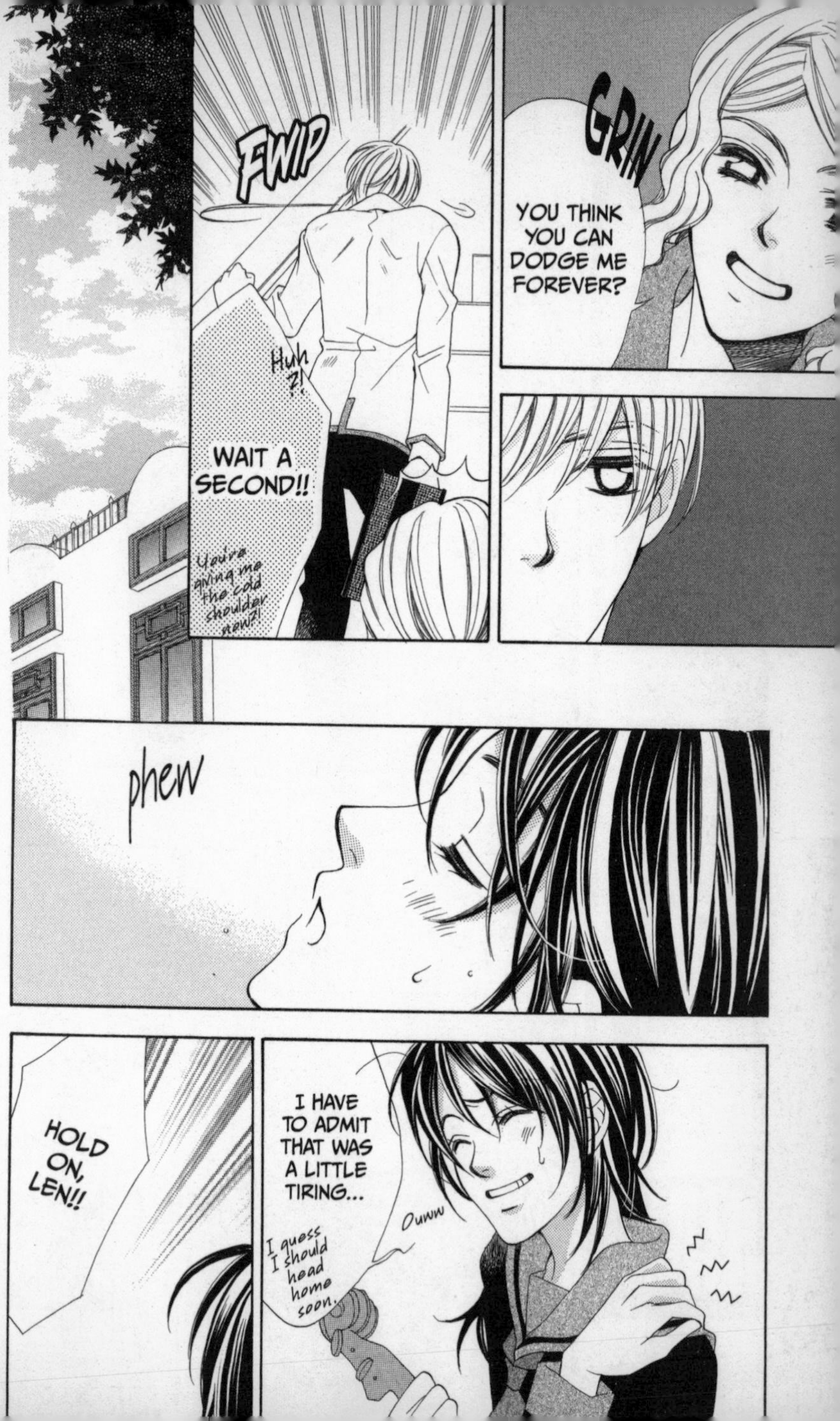
GRIN
YOU THINK YOU CAN DODGE ME FOREVER?
FWIP
Huh?!
WAIT A SECOND!!
You're giving me the cold shoulder now?!
phew
I HAVE TO ADMIT THAT WAS A LITTLE TIRING...
Owww
I guess I should head home soon.
HOLD ON, LEN!!

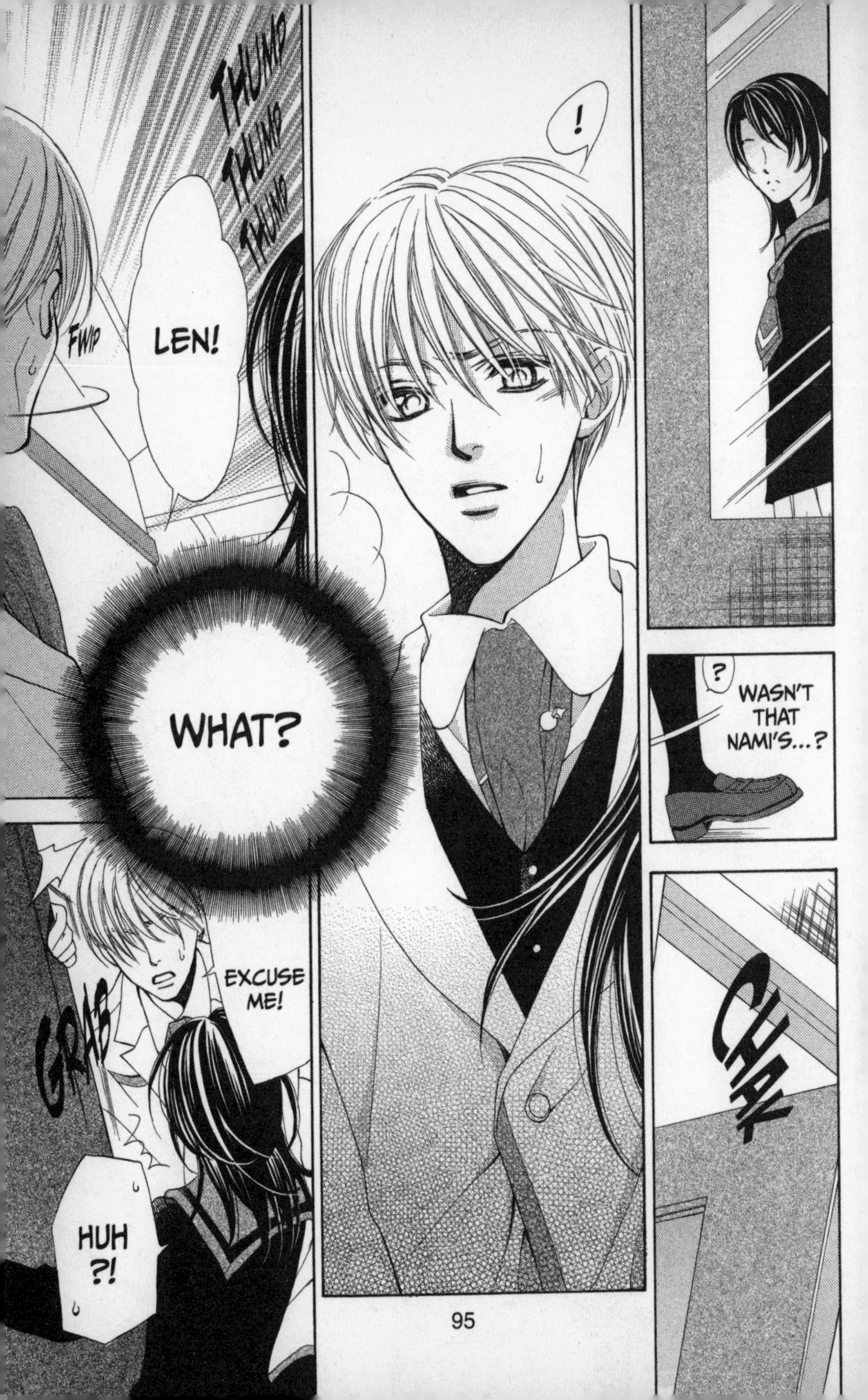
?
WASN'T THAT NAMI'S...?
CHAK
!
THUMP THUMP THUMP
LEN!
FWIP
WHAT?
EXCUSE ME!
GRAB
HUH ?!

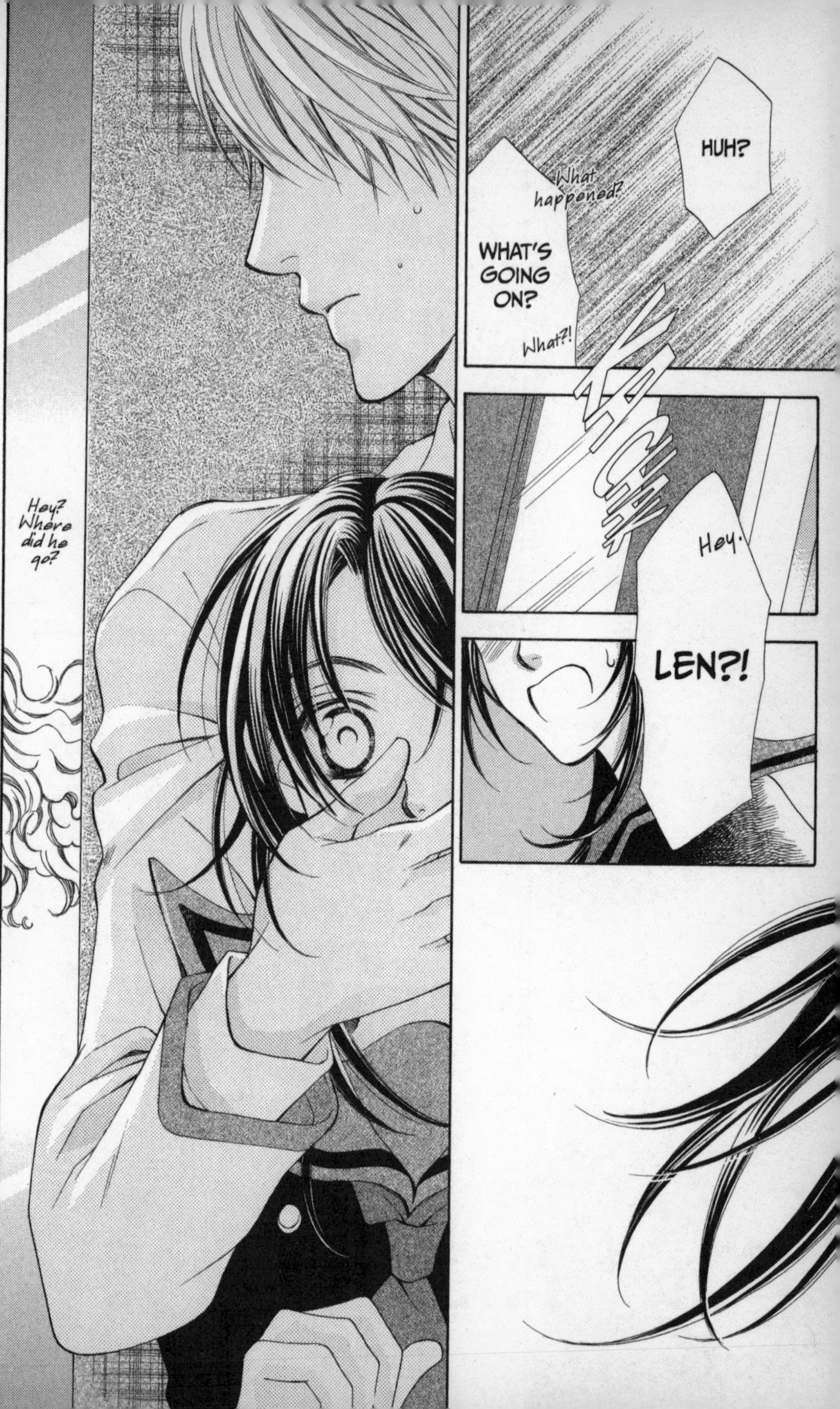
HUH?
What happened?
WHAT'S GOING ON?
What?!
KACHUK
Hey.
LEN?!
Hey? Where did he go?

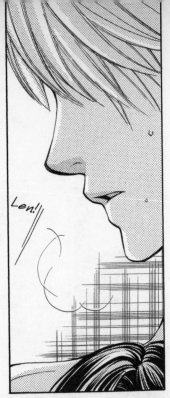

MAKE MY HEART- BEAT SLOW DOWN!!

SWOWWW!! MMMMMM

H... HEY?

KICK KICK

KICK KICK

Len!

th-thump
th-thump
th-thump

SHLP

OH...

pant

pant

WH...

SORRY...

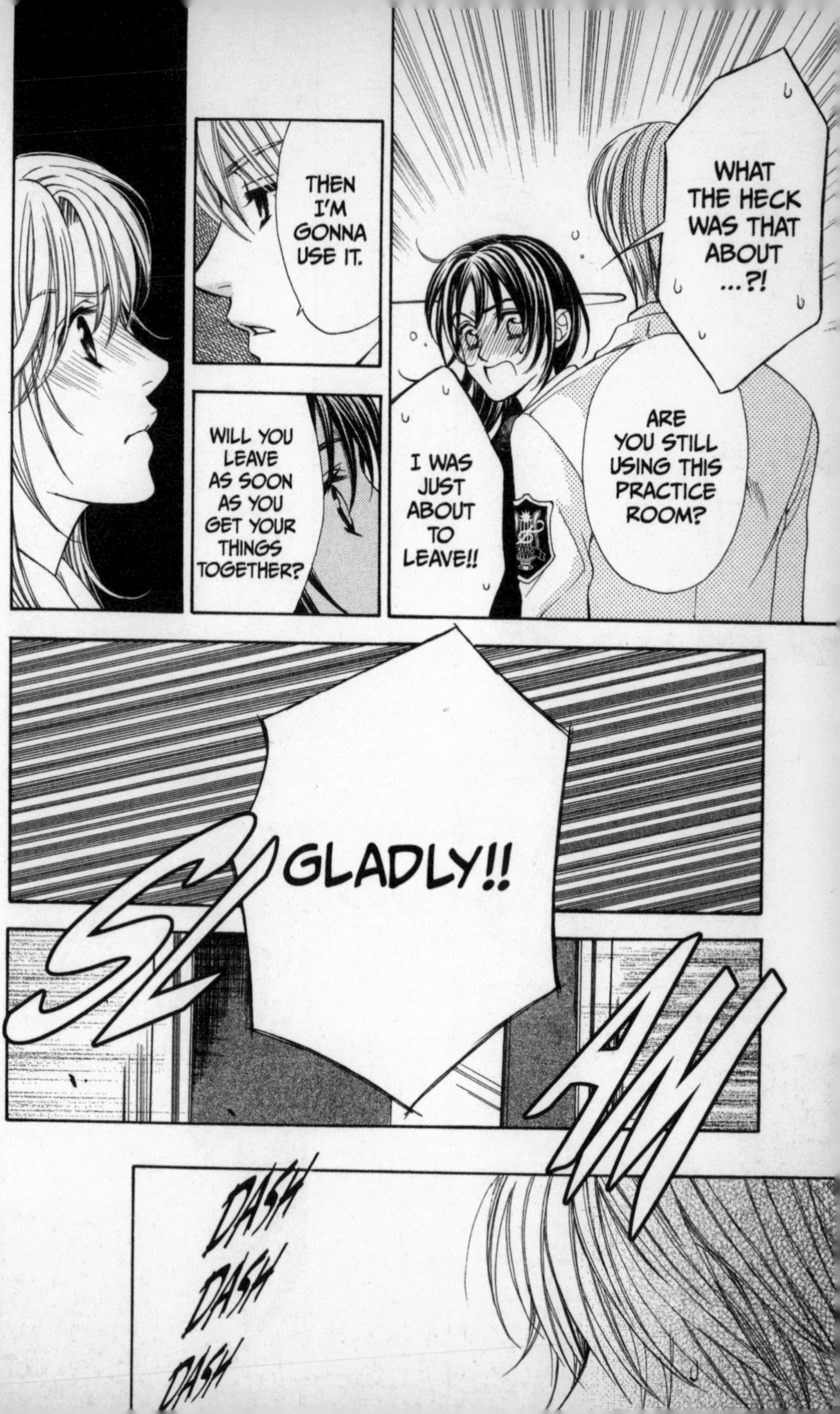
WHAT THE HECK WAS THAT ABOUT ...?!
ARE YOU STILL USING THIS PRACTICE ROOM?
I WAS JUST ABOUT TO LEAVE!!
THEN I'M GONNA USE IT.
WILL YOU LEAVE AS SOON AS YOU GET YOUR THINGS TOGETHER?
GLADLY!!
SLAM
DASH
DASH
DASH

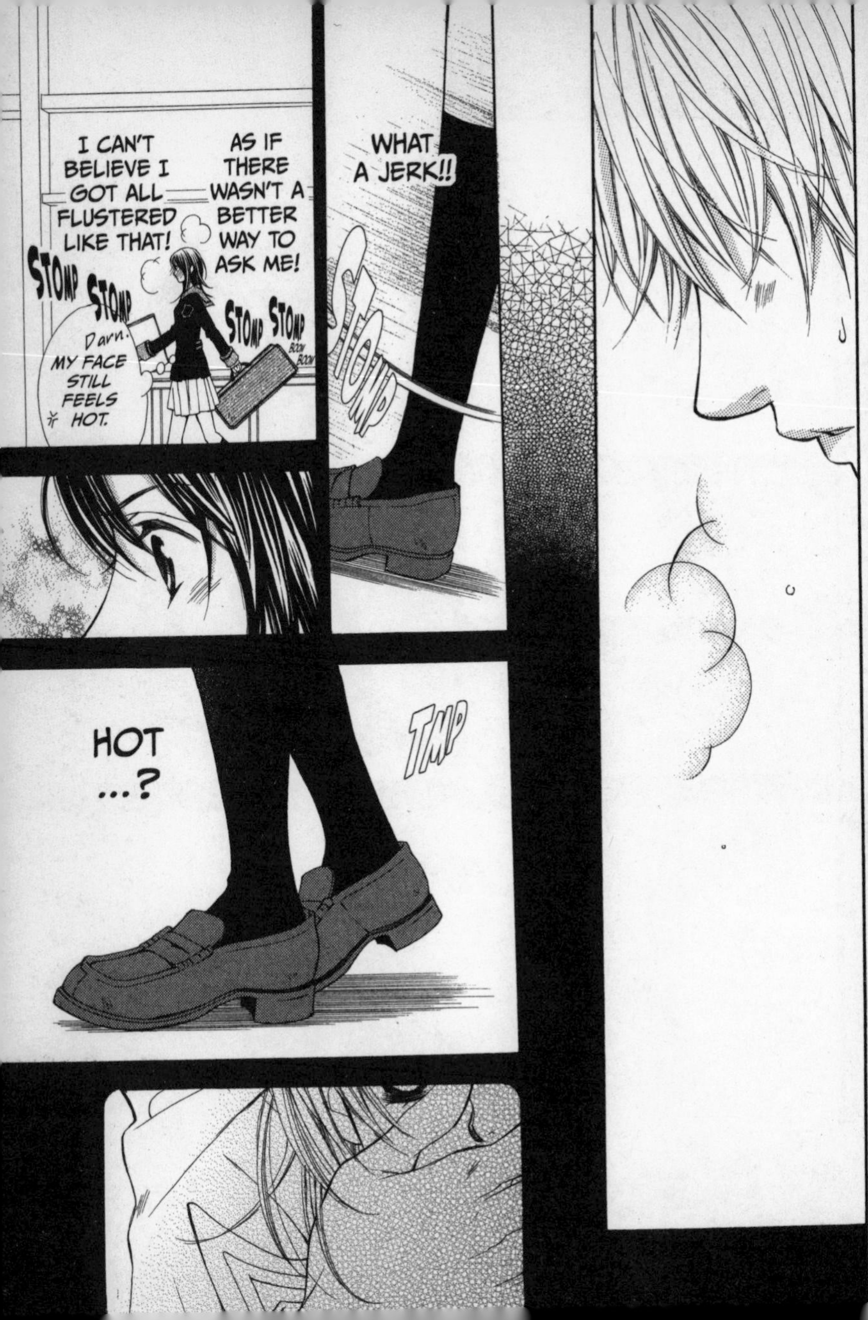
WHAT A JERK!!
STOMP
AS IF THERE WASN'T A BETTER WAY TO ASK ME!
I CAN'T BELIEVE I GOT ALL FLUSTERED LIKE THAT!
STOMP STOMP
STOMP STOMP
BOOM BOOM
Darn. MY FACE STILL FEELS HOT.
TMP
HOT ...?

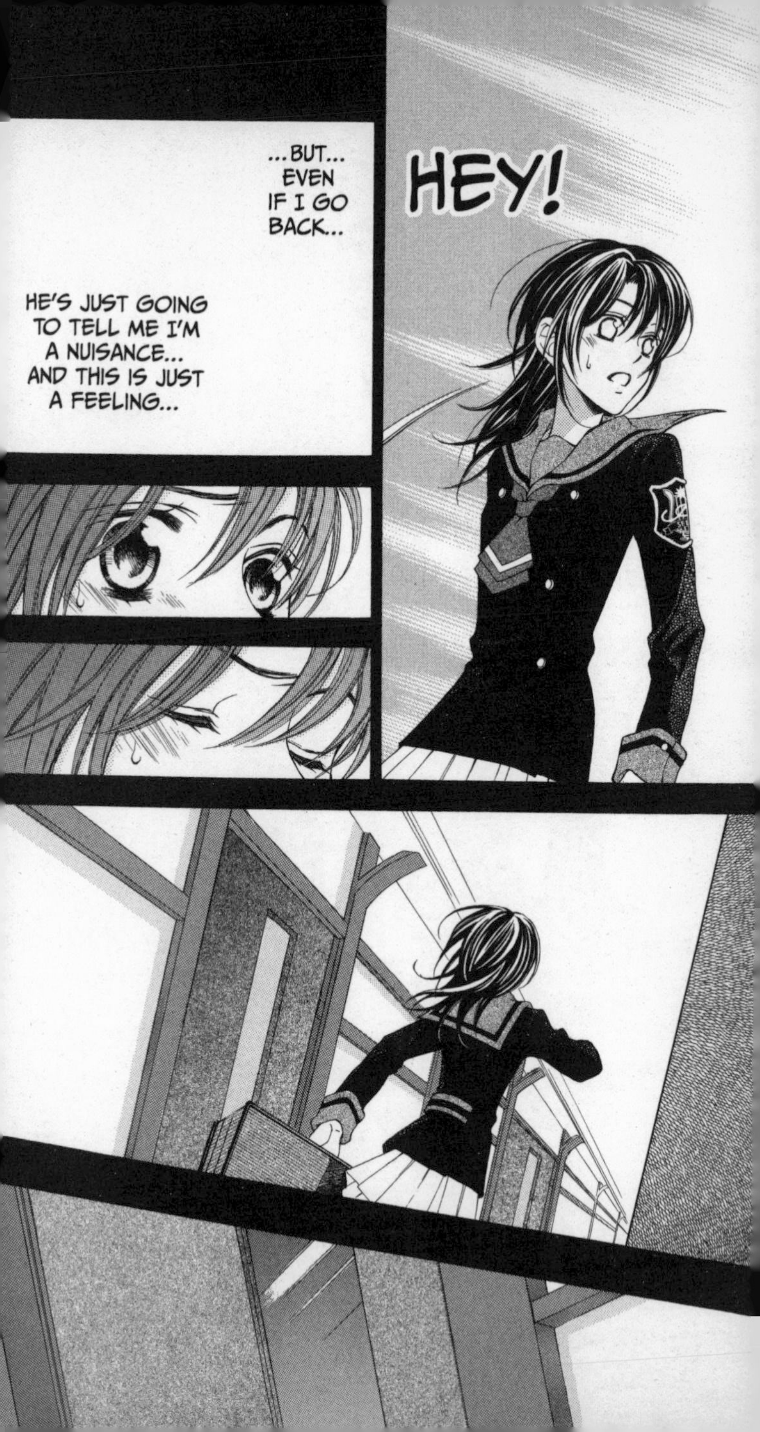
HEY!
...BUT... EVEN IF I GO BACK...
HE'S JUST GOING TO TELL ME I'M A NUISANCE... AND THIS IS JUST A FEELING...

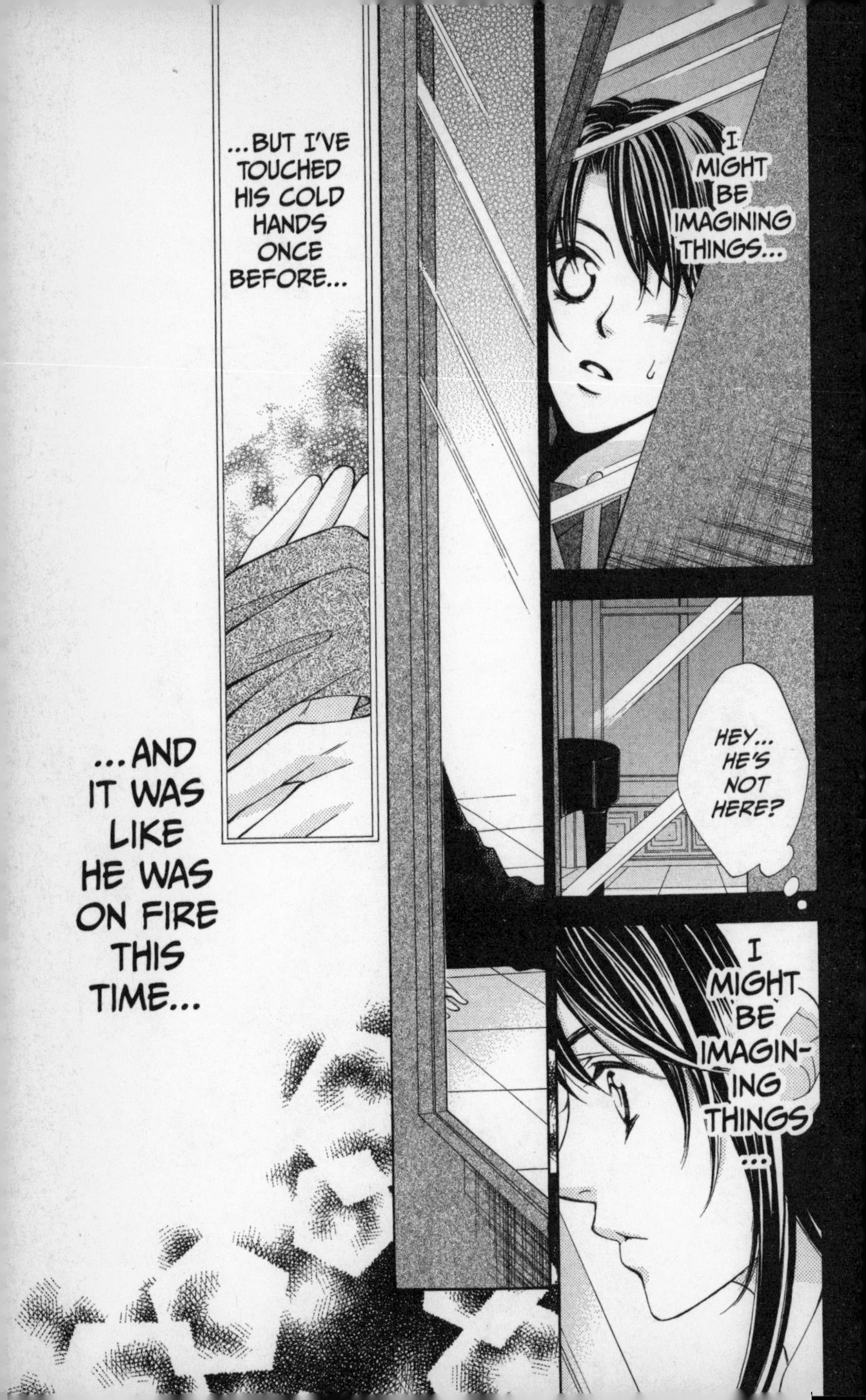
I MIGHT BE IMAGINING THINGS...
HEY... HE'S NOT HERE?
I MIGHT BE IMAGINING THINGS...
...BUT I'VE TOUCHED HIS COLD HANDS ONCE BEFORE...
...AND IT WAS LIKE HE WAS ON FIRE THIS TIME...

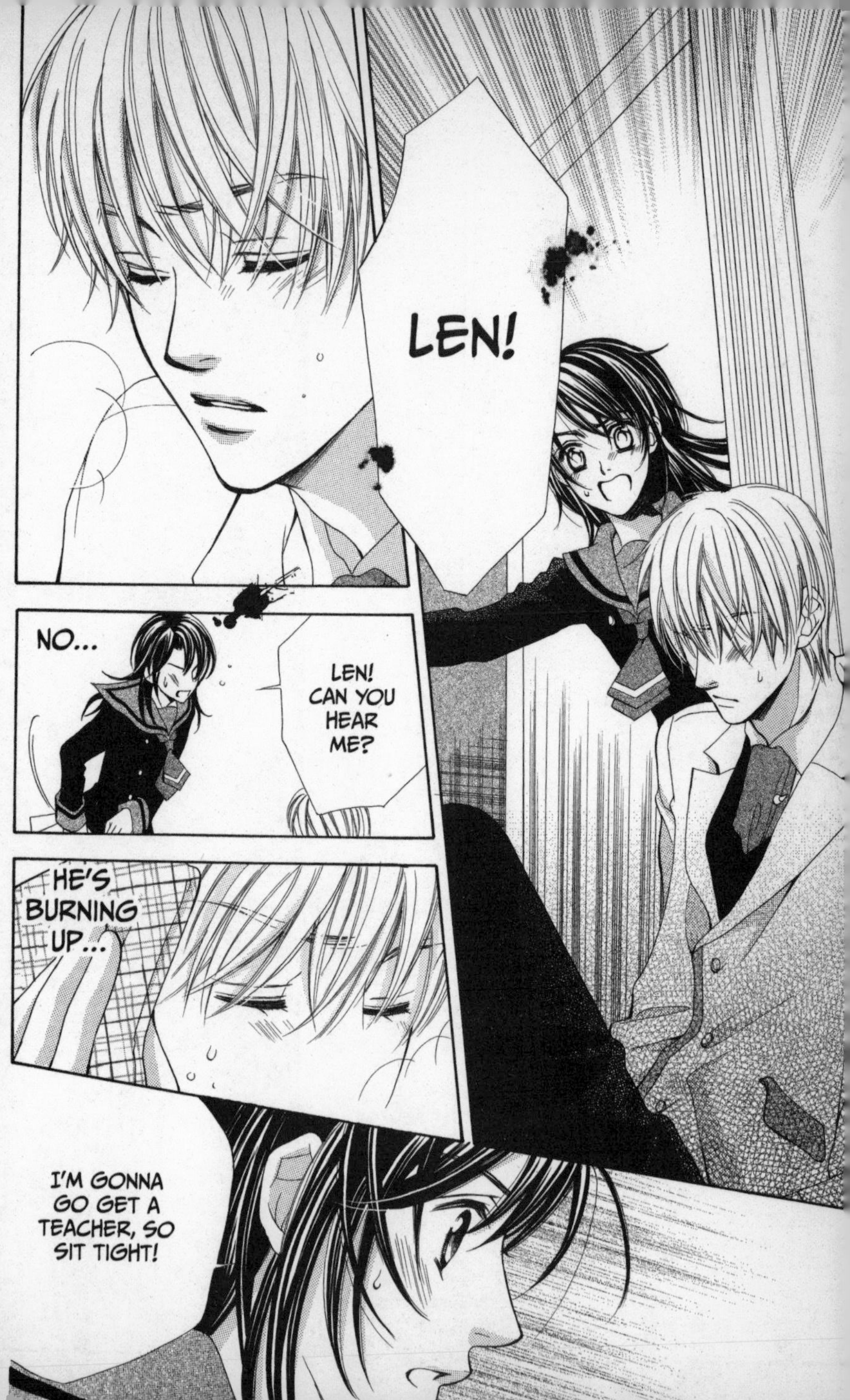
LEN!
LEN! CAN YOU HEAR ME?
NO...
HE'S BURNING UP...
I'M GONNA GO GET A TEACHER, SO SIT TIGHT!

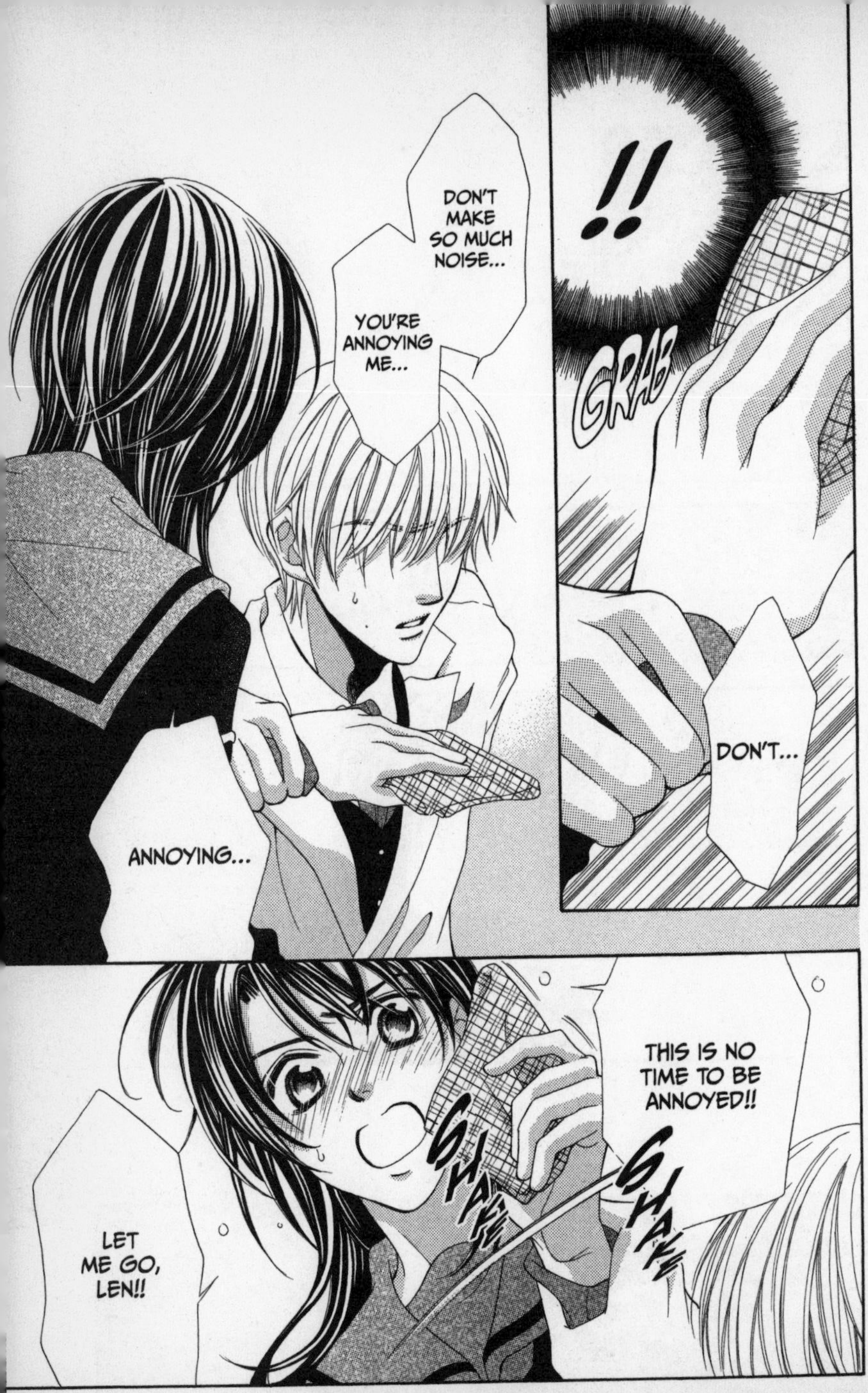
!!
GRAB
DON'T...
DON'T MAKE SO MUCH NOISE...
YOU'RE ANNOYING ME...
ANNOYING...
THIS IS NO TIME TO BE ANNOYED!!
SHAKE
SHAKE
LET ME GO, LEN!!

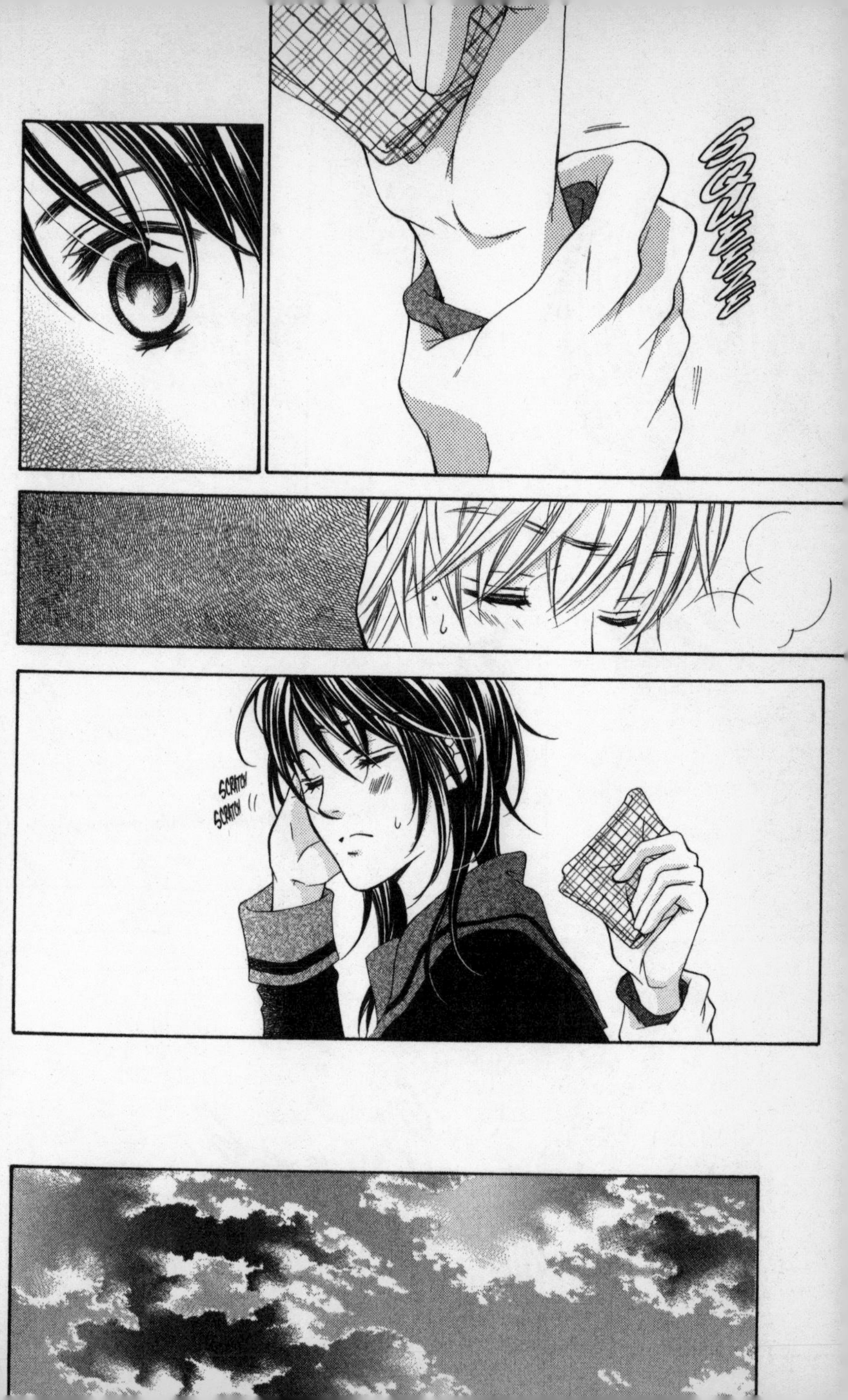
SCRATCH
SCRATCH

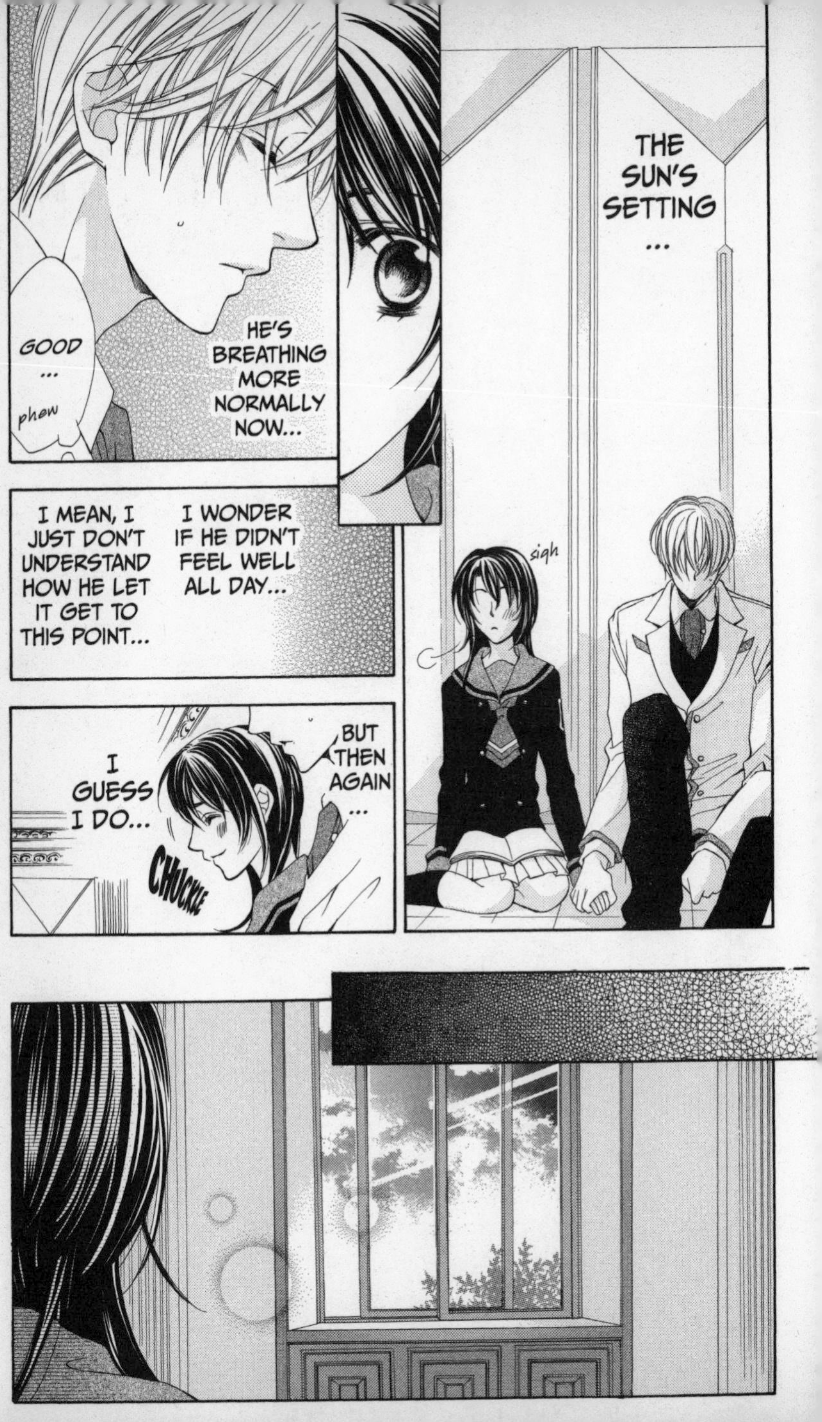
THE SUN'S SETTING ...
sigh
HE'S BREATHING MORE NORMALLY NOW...
GOOD ...
phew
I WONDER IF HE DIDN'T FEEL WELL ALL DAY...
I MEAN, I JUST DON'T UNDERSTAND HOW HE LET IT GET TO THIS POINT...
BUT THEN AGAIN ...
I GUESS I DO...
CHUCKLE

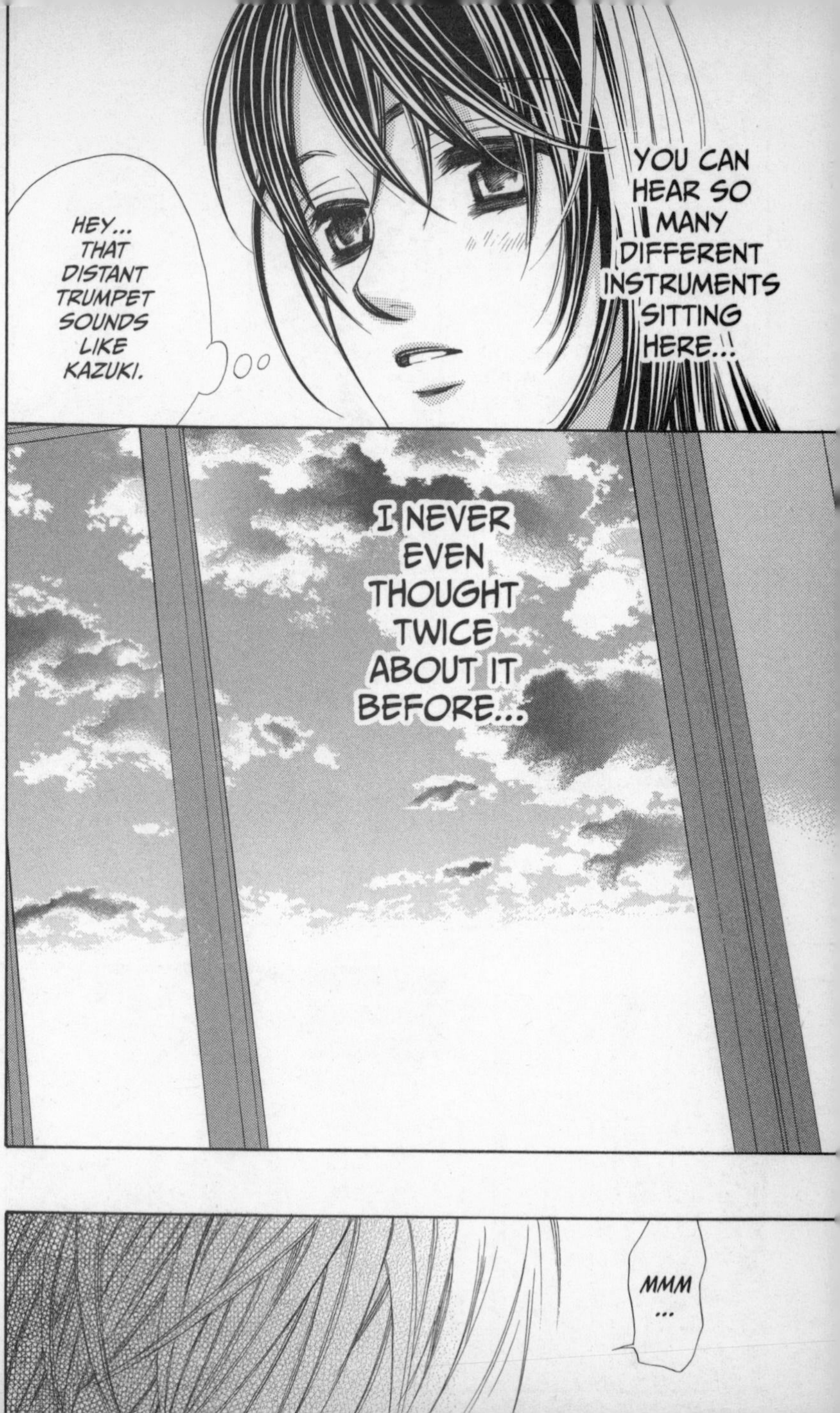
YOU CAN HEAR SO MANY DIFFERENT INSTRUMENTS SITTING HERE...!
HEY... THAT DISTANT TRUMPET SOUNDS LIKE KAZUKI.
I NEVER EVEN THOUGHT TWICE ABOUT IT BEFORE...
MMM...

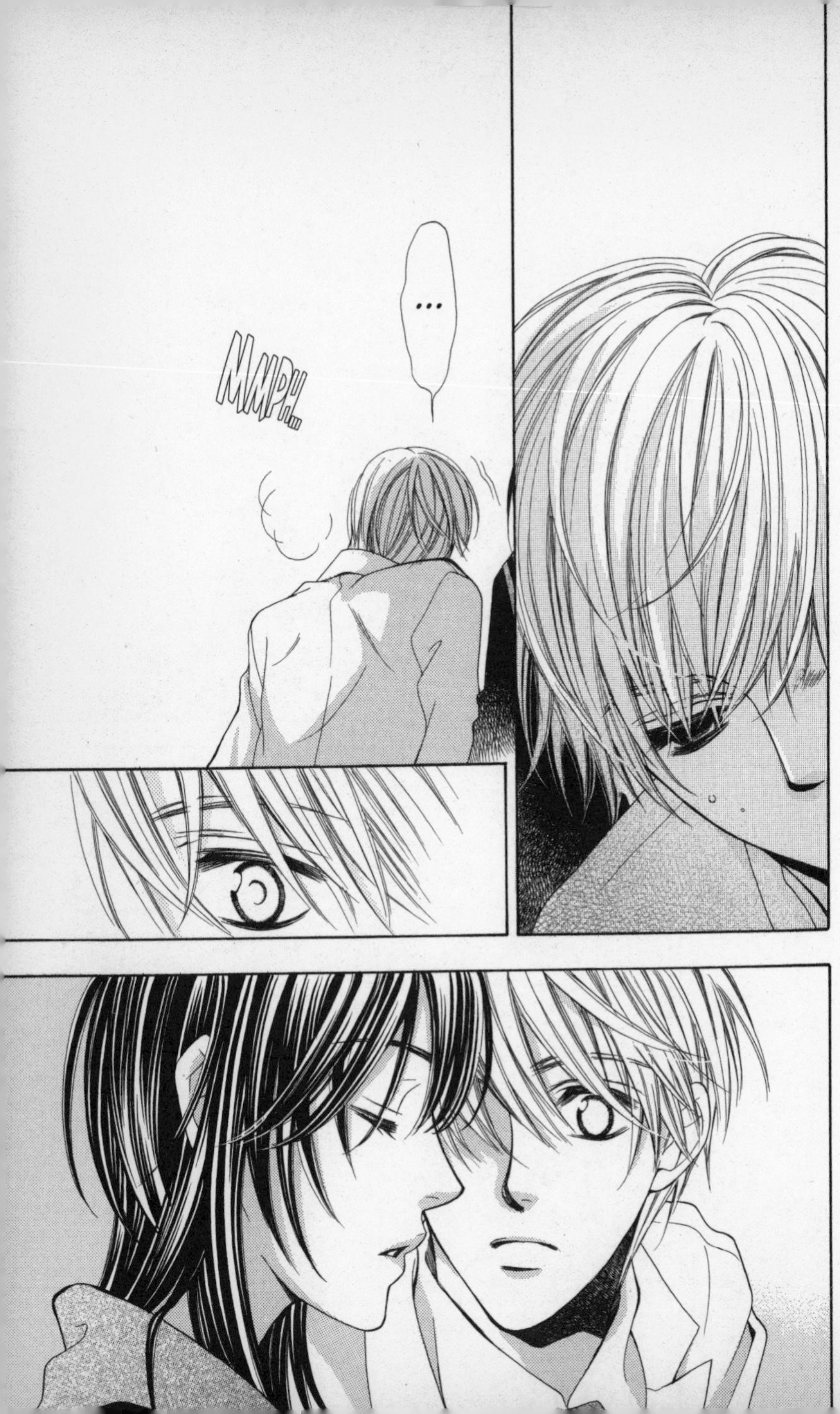
...
MMPH...

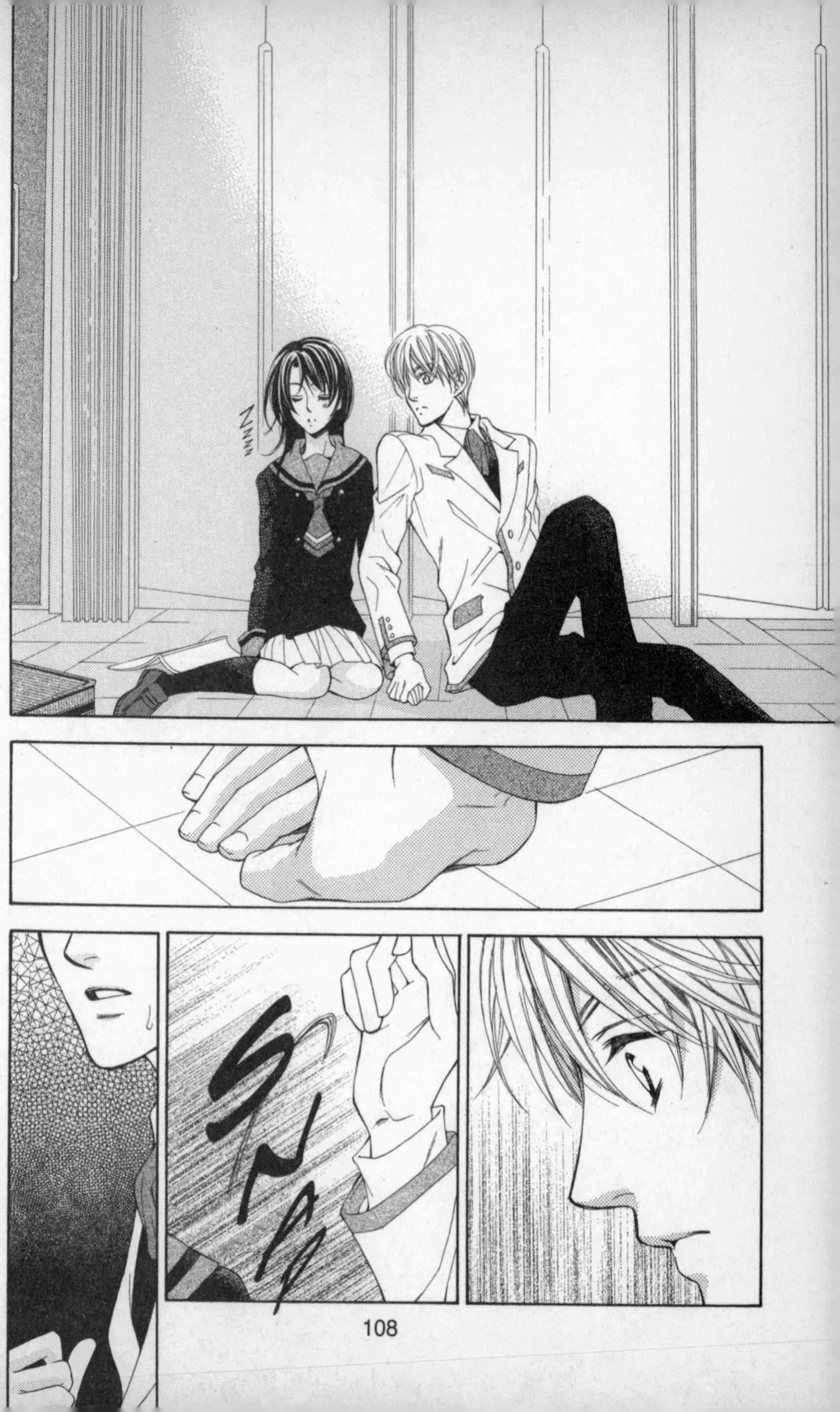
NNN
SNAP

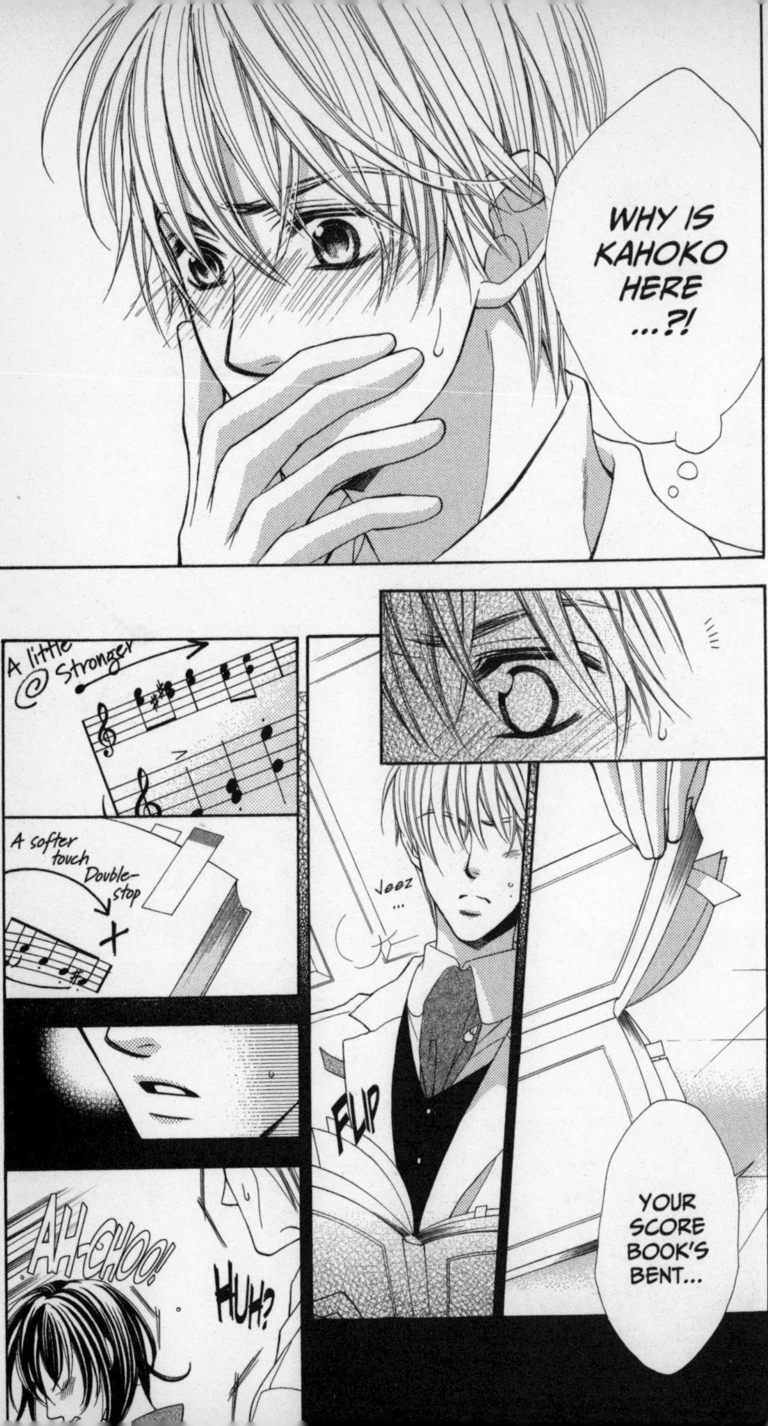
WHY IS KAHOKO HERE ...?!
YOUR SCORE BOOK'S BENT...
Jeez ...
FLIP
A little @ Stronger
A softer touch
Double-stop
AH-CHOO!
HUH?

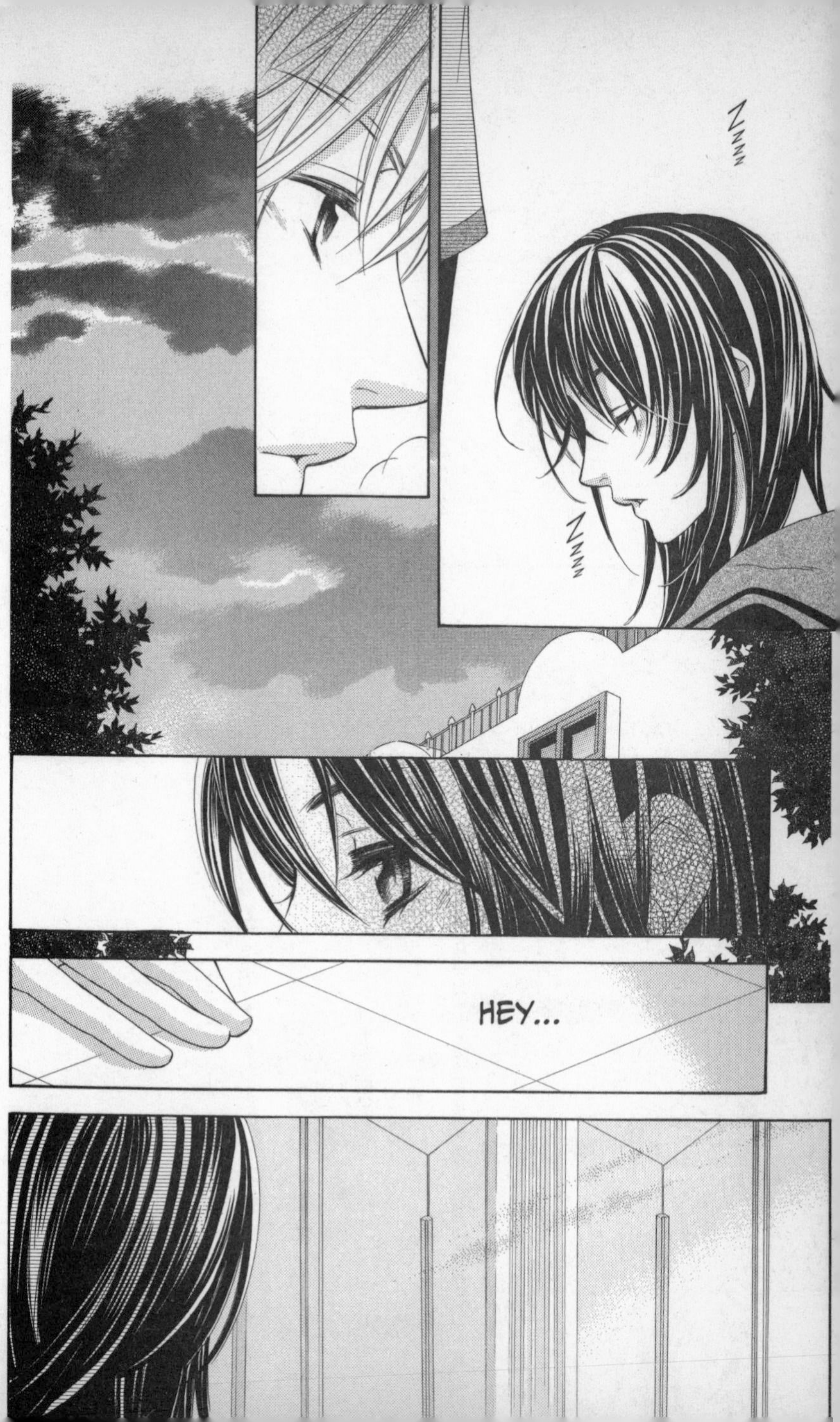
Zzz
Zzz
HEY...

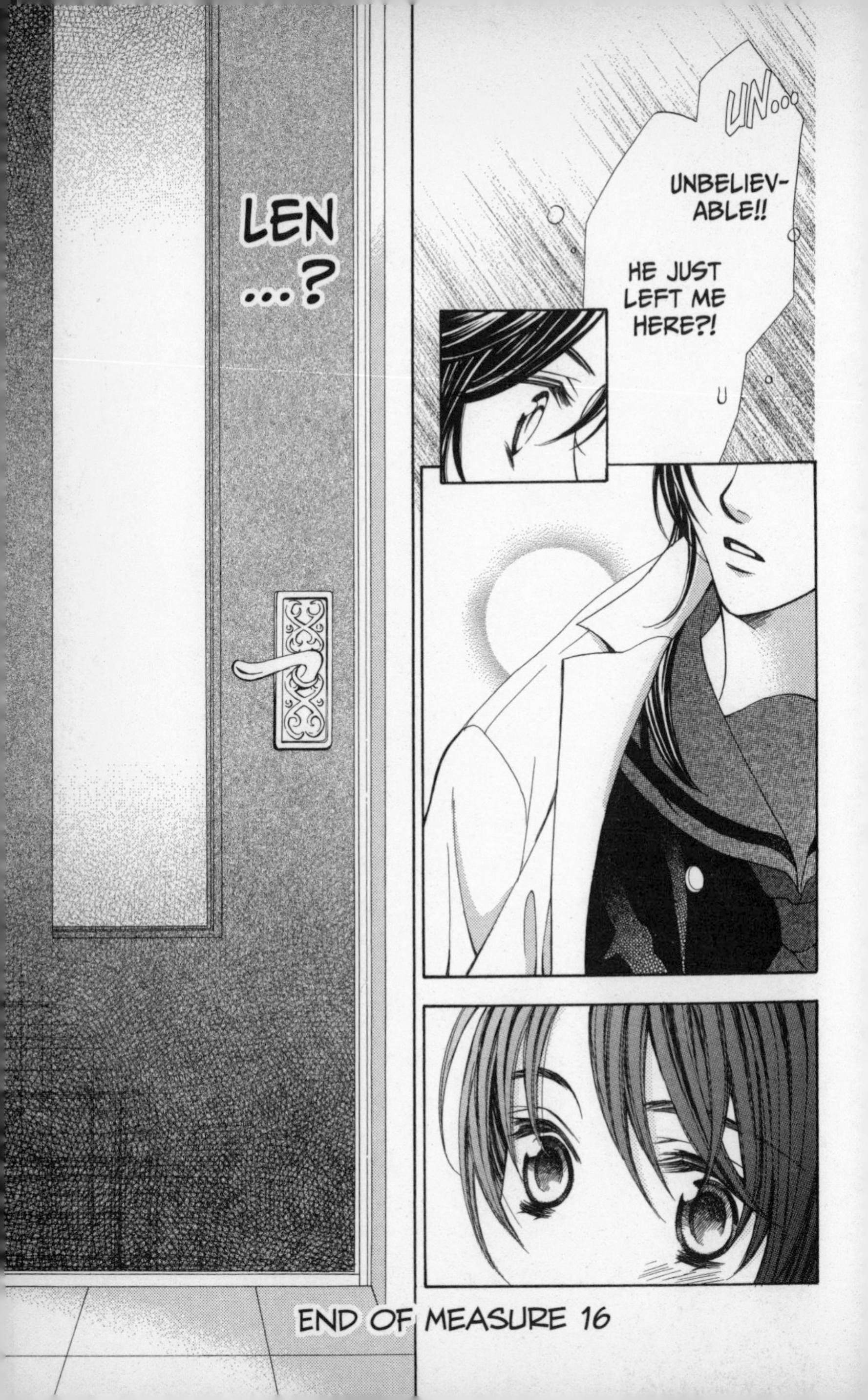
UN...
UNBELIEV-ABLE!!
HE JUST LEFT ME HERE?!
LEN ...?
END OF MEASURE 16

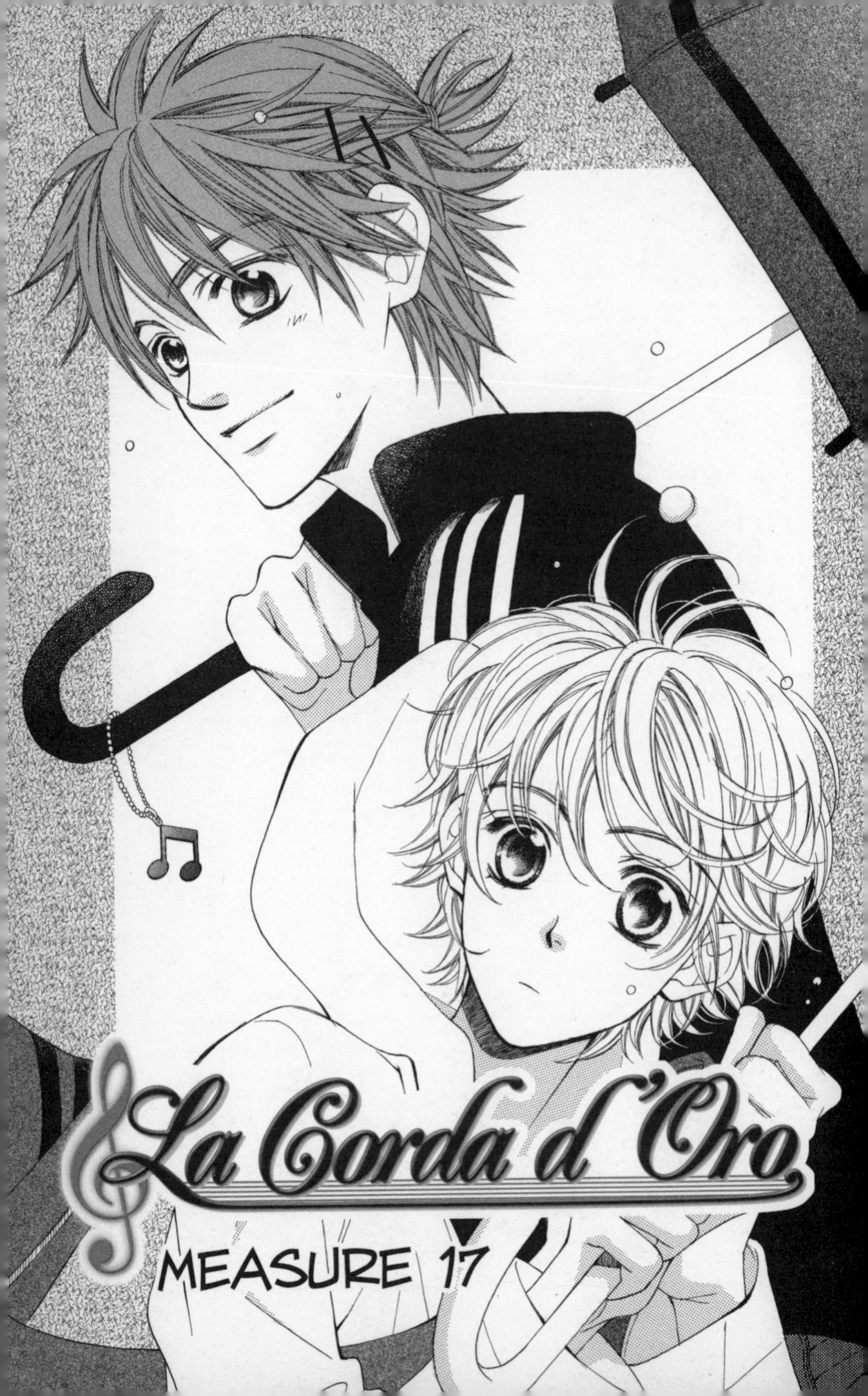
La Corda d'Oro
MEASURE 17

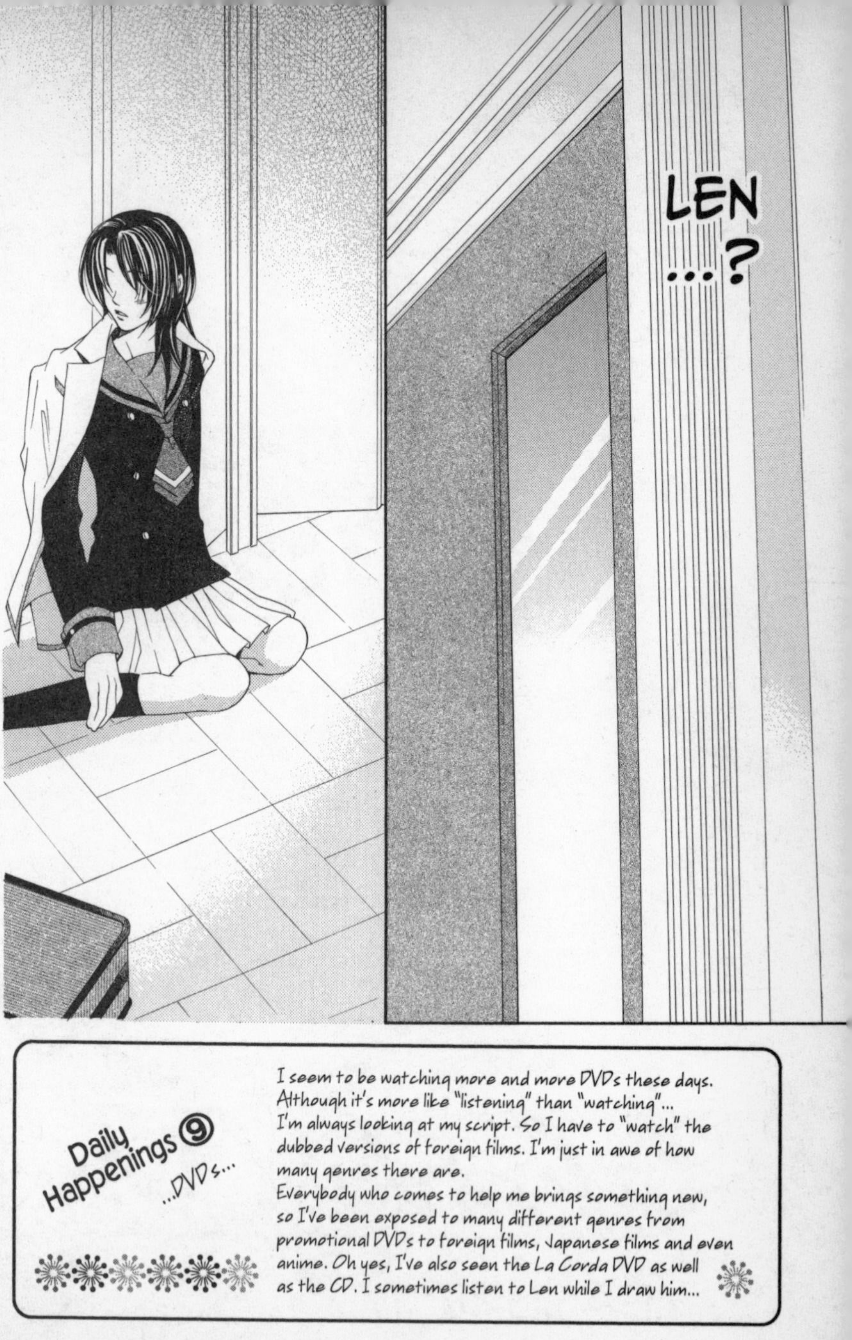
LEN...?

Daily Happenings ⑨

...DVDs...

I seem to be watching more and more DVDs these days. Although it's more like "listening" than "watching"... I'm always looking at my script. So I have to "watch" the dubbed versions of foreign films. I'm just in awe of how many genres there are.

Everybody who comes to help me brings something new, so I've been exposed to many different genres from promotional DVDs to foreign films, Japanese films and even anime. Oh yes, I've also seen the La Corda DVD as well as the CD. I sometimes listen to Len while I draw him...

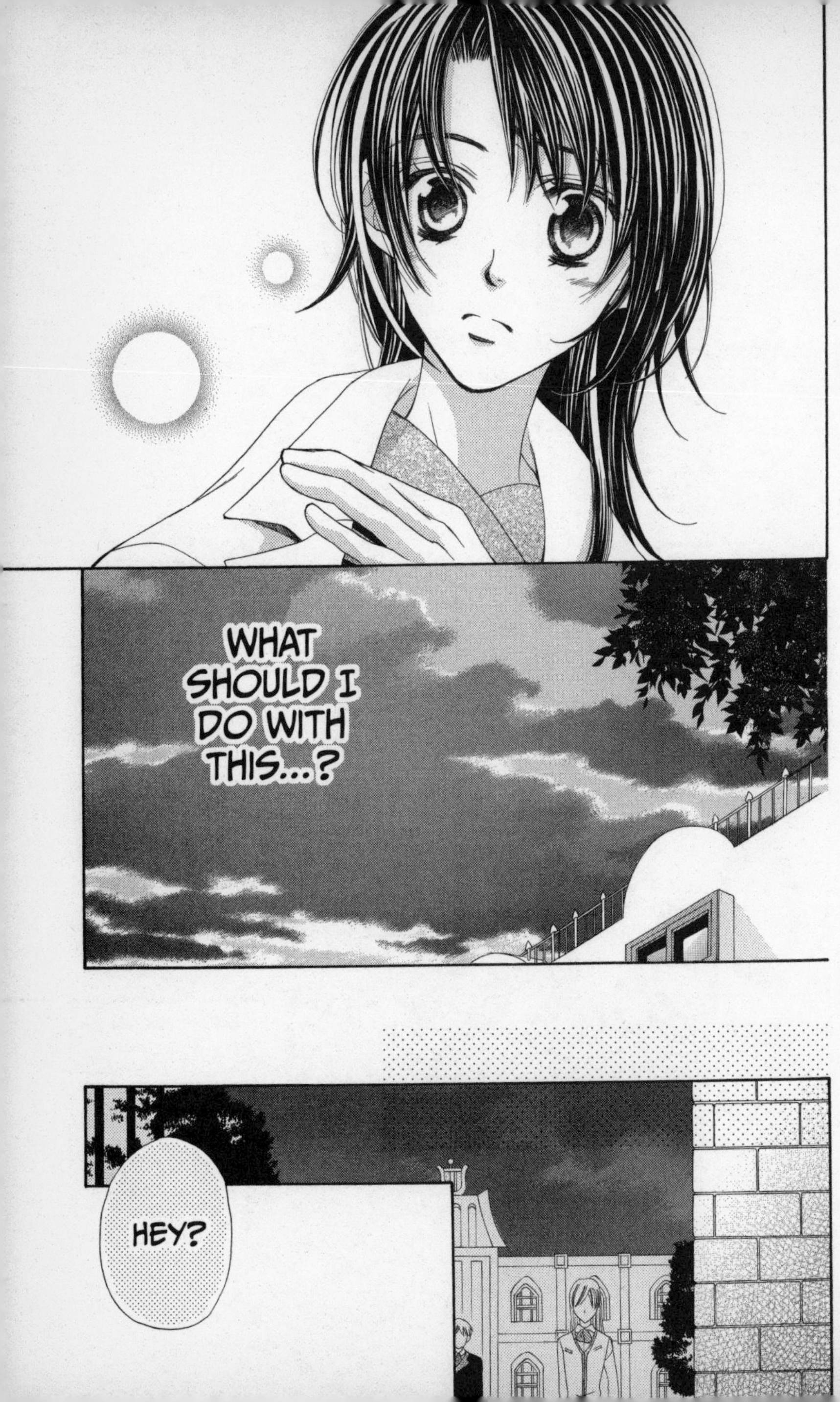
WHAT SHOULD I DO WITH THIS...?
HEY?

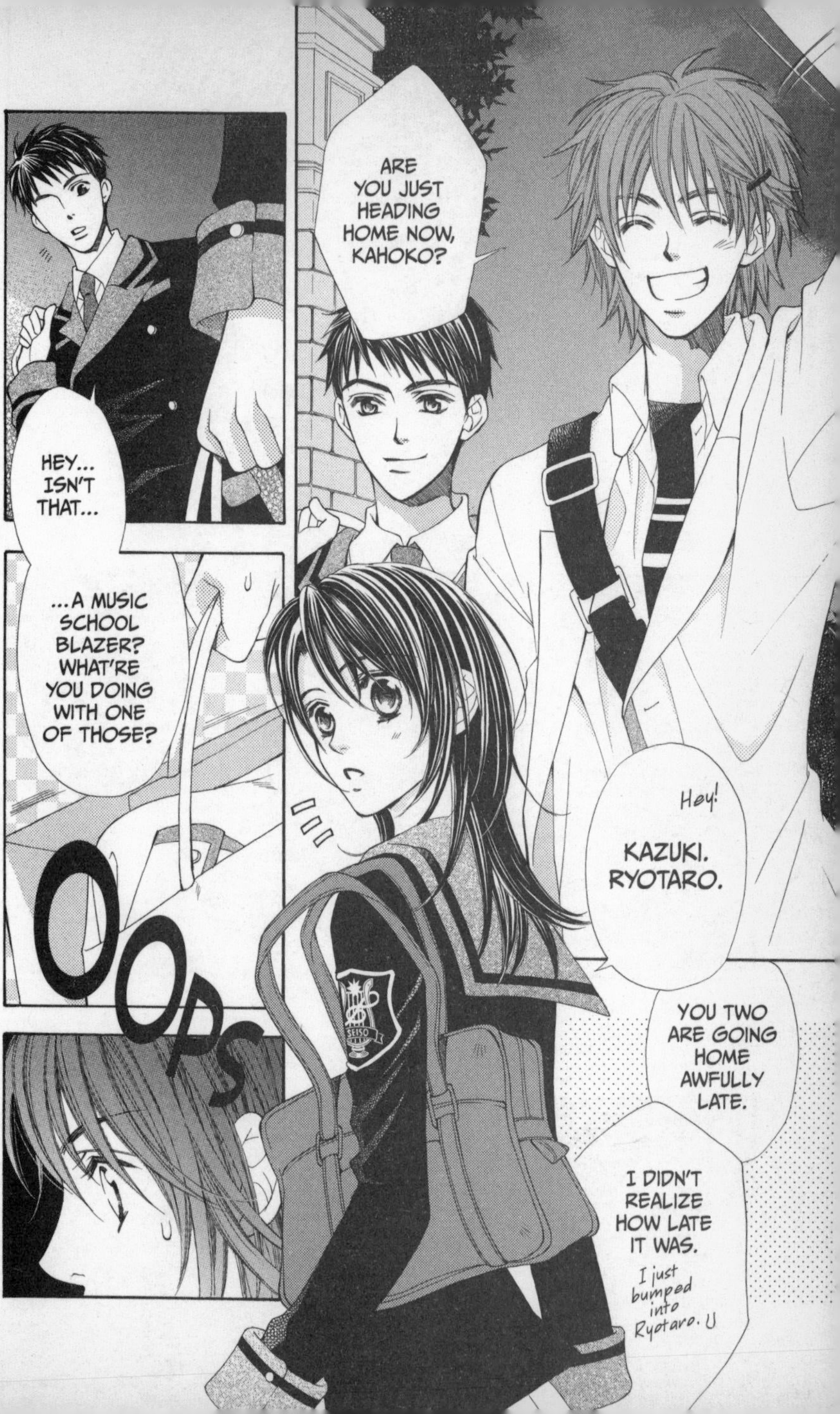
ARE YOU JUST HEADING HOME NOW, KAHOKO?
Hey!
KAZUKI. RYOTARO.
YOU TWO ARE GOING HOME AWFULLY LATE.
I DIDN'T REALIZE HOW LATE IT WAS.
I just bumped into Ryotaro.
HEY... ISN'T THAT...
...A MUSIC SCHOOL BLAZER? WHAT'RE YOU DOING WITH ONE OF THOSE?
OOPS
SEISO

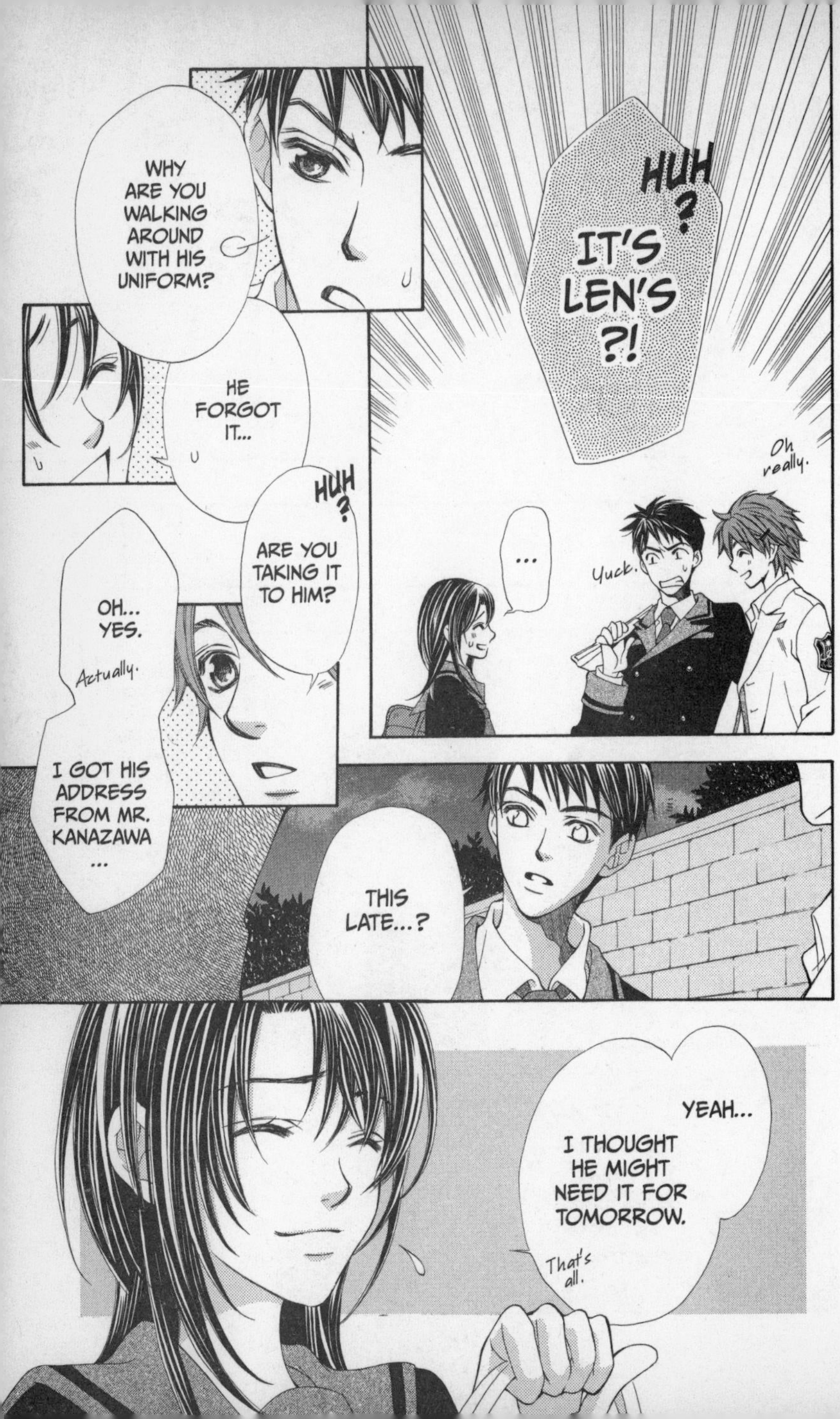
HUH?
IT'S LEN'S?!
Oh really.
Yuck.
...
WHY ARE YOU WALKING AROUND WITH HIS UNIFORM?
HE FORGOT IT...
HUH?
ARE YOU TAKING IT TO HIM?
OH... YES.
Actually.
I GOT HIS ADDRESS FROM MR. KANAZAWA ...
THIS LATE...?
YEAH...
I THOUGHT HE MIGHT NEED IT FOR TOMORROW.
That's all.

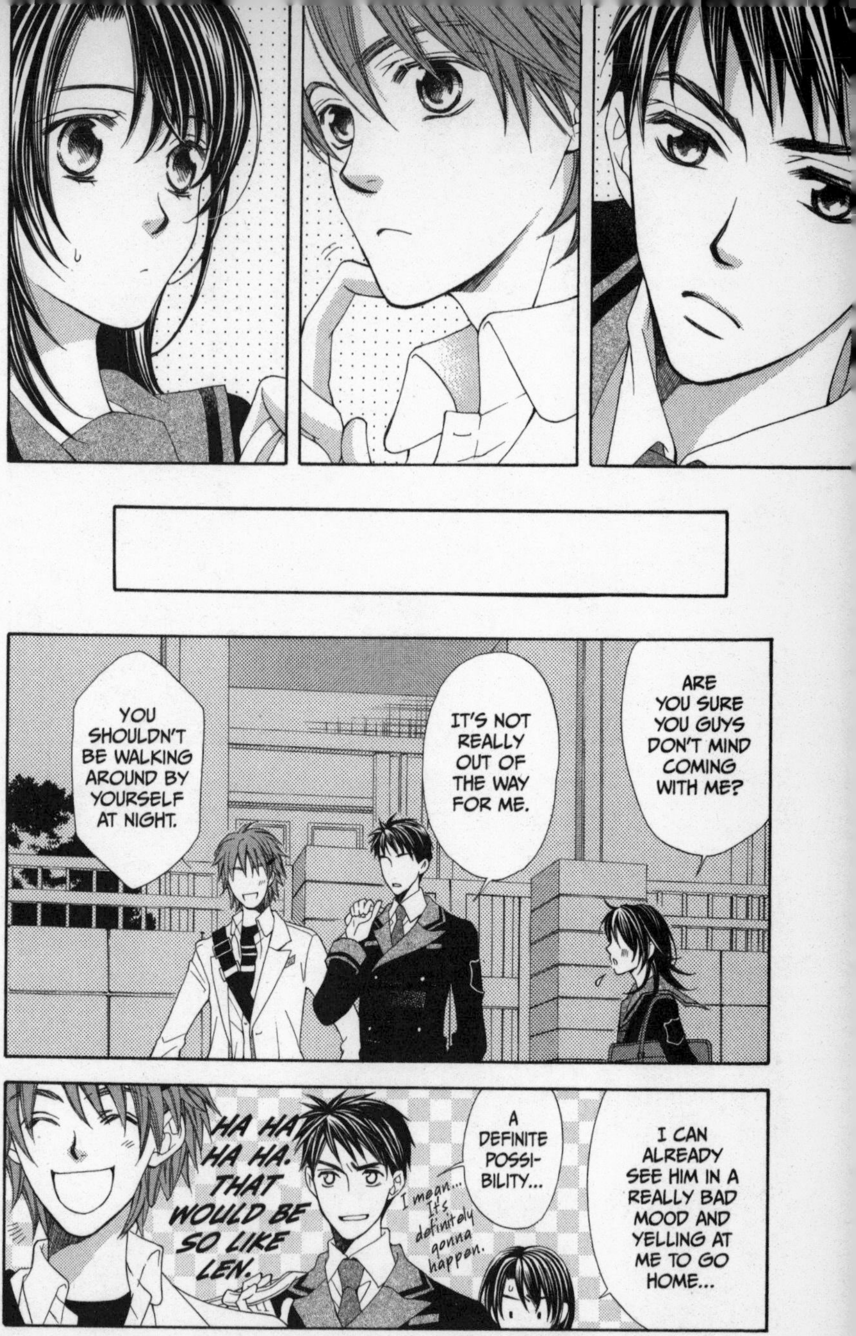
ARE YOU SURE YOU GUYS DON'T MIND COMING WITH ME?
IT'S NOT REALLY OUT OF THE WAY FOR ME.
YOU SHOULDN'T BE WALKING AROUND BY YOURSELF AT NIGHT.
I CAN ALREADY SEE HIM IN A REALLY BAD MOOD AND YELLING AT ME TO GO HOME...
A DEFINITE POSSI-BILITY...
I mean... It's definitely gonna happen.
HA HA HA HA. THAT WOULD BE SO LIKE LEN.

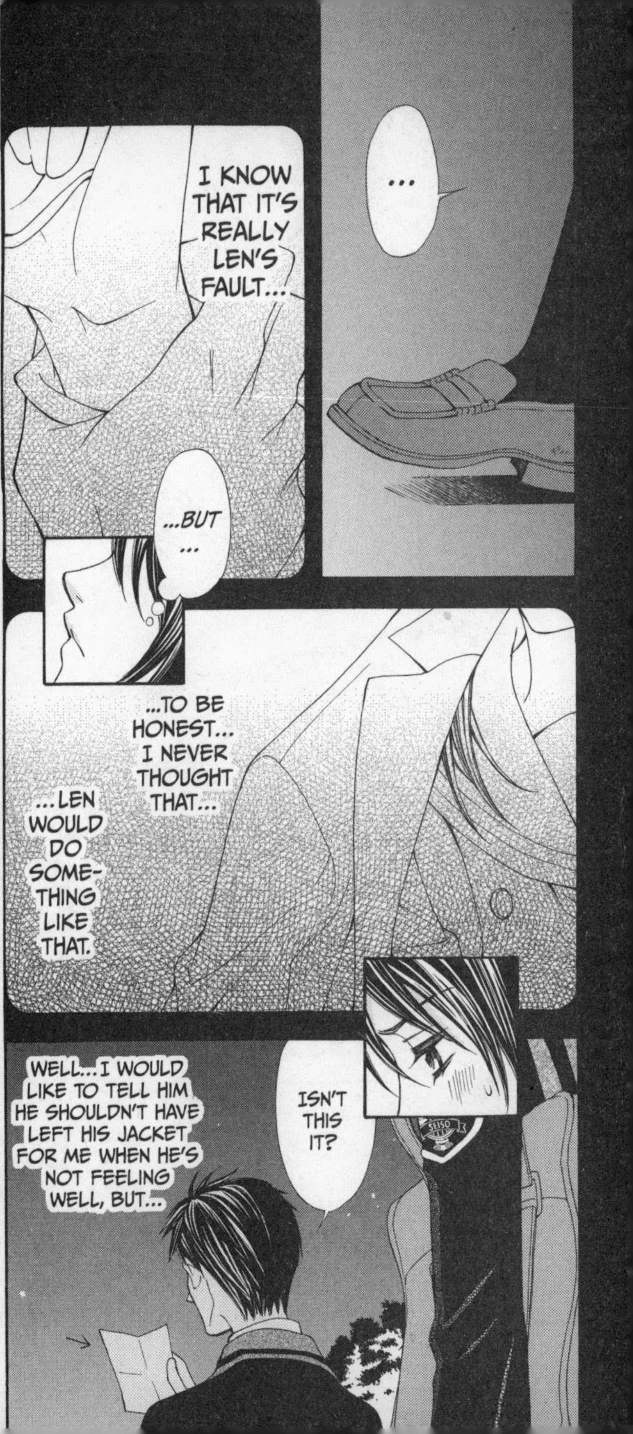
...
I KNOW THAT IT'S REALLY LEN'S FAULT...
...BUT ...
...TO BE HONEST... I NEVER THOUGHT THAT...
...LEN WOULD DO SOME-THING LIKE THAT.
ISN'T THIS IT?
WELL...I WOULD LIKE TO TELL HIM HE SHOULDN'T HAVE LEFT HIS JACKET FOR ME WHEN HE'S NOT FEELING WELL, BUT...

FIVE

♥

The theme for the cover of Measure 17 is "I have to pick you up." It's one of my favorites because it's so cute. I really like drawing Kazuki and Keiichi together. They look so carefree and peaceful. But Kazuki strikes me as the type who would carry around a really cheap umbrella and Keiichi seems like he wouldn't carry one at all...

Len's appearance is on the rise starting in Measure 16, but I feel increasingly fatigued... I know he might be a hard character to warm up to, but I hope you hang in there with him.

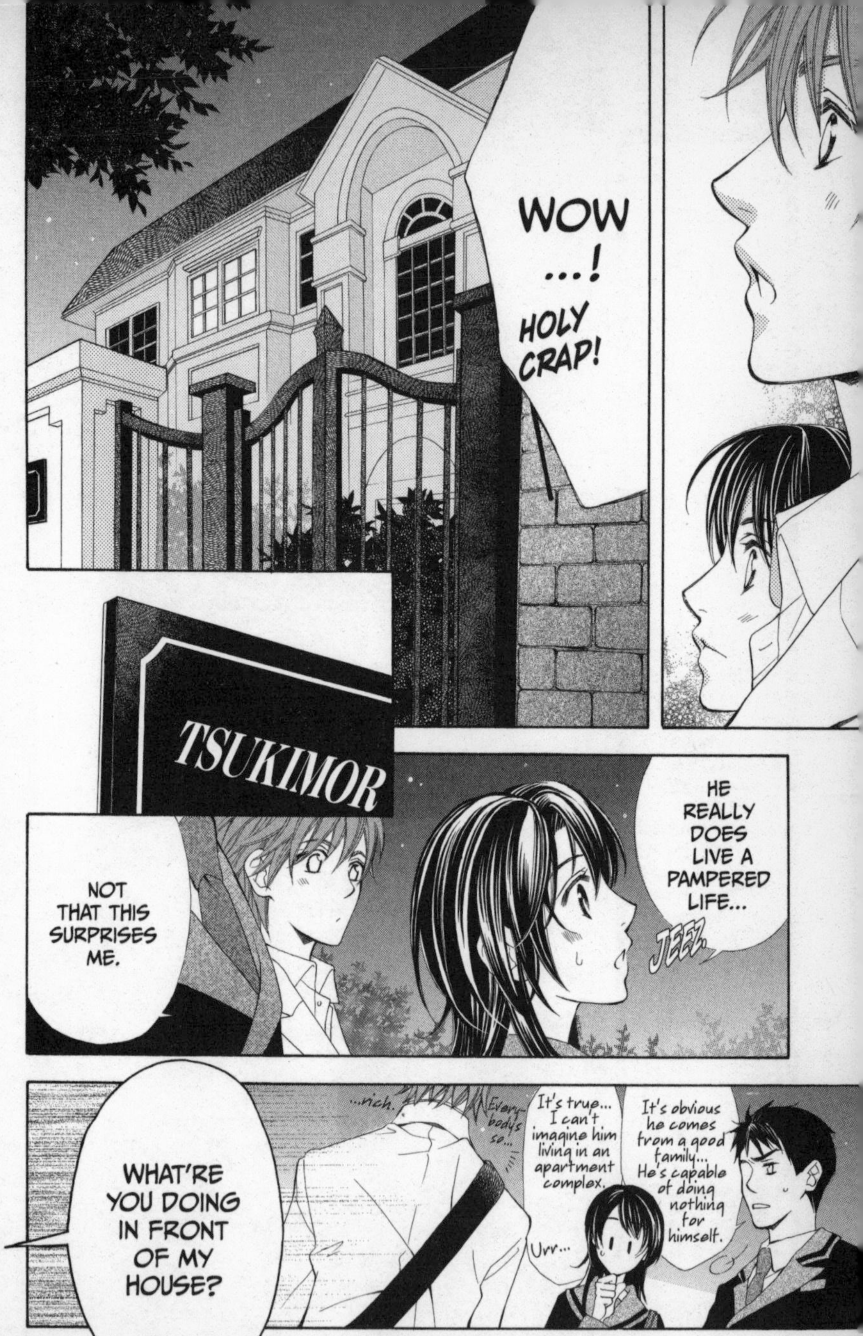
WOW...! HOLY CRAP!
TSUKIMOR
HE REALLY DOES LIVE A PAMPERED LIFE...
JEEZ.
NOT THAT THIS SURPRISES ME.
It's obvious he comes from a good family... He's capable of doing nothing for himself.
It's true... I can't imagine him living in an apartment complex.
Urr...
Everybody's so...
...rich.
WHAT'RE YOU DOING IN FRONT OF MY HOUSE?

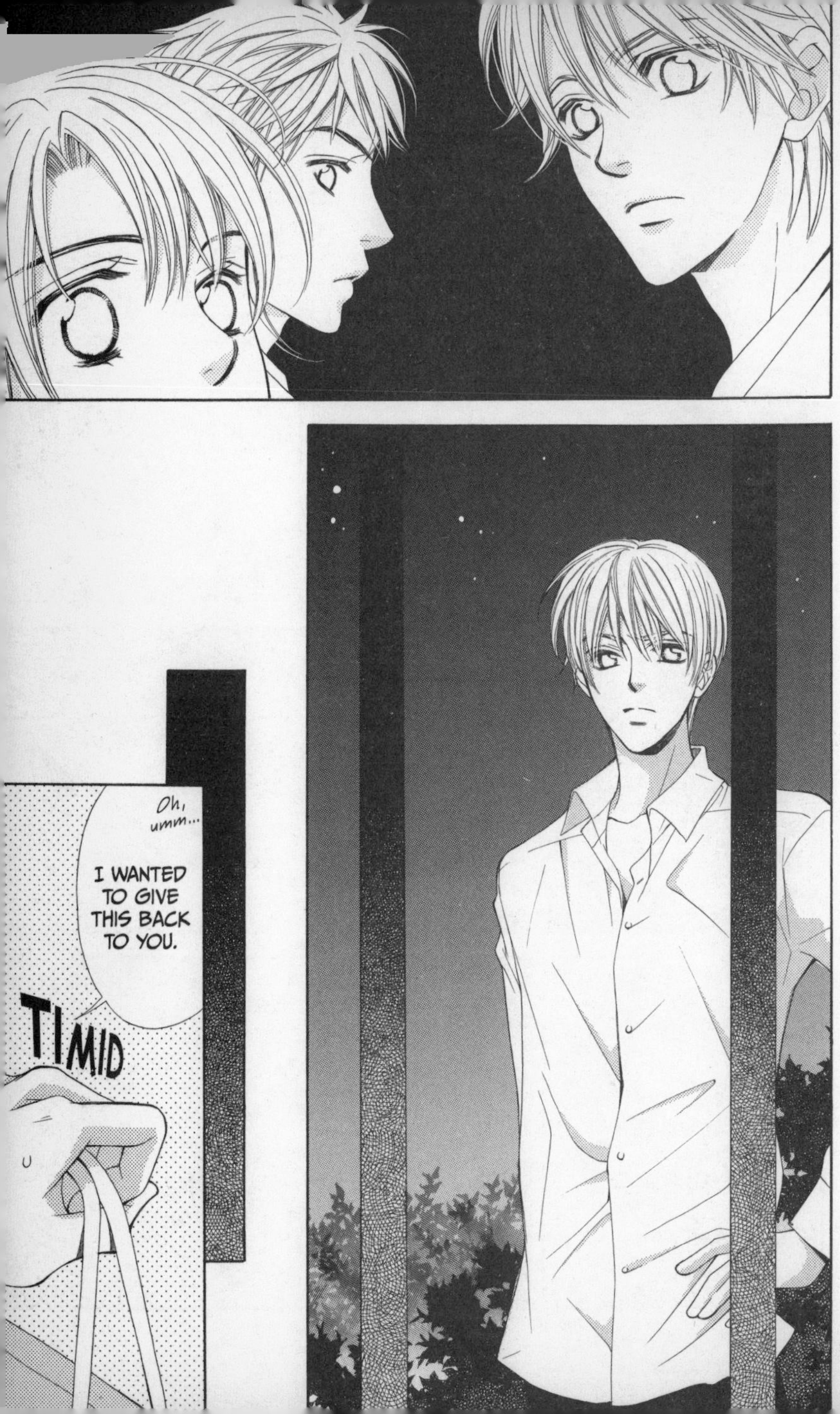
Oh, umm...
I WANTED TO GIVE THIS BACK TO YOU.
TIMID

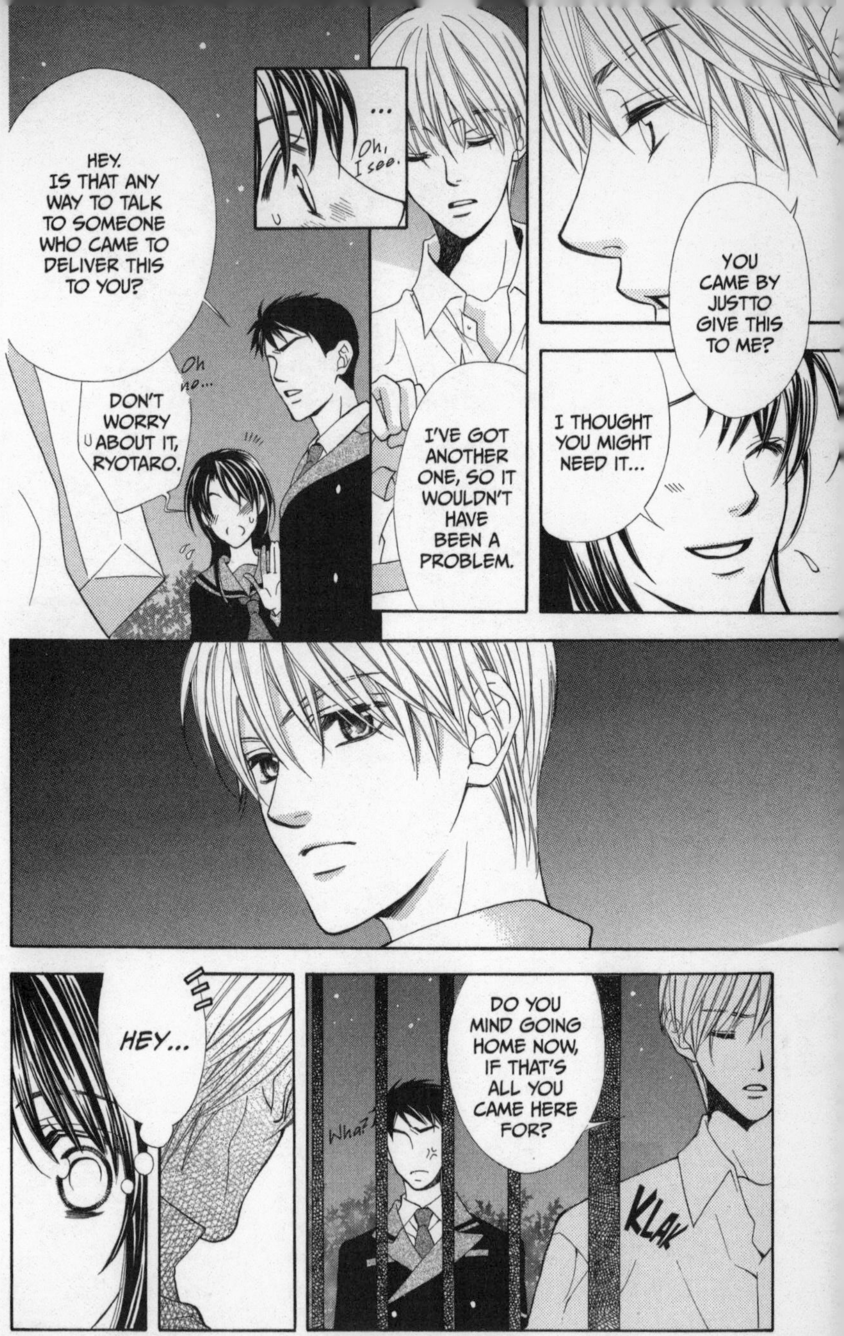
YOU CAME BY JUSTTO GIVE THIS TO ME?
I THOUGHT YOU MIGHT NEED IT...
...
Oh, I see.
I'VE GOT ANOTHER ONE, SO IT WOULDN'T HAVE BEEN A PROBLEM.
HEY. IS THAT ANY WAY TO TALK TO SOMEONE WHO CAME TO DELIVER THIS TO YOU?
Oh no...
DON'T WORRY ABOUT IT, RYOTARO.
DO YOU MIND GOING HOME NOW, IF THAT'S ALL YOU CAME HERE FOR?
KLAK
HEY...

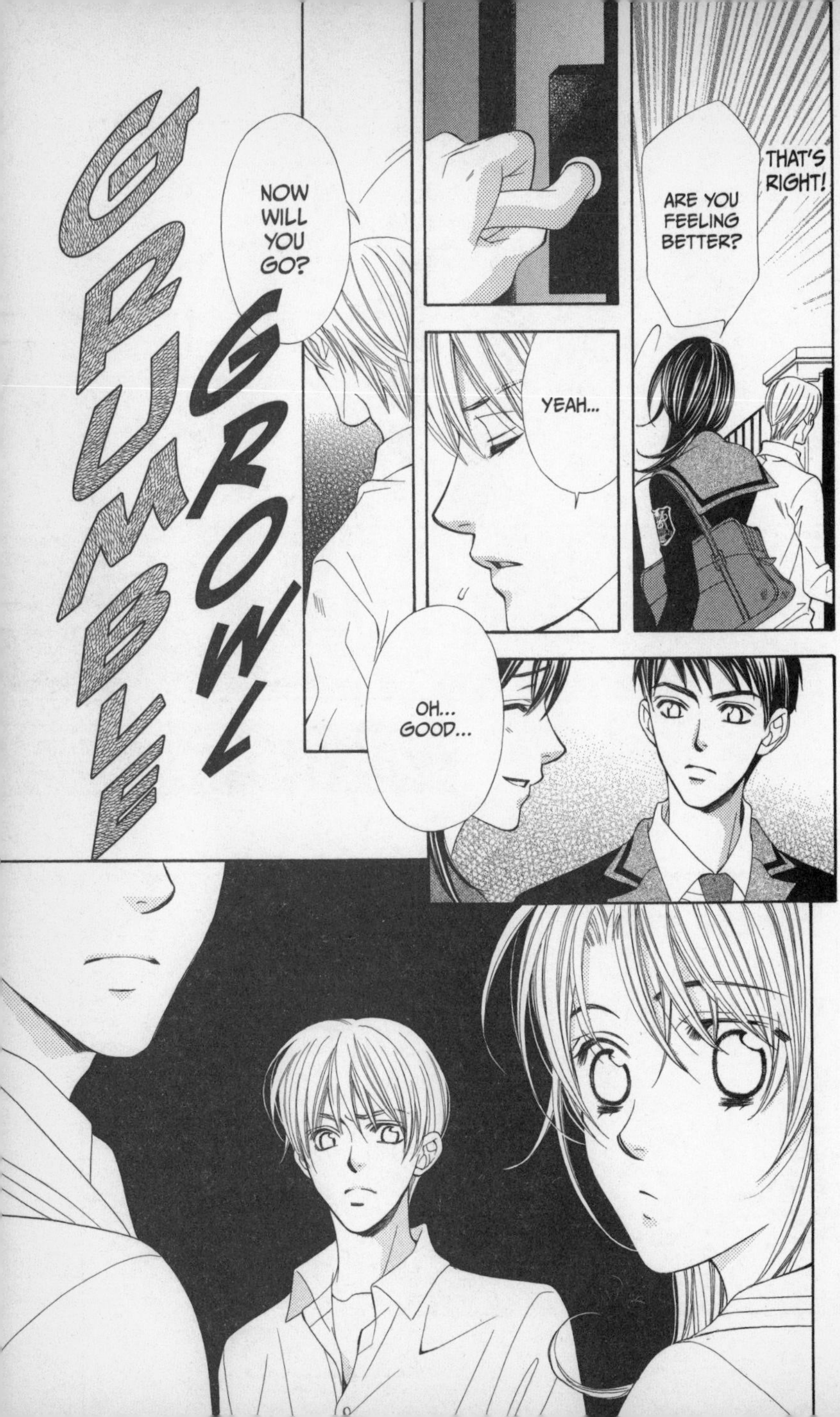
THAT'S RIGHT!
ARE YOU FEELING BETTER?
YEAH...
NOW WILL YOU GO?
GROWL
GRUMBLE
OH... GOOD...

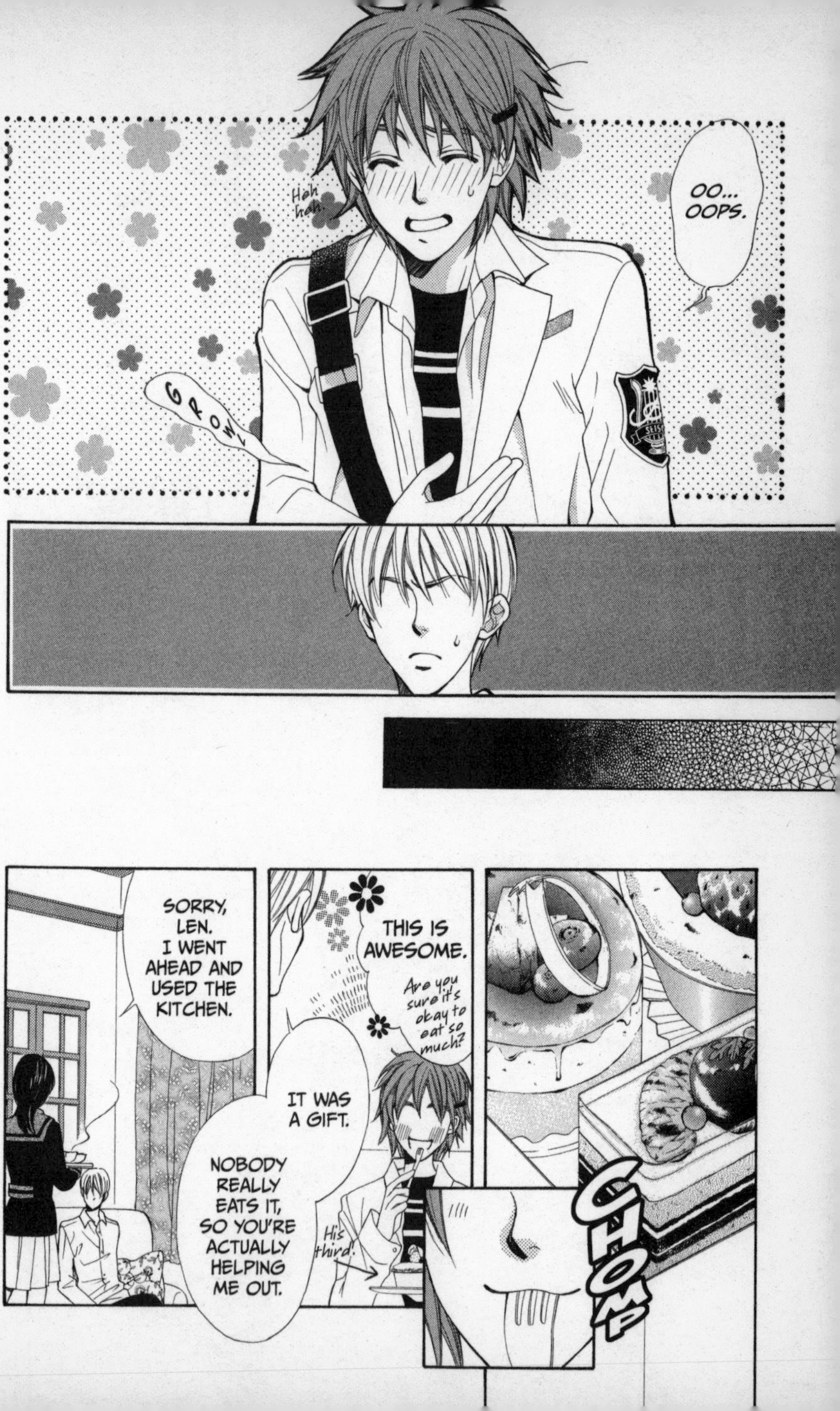
OO... OOPS.
Heh heh.
GROWL
CHOMP
THIS IS AWESOME.
Are you sure it's okay to eat so much?
IT WAS A GIFT.
NOBODY REALLY EATS IT, SO YOU'RE ACTUALLY HELPING ME OUT.
His third!
SORRY, LEN. I WENT AHEAD AND USED THE KITCHEN.

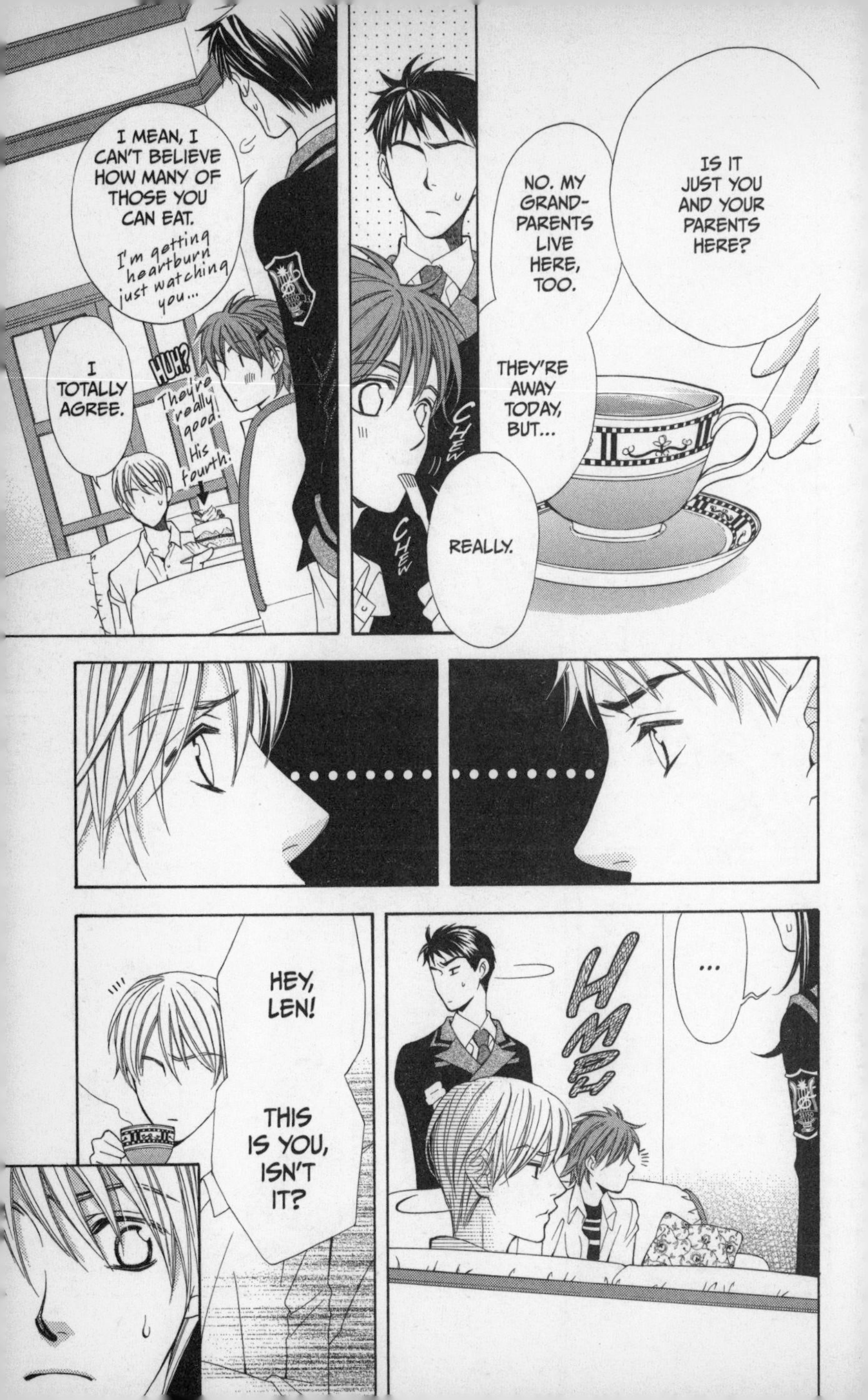
IS IT JUST YOU AND YOUR PARENTS HERE?
NO. MY GRAND-PARENTS LIVE HERE, TOO.
THEY'RE AWAY TODAY, BUT...
CHEW CHEW
REALLY.
I MEAN, I CAN'T BELIEVE HOW MANY OF THOSE YOU CAN EAT.
I'm getting heartburn just watching you...
HUH?
They're really good!
His fourth!
I TOTALLY AGREE.
....
....
...
HMMM
HEY, LEN!
THIS IS YOU, ISN'T IT?

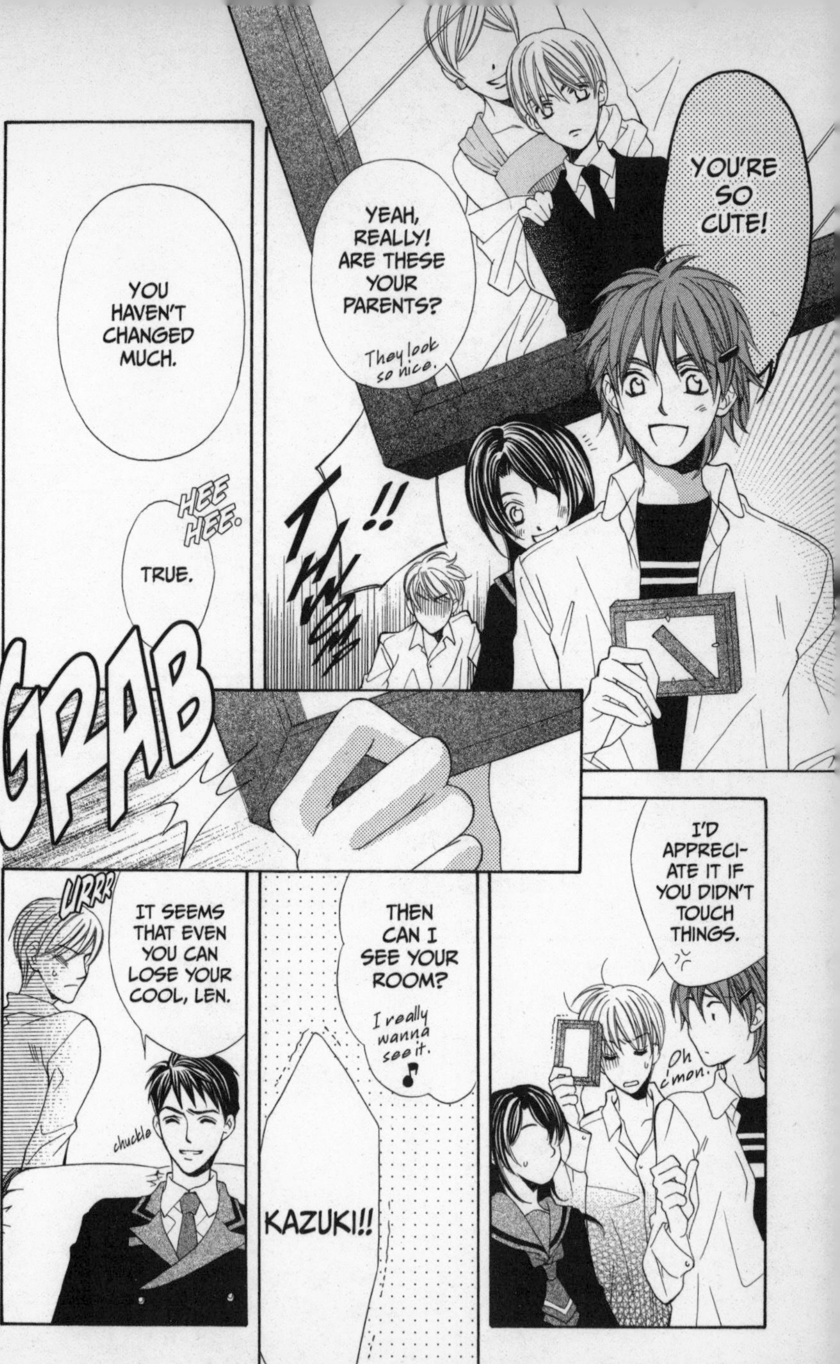

YOU'RE SO CUTE!
YEAH, REALLY! ARE THESE YOUR PARENTS?
They look so nice.
YOU HAVEN'T CHANGED MUCH.
HEE HEE.
TRUE.
GRAB
I'D APPRECIATE IT IF YOU DIDN'T TOUCH THINGS.
Oh c'mon.
THEN CAN I SEE YOUR ROOM?
I really wanna see it. ♪
KAZUKI!!
URRR
IT SEEMS THAT EVEN YOU CAN LOSE YOUR COOL, LEN.
chuckle

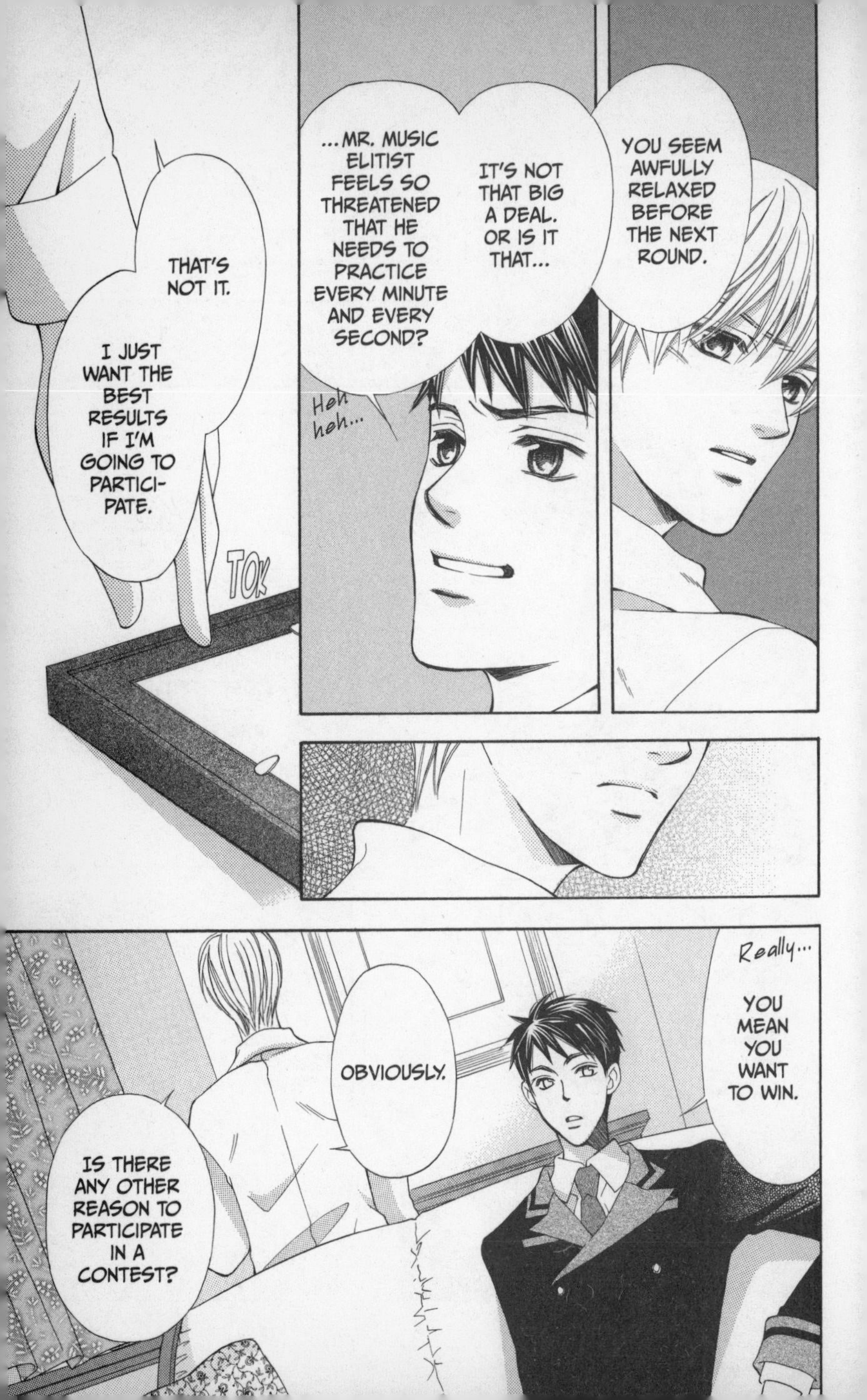
YOU SEEM AWFULLY RELAXED BEFORE THE NEXT ROUND.
IT'S NOT THAT BIG A DEAL. OR IS IT THAT...
...MR. MUSIC ELITIST FEELS SO THREATENED THAT HE NEEDS TO PRACTICE EVERY MINUTE AND EVERY SECOND?
Heh heh...
THAT'S NOT IT.
I JUST WANT THE BEST RESULTS IF I'M GOING TO PARTICI-PATE.
TOK
Really...
YOU MEAN YOU WANT TO WIN.
OBVIOUSLY.
IS THERE ANY OTHER REASON TO PARTICIPATE IN A CONTEST?

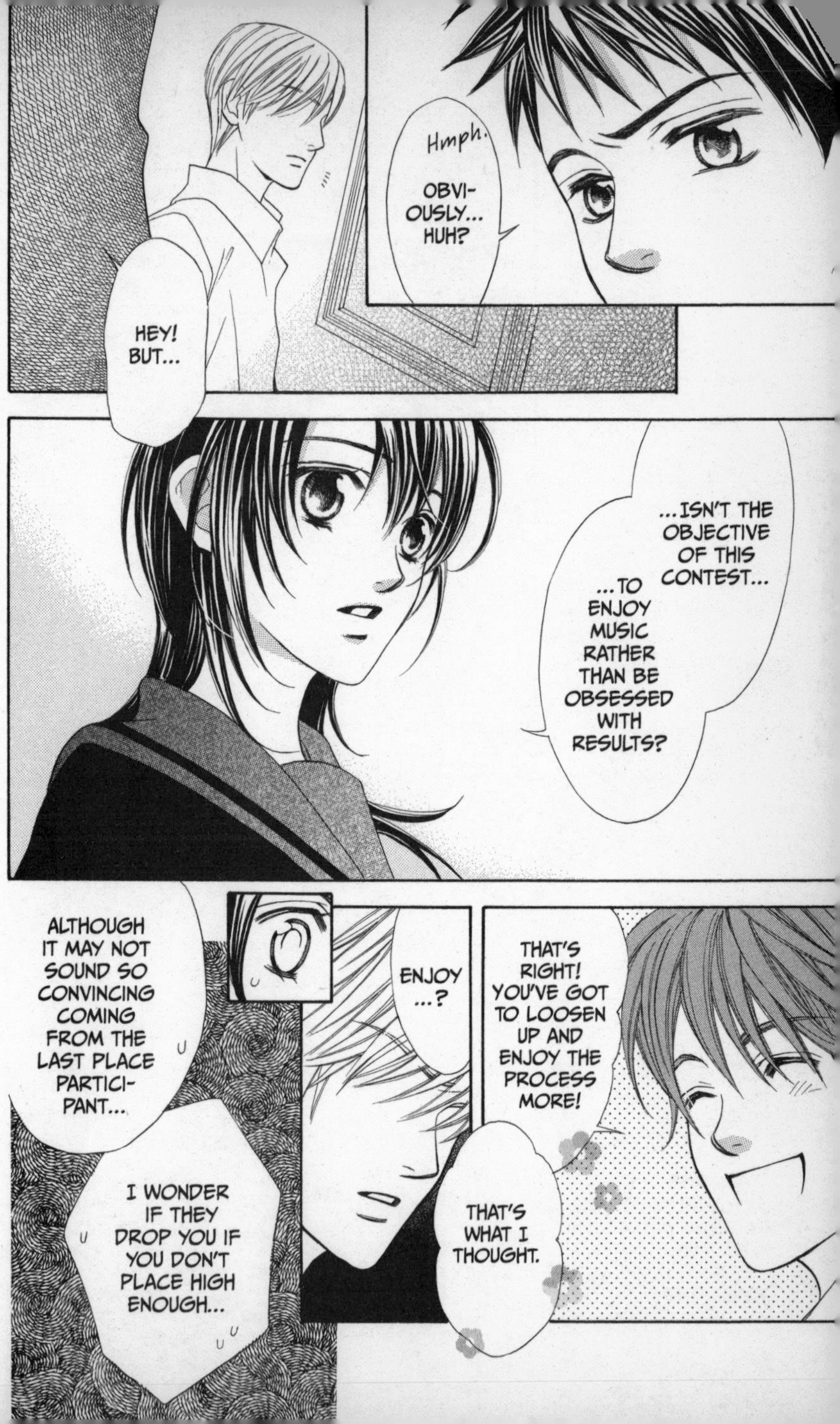
Hmph.
OBVIOUSLY... HUH?
HEY! BUT...
...ISN'T THE OBJECTIVE OF THIS CONTEST...
...TO ENJOY MUSIC RATHER THAN BE OBSESSED WITH RESULTS?
THAT'S RIGHT! YOU'VE GOT TO LOOSEN UP AND ENJOY THE PROCESS MORE!
THAT'S WHAT I THOUGHT.
ENJOY ...?
ALTHOUGH IT MAY NOT SOUND SO CONVINCING COMING FROM THE LAST PLACE PARTICIPANT...
I WONDER IF THEY DROP YOU IF YOU DON'T PLACE HIGH ENOUGH...

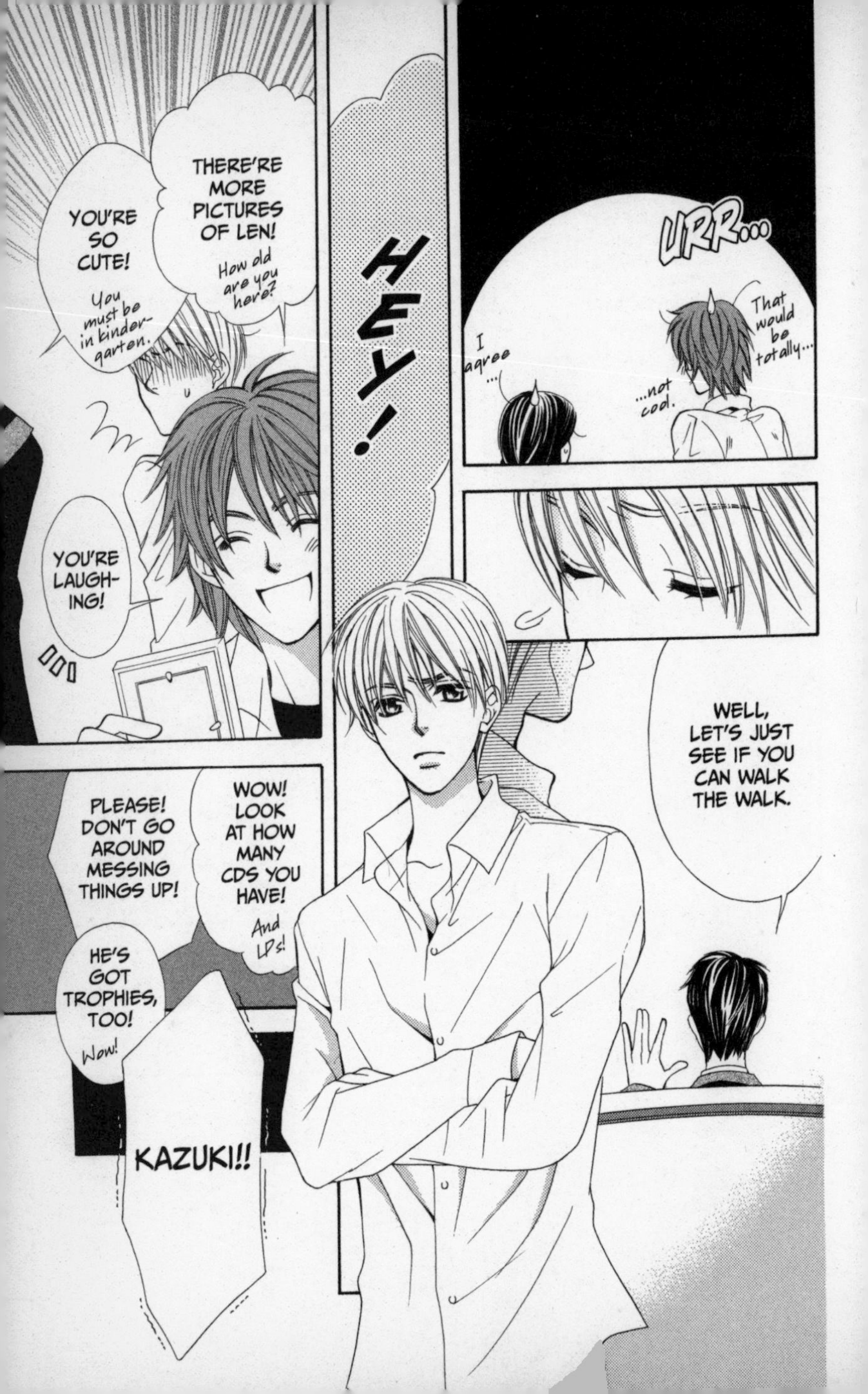
URR...
That would be totally...
...not cool.
I agree...
HEY!
THERE'RE MORE PICTURES OF LEN!
How old are you here?
YOU'RE SO CUTE!
You must be in kinder-garten.
YOU'RE LAUGHING!
WELL, LET'S JUST SEE IF YOU CAN WALK THE WALK.
WOW! LOOK AT HOW MANY CDS YOU HAVE!
And LPs!
PLEASE! DON'T GO AROUND MESSING THINGS UP!
HE'S GOT TROPHIES, TOO!
Wow!
KAZUKI!!

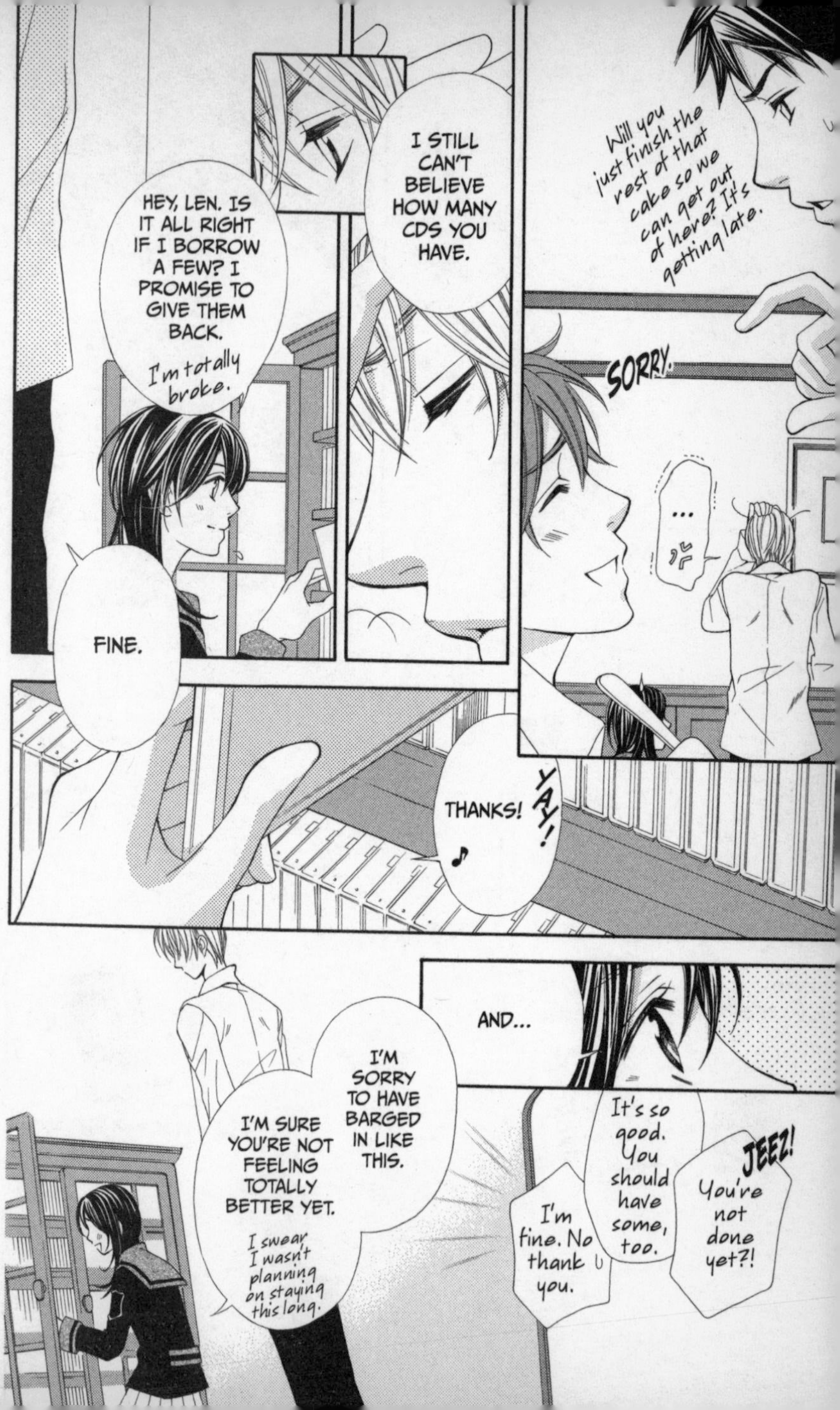
Will you just finish the rest of that cake so we can get out of here? It's getting late.
SORRY.
...
I STILL CAN'T BELIEVE HOW MANY CDS YOU HAVE.
HEY, LEN. IS IT ALL RIGHT IF I BORROW A FEW? I PROMISE TO GIVE THEM BACK.
I'm totally broke.
FINE.
YAY!
THANKS! ♪
AND...
JEEZ!
You're not done yet?!
It's so good. You should have some, too.
I'm fine. No thank you.
I'M SORRY TO HAVE BARGED IN LIKE THIS.
I'M SURE YOU'RE NOT FEELING TOTALLY BETTER YET.
I swear I wasn't planning on staying this long.

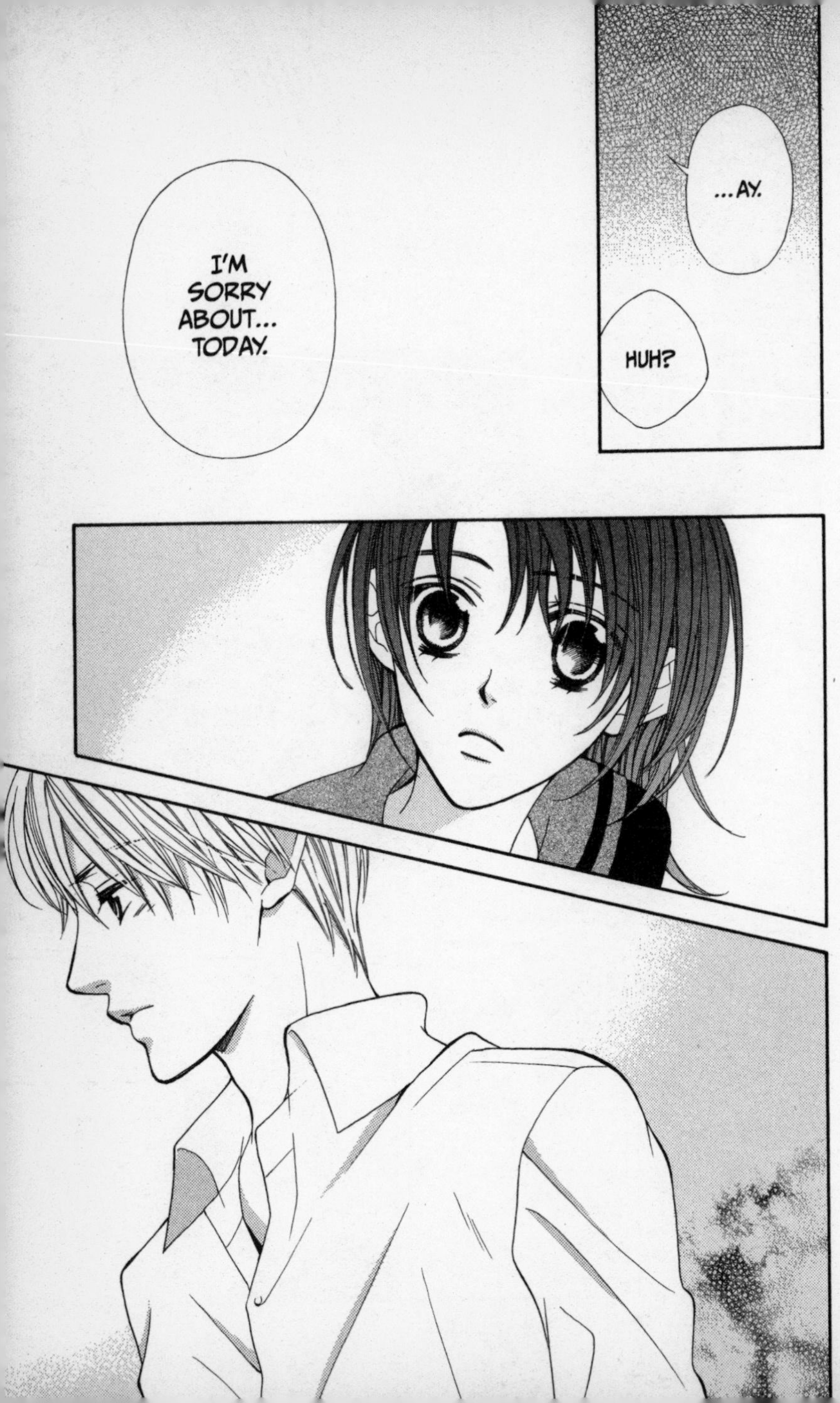
...AY.
HUH?
I'M SORRY ABOUT... TODAY.

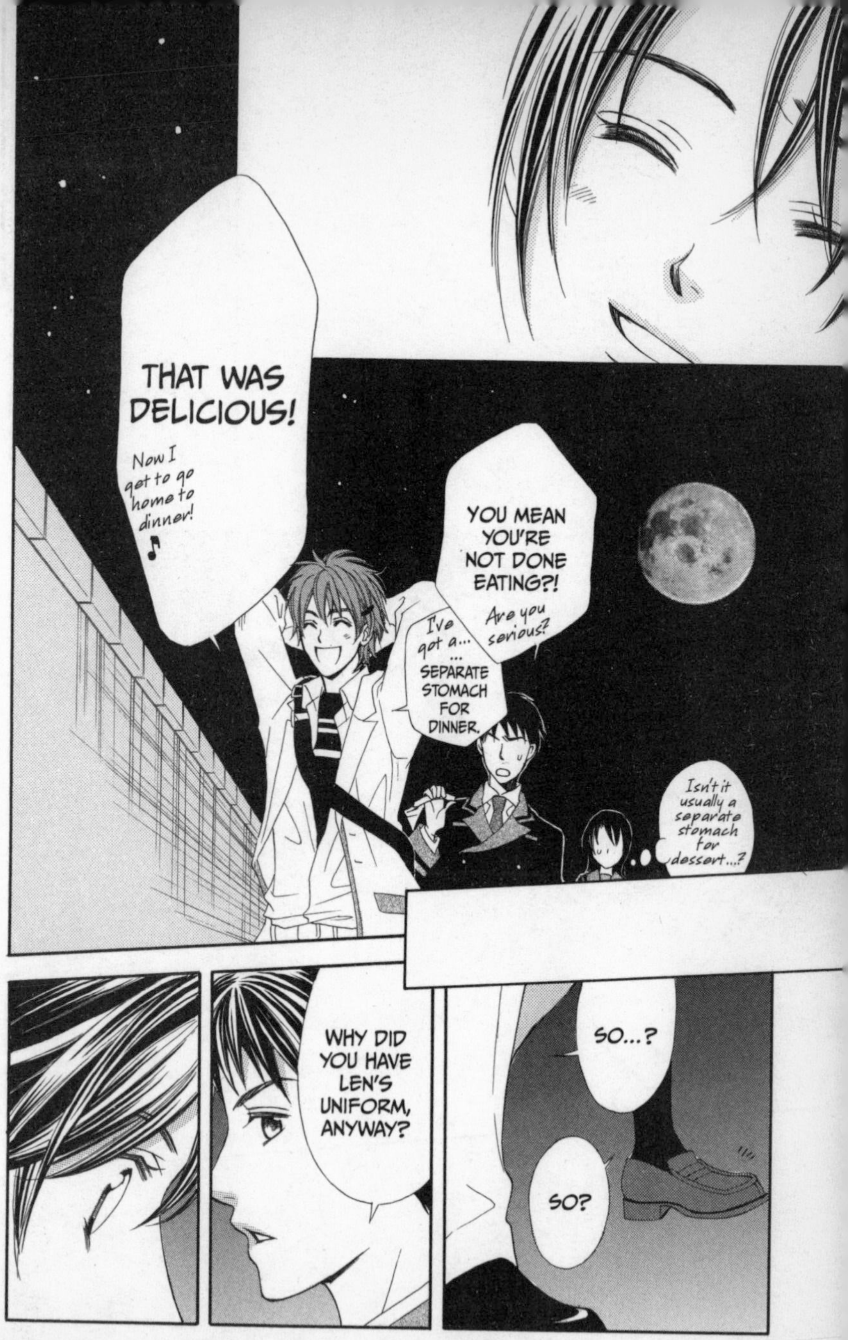
THAT WAS DELICIOUS!
Now I get to go home to dinner! ♪
YOU MEAN YOU'RE NOT DONE EATING?!
Are you serious?
I've got a... ...SEPARATE STOMACH FOR DINNER.
Isn't it usually a separate stomach for dessert...?
SO...?
SO?
WHY DID YOU HAVE LEN'S UNIFORM, ANYWAY?

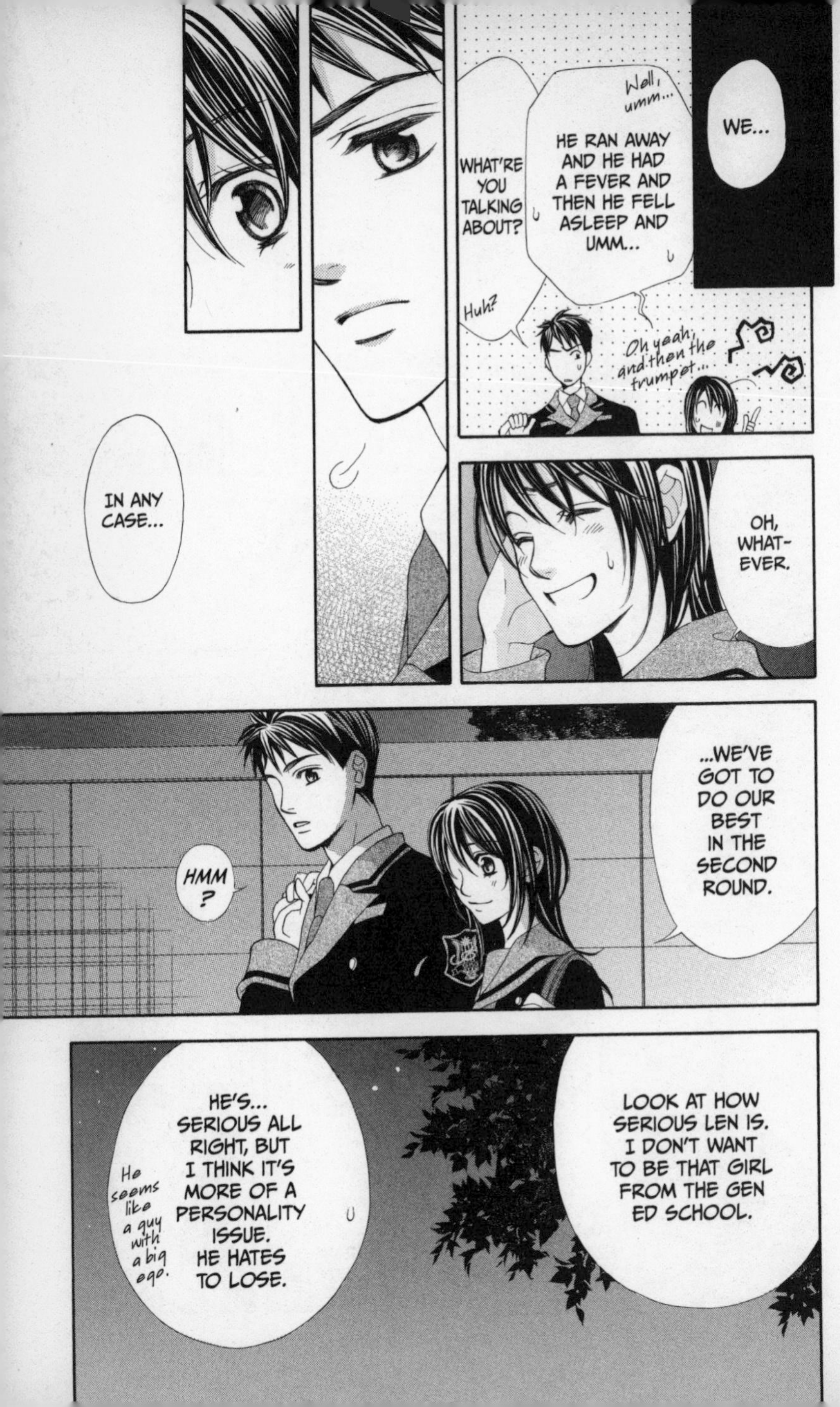
WE...
Well, umm...
HE RAN AWAY AND HE HAD A FEVER AND THEN HE FELL ASLEEP AND UMM...
WHAT'RE YOU TALKING ABOUT?
Huh?
Oh yeah, and then the trumpet...
OH, WHATEVER.
IN ANY CASE...
...WE'VE GOT TO DO OUR BEST IN THE SECOND ROUND.
HMM?
LOOK AT HOW SERIOUS LEN IS. I DON'T WANT TO BE THAT GIRL FROM THE GEN ED SCHOOL.
HE'S... SERIOUS ALL RIGHT, BUT I THINK IT'S MORE OF A PERSONALITY ISSUE. HE HATES TO LOSE.
He seems like a guy with a big ego.

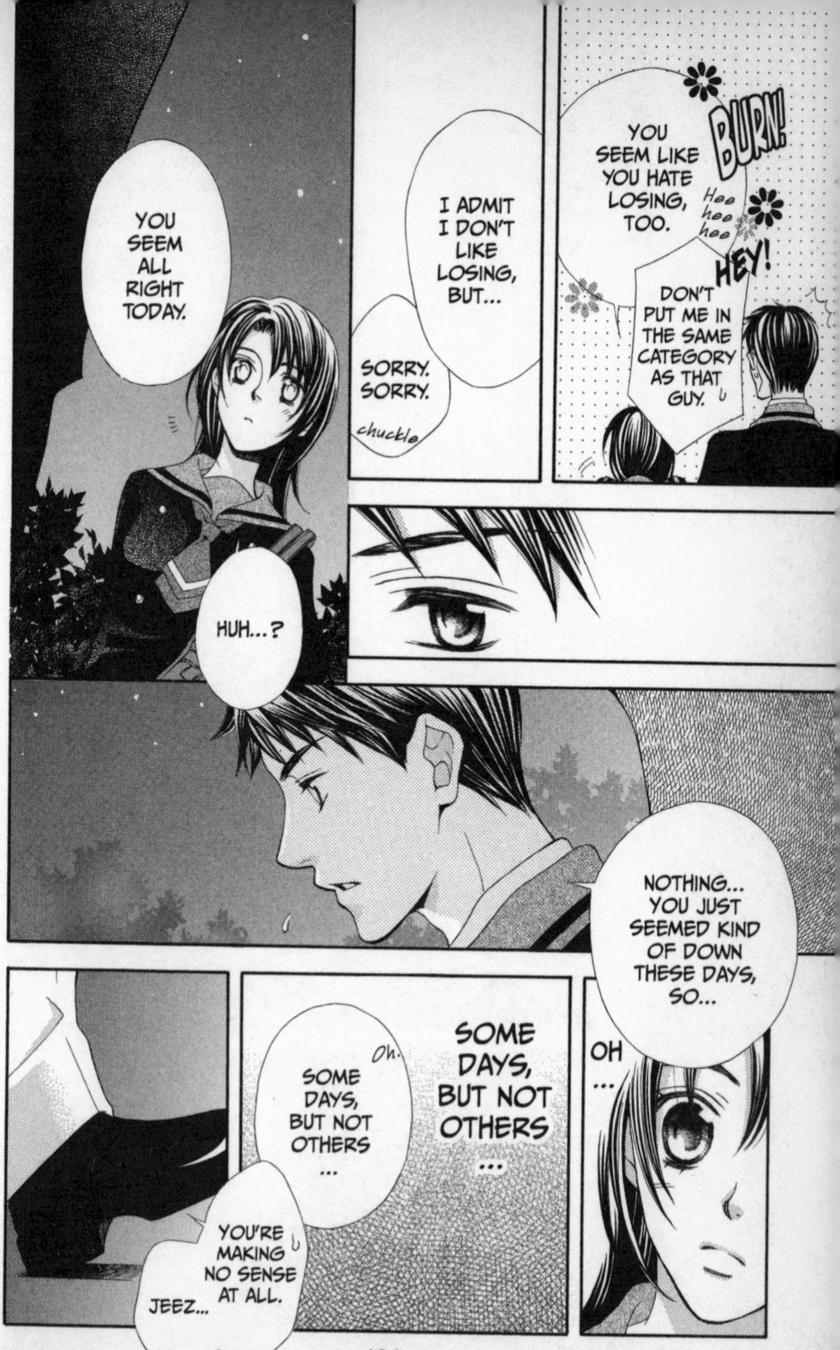
YOU SEEM LIKE YOU HATE LOSING, TOO.
BURN!
Hee hee hee
HEY!
DON'T PUT ME IN THE SAME CATEGORY AS THAT GUY.
I ADMIT I DON'T LIKE LOSING, BUT...
SORRY. SORRY.
chuckle
YOU SEEM ALL RIGHT TODAY.
HUH...?
NOTHING... YOU JUST SEEMED KIND OF DOWN THESE DAYS, SO...
OH ...
SOME DAYS, BUT NOT OTHERS ...
Oh.
SOME DAYS, BUT NOT OTHERS ...
YOU'RE MAKING NO SENSE AT ALL.
JEEZ...

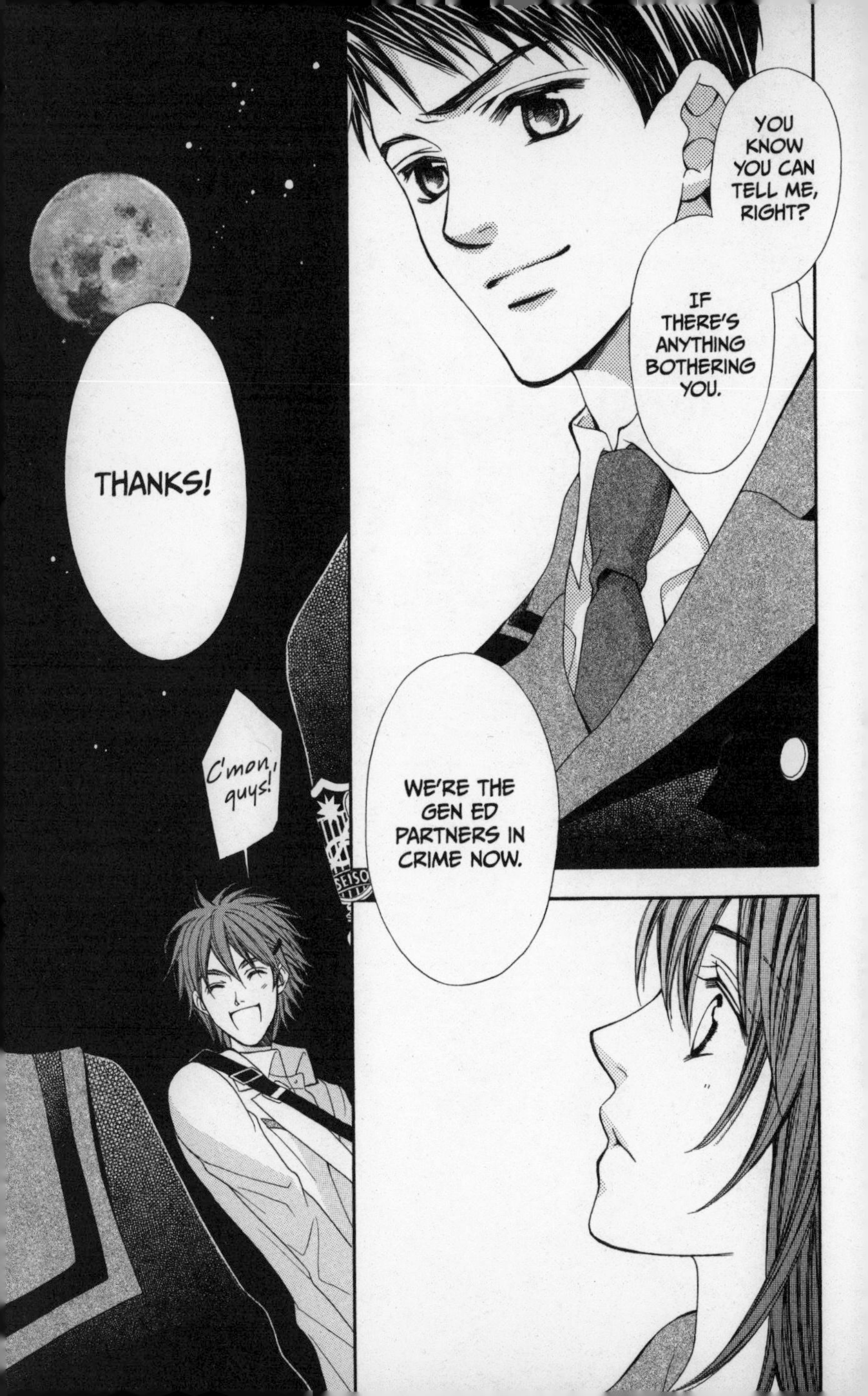
YOU KNOW YOU CAN TELL ME, RIGHT?
IF THERE'S ANYTHING BOTHERING YOU.
WE'RE THE GEN ED PARTNERS IN CRIME NOW.
THANKS!
C'mon, guys!

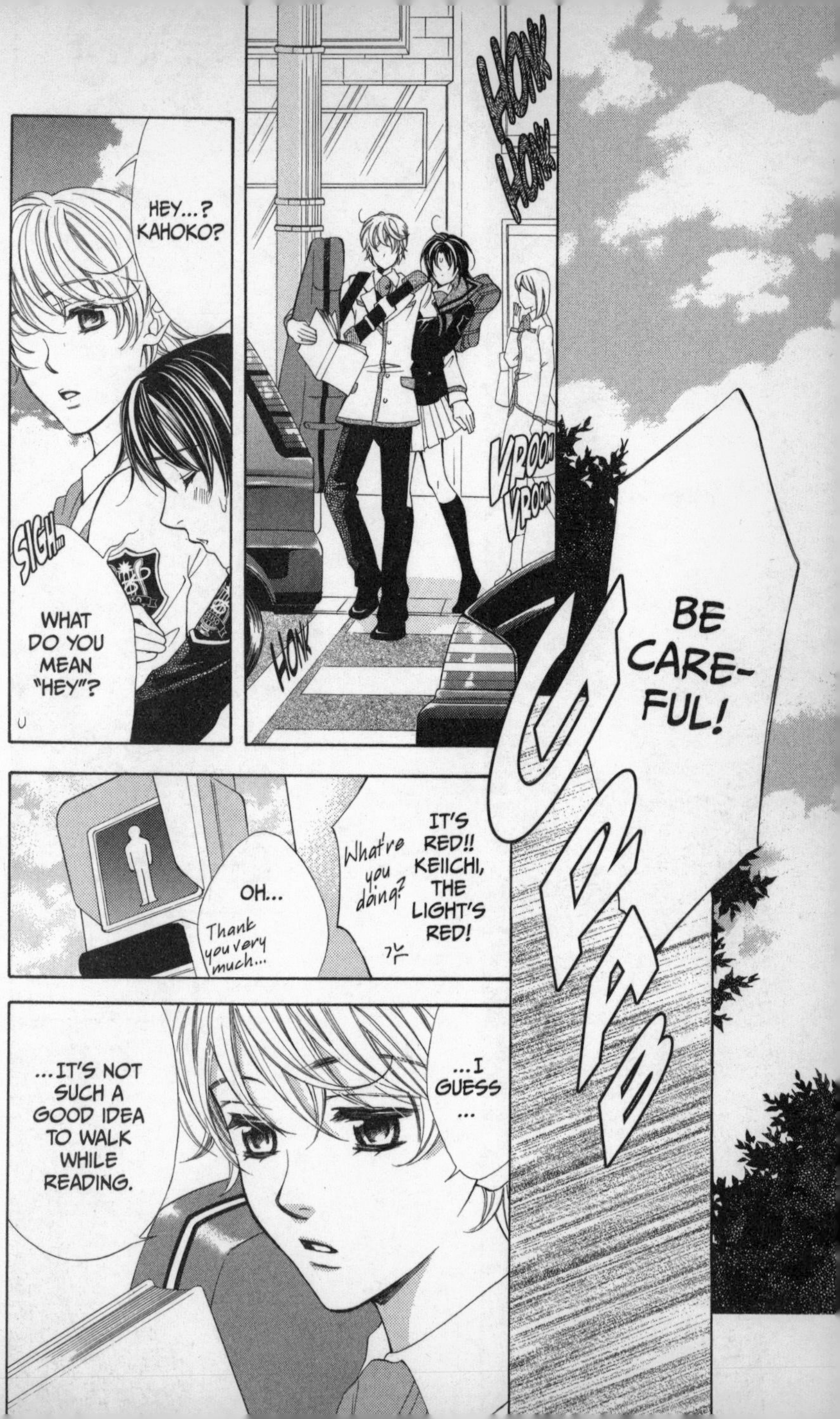
BE CAREFUL!
HONK HONK
VROOM VROOM
HONK
HEY...? KAHOKO?
SIGH
WHAT DO YOU MEAN "HEY"?
IT'S RED!! KEIICHI, THE LIGHT'S RED!
What're you doing?
OH...
Thank you very much...
...I GUESS...
...IT'S NOT SUCH A GOOD IDEA TO WALK WHILE READING.

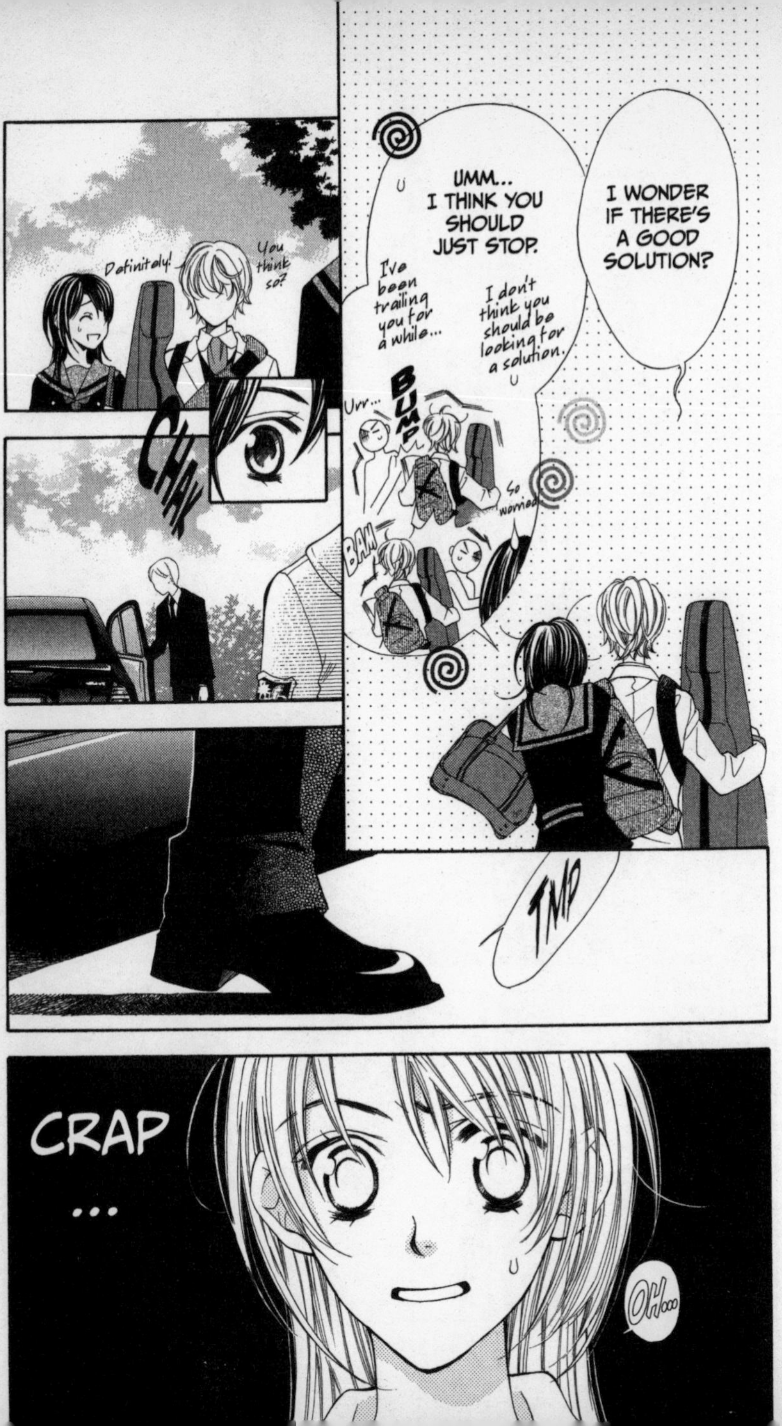
I WONDER IF THERE'S A GOOD SOLUTION?
UMM... I THINK YOU SHOULD JUST STOP.
I don't think you should be looking for a solution.
I've been trailing you for a while...
BUMP
Urr...
So worried
BAM
You think so?
Definitely!
CHAK
TMP
CRAP ...
OH...

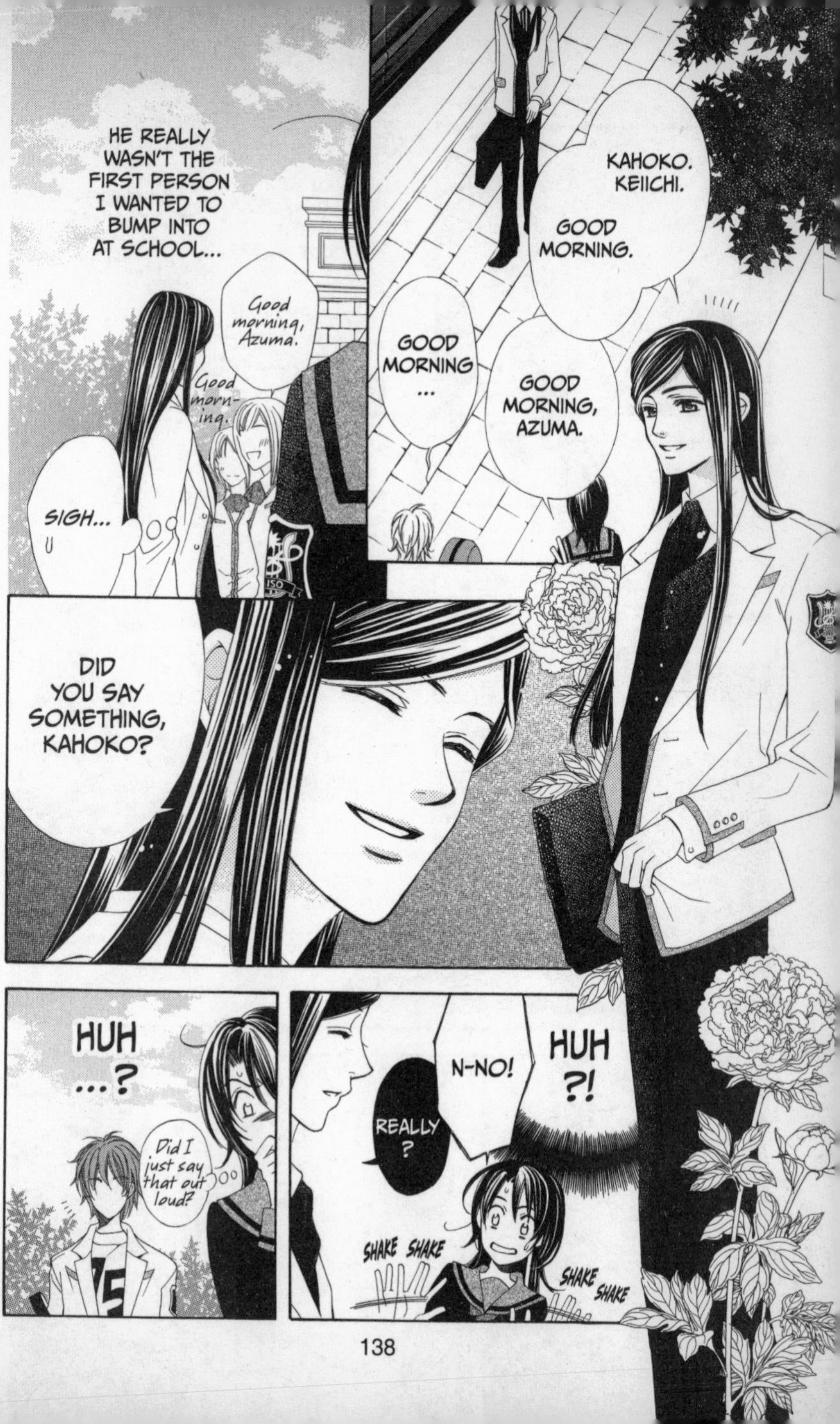
KAHOKO. KEIICHI.
GOOD MORNING.
GOOD MORNING, AZUMA.
GOOD MORNING ...
HE REALLY WASN'T THE FIRST PERSON I WANTED TO BUMP INTO AT SCHOOL...
Good morning, Azuma.
Good morning.
SIGH...
DID YOU SAY SOMETHING, KAHOKO?
HUH ?!
N-NO!
REALLY ?
SHAKE SHAKE
SHAKE SHAKE
HUH ...?
Did I just say that out loud?

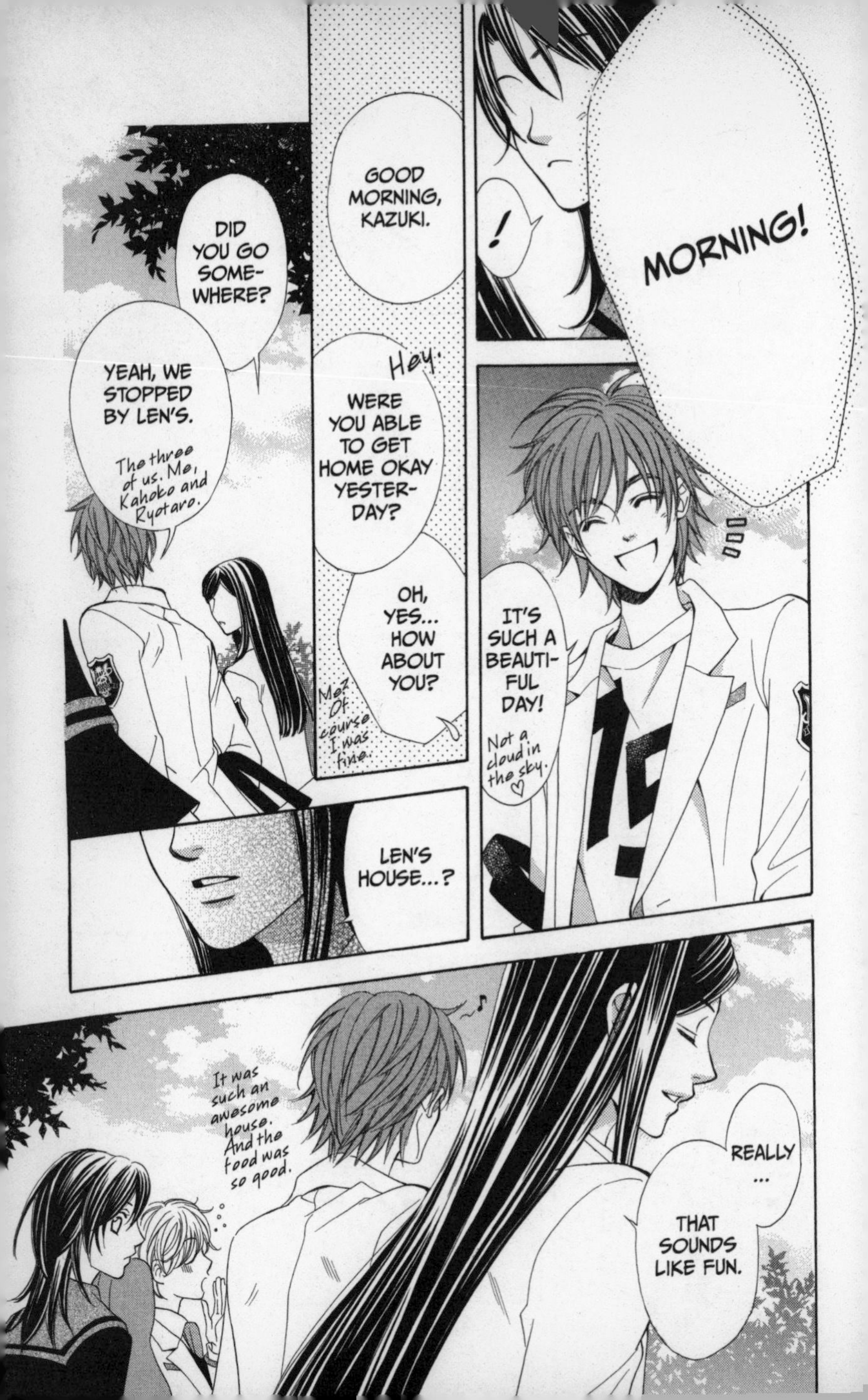
MORNING!
!
IT'S SUCH A BEAUTIFUL DAY!
Not a cloud in the sky. ♡
GOOD MORNING, KAZUKI.
Hey.
WERE YOU ABLE TO GET HOME OKAY YESTERDAY?
OH, YES... HOW ABOUT YOU?
Me? Of course I was fine.
DID YOU GO SOMEWHERE?
YEAH, WE STOPPED BY LEN'S.
The three of us. Me, Kahoko and Ryotaro.
LEN'S HOUSE...?
REALLY... THAT SOUNDS LIKE FUN.
It was such an awesome house. And the food was so good.

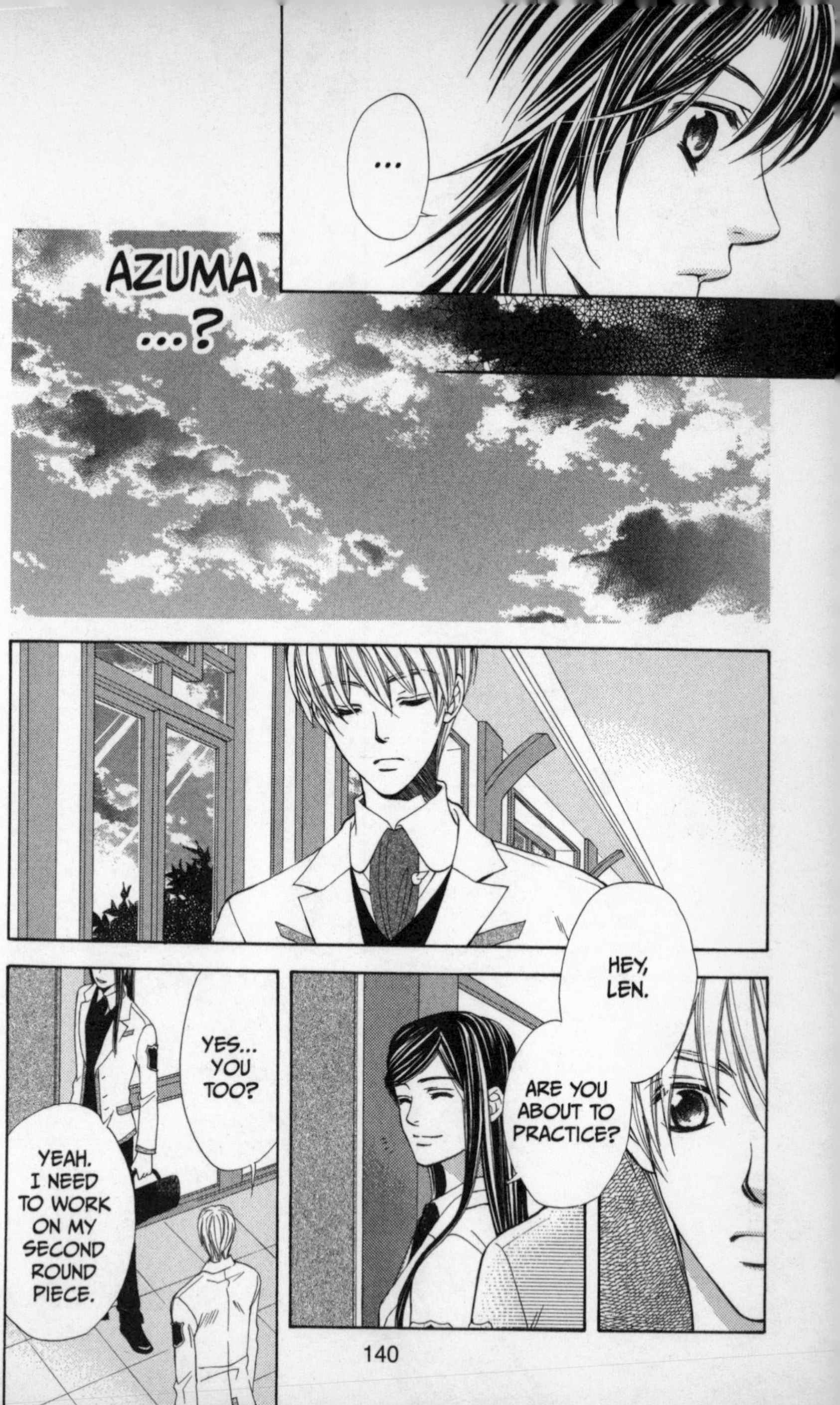
...
AZUMA ...?
HEY, LEN.
ARE YOU ABOUT TO PRACTICE?
YES... YOU TOO?
YEAH. I NEED TO WORK ON MY SECOND ROUND PIECE.

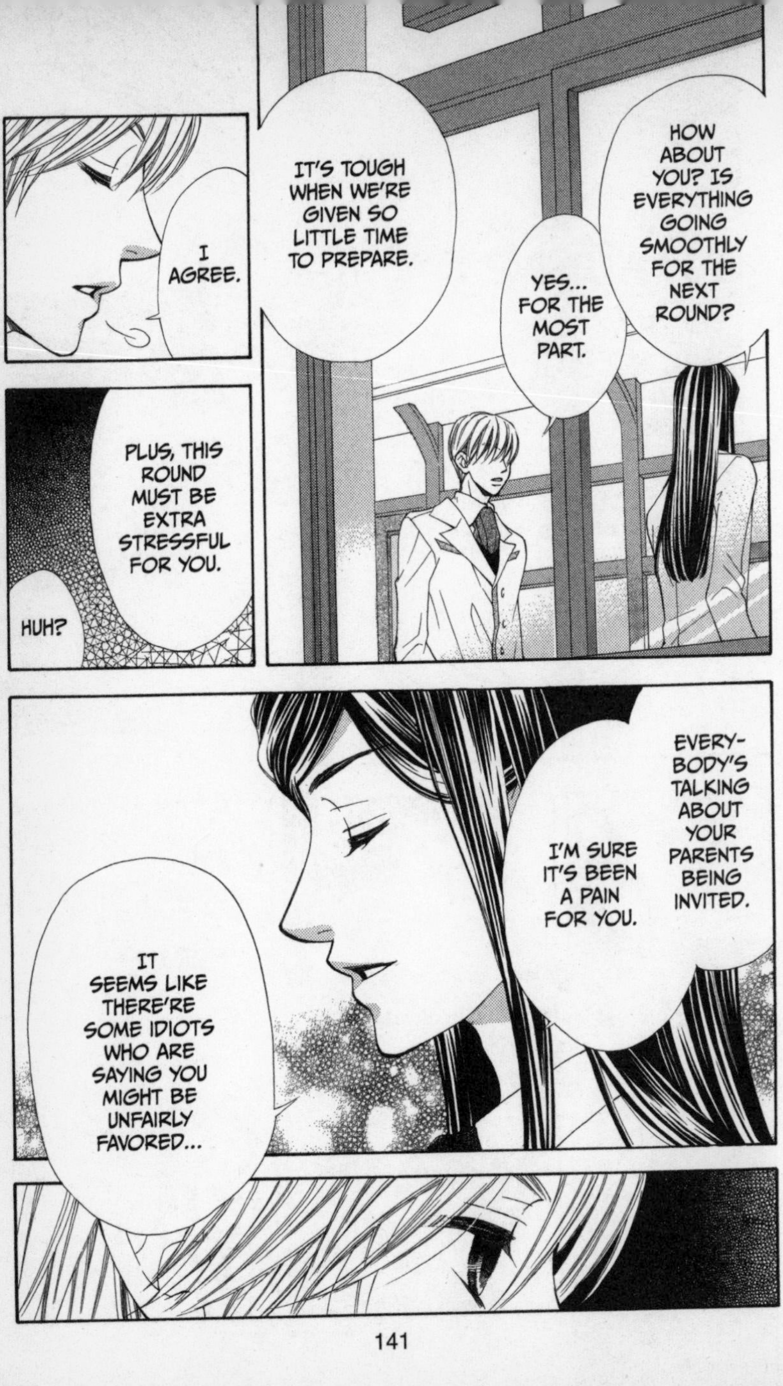
HOW ABOUT YOU? IS EVERYTHING GOING SMOOTHLY FOR THE NEXT ROUND?
YES... FOR THE MOST PART.
IT'S TOUGH WHEN WE'RE GIVEN SO LITTLE TIME TO PREPARE.
I AGREE.
PLUS, THIS ROUND MUST BE EXTRA STRESSFUL FOR YOU.
HUH?
EVERY-BODY'S TALKING ABOUT YOUR PARENTS BEING INVITED.
I'M SURE IT'S BEEN A PAIN FOR YOU.
IT SEEMS LIKE THERE'RE SOME IDIOTS WHO ARE SAYING YOU MIGHT BE UNFAIRLY FAVORED...

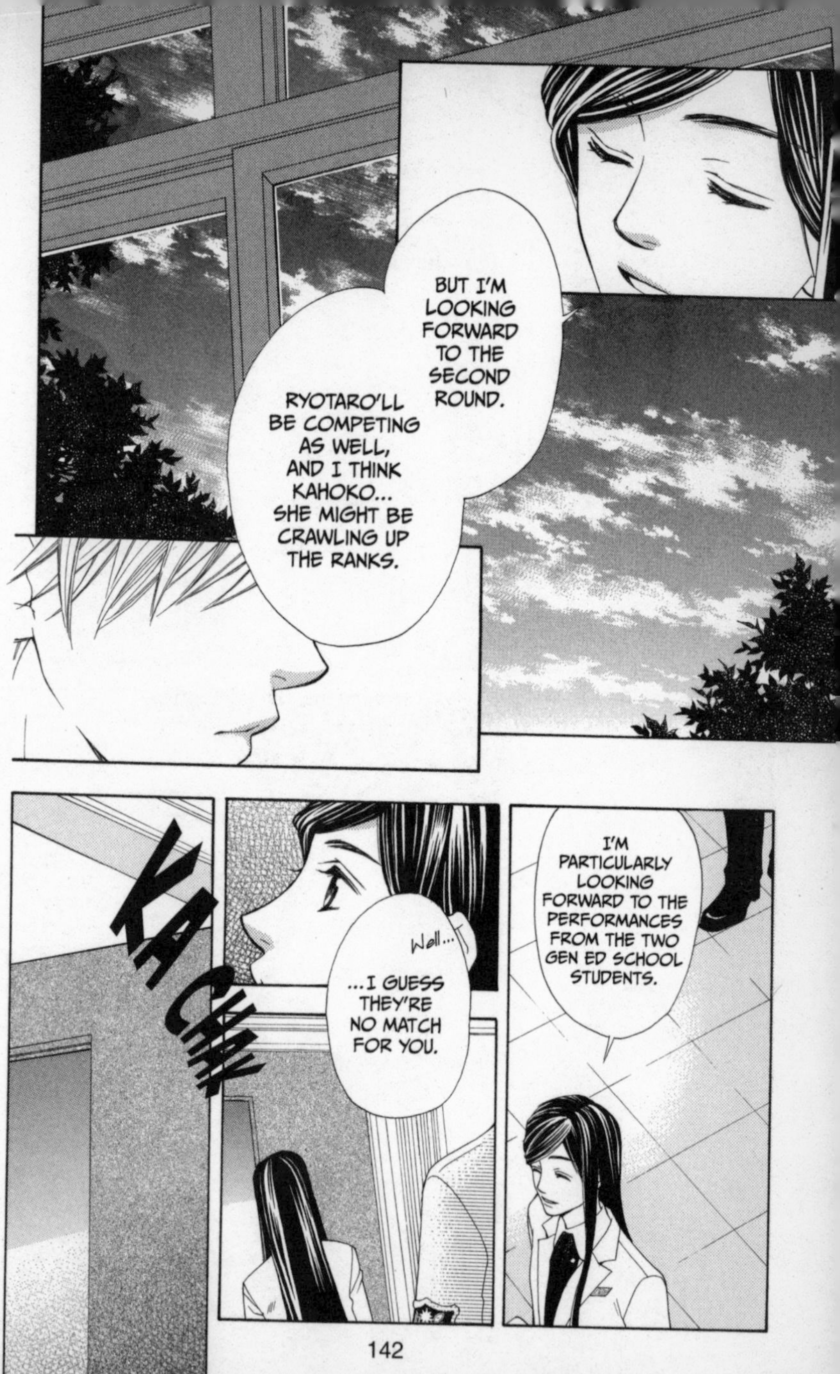
BUT I'M LOOKING FORWARD TO THE SECOND ROUND.
RYOTARO'LL BE COMPETING AS WELL, AND I THINK KAHOKO... SHE MIGHT BE CRAWLING UP THE RANKS.
I'M PARTICULARLY LOOKING FORWARD TO THE PERFORMANCES FROM THE TWO GEN ED SCHOOL STUDENTS.
Well...
...I GUESS THEY'RE NO MATCH FOR YOU.
KA CHAK

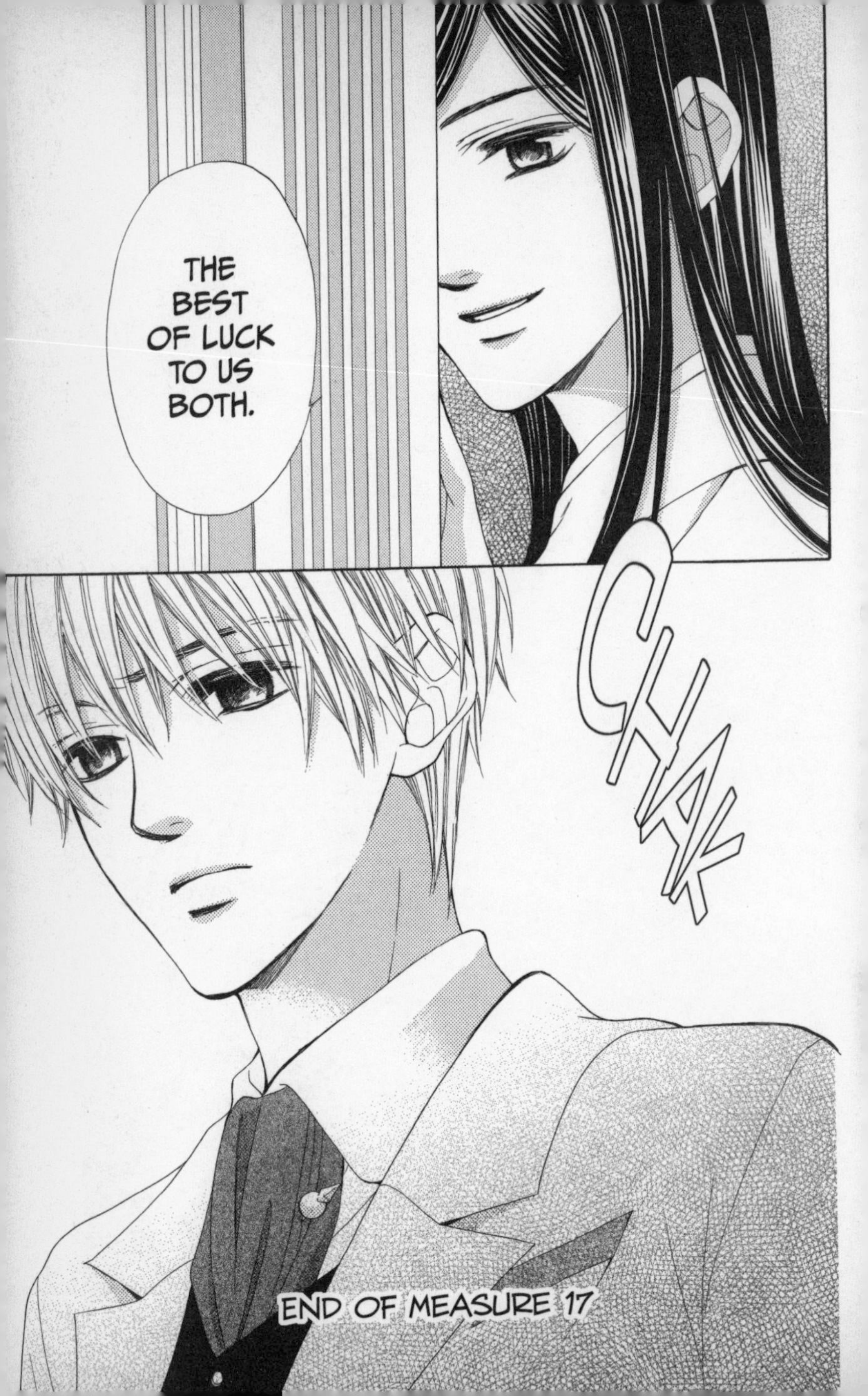
THE BEST OF LUCK TO US BOTH.
CHAK
END OF MEASURE 17

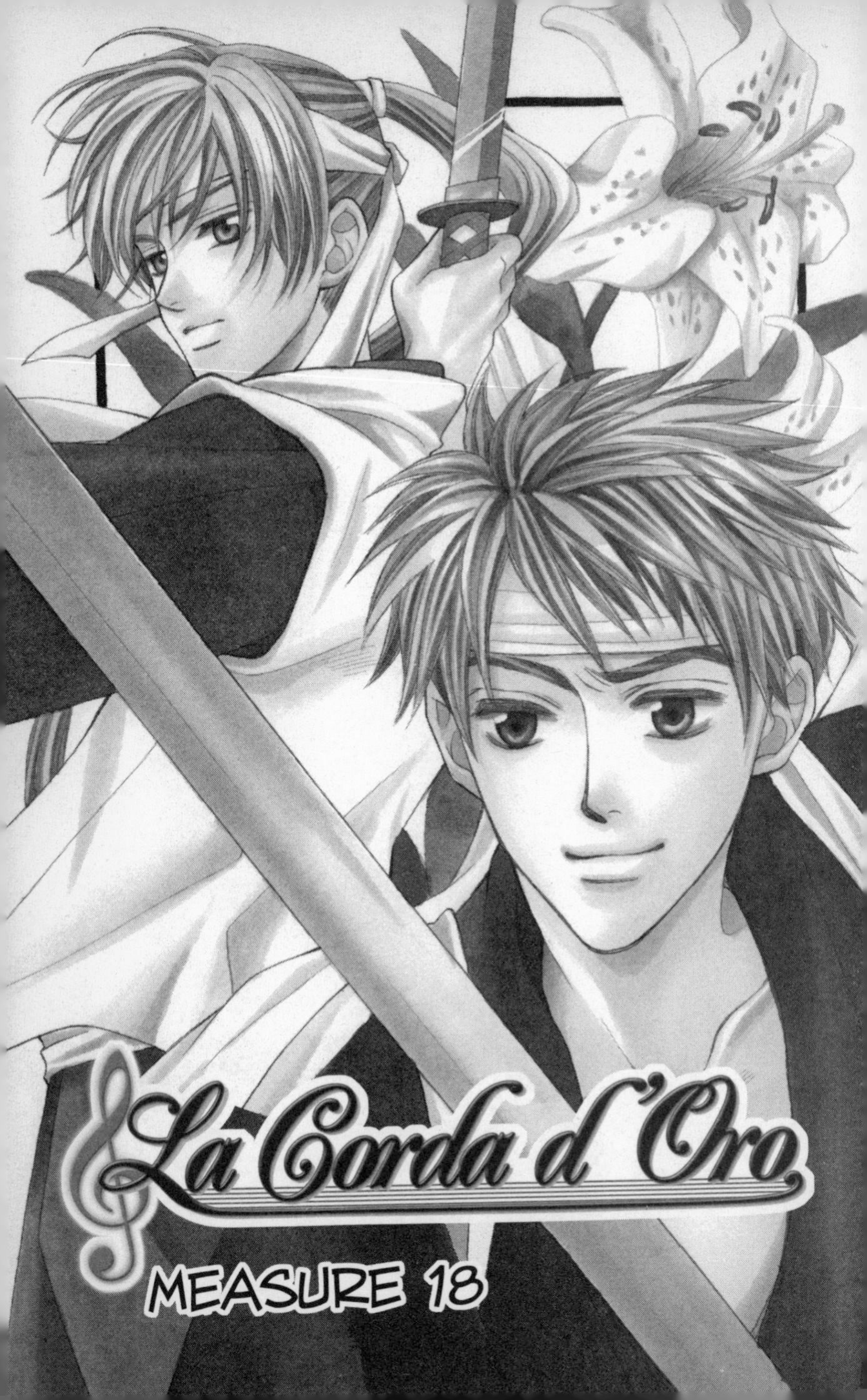
La Corda d'Oro
MEASURE 18

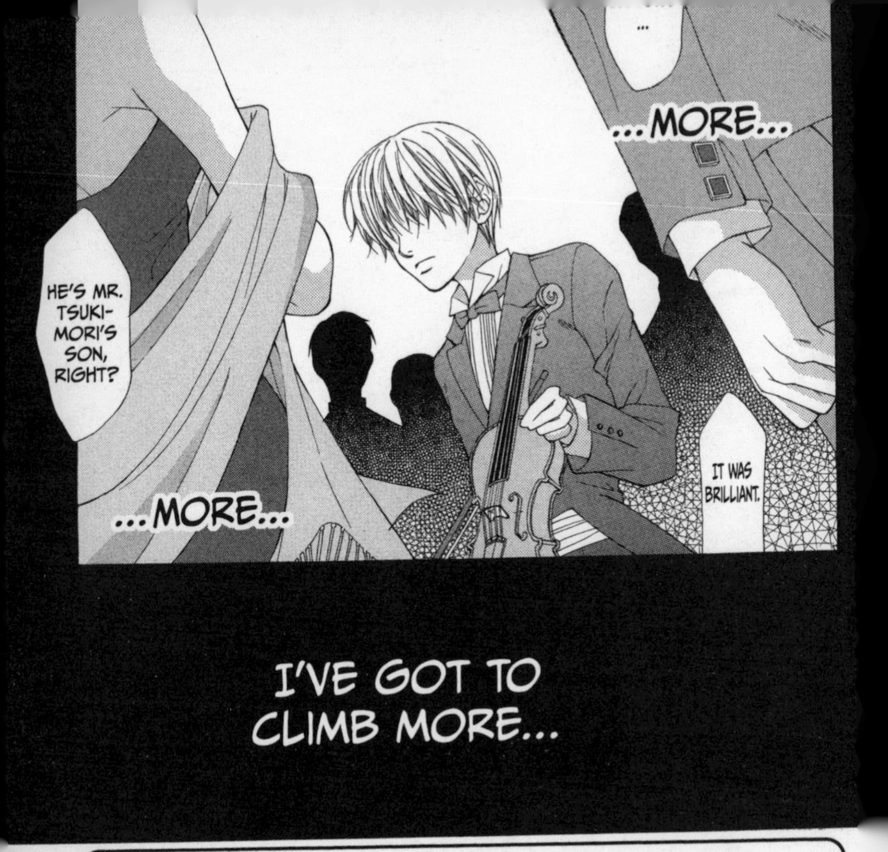
...
...MORE...
IT WAS BRILLIANT.
HE'S MR. TSUKIMORI'S SON, RIGHT?
...MORE...
I'VE GOT TO CLIMB MORE...

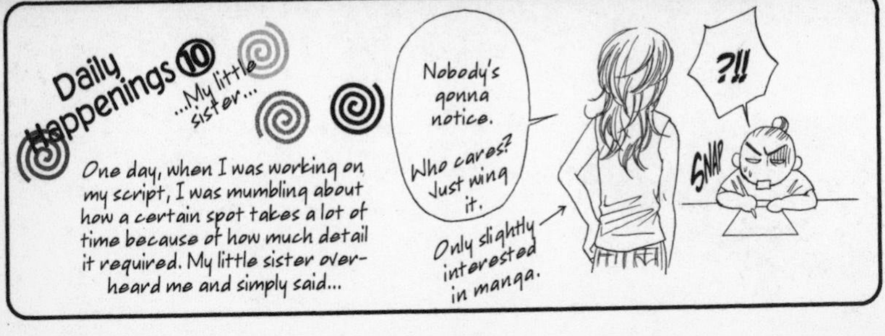
Daily Happenings 10
...My little sister...
One day, when I was working on my script, I was mumbling about how a certain spot takes a lot of time because of how much detail it required. My little sister overheard me and simply said...
Nobody's gonna notice. Who cares? Just wing it.
Only slightly interested in manga.
?!!
SNAP

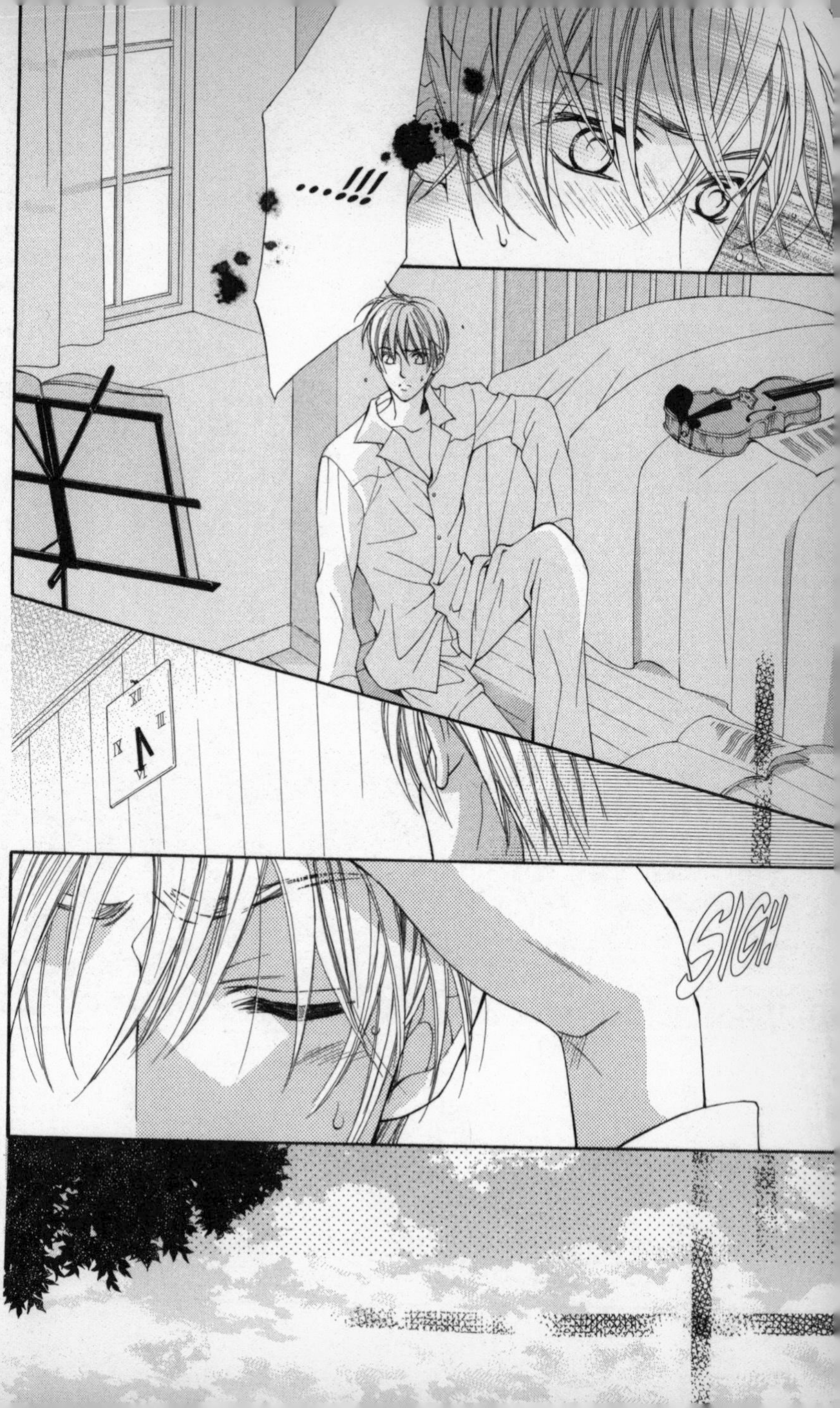

...!!!
SIGH

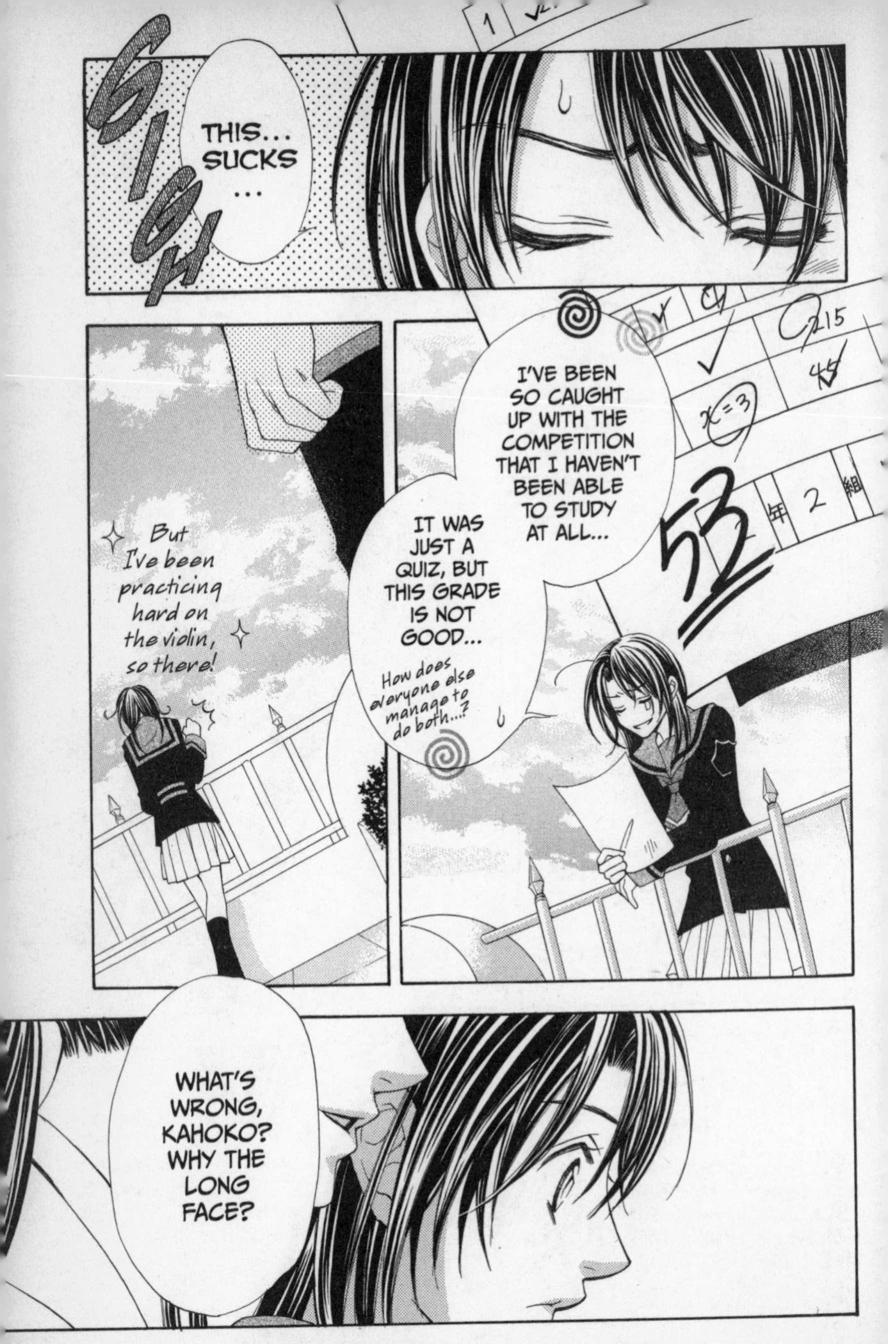
SIGH
THIS... SUCKS ...
53
I'VE BEEN SO CAUGHT UP WITH THE COMPETITION THAT I HAVEN'T BEEN ABLE TO STUDY AT ALL...
IT WAS JUST A QUIZ, BUT THIS GRADE IS NOT GOOD...
How does everyone else manage to do both...?
But I've been practicing hard on the violin, so there!
WHAT'S WRONG, KAHOKO? WHY THE LONG FACE?

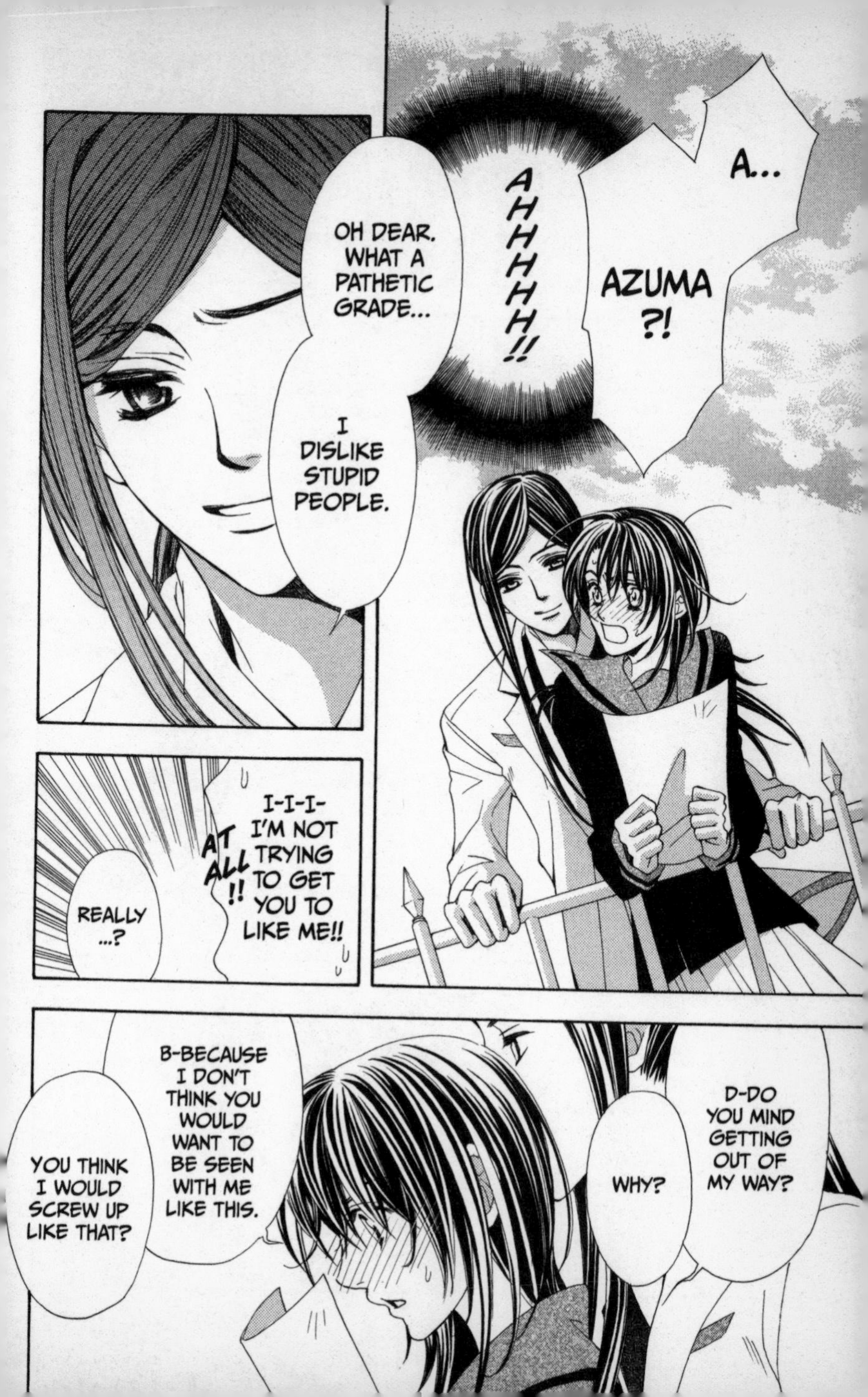
A... AZUMA?!
AHHHHHH!!
OH DEAR. WHAT A PATHETIC GRADE...
I DISLIKE STUPID PEOPLE.
I-I-I- I'M NOT TRYING TO GET YOU TO LIKE ME!!
AT ALL!!
REALLY ...?
D-DO YOU MIND GETTING OUT OF MY WAY?
WHY?
B-BECAUSE I DON'T THINK YOU WOULD WANT TO BE SEEN WITH ME LIKE THIS.
YOU THINK I WOULD SCREW UP LIKE THAT?

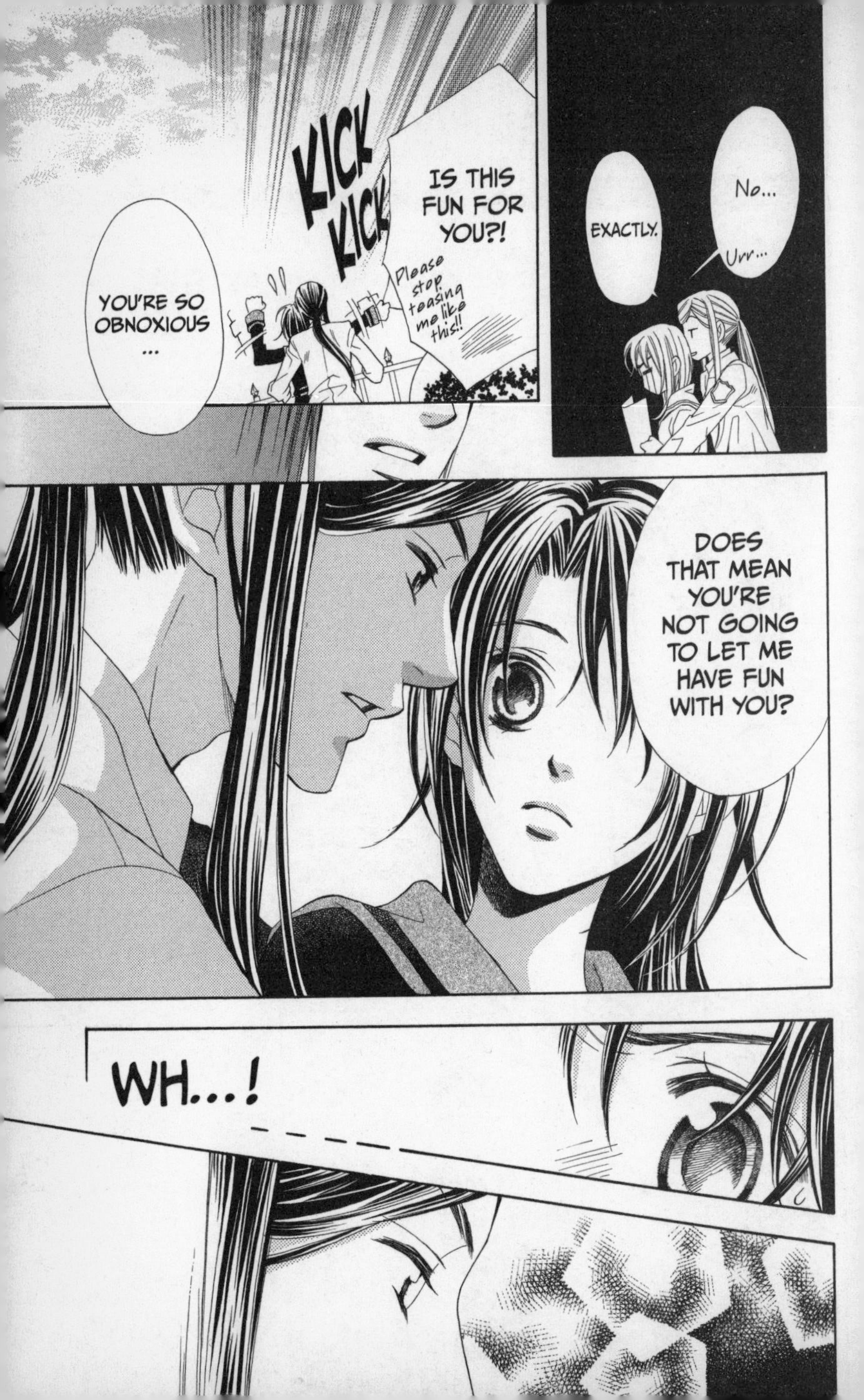
No...
Urr...
EXACTLY.
IS THIS FUN FOR YOU?!
Please stop teasing me like this!!
KICK KICK
YOU'RE SO OBNOXIOUS ...
DOES THAT MEAN YOU'RE NOT GOING TO LET ME HAVE FUN WITH YOU?
WH...!

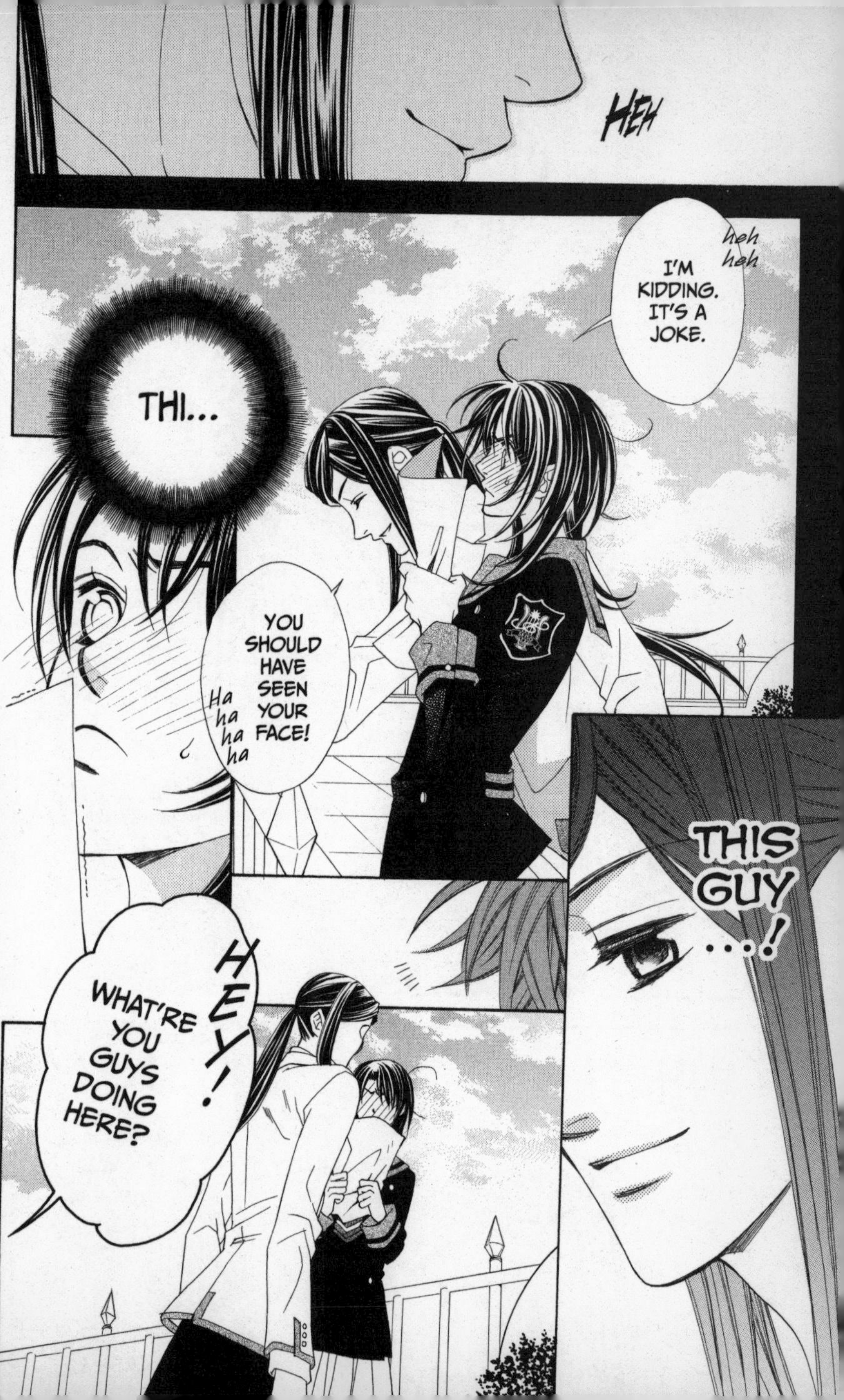
HEH
heh heh
I'M KIDDING. IT'S A JOKE.
THI...
YOU SHOULD HAVE SEEN YOUR FACE!
Ha ha ha ha
THIS GUY ...!
HEY!
WHAT'RE YOU GUYS DOING HERE?

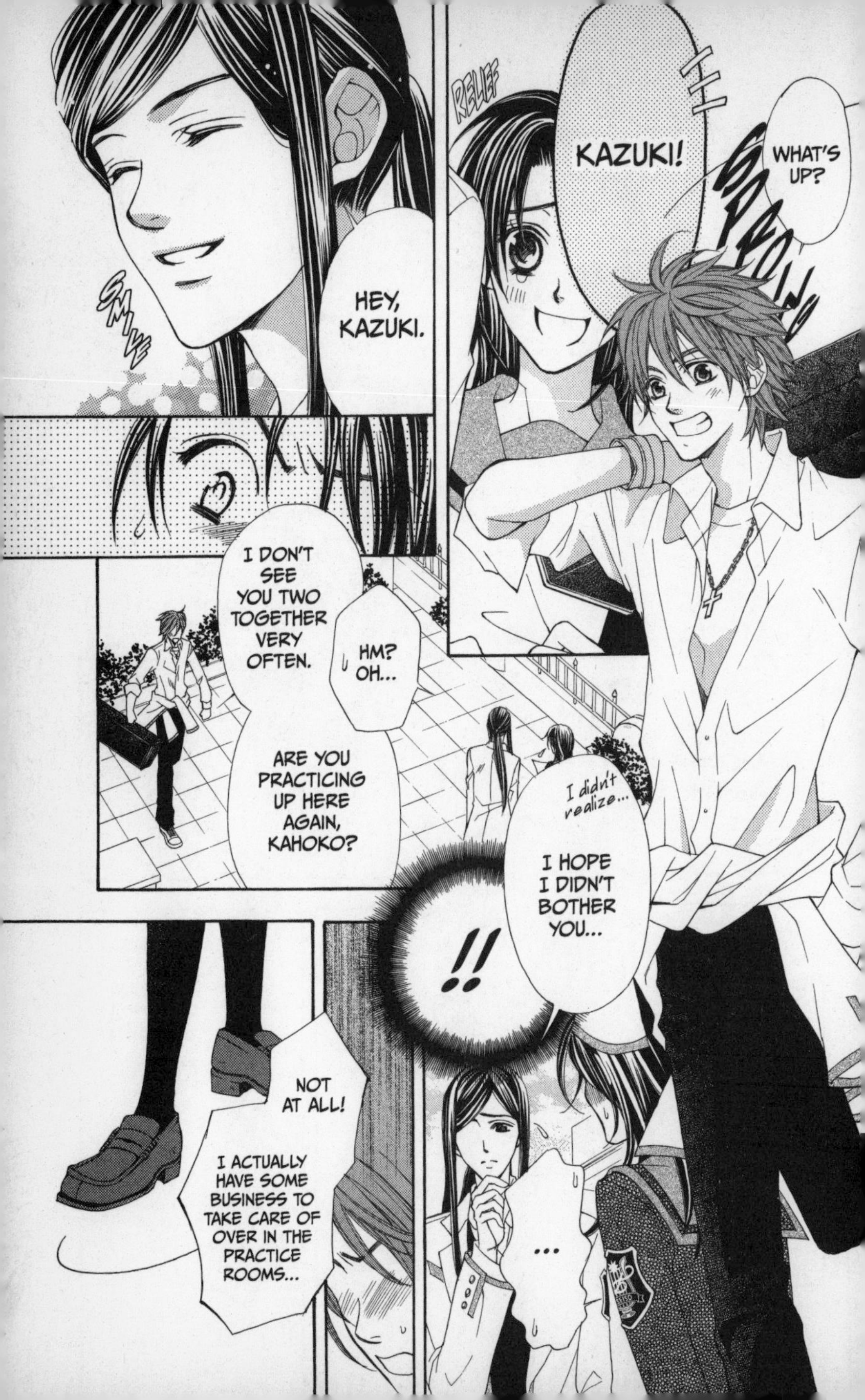
RELIEF
KAZUKI!
WHAT'S UP?
SPROING
SMILE
HEY, KAZUKI.
I DON'T SEE YOU TWO TOGETHER VERY OFTEN.
HM? OH...
ARE YOU PRACTICING UP HERE AGAIN, KAHOKO?
I didn't realize...
I HOPE I DIDN'T BOTHER YOU...
!!
NOT AT ALL!
I ACTUALLY HAVE SOME BUSINESS TO TAKE CARE OF OVER IN THE PRACTICE ROOMS...
...

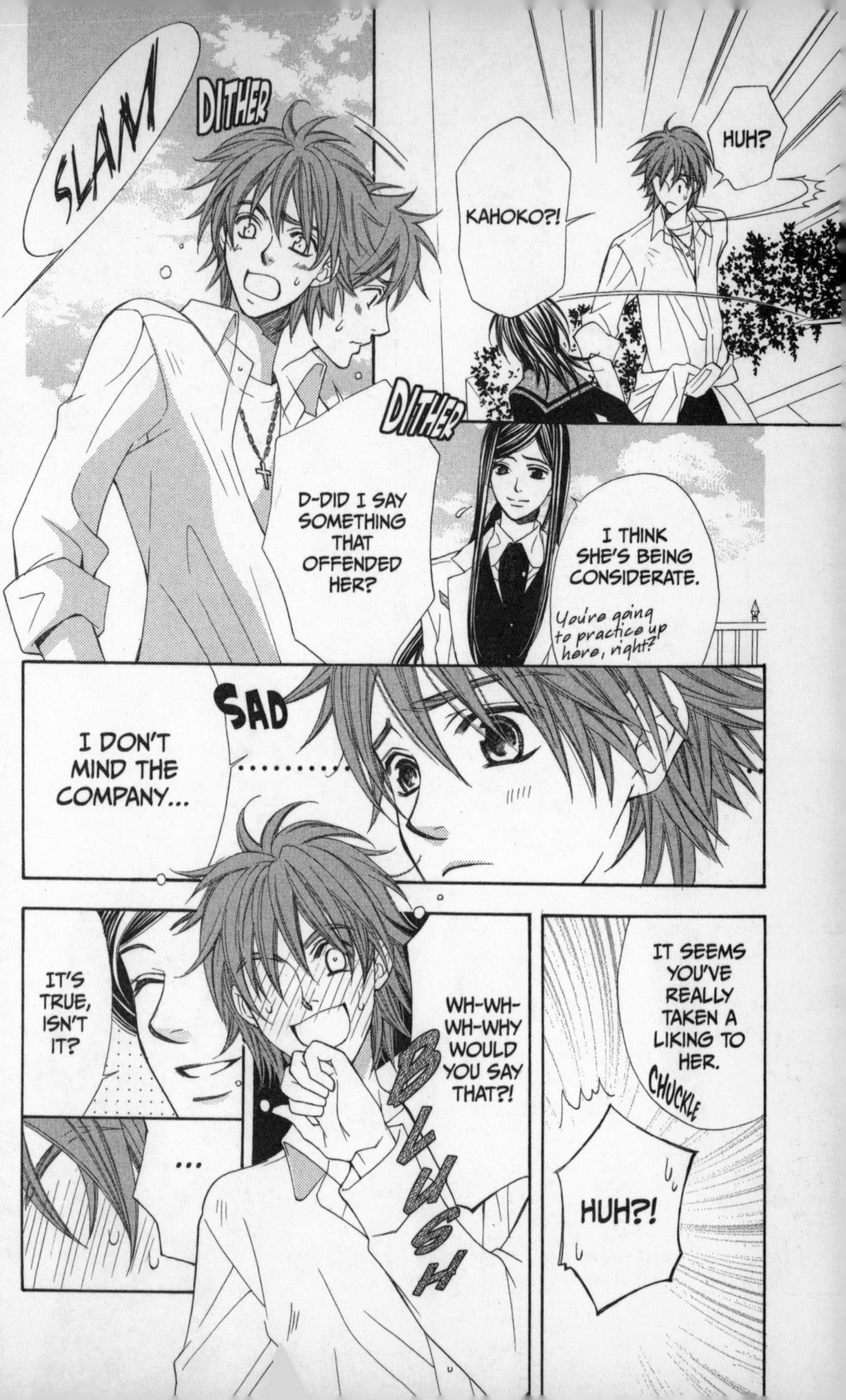

HUH?
KAHOKO?!
I THINK SHE'S BEING CONSIDERATE.
You're going to practice up here, right?
SLAM
DITHER
DITHER
D-DID I SAY SOMETHING THAT OFFENDED HER?
SAD
....
I DON'T MIND THE COMPANY...
IT SEEMS YOU'VE REALLY TAKEN A LIKING TO HER.
CHUCKLE
HUH?!
WH-WH-WH-WHY WOULD YOU SAY THAT?!
BLUSH
IT'S TRUE, ISN'T IT?
...

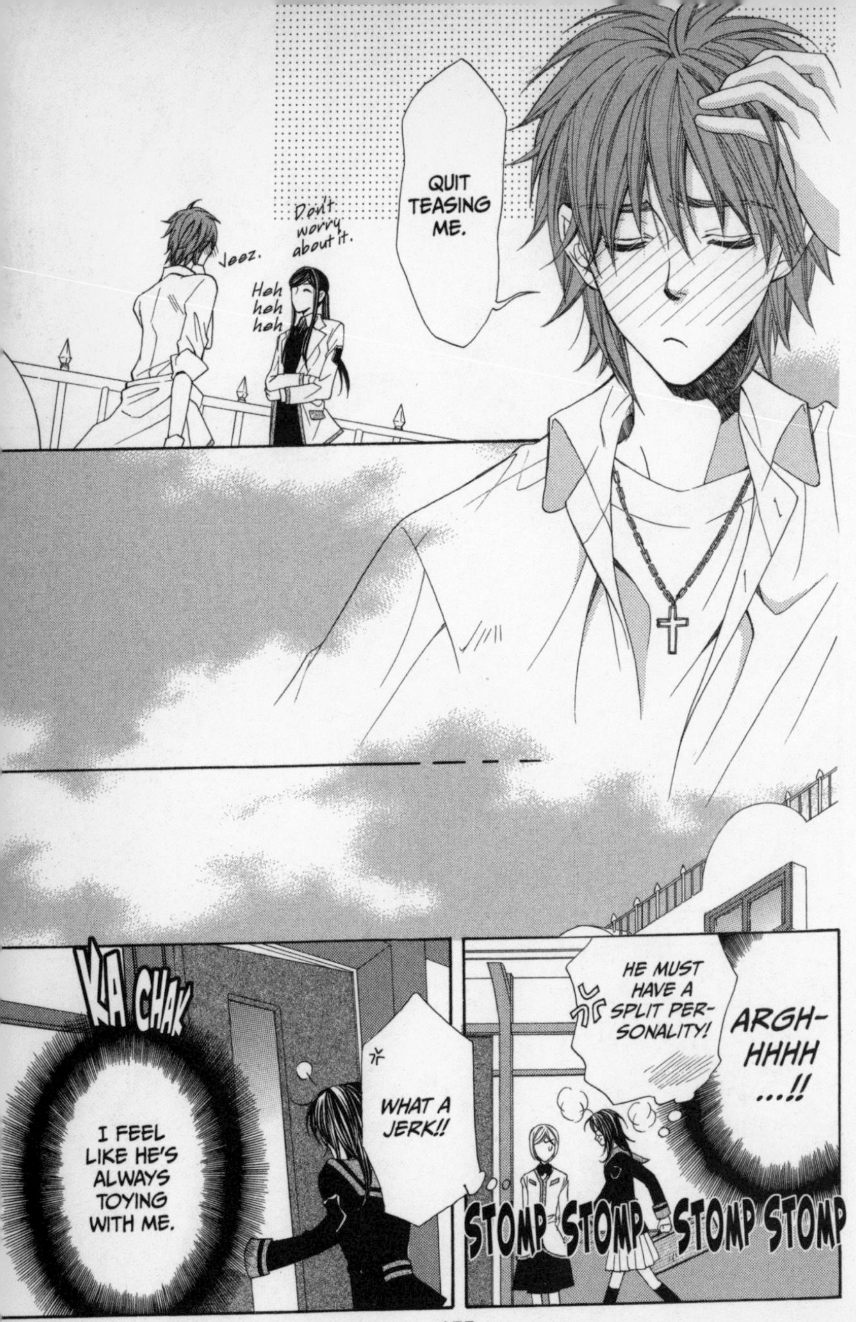
QUIT TEASING ME.
Don't worry about it.
Jeez.
Heh heh heh
ARGH-HHHH ...!!
HE MUST HAVE A SPLIT PER-SONALITY!
STOMP STOMP STOMP STOMP
KA CHAK
WHAT A JERK!!
I FEEL LIKE HE'S ALWAYS TOYING WITH ME.

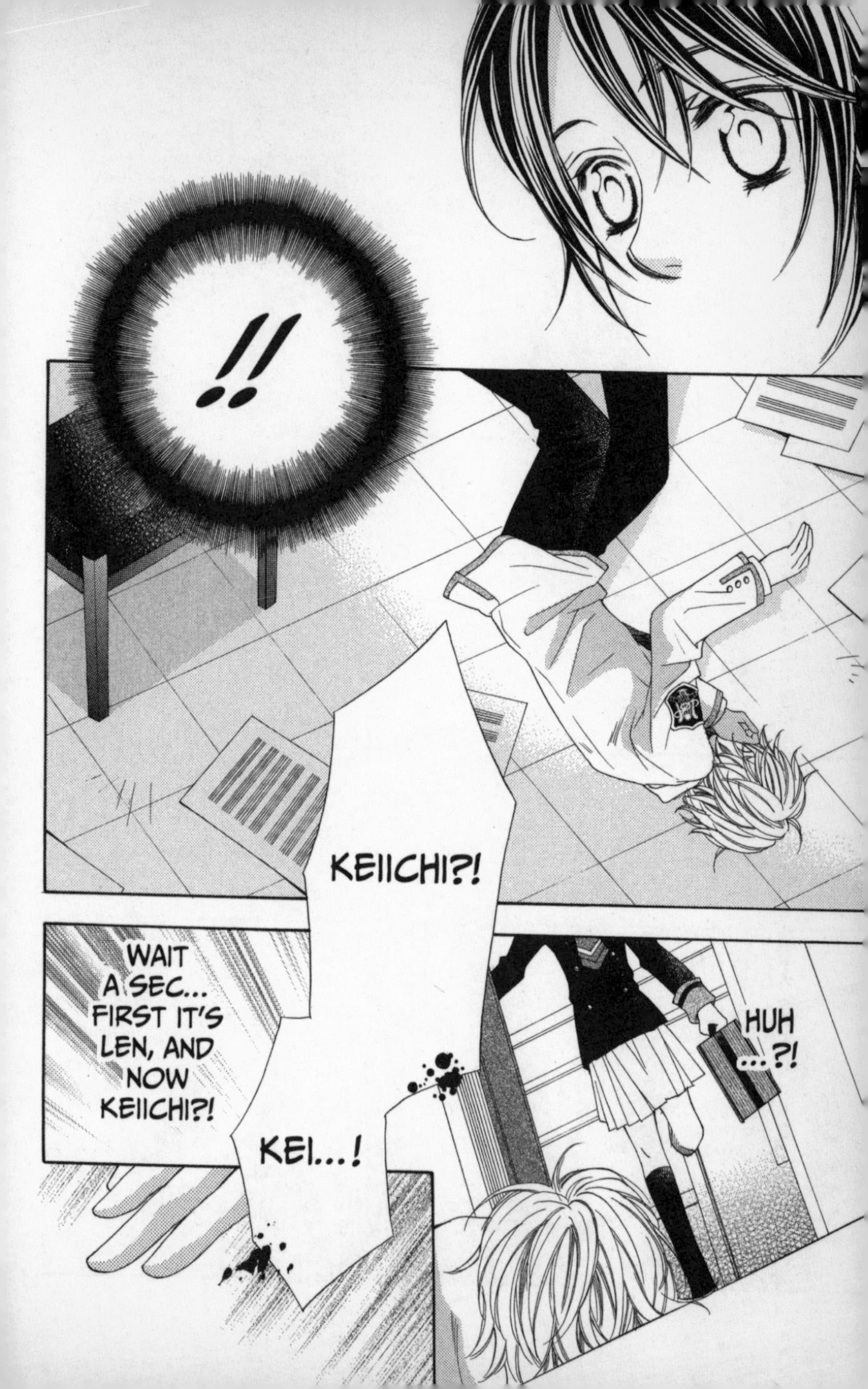
!!
KEIICHI?!
HUH ...?!
KEI...!
WAIT A SEC... FIRST IT'S LEN, AND NOW KEIICHI?!

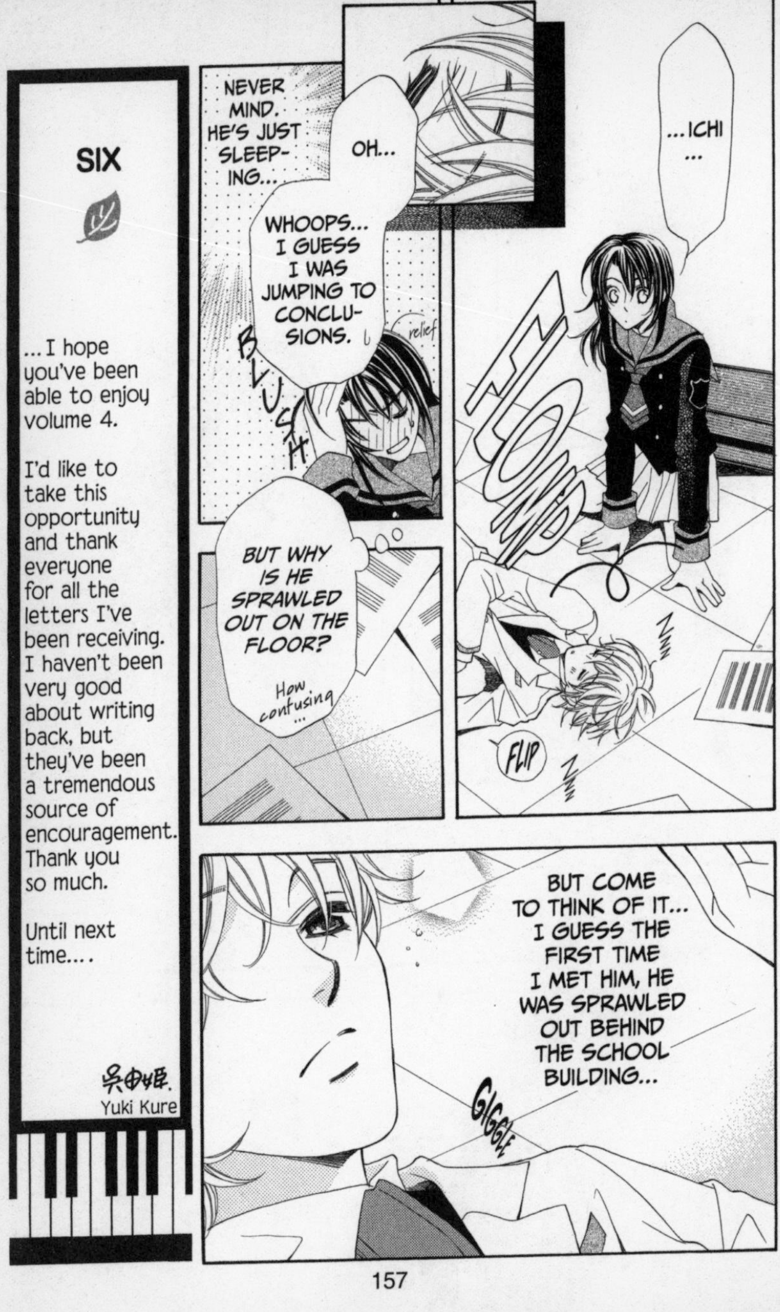
...ICHI ...
FLOMP
ZZZ
FLIP
ZZZ
OH...
NEVER MIND. HE'S JUST SLEEP-ING...
WHOOPS... I GUESS I WAS JUMPING TO CONCLU-SIONS.
relief
BLUSH
BUT WHY IS HE SPRAWLED OUT ON THE FLOOR?
How confusing ...
BUT COME TO THINK OF IT... I GUESS THE FIRST TIME I MET HIM, HE WAS SPRAWLED OUT BEHIND THE SCHOOL BUILDING...
GIGGLE

SIX

...I hope you've been able to enjoy volume 4.

I'd like to take this opportunity and thank everyone for all the letters I've been receiving. I haven't been very good about writing back, but they've been a tremendous source of encouragement. Thank you so much.

Until next time....

呉由姫.
Yuki Kure

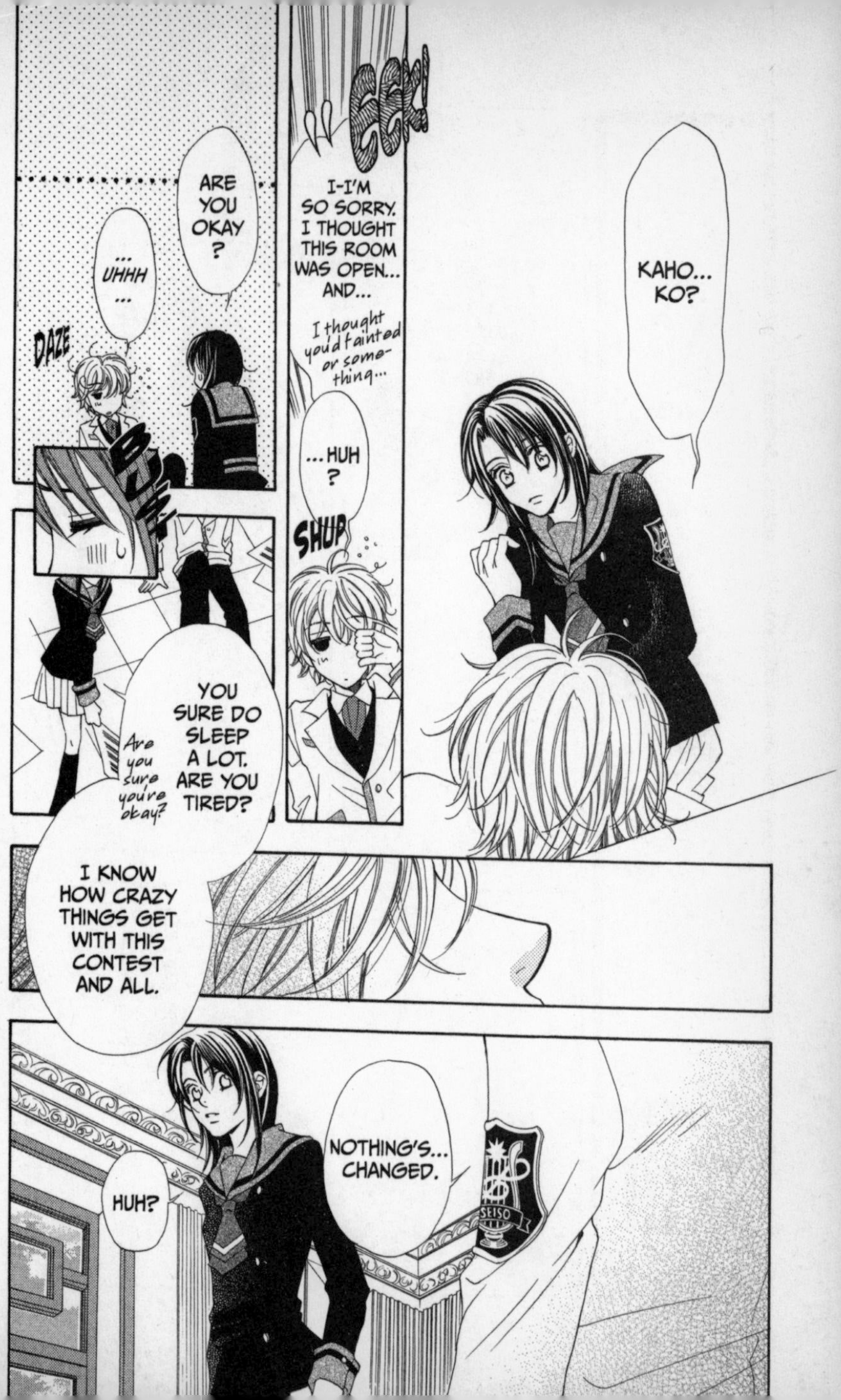
KAHO... KO?
EEK!
I-I'M SO SORRY. I THOUGHT THIS ROOM WAS OPEN... AND...
I thought you'd fainted or something...
...HUH?
SHUP
ARE YOU OKAY?
...UHHH...
DAZE
YOU SURE DO SLEEP A LOT. ARE YOU TIRED?
Are you sure you're okay?
I KNOW HOW CRAZY THINGS GET WITH THIS CONTEST AND ALL.
NOTHING'S... CHANGED.
HUH?
SEISO

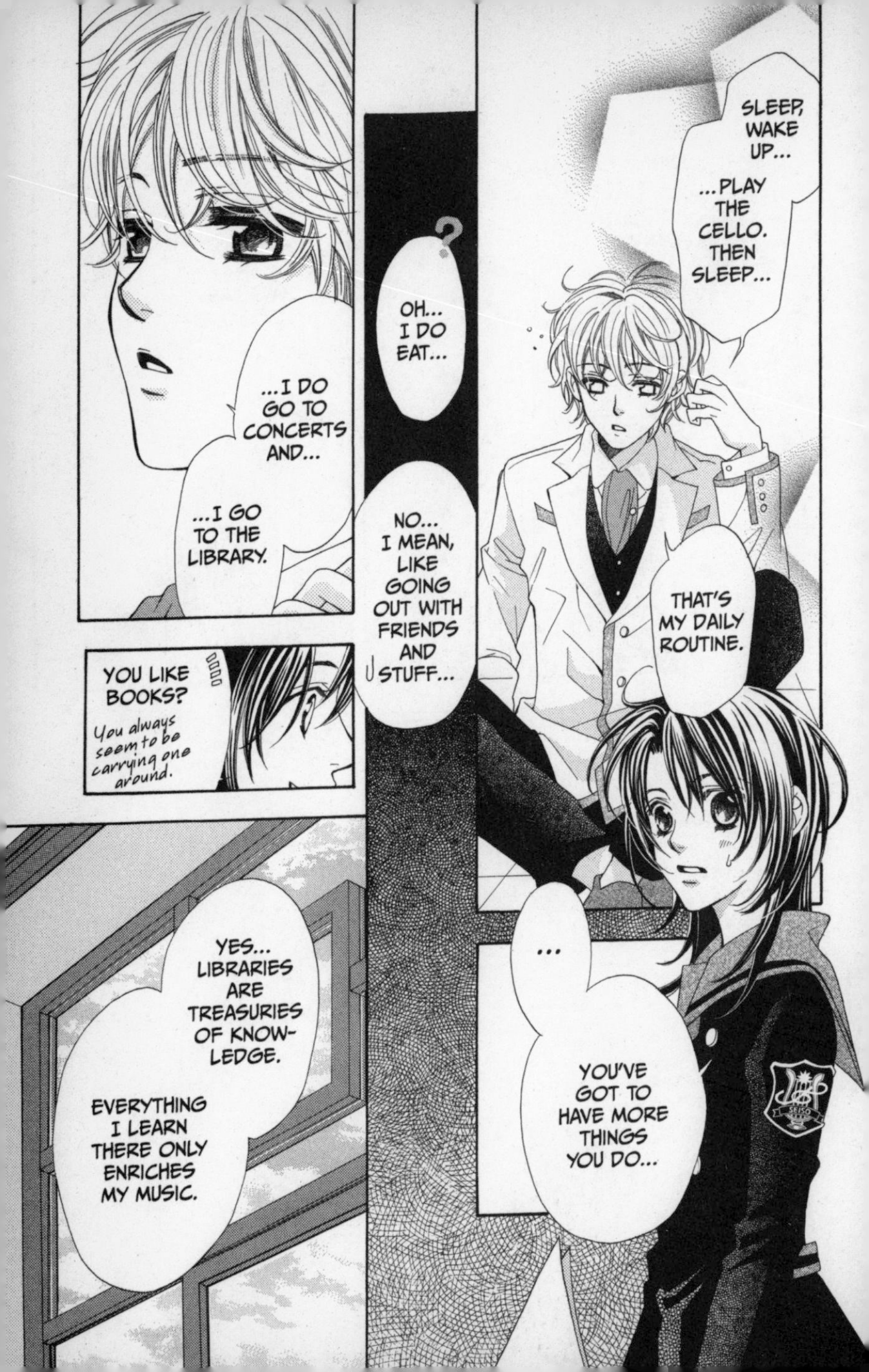
SLEEP, WAKE UP...
...PLAY THE CELLO. THEN SLEEP...
THAT'S MY DAILY ROUTINE.
...
YOU'VE GOT TO HAVE MORE THINGS YOU DO...
?
OH... I DO EAT...
NO... I MEAN, LIKE GOING OUT WITH FRIENDS AND STUFF...
...I DO GO TO CONCERTS AND...
...I GO TO THE LIBRARY.
YOU LIKE BOOKS?
You always seem to be carrying one around.
YES... LIBRARIES ARE TREASURIES OF KNOW-LEDGE.
EVERYTHING I LEARN THERE ONLY ENRICHES MY MUSIC.

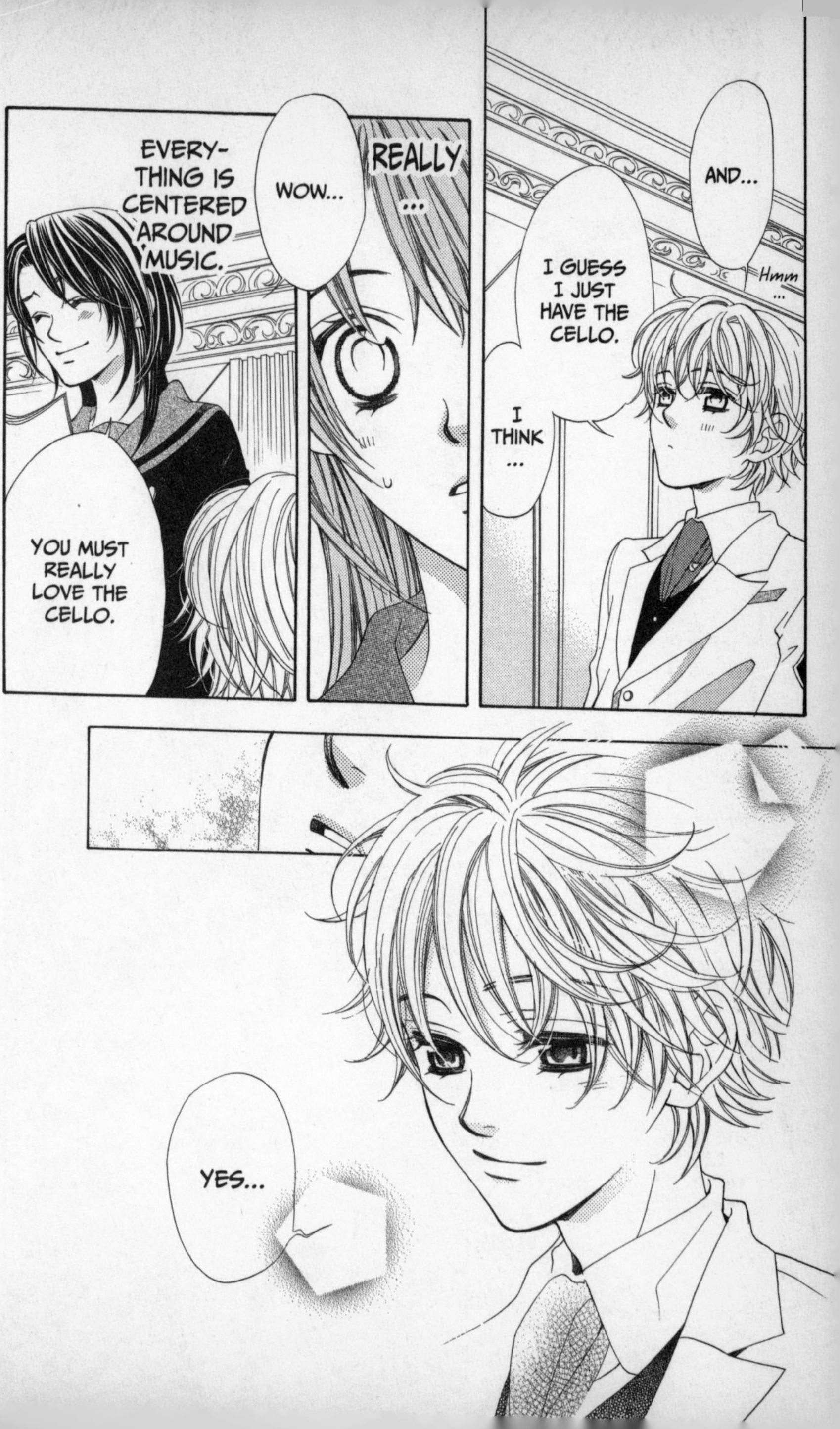
AND...
Hmm...
I GUESS I JUST HAVE THE CELLO.
I THINK...
REALLY...
WOW...
EVERY-THING IS CENTERED AROUND MUSIC.
YOU MUST REALLY LOVE THE CELLO.
YES...

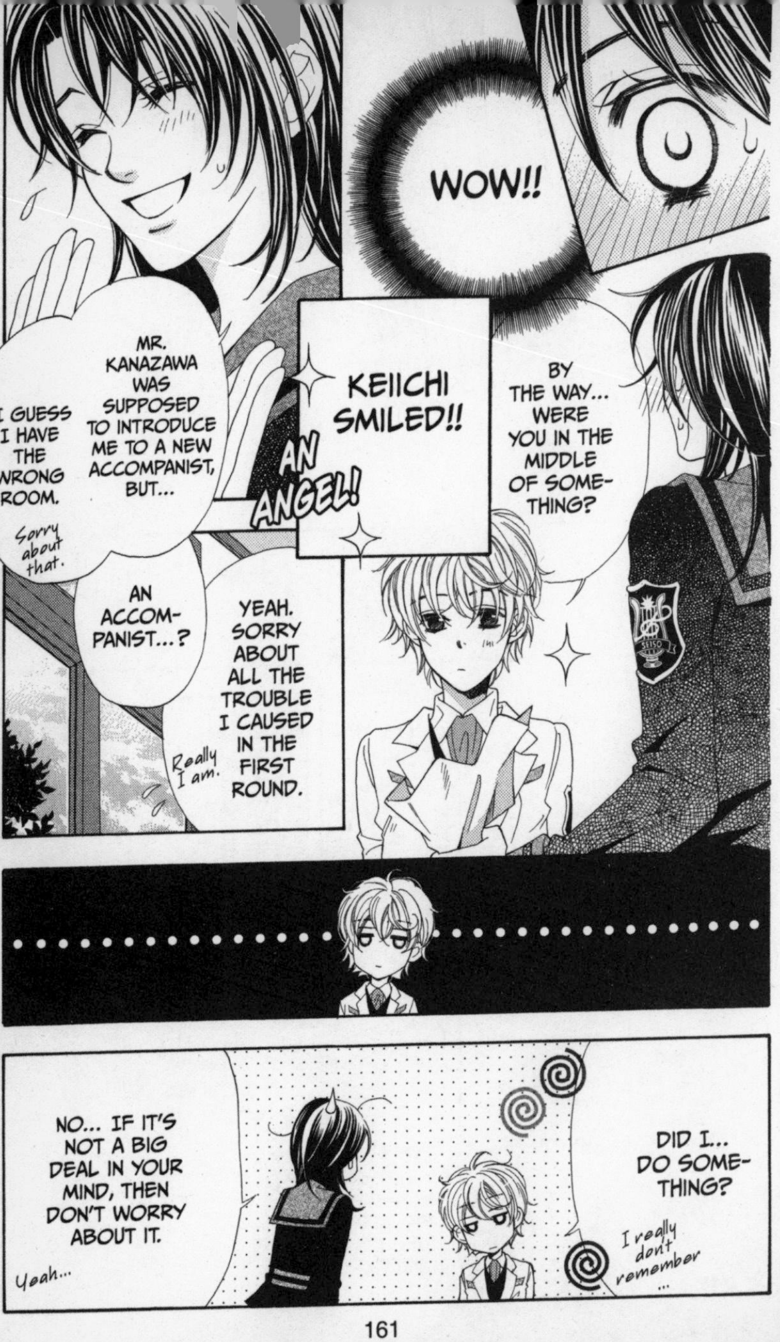
WOW!!
BY THE WAY... WERE YOU IN THE MIDDLE OF SOME-THING?
KEIICHI SMILED!!
AN ANGEL!
MR. KANAZAWA WAS SUPPOSED TO INTRODUCE ME TO A NEW ACCOMPANIST, BUT...
I GUESS I HAVE THE WRONG ROOM.
Sorry about that.
AN ACCOM-PANIST...?
YEAH. SORRY ABOUT ALL THE TROUBLE I CAUSED IN THE FIRST ROUND.
Really I am.
DID I... DO SOME-THING?
I really don't remember ...
NO... IF IT'S NOT A BIG DEAL IN YOUR MIND, THEN DON'T WORRY ABOUT IT.
Yeah...

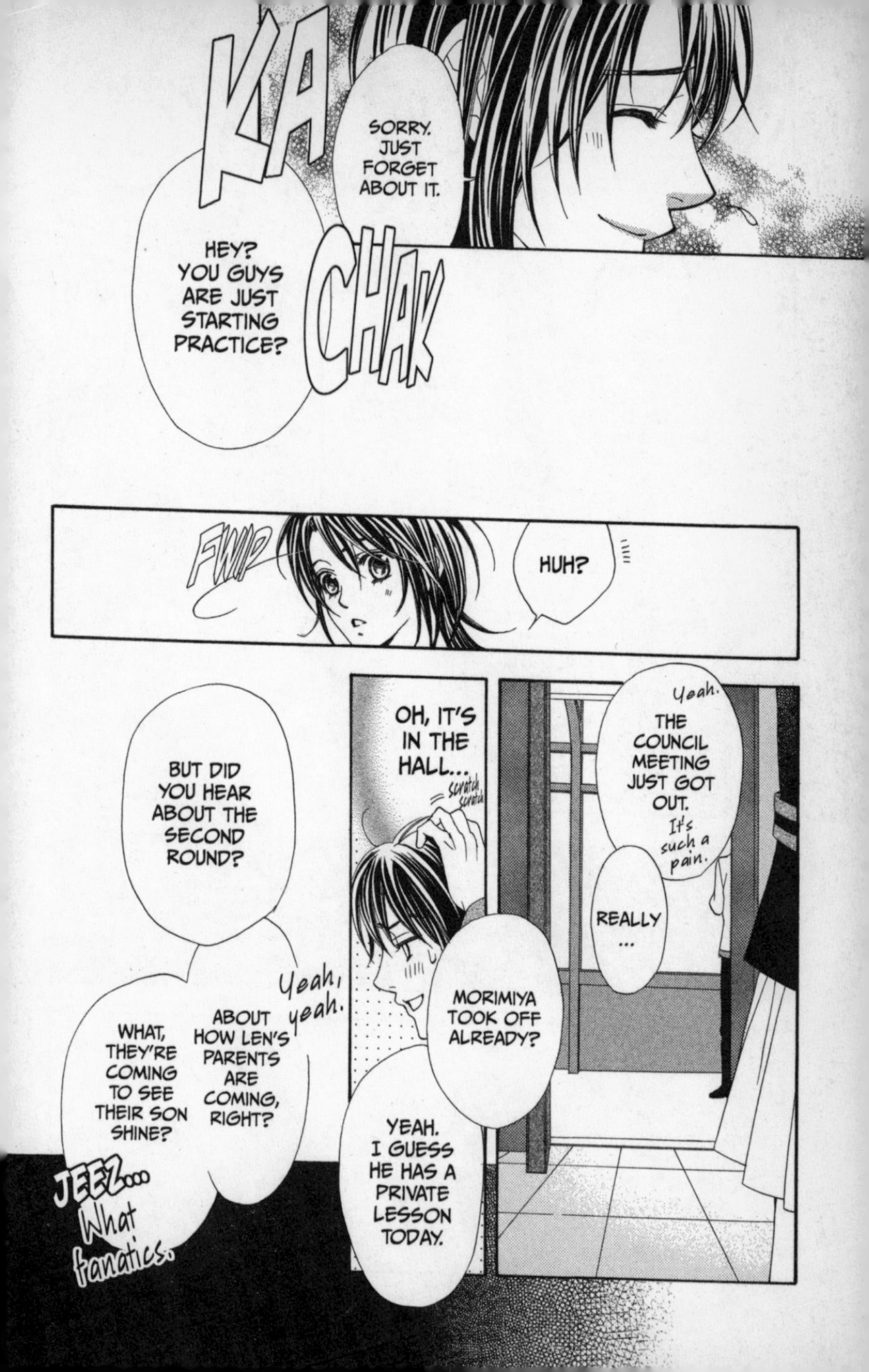

SORRY. JUST FORGET ABOUT IT.
KA
CHAK
HEY? YOU GUYS ARE JUST STARTING PRACTICE?
HUH?
FWIP
Yeah.
THE COUNCIL MEETING JUST GOT OUT.
It's such a pain.
REALLY...
OH, IT'S IN THE HALL...
scratch scratch
MORIMIYA TOOK OFF ALREADY?
YEAH. I GUESS HE HAS A PRIVATE LESSON TODAY.
BUT DID YOU HEAR ABOUT THE SECOND ROUND?
ABOUT HOW LEN'S PARENTS ARE COMING, RIGHT?
Yeah, yeah.
WHAT, THEY'RE COMING TO SEE THEIR SON SHINE?
JEEZ... What fanatics.

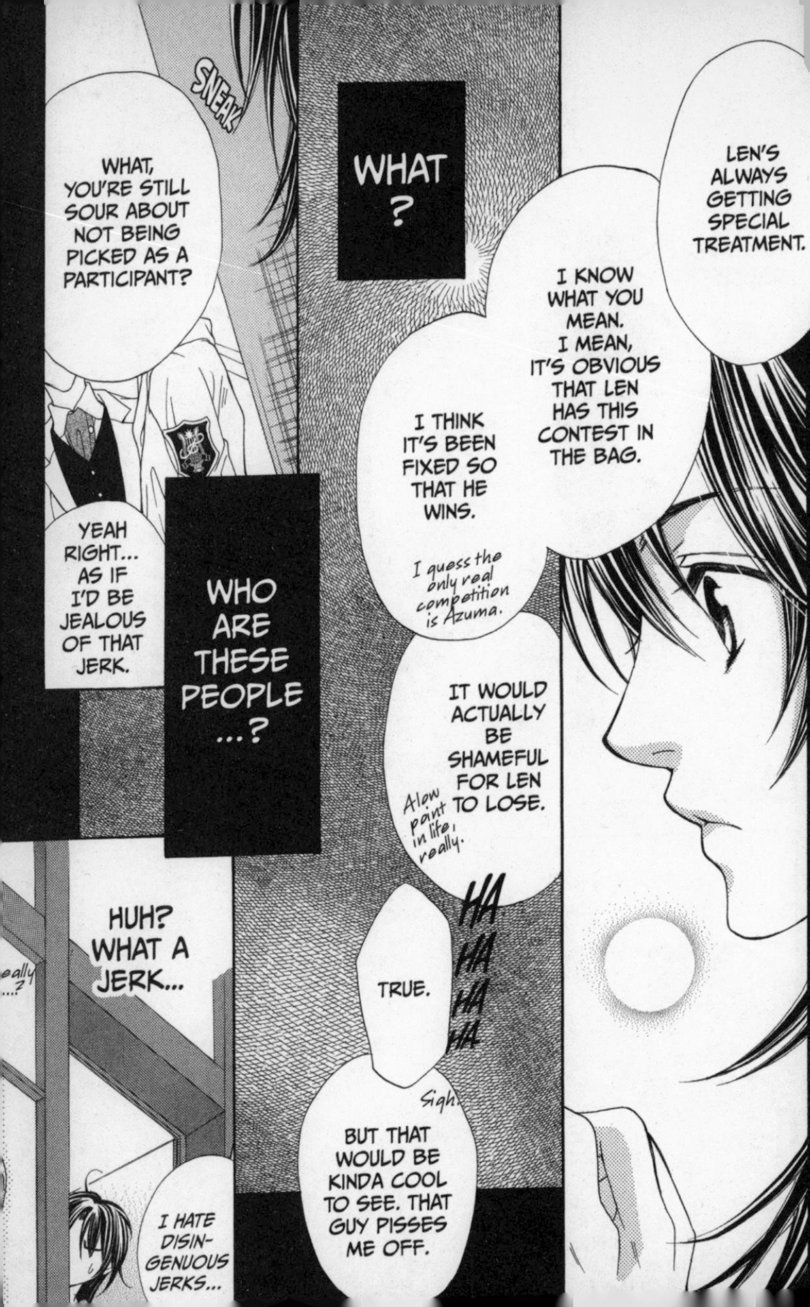
LEN'S ALWAYS GETTING SPECIAL TREATMENT.
I KNOW WHAT YOU MEAN. I MEAN, IT'S OBVIOUS THAT LEN HAS THIS CONTEST IN THE BAG.
I THINK IT'S BEEN FIXED SO THAT HE WINS.
I guess the only real competition is Azuma.
IT WOULD ACTUALLY BE SHAMEFUL FOR LEN TO LOSE.
A low point in life, really.
HA HA HA HA
TRUE.
Sigh.
BUT THAT WOULD BE KINDA COOL TO SEE. THAT GUY PISSES ME OFF.
WHAT ?
WHO ARE THESE PEOPLE ...?
SNEAK
WHAT, YOU'RE STILL SOUR ABOUT NOT BEING PICKED AS A PARTICIPANT?
YEAH RIGHT... AS IF I'D BE JEALOUS OF THAT JERK.
HUH? WHAT A JERK...
I HATE DISIN-GENUOUS JERKS...

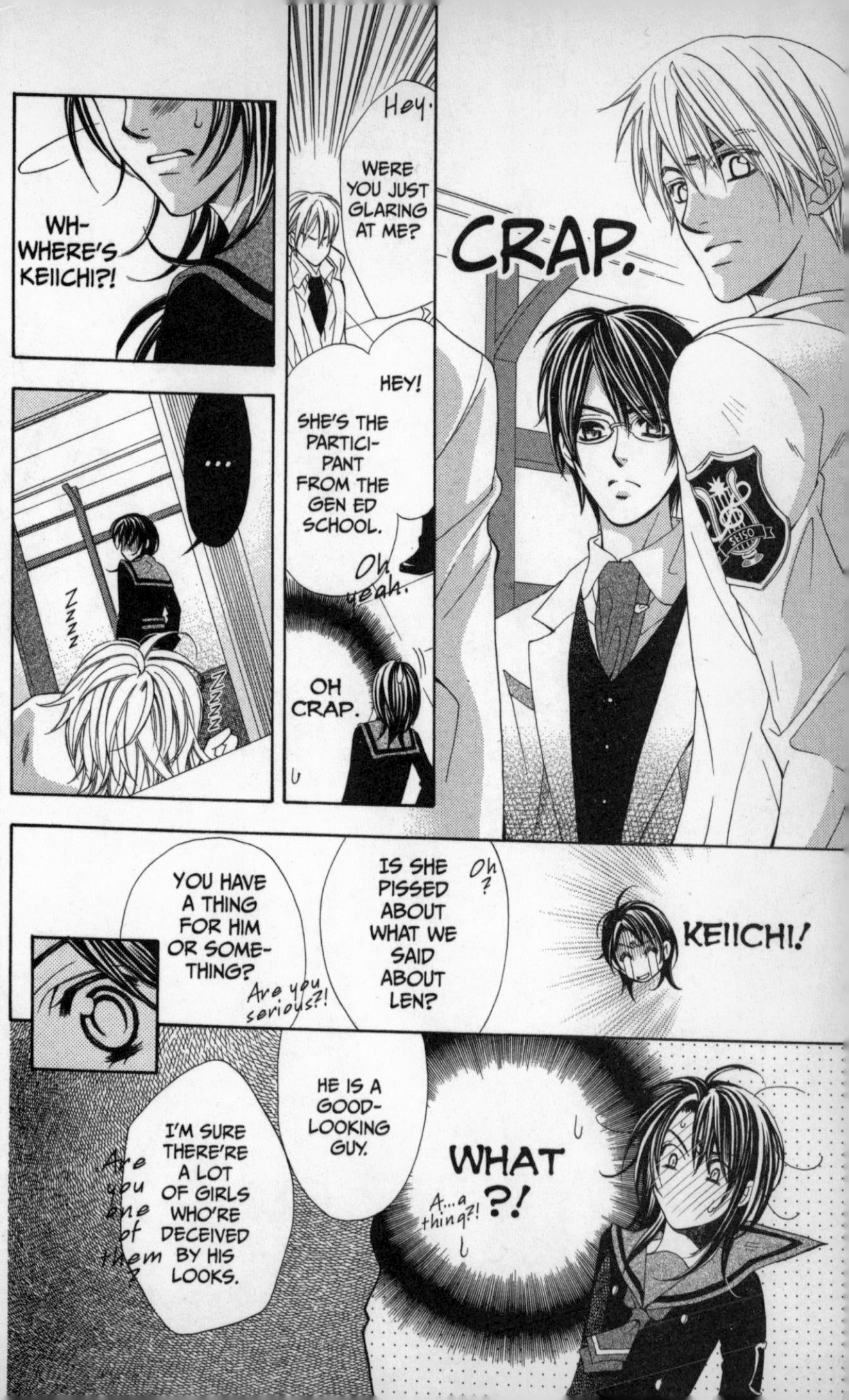
CRAP.
Hey.
WERE YOU JUST GLARING AT ME?
HEY!
SHE'S THE PARTICIPANT FROM THE GEN ED SCHOOL.
Oh yeah.
OH CRAP.
WH- WHERE'S KEIICHI?!
...
Zzzz
Zzzz
KEIICHI!
Oh?
IS SHE PISSED ABOUT WHAT WE SAID ABOUT LEN?
YOU HAVE A THING FOR HIM OR SOMETHING?
Are you serious?!
WHAT?!
A...a thing?!
HE IS A GOOD-LOOKING GUY.
I'M SURE THERE'RE A LOT OF GIRLS WHO'RE DECEIVED BY HIS LOOKS.
Are you one of them?

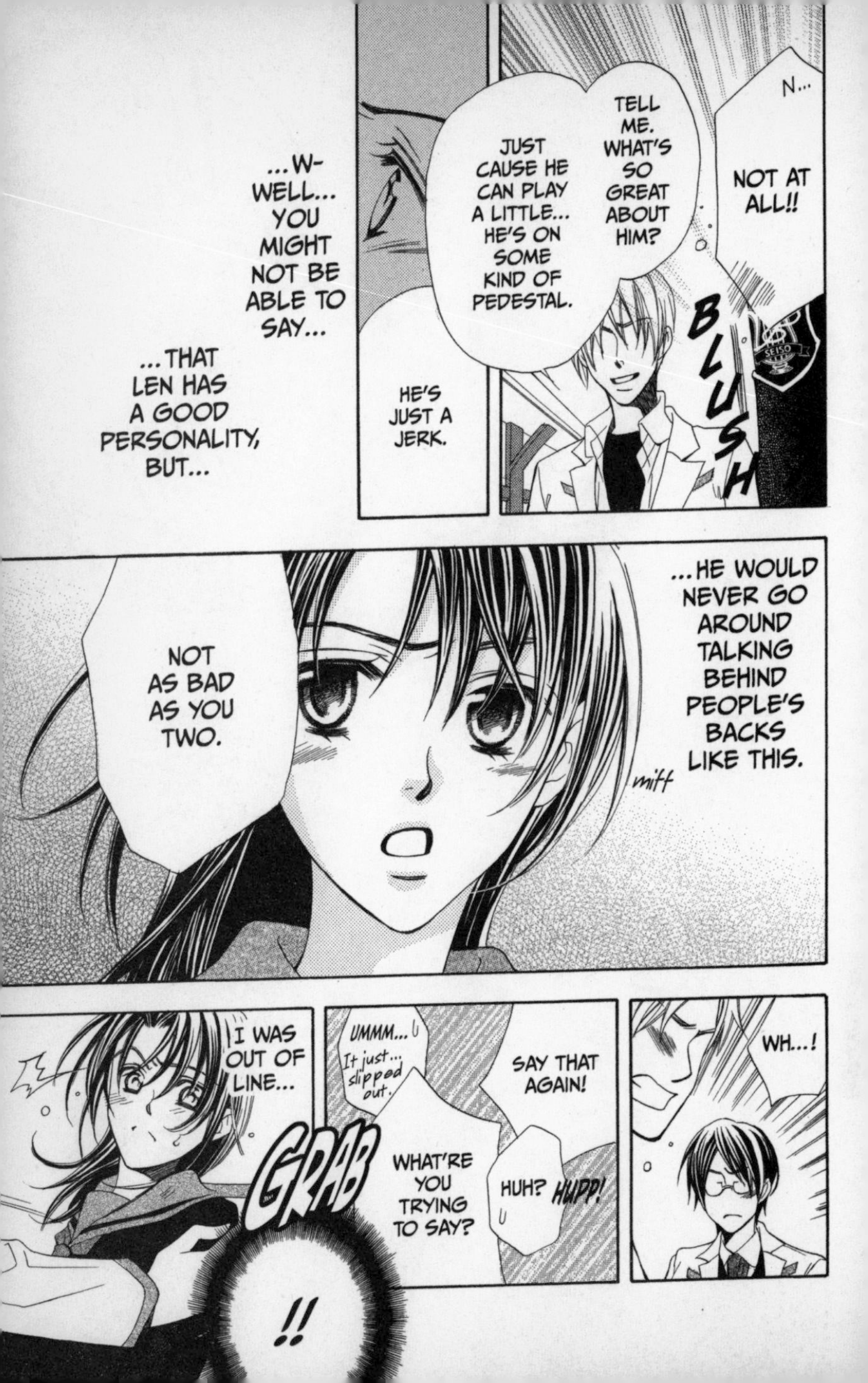
N...
NOT AT ALL!!
BLUSH
TELL ME. WHAT'S SO GREAT ABOUT HIM?
JUST CAUSE HE CAN PLAY A LITTLE... HE'S ON SOME KIND OF PEDESTAL.
HE'S JUST A JERK.
...W-WELL... YOU MIGHT NOT BE ABLE TO SAY...
...THAT LEN HAS A GOOD PERSONALITY, BUT...
...HE WOULD NEVER GO AROUND TALKING BEHIND PEOPLE'S BACKS LIKE THIS.
miff
NOT AS BAD AS YOU TWO.
WH...!
SAY THAT AGAIN!
UMMM...
It just... slipped out.
WHAT'RE YOU TRYING TO SAY?
HUH? HUPP!
I WAS OUT OF LINE...
GRAB
!!

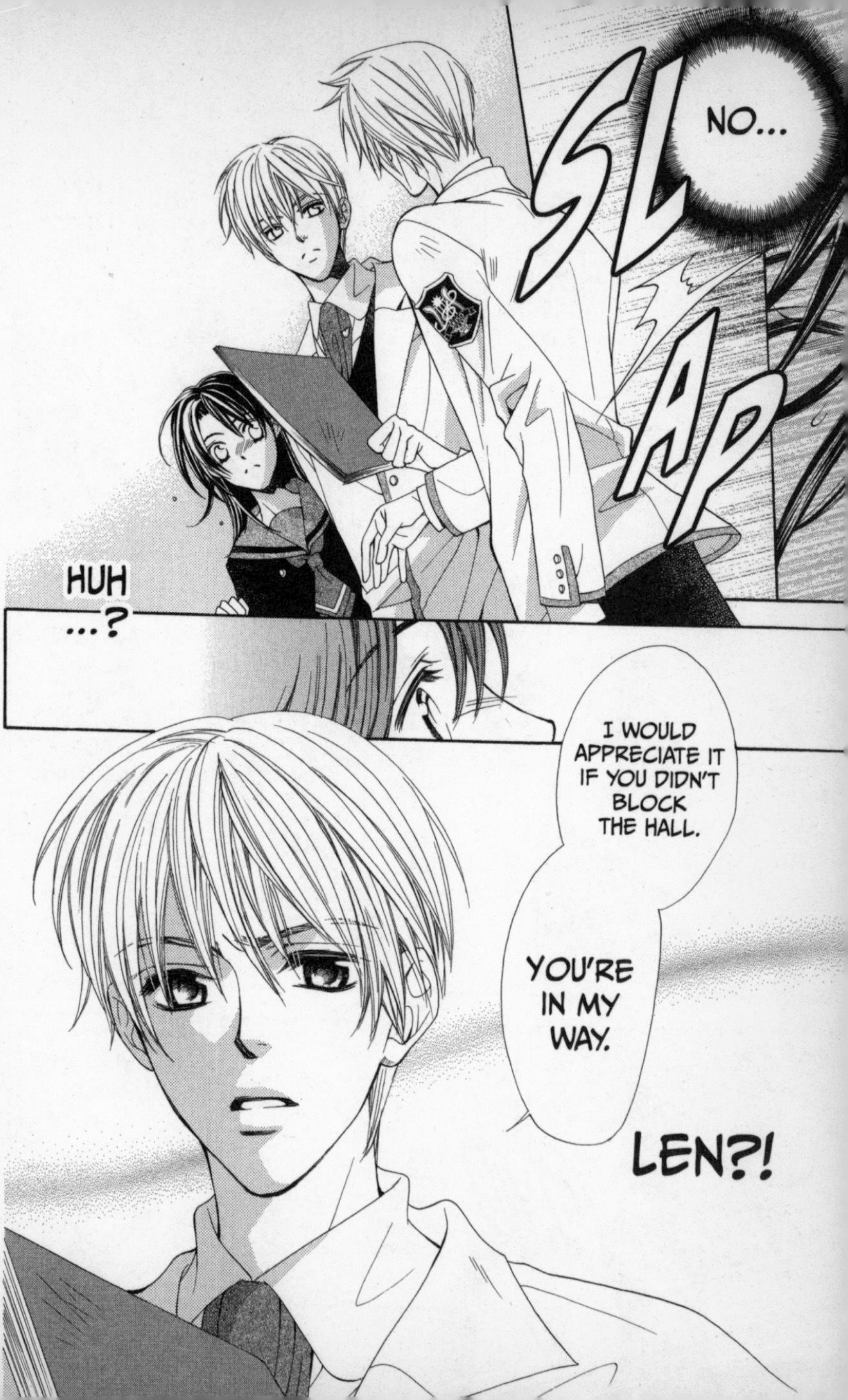
NO...
SLAP
HUH ...?
I WOULD APPRECIATE IT IF YOU DIDN'T BLOCK THE HALL.
YOU'RE IN MY WAY.
LEN?!

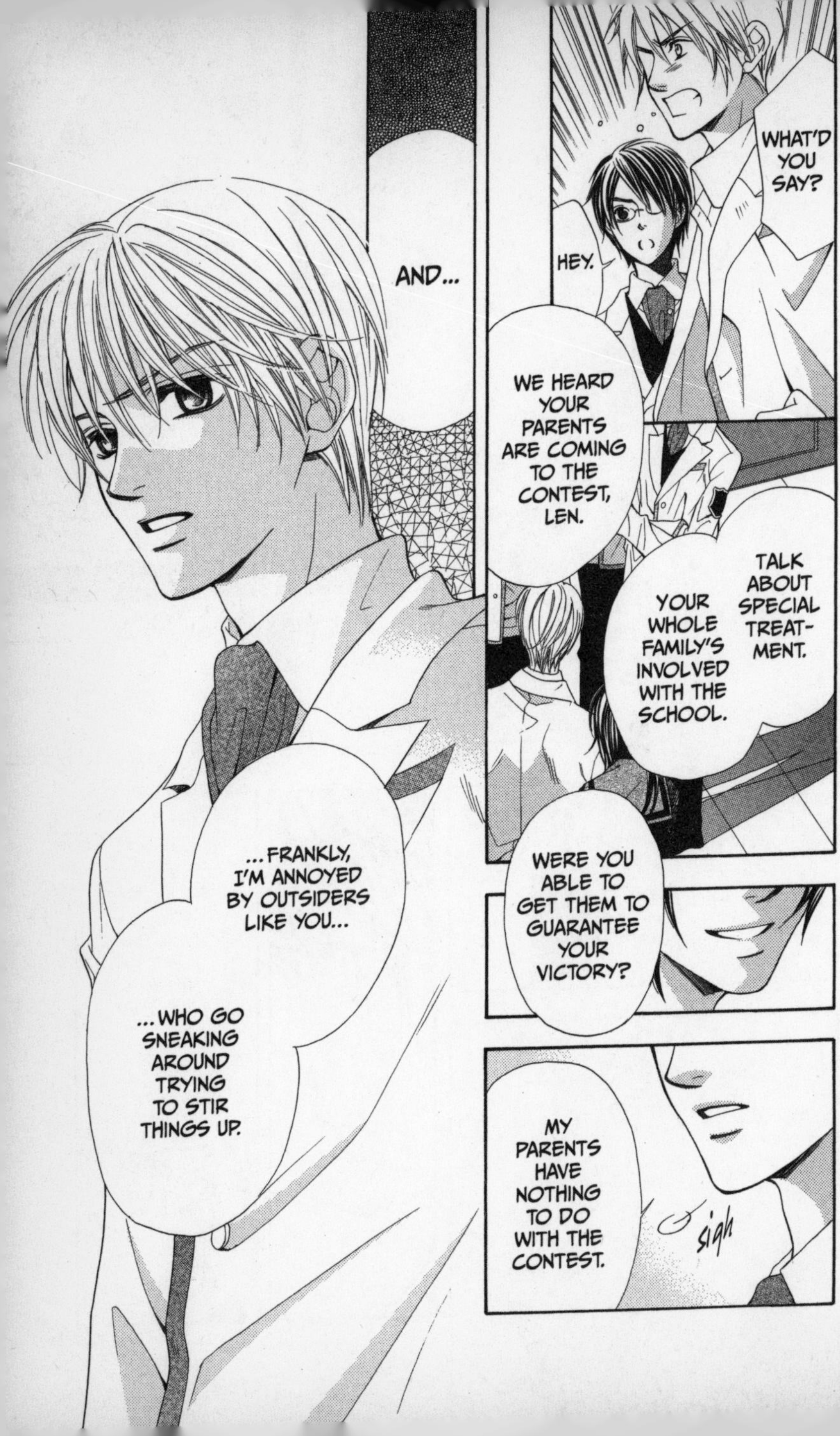
WHAT'D YOU SAY?
HEY.
WE HEARD YOUR PARENTS ARE COMING TO THE CONTEST, LEN.
TALK ABOUT SPECIAL TREATMENT.
YOUR WHOLE FAMILY'S INVOLVED WITH THE SCHOOL.
WERE YOU ABLE TO GET THEM TO GUARANTEE YOUR VICTORY?
sigh
MY PARENTS HAVE NOTHING TO DO WITH THE CONTEST.
AND...
...FRANKLY, I'M ANNOYED BY OUTSIDERS LIKE YOU...
...WHO GO SNEAKING AROUND TRYING TO STIR THINGS UP.

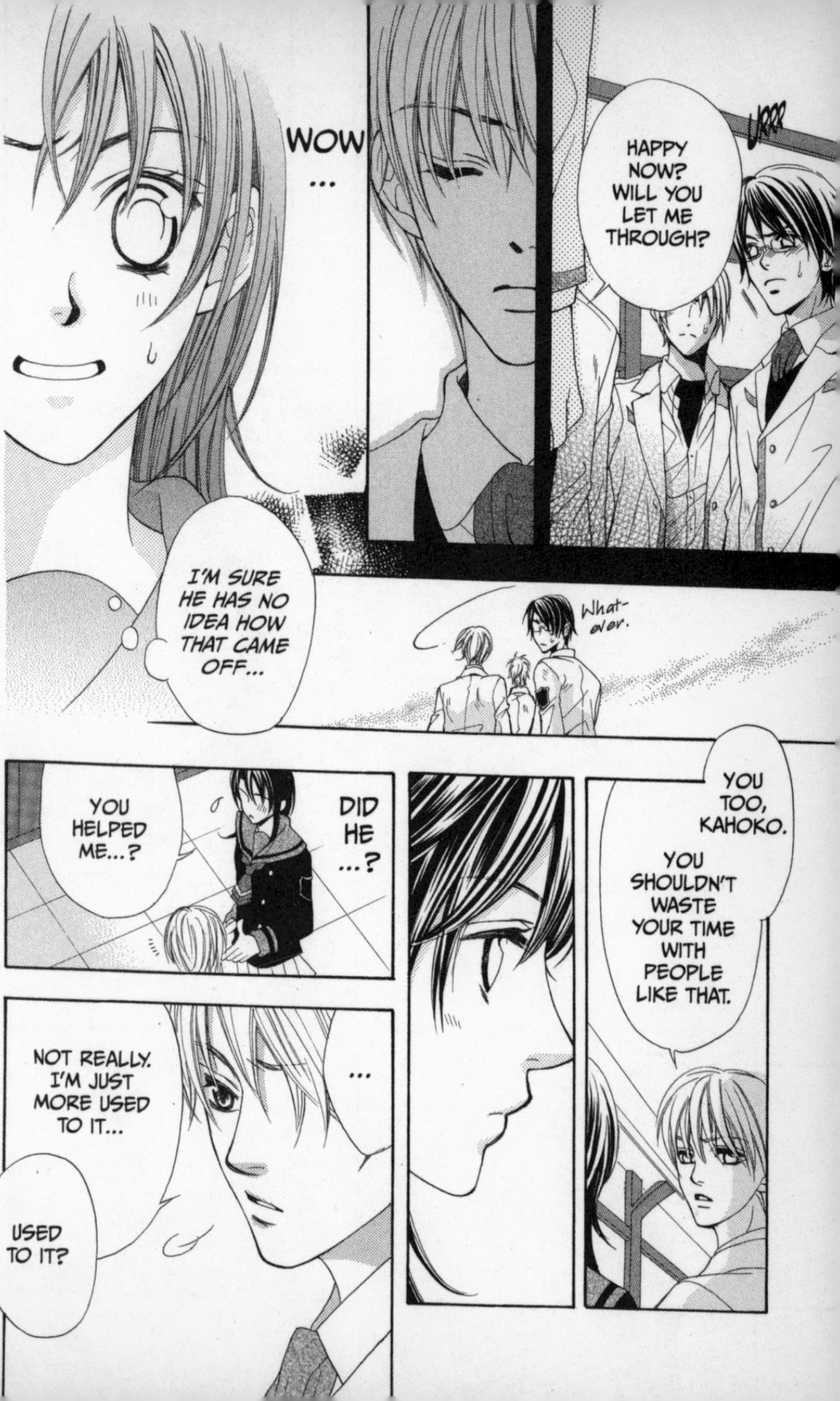
URRR
HAPPY NOW? WILL YOU LET ME THROUGH?
What-ever.
WOW ...
I'M SURE HE HAS NO IDEA HOW THAT CAME OFF...
YOU TOO, KAHOKO.
YOU SHOULDN'T WASTE YOUR TIME WITH PEOPLE LIKE THAT.
DID HE ...?
YOU HELPED ME...?
...
NOT REALLY. I'M JUST MORE USED TO IT...
USED TO IT?

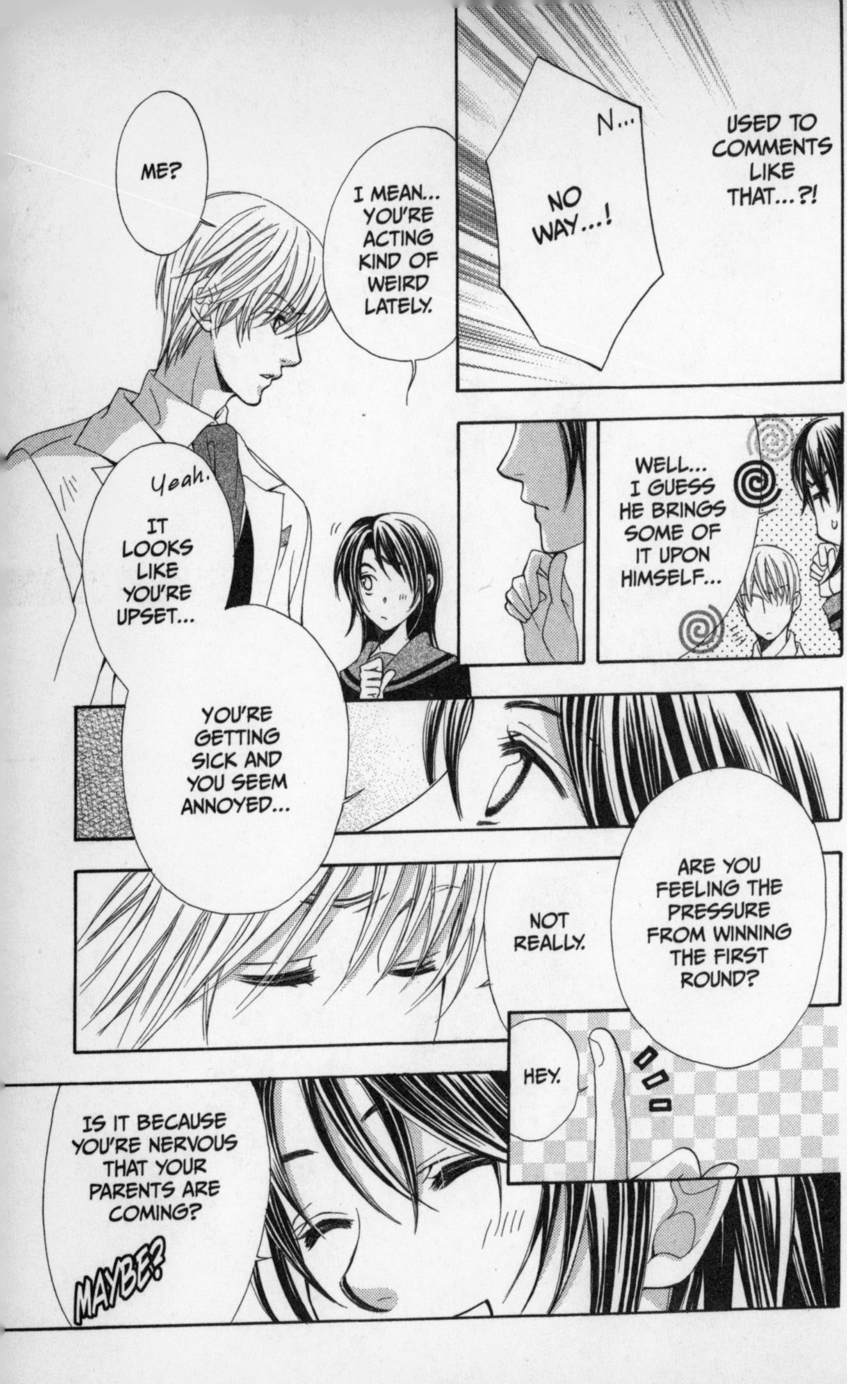
USED TO COMMENTS LIKE THAT...?!
N...
NO WAY...!
WELL... I GUESS HE BRINGS SOME OF IT UPON HIMSELF...
ME?
I MEAN... YOU'RE ACTING KIND OF WEIRD LATELY.
Yeah.
IT LOOKS LIKE YOU'RE UPSET...
YOU'RE GETTING SICK AND YOU SEEM ANNOYED...
ARE YOU FEELING THE PRESSURE FROM WINNING THE FIRST ROUND?
NOT REALLY.
HEY.
IS IT BECAUSE YOU'RE NERVOUS THAT YOUR PARENTS ARE COMING?
MAYBE?

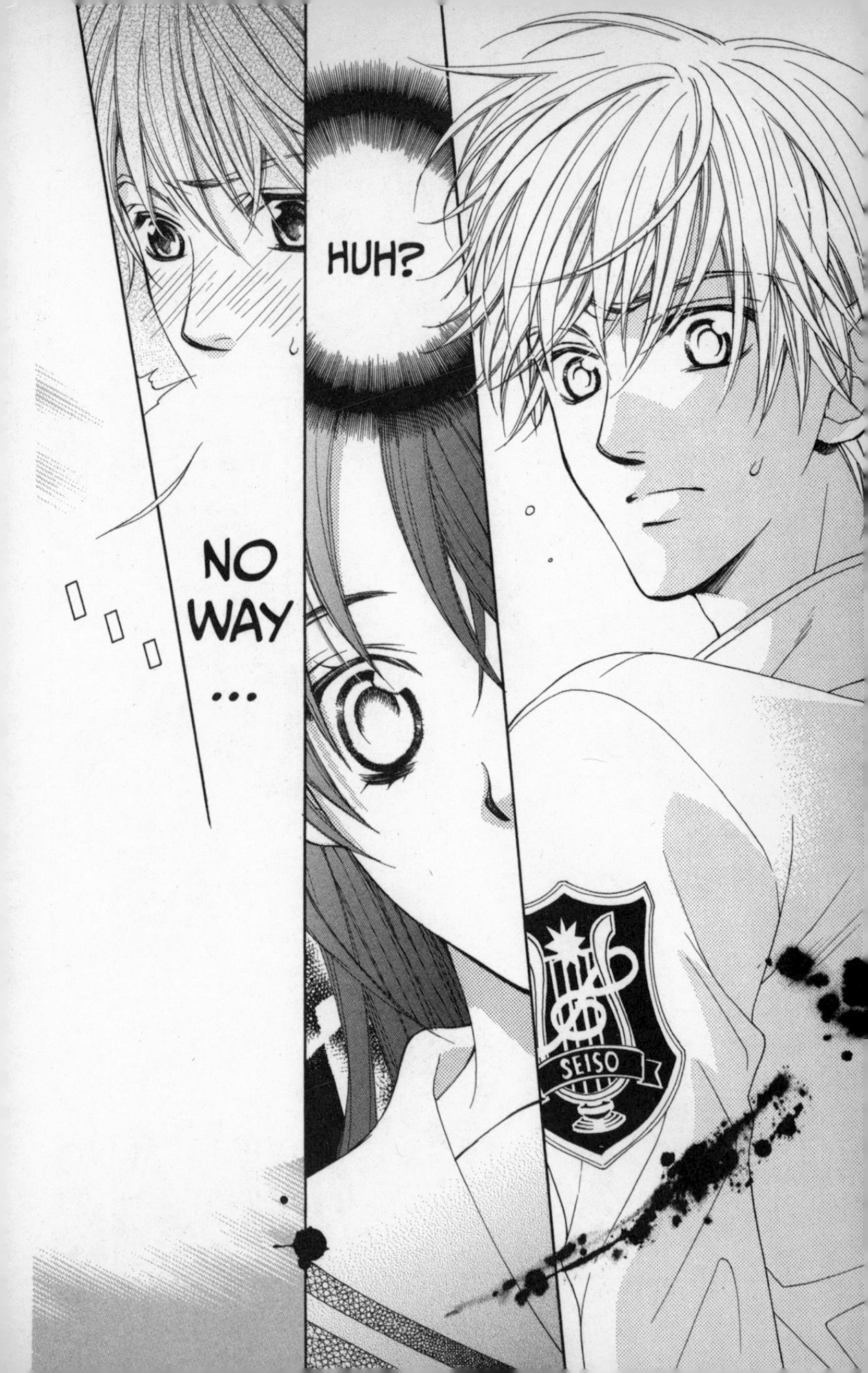
HUH?
NO WAY ...

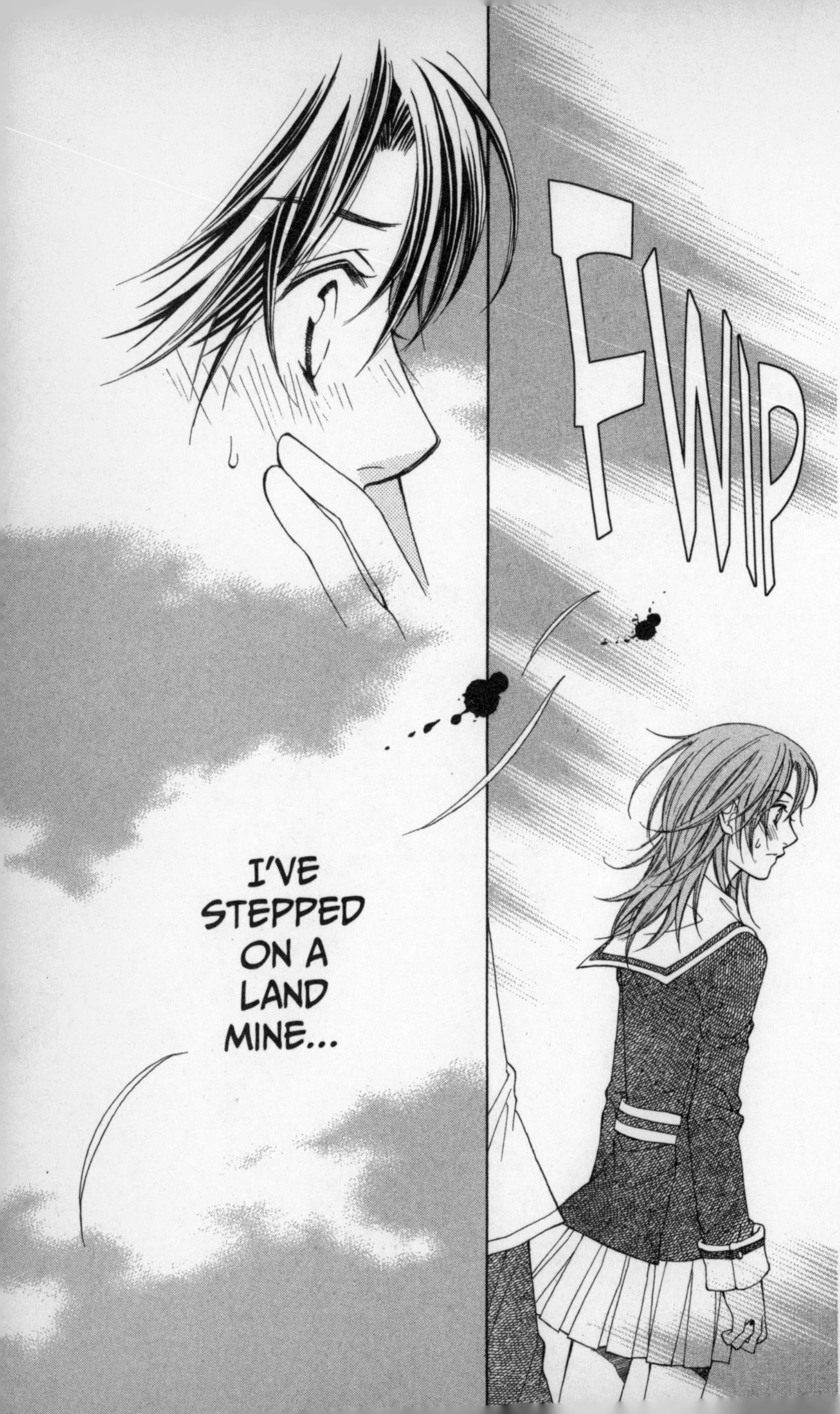
FWIP
I'VE STEPPED ON A LAND MINE...

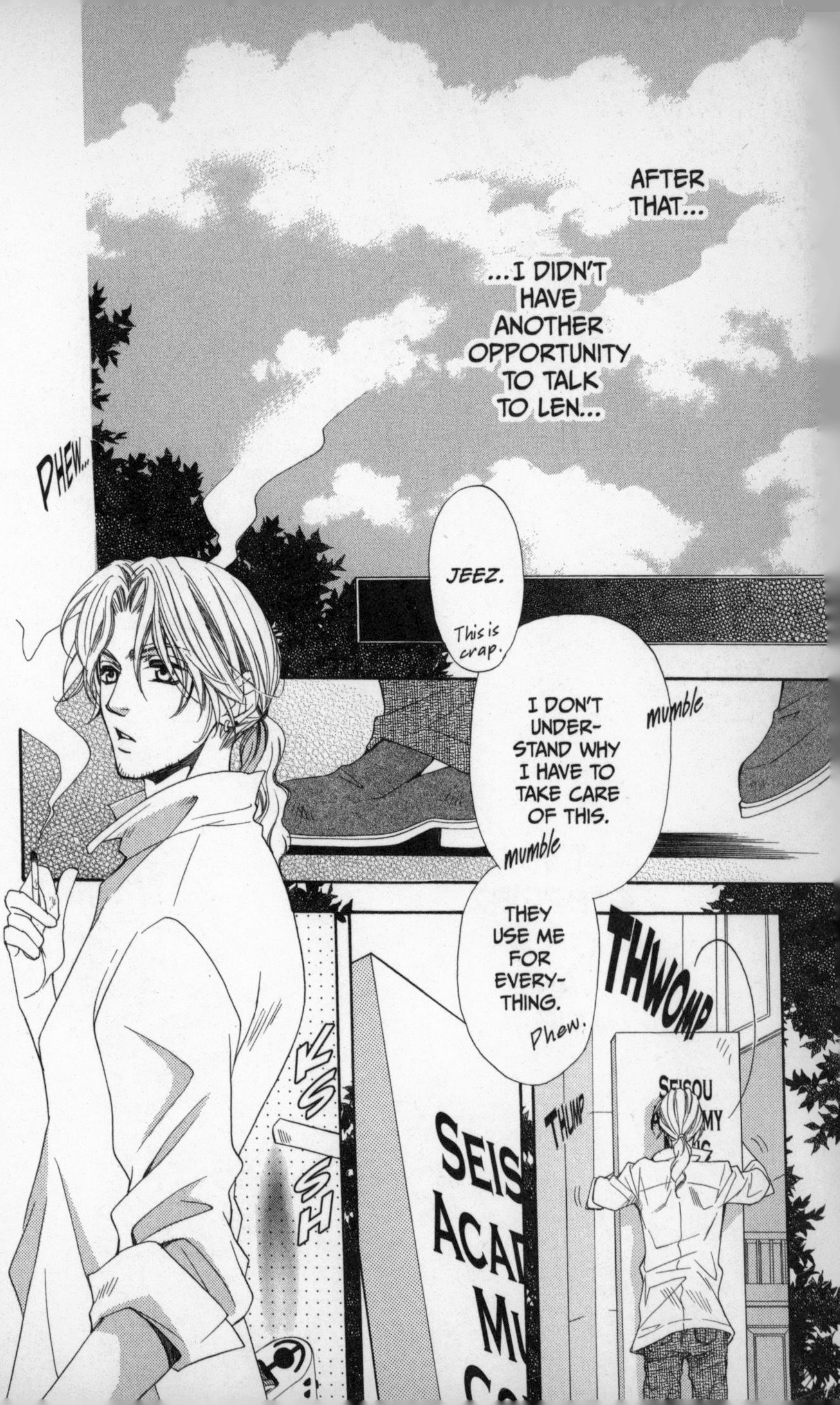
AFTER THAT...
...I DIDN'T HAVE ANOTHER OPPORTUNITY TO TALK TO LEN...
PHEW...
JEEZ.
This is crap.
I DON'T UNDERSTAND WHY I HAVE TO TAKE CARE OF THIS.
mumble
mumble
THEY USE ME FOR EVERYTHING.
Phew.
THWOMP
THUMP

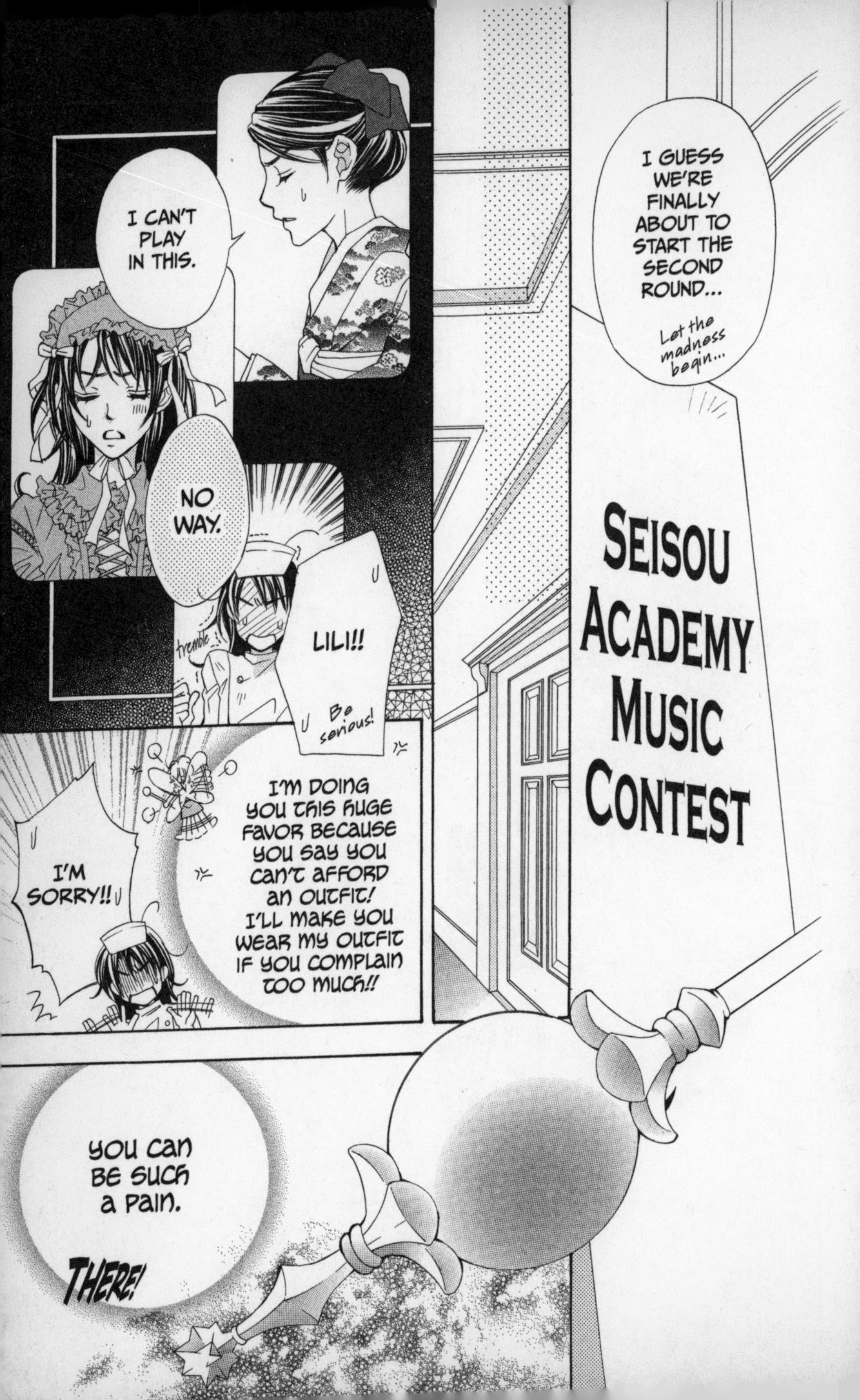
I GUESS WE'RE FINALLY ABOUT TO START THE SECOND ROUND...
Let the madness begin...
SEISOU ACADEMY MUSIC CONTEST
I CAN'T PLAY IN THIS.
NO WAY.
tremble
LILI!!
Be serious!
I'M DOING YOU THIS HUGE FAVOR BECAUSE YOU SAY YOU CAN'T AFFORD AN OUTFIT! I'LL MAKE YOU WEAR MY OUTFIT IF YOU COMPLAIN TOO MUCH!!
I'M SORRY!!
YOU CAN BE SUCH A PAIN.
THERE!

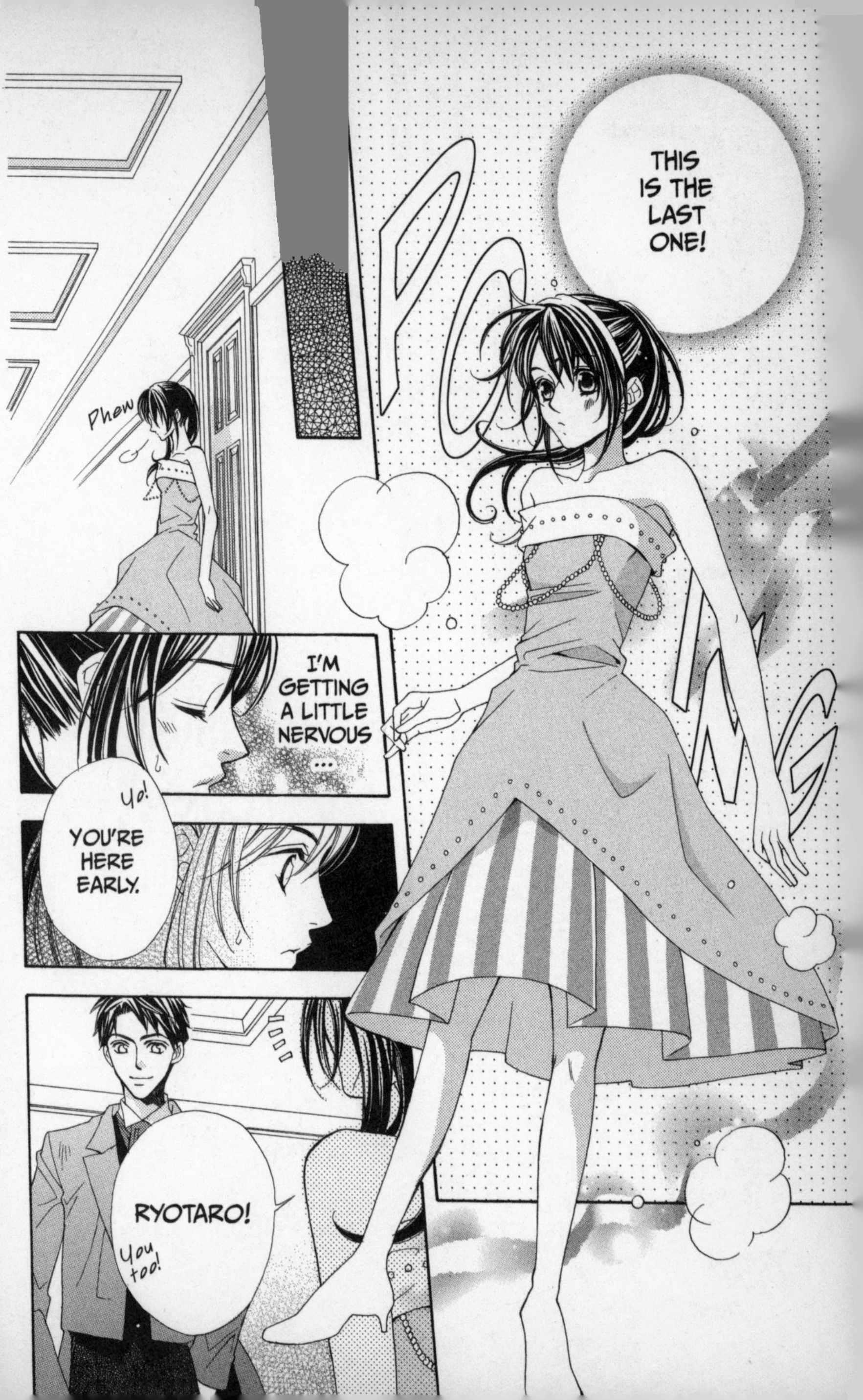
THIS IS THE LAST ONE!
Phew
I'M GETTING A LITTLE NERVOUS...
Yo!
YOU'RE HERE EARLY.
RYOTARO!
You too!

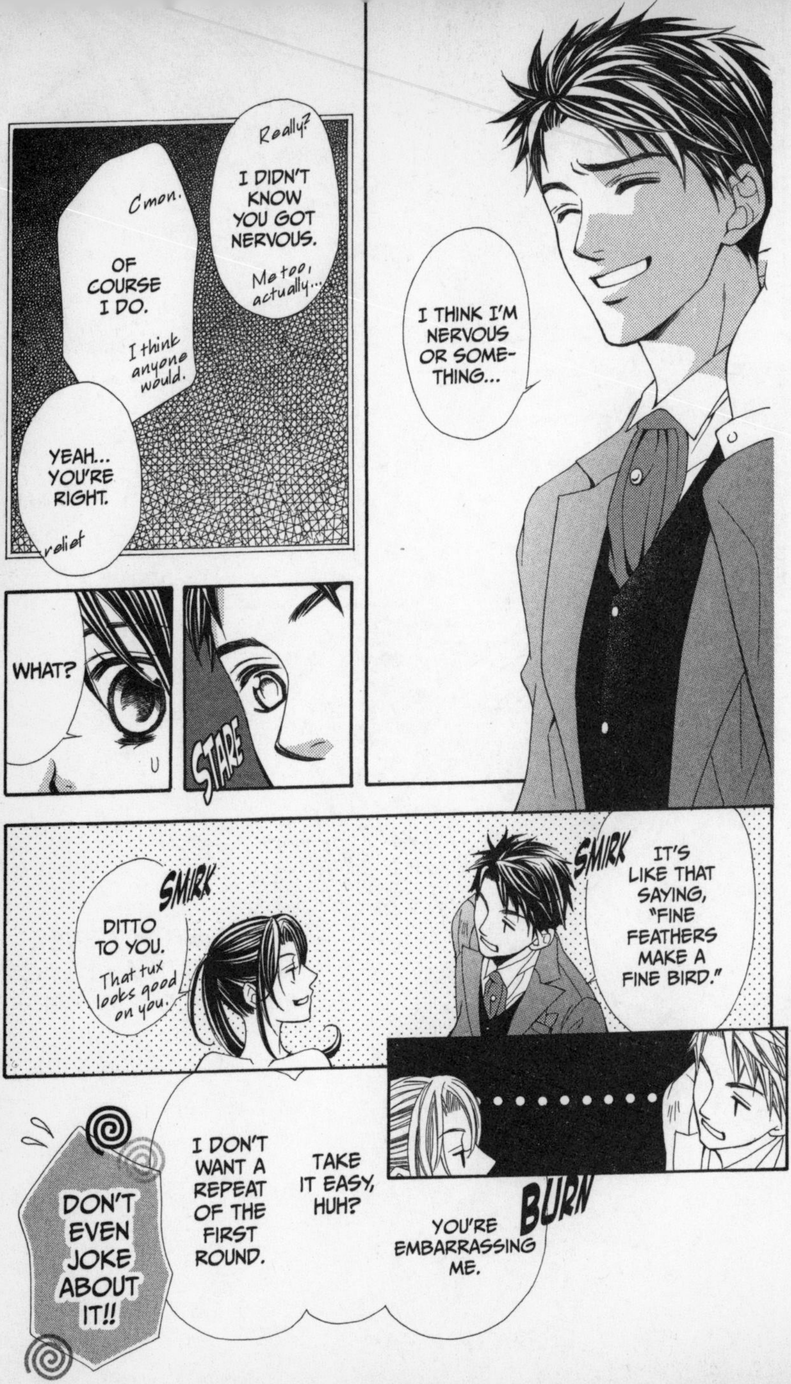
I THINK I'M NERVOUS OR SOME-THING...
Really? I DIDN'T KNOW YOU GOT NERVOUS. Me too, actually...
C'mon. OF COURSE I DO. I think anyone would.
YEAH... YOU'RE RIGHT. relief
STARE
WHAT?
SMIRK
IT'S LIKE THAT SAYING, "FINE FEATHERS MAKE A FINE BIRD."
SMIRK
DITTO TO YOU. That tux looks good on you.
....
BURN
YOU'RE EMBARRASSING ME.
TAKE IT EASY, HUH?
I DON'T WANT A REPEAT OF THE FIRST ROUND.
DON'T EVEN JOKE ABOUT IT!!

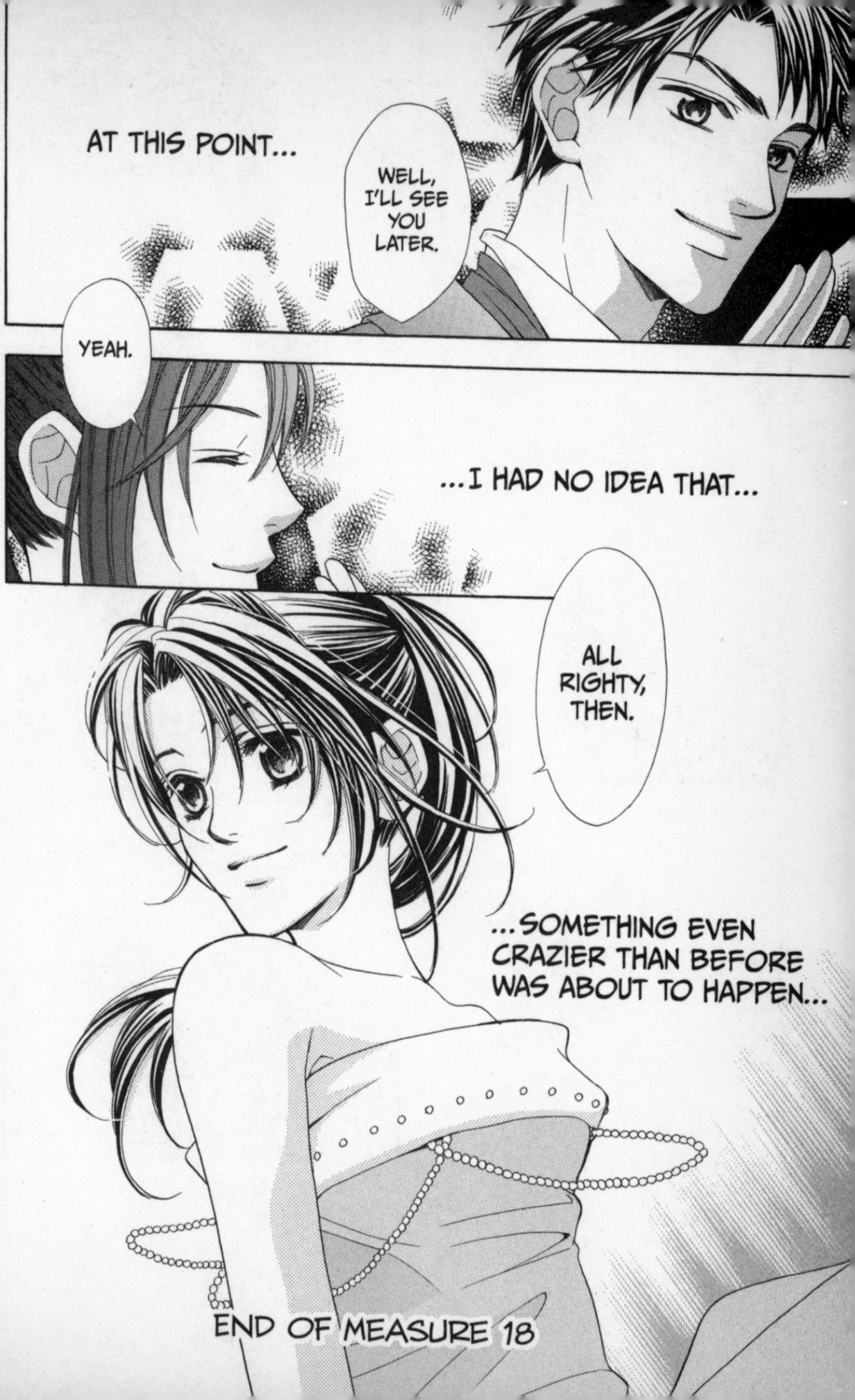
WELL, I'LL SEE YOU LATER.
AT THIS POINT...
YEAH.
...I HAD NO IDEA THAT...
ALL RIGHTY, THEN.
...SOMETHING EVEN CRAZIER THAN BEFORE WAS ABOUT TO HAPPEN...
END OF MEASURE 18

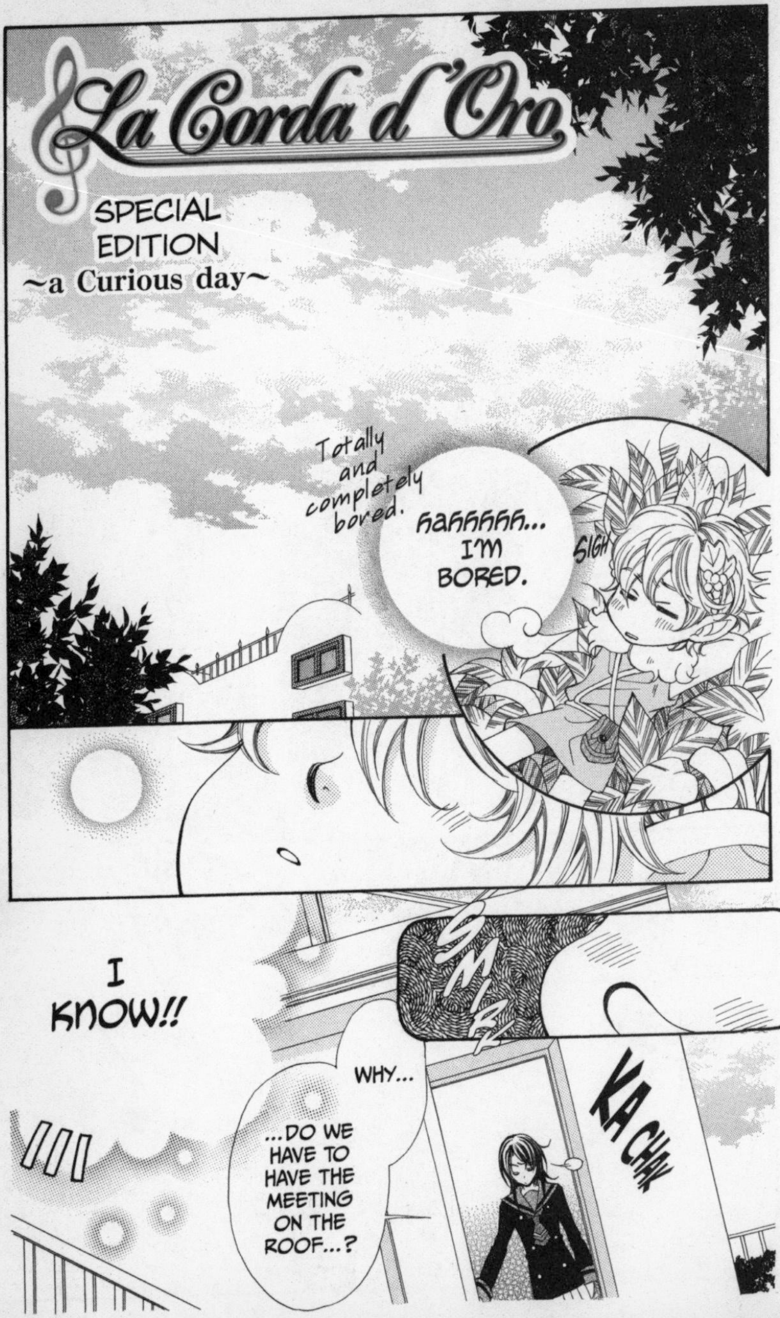
La Corda d'Oro
SPECIAL EDITION
~a Curious day~
SIGH
HAHHHHH... I'M BORED.
Totally and completely bored.
SMIRK
I KNOW!!
KA CHAK
WHY...
...DO WE HAVE TO HAVE THE MEETING ON THE ROOF...?

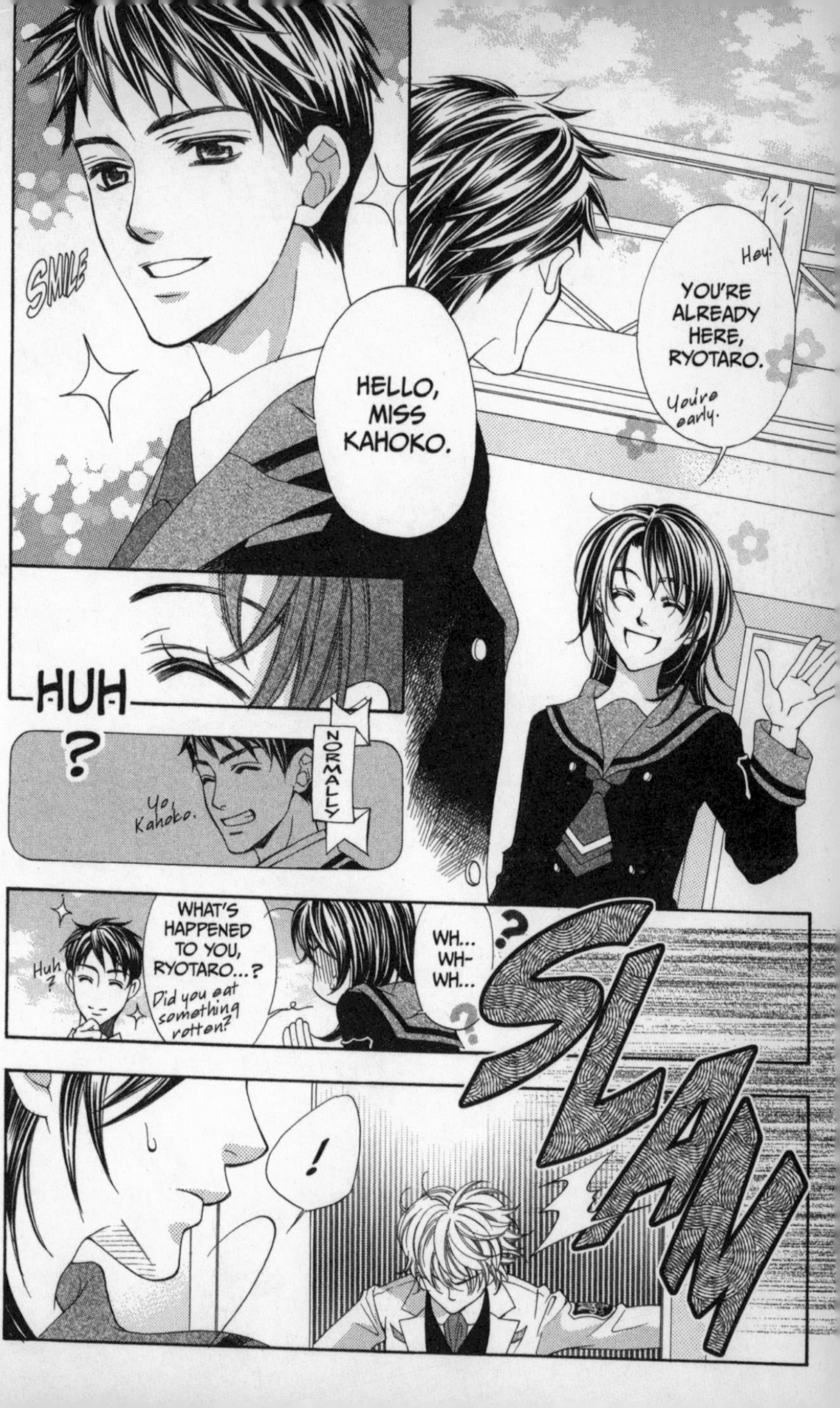
Hey!
YOU'RE ALREADY HERE, RYOTARO.
You're early.
HELLO, MISS KAHOKO.
SMILE
HUH?
NORMALLY
Yo, Kahoko.
WH... WH- WH...
WHAT'S HAPPENED TO YOU, RYOTARO...?
Did you eat something rotten?
Huh?
SLAM
!

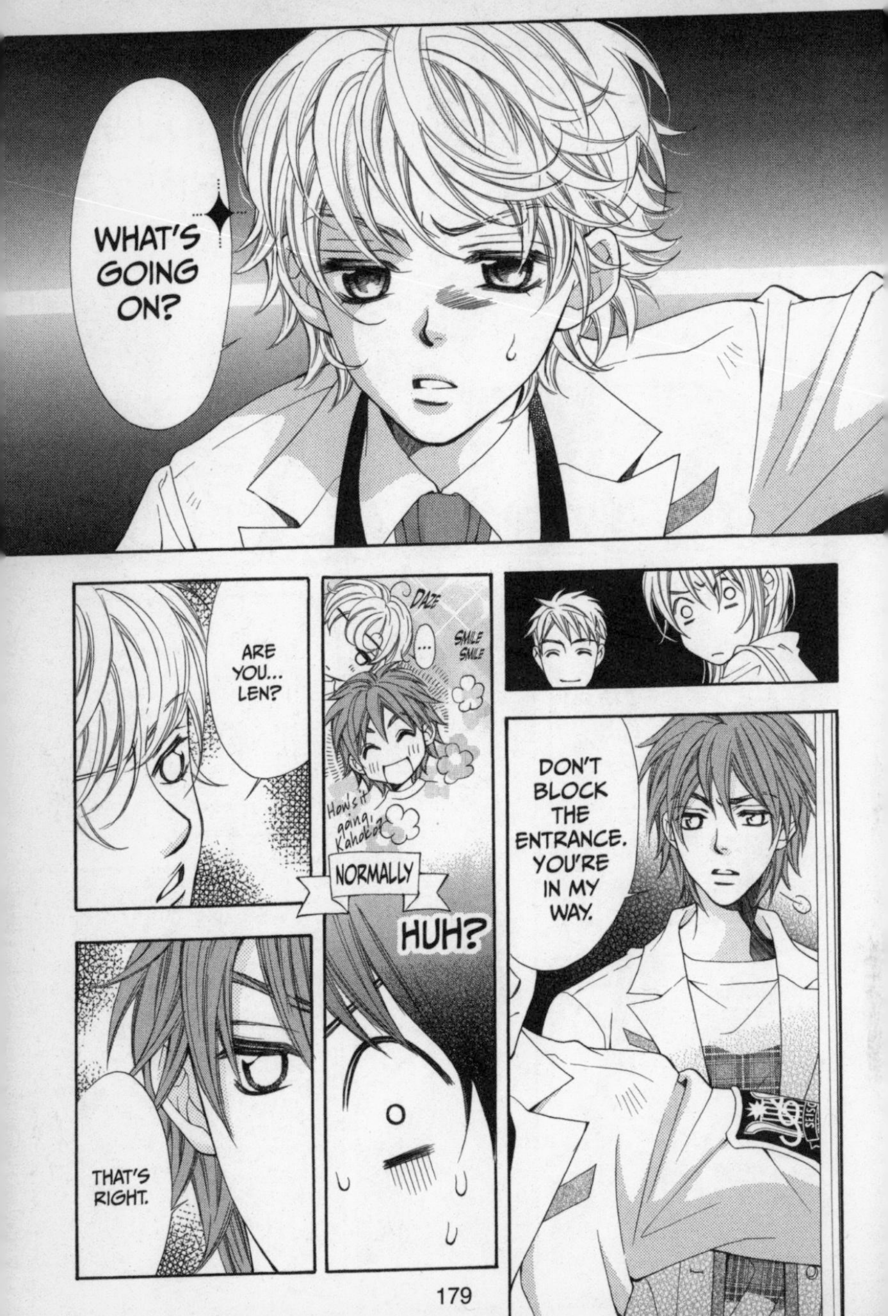
WHAT'S GOING ON?
DON'T BLOCK THE ENTRANCE. YOU'RE IN MY WAY.
DAZE
...
SMILE SMILE
How's it going, Kahoko?
NORMALLY
HUH?
ARE YOU... LEN?
THAT'S RIGHT.

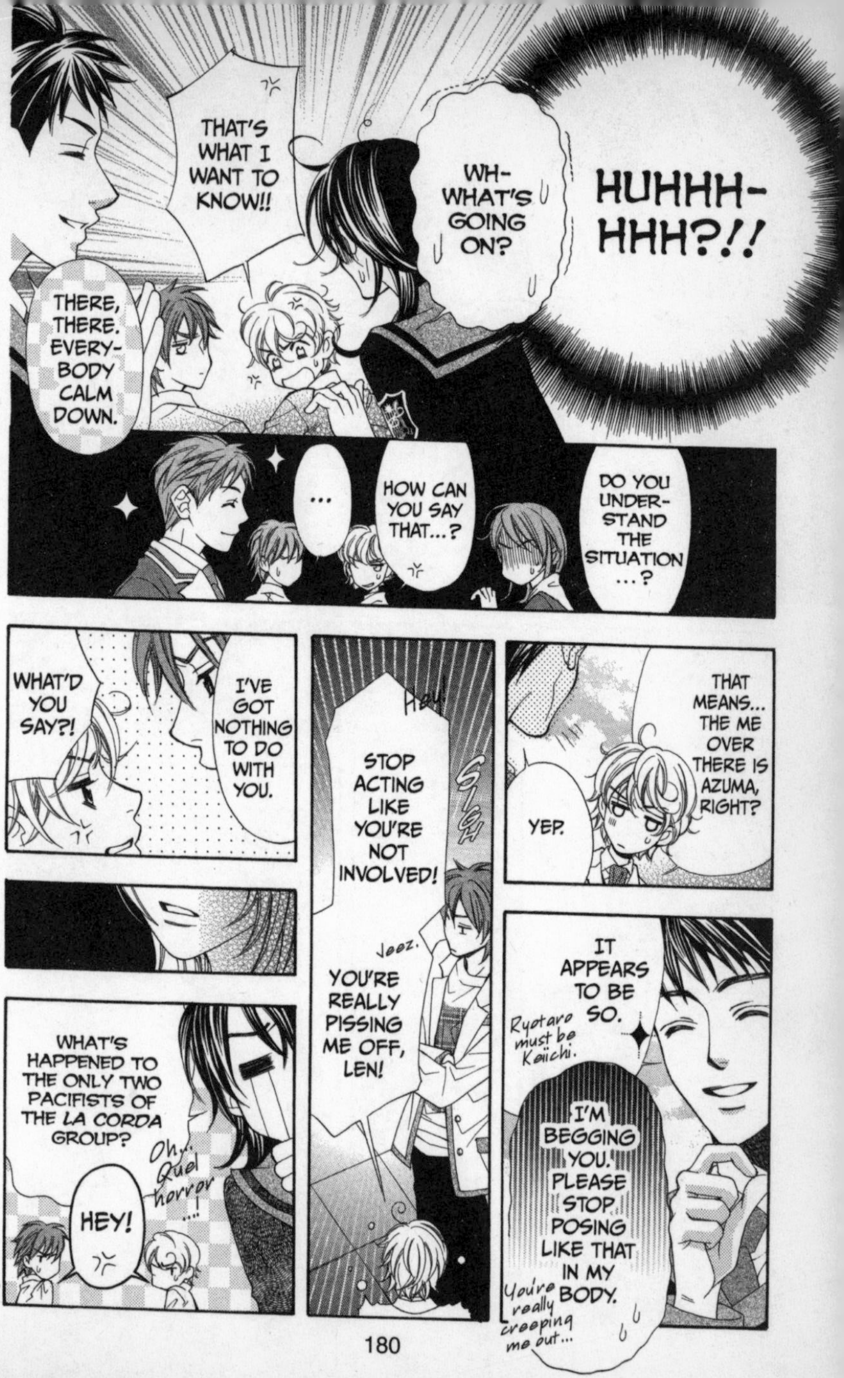
HUHHH-HHH?!!
WH-WHAT'S GOING ON?
THAT'S WHAT I WANT TO KNOW!!
THERE, THERE. EVERYBODY CALM DOWN.
DO YOU UNDERSTAND THE SITUATION...?
HOW CAN YOU SAY THAT...?
...
THAT MEANS... THE ME OVER THERE IS AZUMA, RIGHT?
YEP.
IT APPEARS TO BE SO.
Ryotaro must be Keiichi.
I'M BEGGING YOU. PLEASE STOP POSING LIKE THAT IN MY BODY.
You're really creeping me out...
Hey!
STOP ACTING LIKE YOU'RE NOT INVOLVED!
SIGH
Jeez.
YOU'RE REALLY PISSING ME OFF, LEN!
I'VE GOT NOTHING TO DO WITH YOU.
WHAT'D YOU SAY?!
WHAT'S HAPPENED TO THE ONLY TWO PACIFISTS OF THE *LA CORDA* GROUP?
Oh... Quel horror!...
HEY!

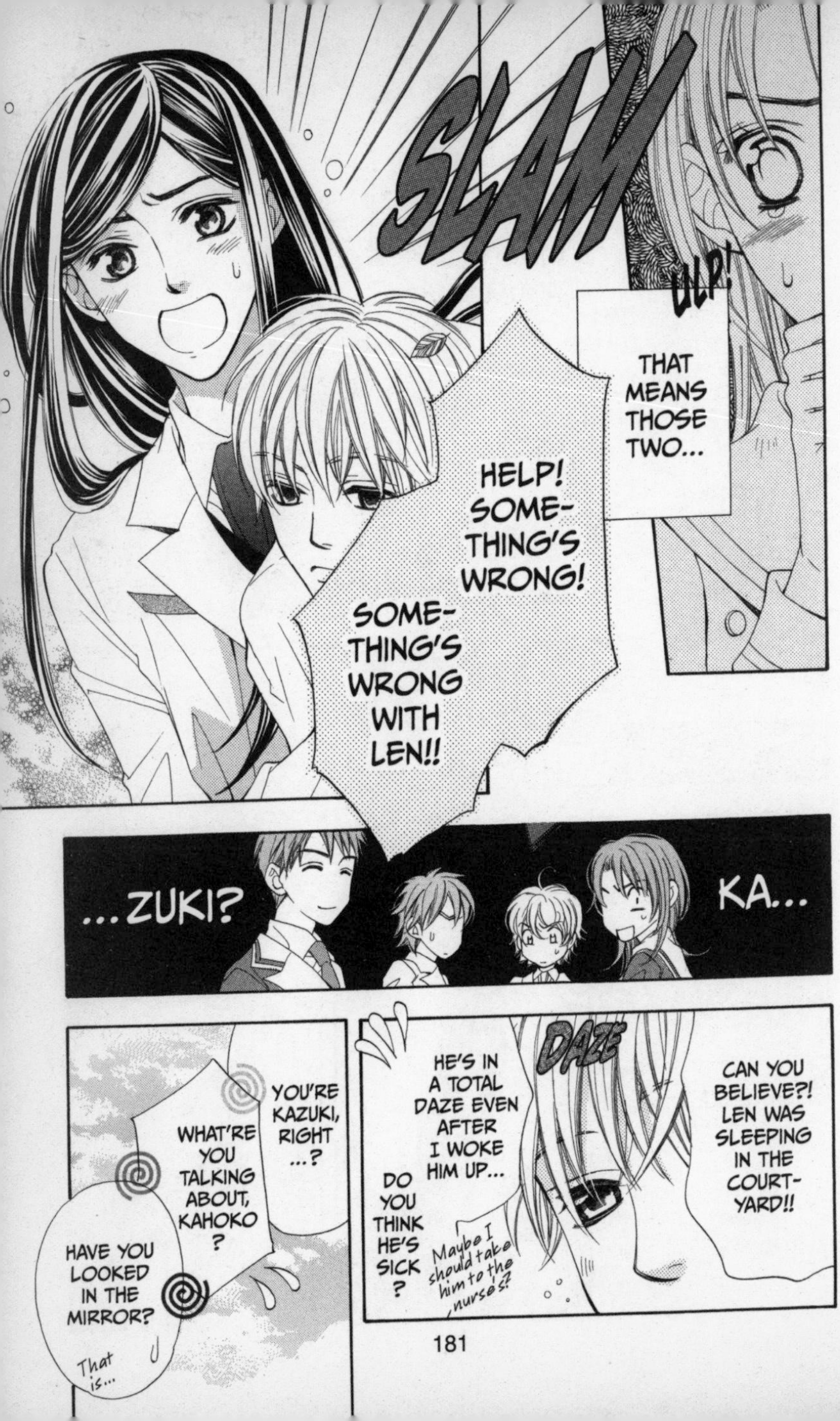
ULP!
THAT MEANS THOSE TWO...
SLAM
HELP! SOMETHING'S WRONG!
SOMETHING'S WRONG WITH LEN!!
KA...
...ZUKI?
CAN YOU BELIEVE?! LEN WAS SLEEPING IN THE COURTYARD!!
DAZE
HE'S IN A TOTAL DAZE EVEN AFTER I WOKE HIM UP...
DO YOU THINK HE'S SICK?
Maybe I should take him to the nurse's?
YOU'RE KAZUKI, RIGHT...?
WHAT'RE YOU TALKING ABOUT, KAHOKO?
HAVE YOU LOOKED IN THE MIRROR?
That is...

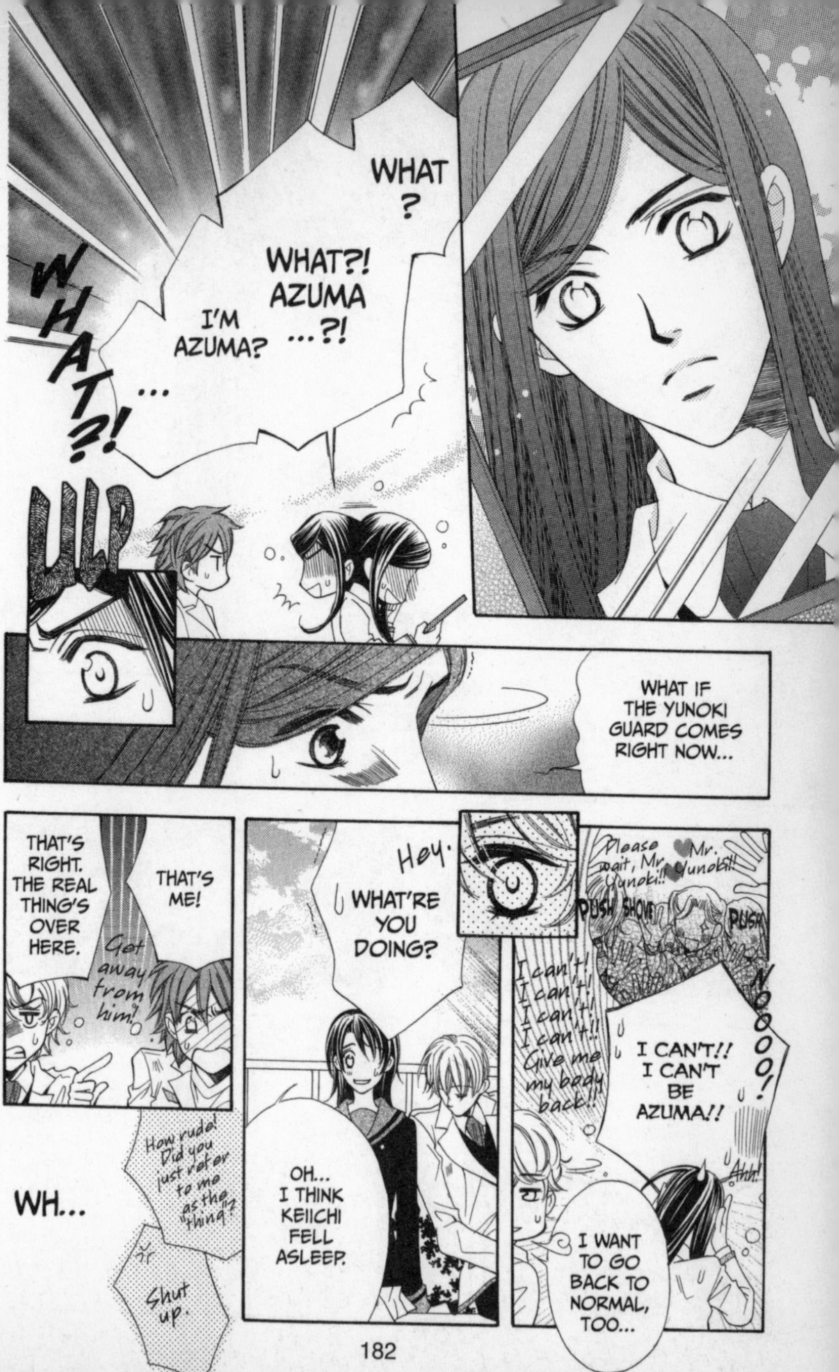
WHAT ?
WHAT?! AZUMA ...?!
I'M AZUMA? ...
WHAT?!
WHAT IF THE YUNOKI GUARD COMES RIGHT NOW...
Please wait, Mr. Yunoki!!
Mr. Yunoki!!
PUSH SHOVE PUSH
NOOOOO!
I can't!! I can't!! I can't!! I can't!! Give me my body back!!
I CAN'T!! I CAN'T BE AZUMA!!
Ahh!
I WANT TO GO BACK TO NORMAL, TOO...
Hey.
WHAT'RE YOU DOING?
OH... I THINK KEIICHI FELL ASLEEP.
THAT'S ME!
THAT'S RIGHT. THE REAL THING'S OVER HERE.
Get away from him!
How rude! Did you just refer to me as the "thing"?
Shut up.
WH...

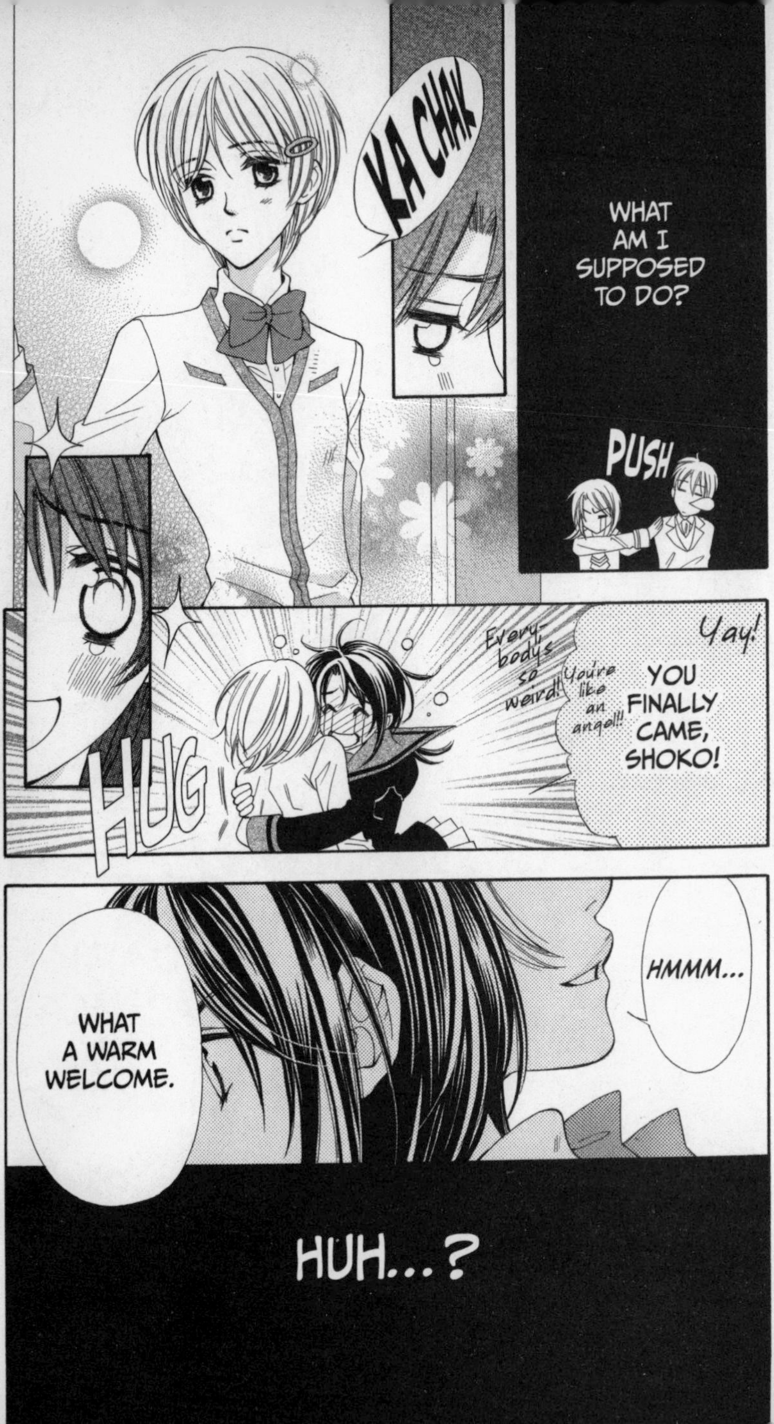
WHAT AM I SUPPOSED TO DO?
KA CHAK
PUSH
Yay!
YOU FINALLY CAME, SHOKO!
You're like an angel!!
Everybody's so weird!!
HUG
HMMM...
WHAT A WARM WELCOME.
HUH...?

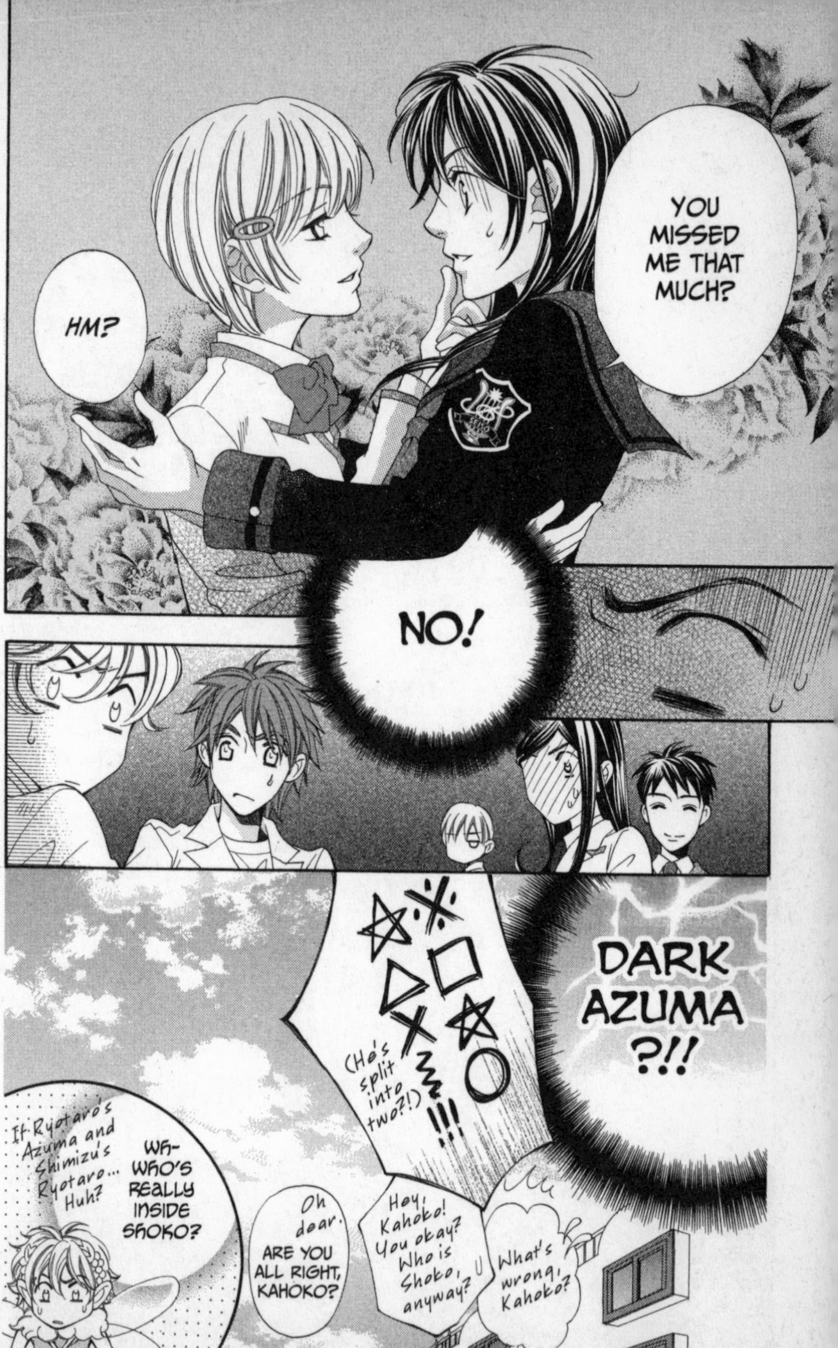
YOU MISSED ME THAT MUCH?
HM?
NO!
DARK AZUMA ?!!
(He's split into two?!)
What's wrong, Kahoko?
Hey, Kahoko! You okay? Who is Shoko, anyway?
Oh dear. ARE YOU ALL RIGHT, KAHOKO?
WH-WHO'S REALLY INSIDE SHOKO?
If Ryotaro's Azuma and Shimizu's Ryotaro... Huh?

BACKSTAGE WITH THE JOURNALISM CLUB #3

HELLO.

HI, EVERY-BODY. ♡

I FINALLY HAD AN APPEARANCE IN VOLUME 4.

NOT THAT IT WAS A LOT, BUT...

La Corda ④ →

WELL, THEN! I'D LIKE TO INTRODUCE SOME PROFILES AGAIN!

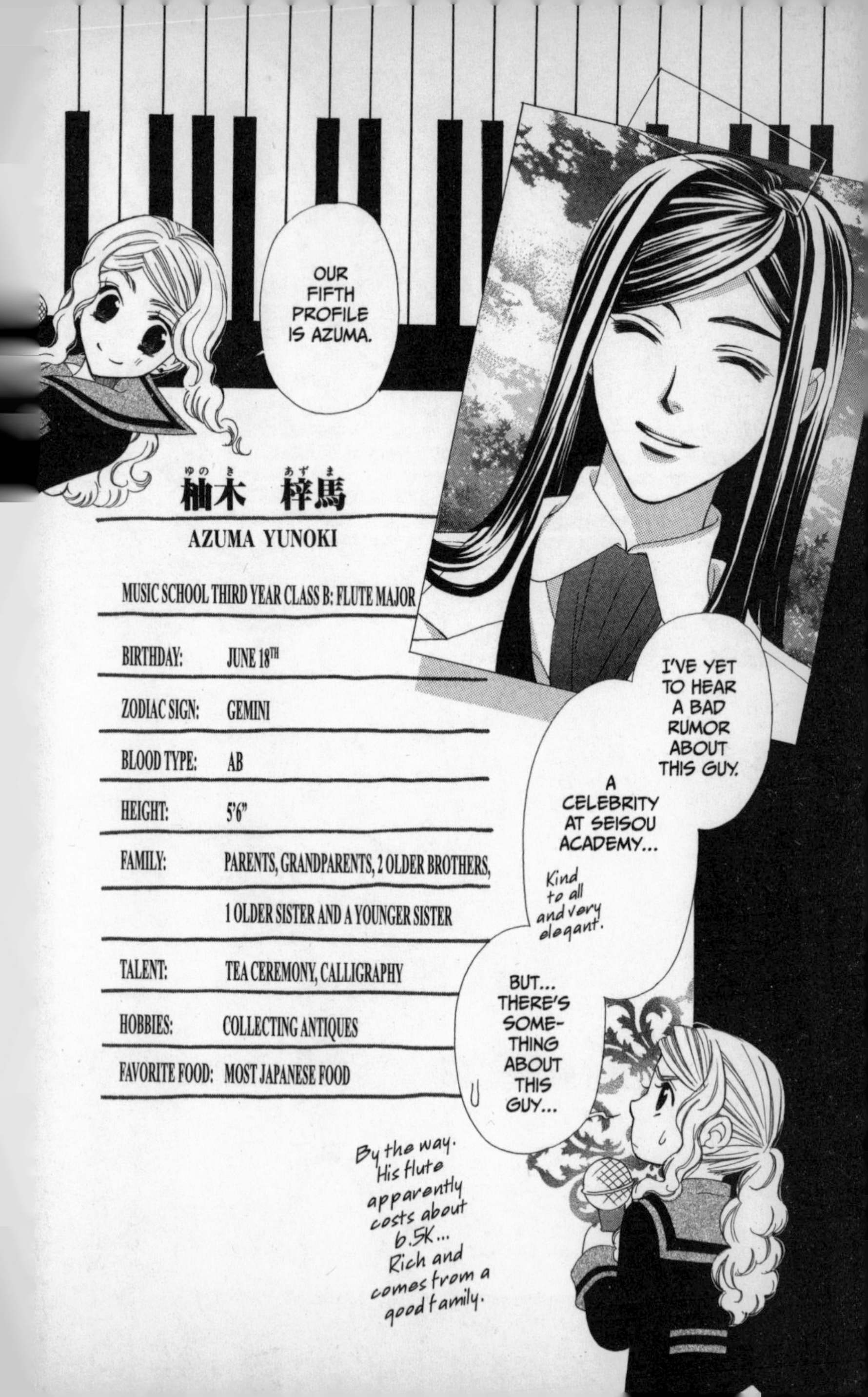
OUR FIFTH PROFILE IS AZUMA.
I'VE YET TO HEAR A BAD RUMOR ABOUT THIS GUY.
A CELEBRITY AT SEISOU ACADEMY...
Kind to all and very elegant.
BUT... THERE'S SOME-THING ABOUT THIS GUY...
By the way. His flute apparently costs about 6.5K... Rich and comes from a good family.
ゆのき あずま
柚木 梓馬
AZUMA YUNOKI
MUSIC SCHOOL THIRD YEAR CLASS B: FLUTE MAJOR
BIRTHDAY: JUNE 18TH
ZODIAC SIGN: GEMINI
BLOOD TYPE: AB
HEIGHT: 5'6"
FAMILY: PARENTS, GRANDPARENTS, 2 OLDER BROTHERS, 1 OLDER SISTER AND A YOUNGER SISTER
TALENT: TEA CEREMONY, CALLIGRAPHY
HOBBIES: COLLECTING ANTIQUES
FAVORITE FOOD: MOST JAPANESE FOOD

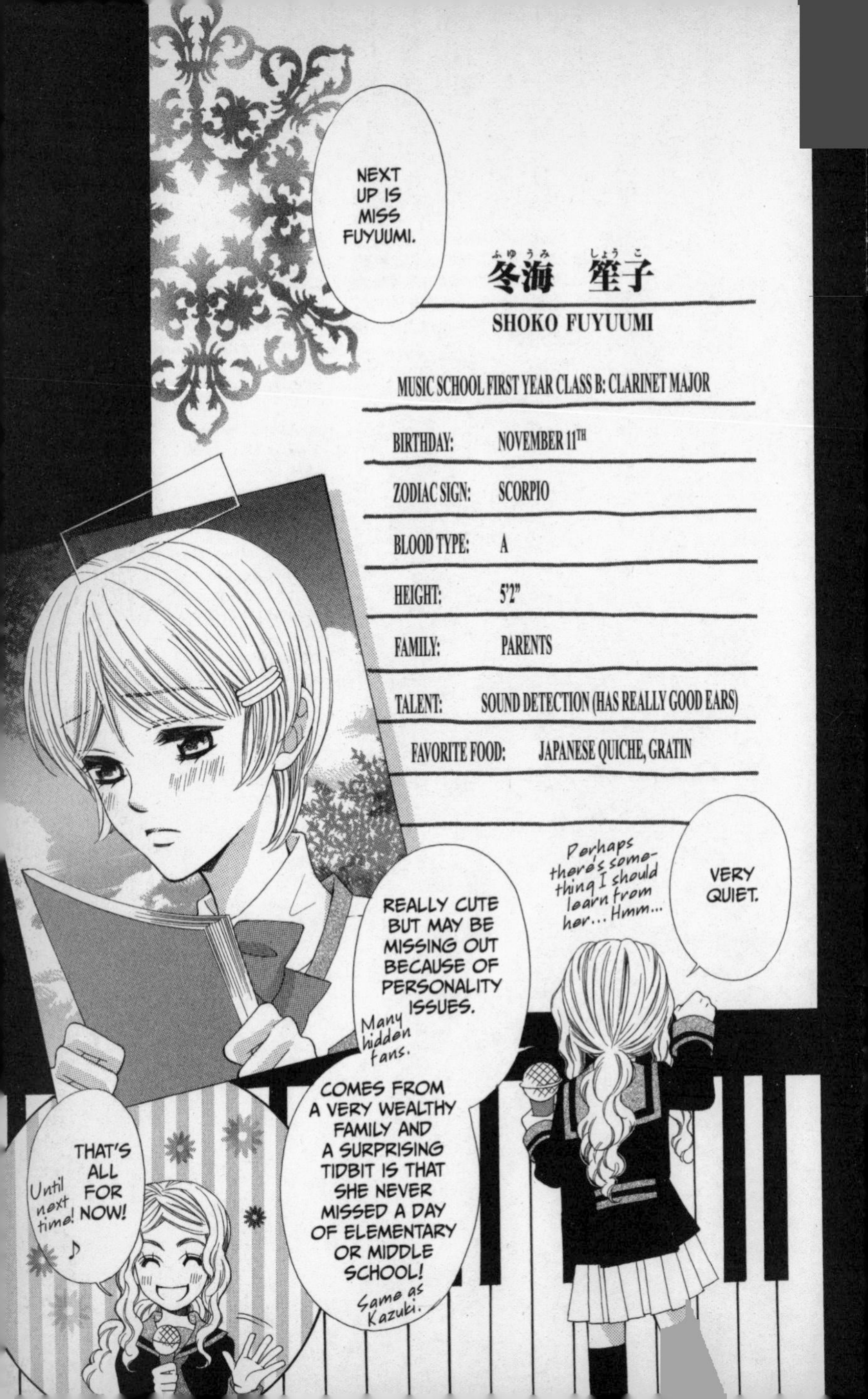
NEXT UP IS MISS FUYUUMI.
ふゆうみ　しょうこ
冬海　笙子
SHOKO FUYUUMI
MUSIC SCHOOL FIRST YEAR CLASS B: CLARINET MAJOR
BIRTHDAY: NOVEMBER 11TH
ZODIAC SIGN: SCORPIO
BLOOD TYPE: A
HEIGHT: 5'2"
FAMILY: PARENTS
TALENT: SOUND DETECTION (HAS REALLY GOOD EARS)
FAVORITE FOOD: JAPANESE QUICHE, GRATIN
VERY QUIET.
Perhaps there's something I should learn from her... Hmm...
REALLY CUTE BUT MAY BE MISSING OUT BECAUSE OF PERSONALITY ISSUES.
Many hidden fans.
COMES FROM A VERY WEALTHY FAMILY AND A SURPRISING TIDBIT IS THAT SHE NEVER MISSED A DAY OF ELEMENTARY OR MIDDLE SCHOOL!
Same as Kazuki.
THAT'S ALL FOR NOW!
Until next time! ♪

POSTSCRIPT

Hello again.
The cover for volume 4 is the two third years, since I used the two second years in the cover for volume 3.

Since the duo on volume 3 seemed so cold, I decided to make the duo on volume 4 extra friendly.

Especially the guy on the right, who has the world's friendliest smile. (Perhaps a talent or a special skill...?) I tried to make them smile as naturally as possible, but it came out looking like they have a suppressed smile... Hee hee.

Lastly, to my readers, my editors who work tirelessly with me, Koei, parents and friends... I'd like to extend my sincerest gratitude to you all. Thank you very much.

Thank you all for reading this volume through.

呉由姫
Yuki Kure

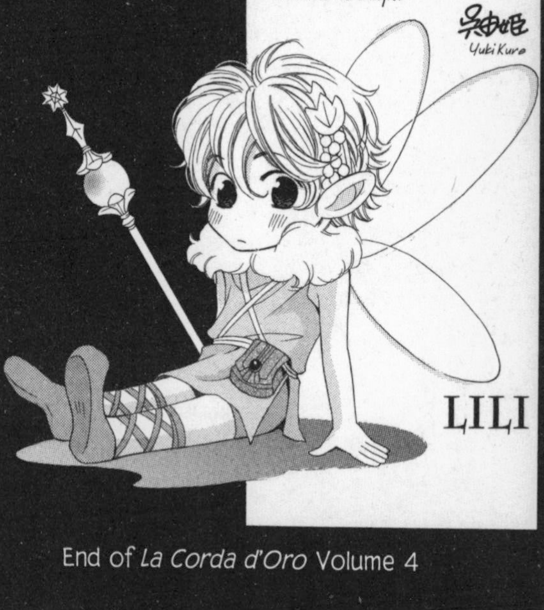
LILI

End of *La Corda d'Oro* Volume 4

SPECIAL THANKS

A.Kashima
A.Shimaya
M.Shiino
N.Sato
Kugaru

A.Izumi
A.Hagio
C.Karasawa

C.Sawanobori
Y.Uruno

Yuki Kure made her debut in 2000
with the story *Chijo yori Eien ni*
(Forever from the Earth), published
in monthly *LaLa* magazine.
La Corda d' Oro is her first manga
series published. Her hobby is
watching soccer games and
collecting small goodies.

LA CORDA D'ORO
Vol. 4
The Shojo Beat Manga Edition

STORY AND ART BY
YUKI KURE
ORIGINAL CONCEPT BY
RUBY PARTY

English Translation & Adaptation/Mai Ihara
Touch-up Art & Lettering/Gia Cam Luc
Design/Yukiko Whitley
Editors/Pancha Diaz and Shaenon K. Garrity

Editor in Chief, Books/Alvin Lu
Editor in Chief, Magazines/Marc Weidenbaum
VP of Publishing Licensing/Rika Inouye
VP of Sales/Gonzalo Ferreyra
Sr. VP of Marketing/Liza Coppola
Publisher/Hyoe Narita

Kiniro no Corda by Yuki Kure © Yuki Kure, KOEI Co., Ltd. 2005
All rights reserved.
First published in Japan in 2005 by HAKUSENSHA, Inc., Tokyo.
English language translation rights in America and Canada arranged
with HAKUSENSHA, Inc., Tokyo.
New and adapted artwork and text © 2007 VIZ Media, LLC.
The LA CORDA D'ORO logo is a trademark of VIZ Media, LLC.
The stories, characters and incidents mentioned in this publication are entirely fictional.

Printed in Canada

Published by VIZ Media, LLC
P.O. Box 77010
San Francisco, CA 94107

Shojo Beat Manga Edition
10 9 8 7 6 5 4 3 2
First printing, July 2007

store.viz.com

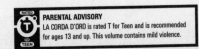

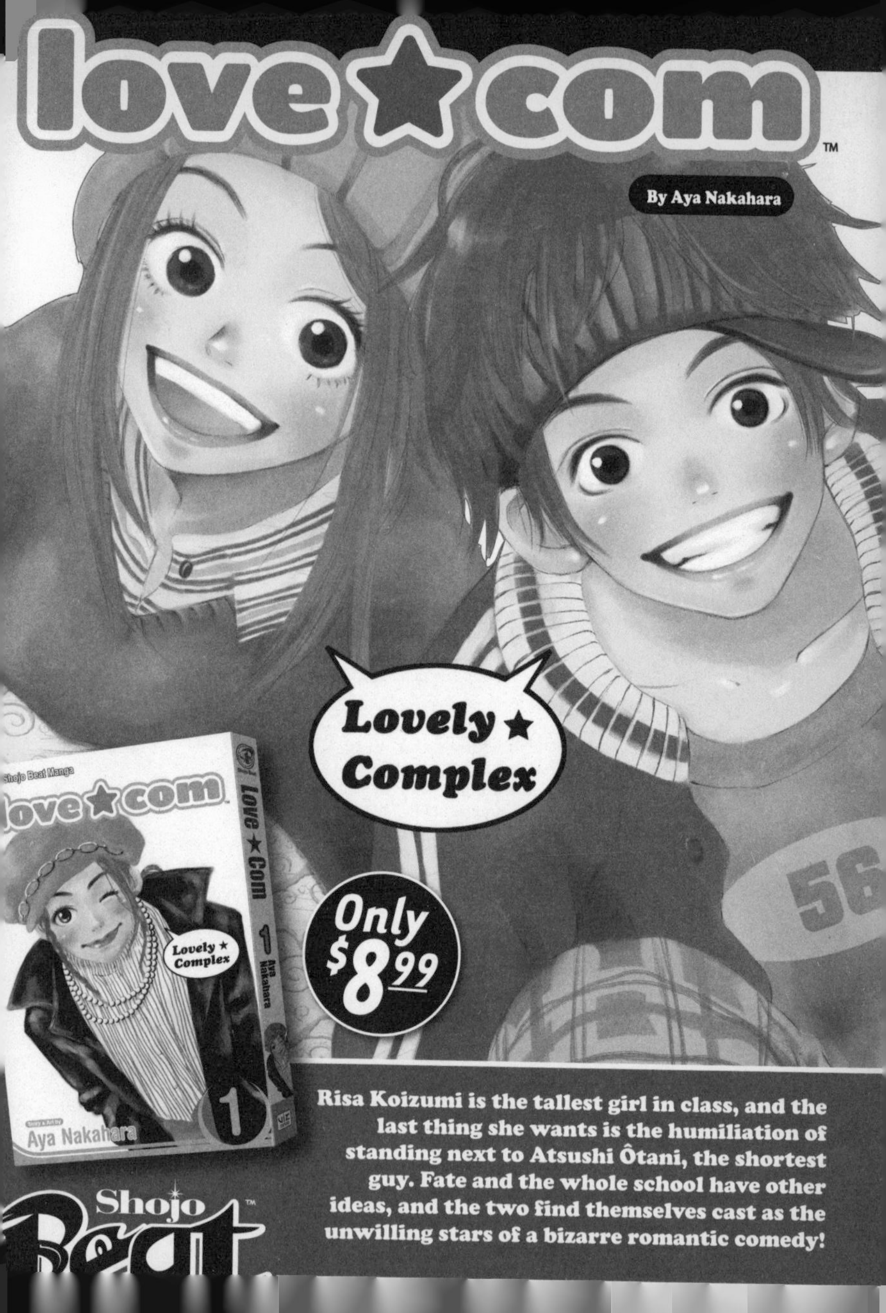
love★com™
By Aya Nakahara
Lovely★ Complex
Shojo Beat Manga
love★com
Love★Com
1
Aya Nakahara
Lovely★ Complex
Story & Art by
Aya Nakahara
1
Only $8.99
56
Risa Koizumi is the tallest girl in class, and the last thing she wants is the humiliation of standing next to Atsushi Ôtani, the shortest guy. Fate and the whole school have other ideas, and the two find themselves cast as the unwilling stars of a bizarre romantic comedy!
Shojo Beat™

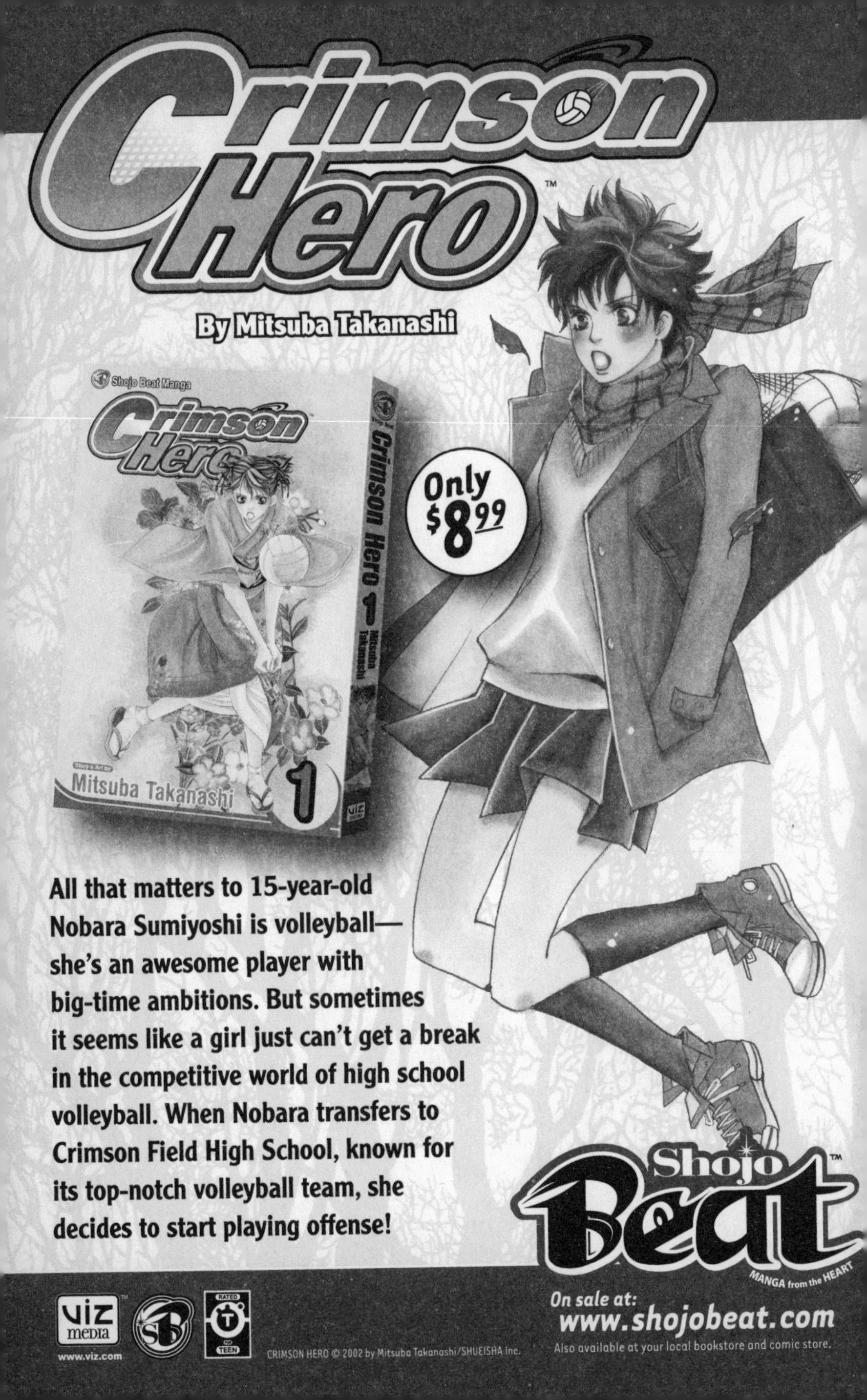
Crimson Hero™
By Mitsuba Takanashi
Shojo Beat Manga
Crimson Hero
Crimson Hero 1 Mitsuba Takanashi
Mitsuba Takanashi
1
Only $8.99
All that matters to 15-year-old Nobara Sumiyoshi is volleyball—she's an awesome player with big-time ambitions. But sometimes it seems like a girl just can't get a break in the competitive world of high school volleyball. When Nobara transfers to Crimson Field High School, known for its top-notch volleyball team, she decides to start playing offense!
Shojo Beat™
MANGA from the HEART
viz media
www.viz.com
RATED T FOR TEEN
CRIMSON HERO © 2002 by Mitsuba Takanashi/SHUEISHA Inc.
On sale at:
www.shojobeat.com
Also available at your local bookstore and comic store.

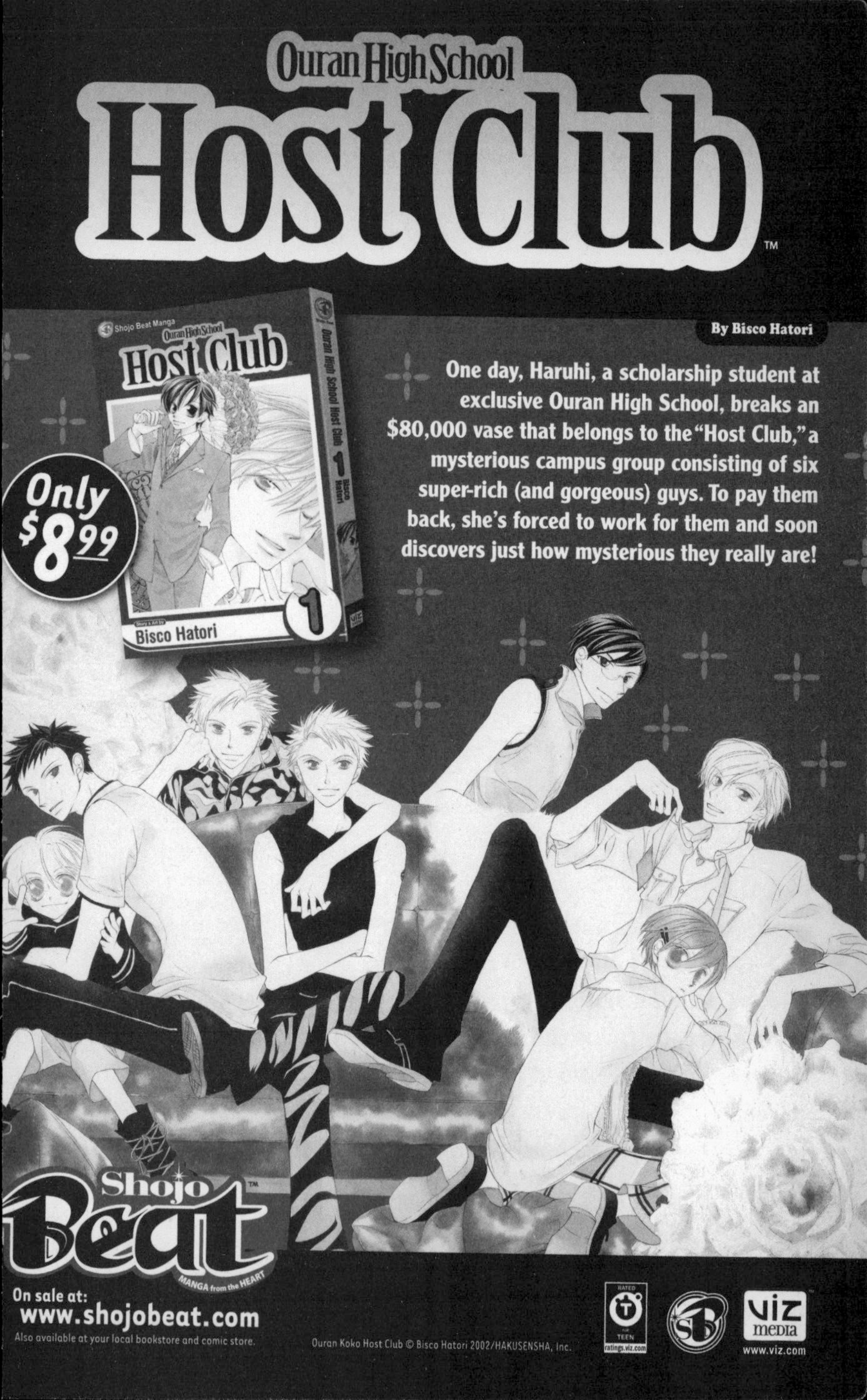
Ouran High School
Host Club™
Shojo Beat Manga
Ouran High School Host Club 1
Bisco Hatori
Story & Art by Bisco Hatori
Only $8.99
By Bisco Hatori
One day, Haruhi, a scholarship student at exclusive Ouran High School, breaks an $80,000 vase that belongs to the "Host Club," a mysterious campus group consisting of six super-rich (and gorgeous) guys. To pay them back, she's forced to work for them and soon discovers just how mysterious they really are!
Shojo Beat™
MANGA from the HEART
On sale at:
www.shojobeat.com
Also available at your local bookstore and comic store.
Ouran Koko Host Club © Bisco Hatori 2002/HAKUSENSHA, Inc.
RATED T FOR TEEN
ratings.viz.com
VIZ media
www.viz.com

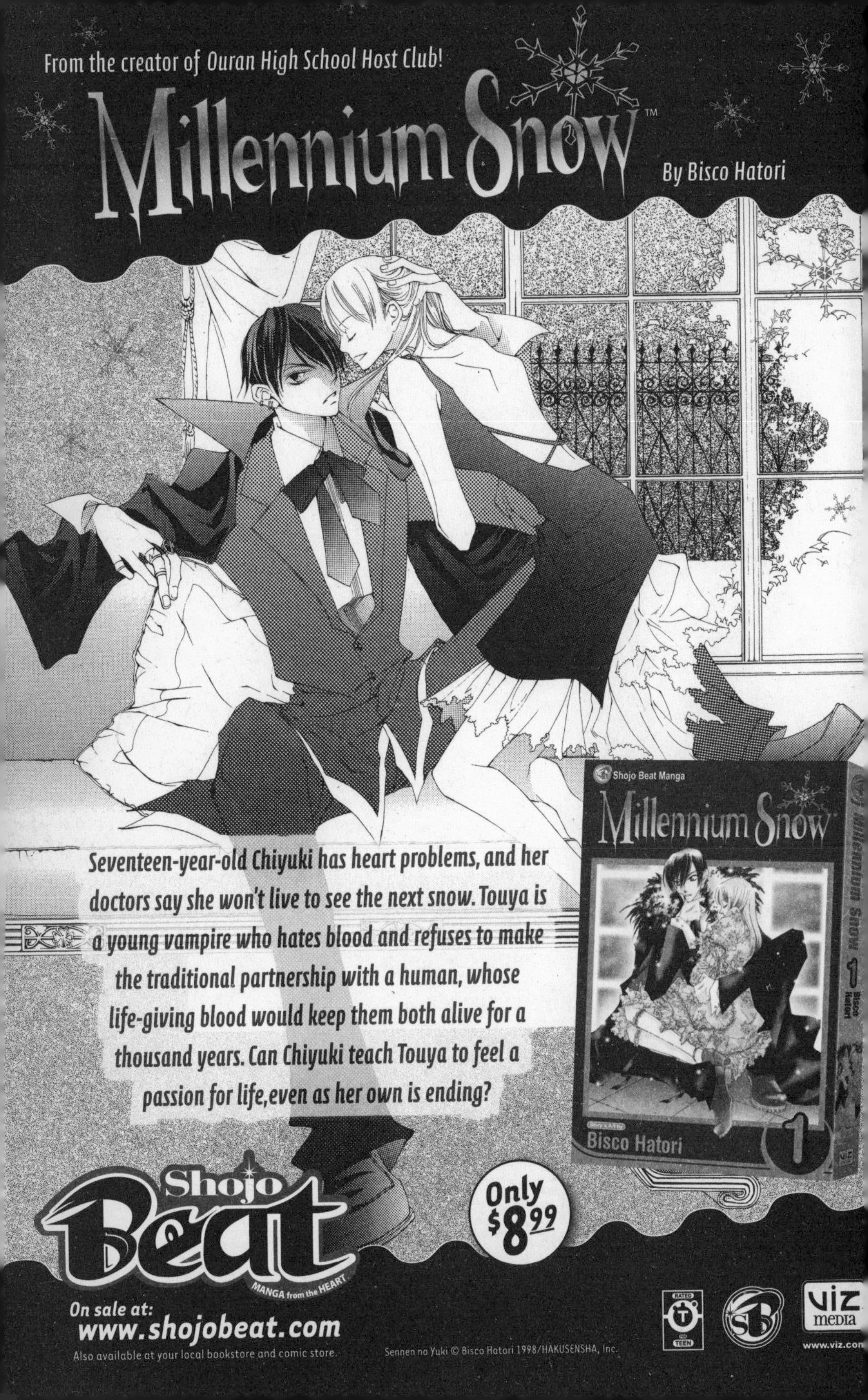
From the creator of Ouran High School Host Club!
Millennium Snow™
By Bisco Hatori
Seventeen-year-old Chiyuki has heart problems, and her doctors say she won't live to see the next snow. Touya is a young vampire who hates blood and refuses to make the traditional partnership with a human, whose life-giving blood would keep them both alive for a thousand years. Can Chiyuki teach Touya to feel a passion for life, even as her own is ending?
Shojo Beat Manga
Millennium Snow
1
Bisco Hatori
Only $8.99
Shojo Beat
MANGA from the HEART
On sale at:
www.shojobeat.com
Also available at your local bookstore and comic store.
Sennen no Yuki © Bisco Hatori 1998/HAKUSENSHA, Inc.
RATED T TEEN
VIZ media

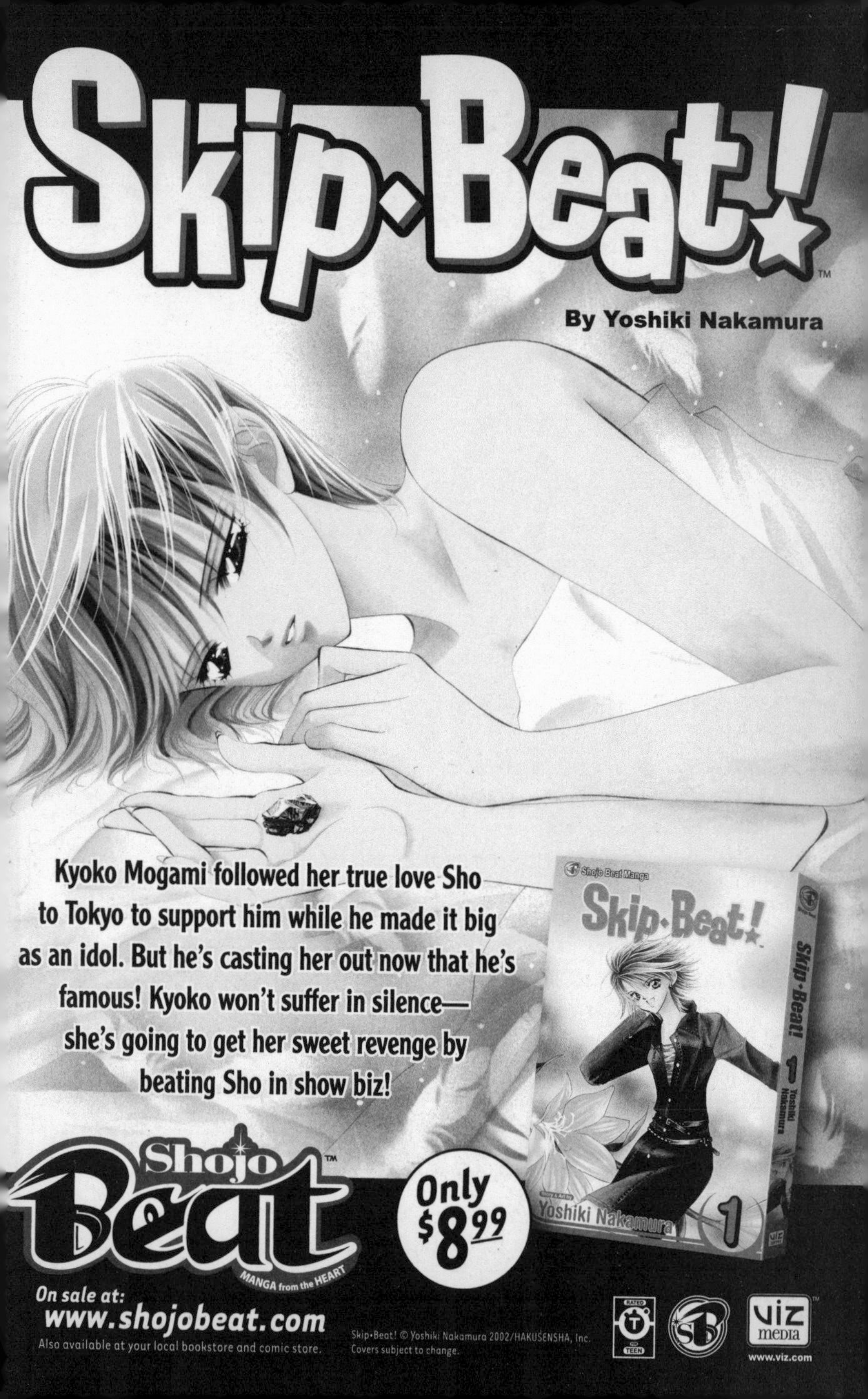
Skip·Beat!™
By Yoshiki Nakamura
Kyoko Mogami followed her true love Sho to Tokyo to support him while he made it big as an idol. But he's casting her out now that he's famous! Kyoko won't suffer in silence—she's going to get her sweet revenge by beating Sho in show biz!
Shojo Beat Manga
Skip·Beat!
1
Yoshiki Nakamura
Shojo Beat™
MANGA from the HEART
Only $8.99
On sale at:
www.shojobeat.com
Also available at your local bookstore and comic store.
Skip·Beat! © Yoshiki Nakamura 2002/HAKUSENSHA, Inc.
Covers subject to change.
RATED T TEEN
viz media
www.viz.com

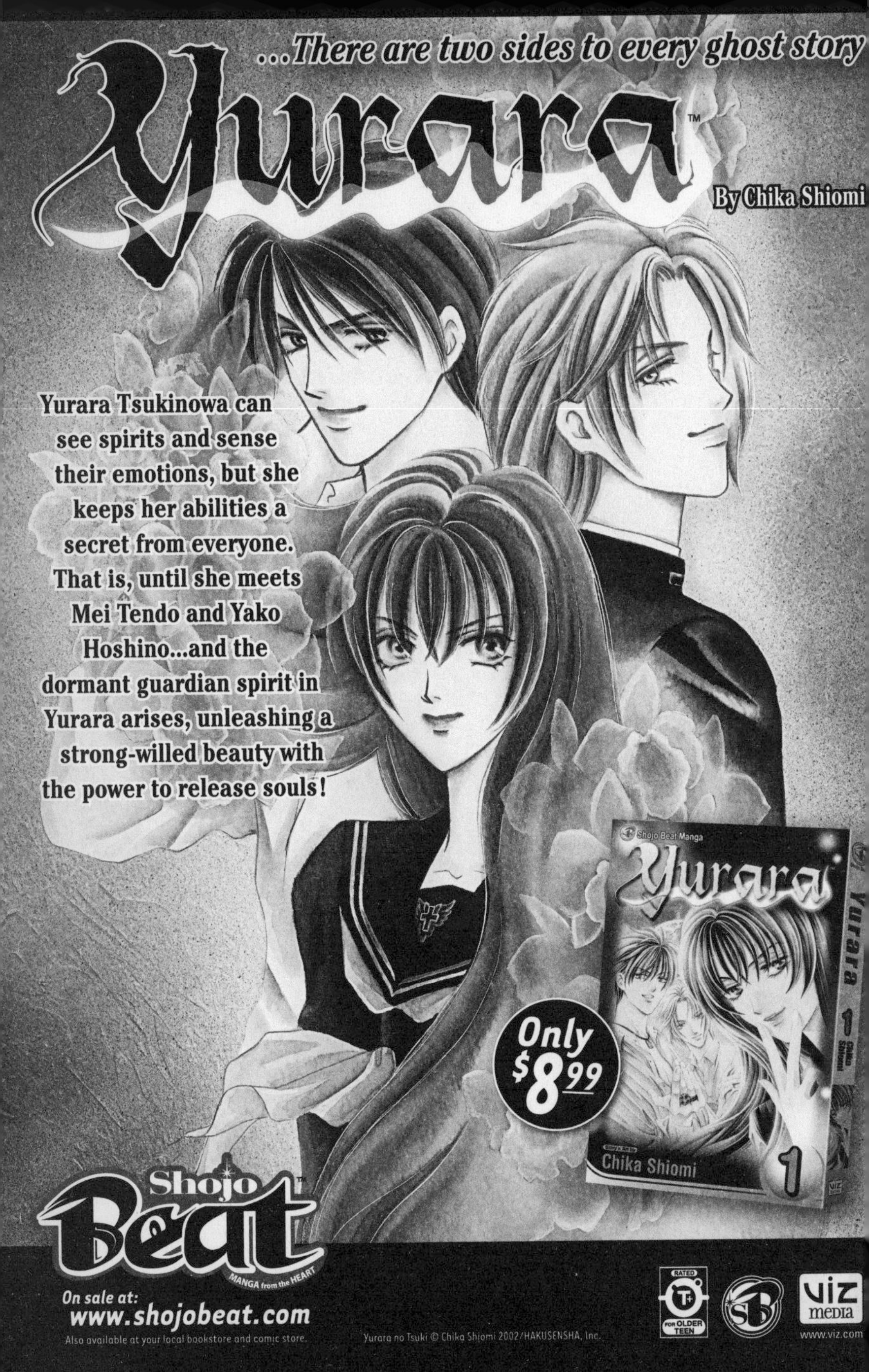

...There are two sides to every ghost story
Yurara™
By Chika Shiomi
Yurara Tsukinowa can see spirits and sense their emotions, but she keeps her abilities a secret from everyone. That is, until she meets Mei Tendo and Yako Hoshino...and the dormant guardian spirit in Yurara arises, unleashing a strong-willed beauty with the power to release souls!
Shojo Beat Manga
Yurara
Chika Shiomi
1
Only $8.99
Shojo Beat™
MANGA from the HEART
On sale at:
www.shojobeat.com
Also available at your local bookstore and comic store.
Yurara no Tsuki © Chika Shiomi 2002/HAKUSENSHA, Inc.
RATED T+ FOR OLDER TEEN
VIZ media
www.viz.com